Ennobling Love

THE MIDDLE AGES SERIES

Ruth Mazo Karras, General Editor
Edward Peters, Founding Editor

A complete list of books in the series
is available from the publisher.

Ennobling Love

In Search of a Lost Sensibility

C. STEPHEN JAEGER

PENN

University of Pennsylvania Press

Philadelphia

10 9 8 7 6 5 4 3 2 1

Published by
University of Pennsylvania Press
Philadelphia, Pennsylvania 19104-4011

Library of Congress Cataloging-in-Publication Data
Jaeger, C. Stephen.
    Ennobling love : in search of a lost sensibility / C. Stephen
Jaeger.
        p.   cm. — (The Middle Ages series)
    Includes bibliographical references and index.
    ISBN 0-8122-3494-4 (alk. paper). —
ISBN 0-8122-1691-1 (pbk, alk. paper)
    1. Literature, Medieval — History and criticism.   2. Love in
literature. 3. Literature, Medieval Translations into English.
4. Nobility of character, Literary collections. 5. Nobility of
character in literature.   6. Love, Literary collections.   I. Title.
II. Series.
PN682.L68J34   1999
809'.933543 — dc21   99-24084
                                                        CIP

For Stephanie

Contents

Preface

With this book now out of my hands and in those of readers I can say with Richard of St. Victor, "What a happy and inexhaustible subject love is. No writer tires and no reader wearies of it."[1] He (and I) did not mean to foist benevolence on our readers with that last phrase, but to speak as readers ourselves, who had the good fortune to spend several years studying the subject. I would only add, "No teacher tires of teaching it!"

The "Search" of my subtitle is not just mood music. I sensed in a few texts a way of loving that seemed to me as strange as unicorns and stigmata, and just as alien to my experience and that of my world. Over the years I tracked it like an archeologist of the emotions gathering fragments from some layer of the human psyche that had shattered and dispersed centuries ago and was detectable only like rock traces on the top of a buried site.

How "lost" the sensibility is that I've tried to reconstruct was brought home to me every day in the year of an American president caught up in a scandalous affair with a young woman drunk on love, lust, and power. The culture of love this study deals with found ennobling force in the erotic attraction that power and charisma exert. The counterpoint of degrading and exalting love was for me a lesson in the usefulness, in fact the pragmatism, of a social value which molds the erotic into an instrument for the exercise of power, parallel to wisdom and strength of character as a ruler's virtue, and which thrusts degradation back onto those who see shame and not nobility in the muted eroticism of kings, queens, princes, knights, bishops, and saints in love with their "minions."

This book is about a kind of love that conferred honor on those who practiced it. The book's goal is limited; it aims at one strain of love among many. I do not want to suggest exclusivity by putting this strain in the foreground. In the background at varied distances, interlaced with my main subject, are other forms of love: sexuality of any gender combination, romance, wedded love. Ennobling love is an important strain because it links politics, the social life, and the emotions. It is a means of peace-making, treaty-making, and treaty-keeping, of giving and receiving prestige, rank, and standing, and of recognizing "virtue." It is the source of a morality and a heroism of self-control and self-mastery. Studying it shows how passion and social action, love and the exercise of power, make common cause. Aristotle said that love and friendship are important to the *polis*, because the more human interactions are regulated by friendship, the less they require regulation by the law. That makes love and friendship alternate and higher forms of governing. The insight and the experience were not lost on the Middle Ages, though not linked to the name and the work of Aristotle. A law code from the early twelfth century states the common human experience that "Agreement is better than litigation and love is better than a judge's edict" ("Pactum legem vincit et amor iudicium.")[2]

A "culture of love and friendship" developed in medieval Europe based on underlying conceptions that link works as disparate as letters of friendship from monasteries and cathedral communities, courtly romances, the biography of the English visionary recluse Christina of Markyate, love lyric in Latin and the vernacular, Ailred of Rievaulx's tract on friendship, and the treatises on love by Andreas Capellanus and Baldesar Castiglione in the fourth book of his *Book of the Courtier*.

One of the premises of this study is that the love literature of the western European aristocracy from the early Middle Ages to the Renaissance, across a wide spectrum of genre and social origin, has common features and common roots in antiquity. The documentation of the cult of love and friendship is ordinarily considered in discrete packets, for each period, for each genre, and for each social order its own packet. My purpose is partly to argue a fundamental coherence and partly to show the distortions that can arise from too tight a focus on a particular section of the nobility.

*   *   *

I owe special thanks to John Baldwin and Brian McGuire, both of whom read the manuscript and made valuable comments that changed the complexion of the book. Ruth Mazo Karras, Ullrich Langer, Eugene Vance, Raymond Cormier, Robert Tobin, and an anonymous reviewer of University of Pennsylvania Press also helped refine many of my analyses. Two good friends gave me invaluable help both in the research stage and in the formulation of the manuscript: to Sieglinde Pontow and Stephanie Pafenberg I owe more than can be confessed or repaid in a few words. Horst Wenzel is both patron saint and muse of this project. He nominated me for a Research Prize of the Humboldt Foundation and acted as my gracious host and stimulating conversation partner in Berlin when the nomination was successful. The Humboldt Foundation is a generous and courteous Maecenas to whom I am particularly grateful. A summer grant from the Royalties Research Fund of University of Washington supported my work at an early stage. Paul Pascal was generous with help on

Latin. JoAnn Taricani and Thomas Mathiesen helped me with some technical terms of music in the "Metamorphosis of Golias." Thanks also to my colleague Anna Kartsonis for the conversation that gave me the motto for this book.

My students were and always are some of the greatest inspirers and supporters of my work. My particular thanks to Kelley Kucaba, Britta Simon, and Mike McArthur at University of Washington. In 1995 I taught courses on Love in the Middle Ages at UCLA, and it was for me the happiest combination of research and teaching. I am especially grateful to Zaia Alexander and Gabriele Dillman, also to Pat Geary, then director of the UCLA Center of Medieval and Renaissance Studies, who invited me as a guest of the Center.

My warm thanks are also due to my colleagues in Dresden, Gert Melville and Peter Strohschneider; to Ursula Peters and Joachim Bumke in Cologne; Fritz Wagner, Wolfgang Maaz, and Angela Lozar at the Mittellateinisches Institut of the Free University, Berlin; Gert Althoff of Münster; Wolfgang Harms of Munich; Burghart Wachinger and Christoph Huber of Tübingen; Klaus Speckenbach of University of Münster; Paul Dutton of Simon Fraser University; the members of the "Court Culture East and West" research group; Fred Cheyette of Amherst College; Klaus Van Eickel of Bamberg; Robert Lerner of Northwestern University for support and encouragement over many years; Barbara Rosenwein, her colleagues and students at Loyola University, Chicago.

Alison, Katie, and Rosalind Jaeger were the constant companions and supporters of my "searches," and I thank them for their love and friendship.

* * *

All translations in the text are mine unless otherwise noted. I have included Latin passages along with the translation in cases where the wording is important for the argument and where the translation was difficult, especially in translations of lyric.

There are more uses of the erotic
than just erotic ones.

— ANNA KARTSONIS

Introduction: Cordelia on Trial

A long time ago, before I had any idea where this irritation might take me, two texts got under my skin, stuck there, and were the seeds from which this book eventually grew. One was a passage from a chronicle of the reign of Henry II of England, which is the subject of Chapter 1; the other the opening scene of *King Lear*. In the first, the writer tells how the French siege of the English at Châteauroux in 1187 was ended when the king of France fell in love with the duke of Aquitaine and future king of England, Richard Lionheart. The king loved him "as his own soul" and so honored him that they slept together in the same bed and ate from the same dish at table.

In the beginning of *King Lear*, the old king divides his kingdom among his three daughters, measuring out their inheritance according to the extent of their love for him. He gives Goneril and Regan, who claim to love him fervently, large divisions, and he disowns Cordelia, who refuses to express her love publicly.

I came to see the two texts as relics of a sensibility now dead and buried, which needed historical excavation. I also saw and see them as framing this sensibility in its historical trajectory, significant routing signs in a history of ennobling love.[1] It is at a high point when the king's love ends war, and it has reached a serious crisis when a king's daughter can confuse official arrangements for succession to the throne by letting personal considerations intrude.

In the course of my reading I came across hosts of courtiers and aspirants to office declaring their love of kings and receiving rewards from them. These men would probably react with nearly as much alarm to Cordelia's refusal as did her father. Even allowing for historical kings with better sense than Lear, and allowing that even stupid kings probably would not appoint their successors by a staged love contest,[2] a king's daughter who refused to express her love for the king her father, when asked point blank and publicly to do so, would be in trouble. A trial against Cordelia on charges of insult of majesty would almost certainly go against her. At least it would be easy for the prosecution to assemble a jury of medieval bishops, abbots, courtiers, pretenders, princes, clerics, who either indeed loved and were loved by the kings they served, or pretended to, and it would be hard for the defense to find anyone who thought public displays of fervent love for the king foolish. Here are some from that large jury pool, quickly and easily culled from the "minions" of various kings, bishops, archbishops, and their officers, whose loves are in part the subject of the following chapters.

Venantius Fortunatus wrote a panegyric poem to the Merovingian king Sigibert I, "spurred on by love" of the king; he praised Sigibert's choice of Gogo as counselor since, "being a lover he has chosen one who loves."

Smaragd of St. Mihiel received an important abbacy from Charlemagne and as thanks wrote,

Those embraces which your royal arm has sweetly bestowed on us are painted on the secret surfaces of our mind, your honey-dripping kisses carved on the tablets of our heart, your words — kingly, honey-flowing, sweet and gentle — we treasure in the inner-most recess of the mind.

The Frankish poet and courtier Angilbert declared his love for Charle-magne in a poem to his court, urging the court poets to let the king's love fill their hearts and inspire their songs; he became the lover of Charlemagne's daughter Bertha and father of her children, and later abbot of Saint-Riquier.

Alcuin, Charlemagne's tutor and favorite, told the king,

the sweetness of your sacred love abundantly refreshes and soothes the ardor of my breast every hour, every minute; and the beauty of your face, which I constantly dwell upon in loving thoughts, fills all the channels of my memory with desire and an im-mense joy, and in my heart the beauty of your goodness and your appearance enriches me as with great treasures.

He eventually became abbot of Tours.

The court poet Theodulf pined for Charlemagne's son, Charles: "My eyes thirst for the sight of you with unquenchable longing, and the lofty love in my breast desires you." He became bishop of Orleans.

Bebo of Bamberg, former tutor of Henry II, despaired (like Lear's daugh-ter Goneril) that "mere words can express, most beloved emperor, how much I love you" — a prelude to requesting a promotion.

Meinwerk of Paderborn showed Henry II "the flames of his intimate love," and was promoted to bishop of Paderborn.

Aelred of Rievaulx "embraced in love" King David of Scotland, who in turn "vehemently loved" Aelred, made him his steward, and planned to make him a bishop.

And finally, Richard Lionheart loved King Philip Augustus of France, shared his bed, and was loved by him "as his own soul."

There are many others. Courtiers and pretenders, aspiring abbots and bishops, and even officers who wanted the king or queen to pay the bills for their military campaigns,[3] declared their love for the monarch. Their rhetoric can make that of Regan and Goneril seem tepid. It was not just self-serving flattery or empty good manners; it was a recognition of royal charisma, or virtue, or divinity. An aura beamed from a true king as brightly as the sun gleamed from his crown, and the response in his retinue that credited it and bowed to it was powerful and passionate love.

Packing the jury with kings' lovers in this way assures the result: all those courtiers who in the course of the Middle Ages did gladly and out of a sense of devotion and duty what Cordelia refused to do would surely convict her of the charges.

Of course, her strong defender is William Shakespeare, and he located the defense beyond refutation: in the characters and the events. He set up two callous hypocrites as king's lovers, reduced their love to a mask for utility and ambition, and made the king blinded, rash, and foolish. He also infused a new high value into private emotions as distinct from public emotions, so that his readers admire characters like Cordelia and Hamlet who show contempt for "actions that a man might play" and who have "that within which passeth show." The medieval jury found "show" and "played actions" vitally impor- tant, — and hoped that they corresponded to "that within."

But apart from the particular characters playing out their particular desti- nies, the principle remains. Cordelia's father may have overreacted, but to refuse a confession of love for the king in a solemn public forum charged with destiny for the kingdom is a little like knocking his crown off his head. When Cordelia says,

I love your majesty
According to my bond; nor more nor less,

she is, in the eyes of our packed jury, putting on public display a denial of his royalty. That is bad enough coming from any citizen, but coming from his favorite daughter it is a terrible breach of etiquette. It may be all right to love him as father and private person "according to her bond" and no more, but to love "his majesty" so cold-bloodedly is to reduce it. The forum is not only charged with state policy, it is a stage for giving and receiving "face," and Cor- delia's posture makes the king lose face publicly. Our anachronistic jury would also understand the king's next gesture: he gives his two "loving" daughters his

. . . power,
Pre-eminence and all the large effects
That troop with majesty.

but disowns Cordelia and strips her of her dowry, since "now her price is fallen." Lear's "worth" sinks because of her "proud" words, and it follows that the king lowers Cordelia's "worth" in response.

What makes a study of ennobling love especially difficult is that after the sixteenth century most available jurors would view Lear's methods of succession through the filter of a new paradigm; there would be very few who fully understood how the love of the king translated directly into political favor, *overriding any personal feelings*.[4] Increasing numbers would acquit Cordelia of the charges, in fact would see only a foolish father and a genuinely loving daughter, and in public confessions of love only bunk, flattery, and empty ceremony. By Shakespeare's time, the love of kings had moved to the status of an atavistic and slightly dubious form of royal representation, not to be taken seriously as sensibility and genuine emotion. Love no longer was necessarily one of "the large effects that troop with majesty." The western culture of love increasingly privatized the experience, idealized it when turned inward and fastened nontransferably on a single object, made it subjective and deeply individual. Loving became something like praying, and public displays of it had to seem, as they did to Cordelia, a kind of hypocrisy.

*   *   *

This book studies the conception of love that Cordelia violated. It is a spiritualized love that responds to the "virtue," the "majesty," the charisma, the saintliness, of the beloved, to some inner force of authority or amiability or sanctity. It occurs in various sites of aristocratic life. I have set it here in the main context I find it in prior to the twelfth century, the love of kings, but it is important to stress that kings as the bearers of majesty are just the largest object of what I will call "charismatic love." There were many others. Any exceptional human being inspires it. The greatest kings had it along with abbots, bishops, courtiers, and the most humble saints.

It is also important to stress that charismatic love is a genuine mode of loving. At a king's court love and devotion are never, or hardly ever, separable from ambition and material rewards. Still, there was a mode of loving that flourished in the presence of concentrated authority, power, or divine force, a love that was or could be heartfelt even when mixed with awe or terror or conniving ambition. Everyone who observed or reflected on it (like Aristotle, Cicero, Ambrose of Milan, Aelred of Rievaulx, and Peter of Blois) saw the dangers of love masking ambition, but none of them imagined that the genuine love of exceptional men was diminished in its value when its by-product was material gain or advancement in a career.

The love of virtue in another person is distorted if we imagine it as essentially the same as the emotions we call love, a private experience attended by romantic aspirations, taboos, sexual hangups, and attitudes to marriage very much like our own. Our sensibilities, formed beyond the Cordelian turn, need to clear their view of a filter that makes the only good love private and nontransferable. For the purpose of this study it is good to assume with an anthropologist's distancing that all the rich documentation on ennobling love from antiquity to the nineteenth century are voices from an alien, exotic culture and to study it with minimal contamination from ideas and social practices not its own.

This is not to argue that ennobling love somehow died out after the Middle Ages. It has not. It is still alive. Some of its basic assumptions, its passion, its elitism, are evident in Honoré Balzac's novel *Lily of the Valley*, which I discuss in the last chapter. One of the characters, Lady Arabella, passionately in love with the novel's hero, intones them in a speech in praise of the Indian practice of wife immolation, suttee:

"You must confess . . . that in the dead level of our modern manners the aristocracy cannot resume its place unless by exceptional feelings. How can I show the middle class that the blood flowing in my veins is not the same as theirs if not in dying in another way than they die? Women of no birth can have diamonds, silks, horses, even coats-of-arms, which ought to be ours alone, for a name can be purchased! — But to love, unabashed, in opposition to the law, to die for the idol she has chosen, and make a shroud of the sheets off her bed; to bring earth and heaven into subjection to a man, and thus rob the Almighty of His right to make a god, never to be false to him not even for virtue's sake . . . these are the heights to which vulgar women cannot rise."[5]

Whatever this hymn to suicide out of love owes to the plebeian would-be aristocrat Balzac, it states some important principles of aristocratic life. Love even in its most passionate manifestation is a form of show ("how can I show . . . ?"); it asserts class privilege and appears, not only to this rhapsode, as an instrument that stabilizes hierarchy in favor of an aristocratic elite. "Exceptional feelings" are a means of establishing superiority, a form of aristocratic self-representation; love is the most exceptional.

The Western aristocracy always invested heavily in the emotional life, as they did in jewels, chariots, and palaces. Rare and exceptional feelings are a higher, purer investment, adding to the capital in virtue, a greater source of respect, self-definition, and self-representation than the comparatively contemptible outward show.[6] Probably everyone can be persuaded that human dignity resides in the mind, the soul, and the emotions. The European aristocracy since antiquity built a culture of the self and, in part, an educational system on this conviction.

The exalting love of men for men in antiquity, "spiritual friendship" in the Middle Ages and "courtly love" from the twelfth century, are ordinarily seen within the confines of individual disciplines: history of ancient philosophy,

Christian monastic spirituality, medieval literary history. The one perspective that has seen and shown a common social tradition linking these diverse forms of love is history of homosexuality. But being focused on male-male love, gay history cannot include the other major manifestation of aristocratic culture of love in the premodern west, courtly love. The interrelatedness becomes clearer if we put the question of sexuality to one side and ask about the social function of ennobling love. This approach softens the borders that trenchant categories like "homosexuality," "Hellenic pederasty," "courtly love," and "spiritual friendship" create, and when transit across those borders becomes allowable, their relatedness as branchings of an aristocratic social ideal becomes evident.

In the Middle Ages "ennobling love" emerges in court society, in cathedral communities, and in monastic communities. They share common conceptions and formulations, drawing on Cicero's *De amicitia*, also on the Song of Songs and the Psalms, on the gospels, the letters of St. Paul, on the Acts of the Apostles, and on various Latin sources from late antiquity.

This ideal had a powerful influence on educational values and on ideals of behavior in the Middle Ages. Since the twelfth century it also created, at least participated in the creation of, a rich imaginative literature of love.

The argument of this book can be summarized in five theses:

1. Friendship and love were social ideals of the aristocracy in the Middle Ages, lay, clerical, and monastic. Varied as they were in these various sites of noble life, there are common threads, bundled in this study in the term "ennobling love."

2. Ennobling love is primarily a public experience, only secondarily private.

3. It is primarily a way of behaving, only secondarily a way of feeling.

4. It is a form of aristocratic self-representation. Its social function is to show forth virtue in lovers, to raise their inner worth, to increase their honor and enhance their reputation. It is, or is seen as, a response to the virtue, charisma, saintliness of the beloved, and must be distinguished from the monastic ideal of communal friendship (*caritas*), which is given as a social duty to all alike.

5. From antiquity until the late eleventh century this ideal of a social elite was restricted to men. Before that time the love of men for women and of women for men belonged with few exceptions to the private sphere. It had no public discourse, at least none, or virtually none, in which woman's love was ennobling. From the late eleventh century on women emerge in both the courtly and the monastic spheres as participants in this exclusive mode of behaving.

By itself this point of departure shows my "social constructivist" position.

I am looking at a society whose values were established prior to the great modern schism in the romantic life; it is a society in which men who loved men were not "homosexuals," even if they had sex with them; in which also men who loved women were not "heterosexuals." I try to explore here the territory stretching between spiritual and carnal love. I have tried hard to articulate the attitude to sex and gender implied or expressed in the texts themselves, not forcing modern conceptions onto them.[7]

The dilemma of romantic love is created by the tensions between sexuality and an ideal of virtuous love. In order to ennoble, love had to be a subject of virtue; it had to derive from virtue and in some sense also be its source. And so ennobling love had to manage sexuality, hold it in its place by severe discipline, or — the most ascetic position — banish it altogether, demonize it, lay heavy taboos on it. That meant that any love that incorporated and included sex was not ennobling. That excluded marital love by and large (though not invariably: Aristotle thought that love based on virtue could exist between spouses, and the Roman matron at a certain period became the bearer of virtuous love). But with very few exceptions the love of men for women could not ennoble, since sexuality was its natural fulfillment. Love and friendship of men for women that claimed "virtue" and innocence inevitably roused suspicion.

What I will call "the romantic dilemma" arises out of the attempt to reconcile virtue with sex. It became acute from the end of the eleventh century on, when women emerged in the discourse of ennobling love, and a kind of love joined naturally with sexuality asserted its ability to ennoble. Virtue and sex formed a precarious union; it was constantly falling apart, showing its destructive nature, crushing those who claimed its ennobling force. From the High Middle Ages on, the romantic dilemma created a great literature of romantic love, rich in ambiguities, full of tragic, destructive passion.

PART I

CHARISMATIC LOVE AND FRIENDSHIP

I

Problems of Reading the Language of Passionate Friendship

Two Kings in Love

Henry II's campaign in France in 1187 bogged down when his son, Richard Lionheart, to whom he had entrusted a large part of the English army, fell in love with the enemy king, the young Philip Augustus of France. Without giving the incident any particular highlight, the chronicler, Roger of Hovedon, writing at the turn of the twelfth to the thirteenth century, describes the end of the French siege at Châteauroux as follows:

Richard, Duke of Aquitaine, son of the King of England, remained with Philip, the King of France, who so honored him for so long that they ate every day at the same table and from the same dish, and at night their beds did not separate them. And the King of France loved him as his own soul; and they loved each other so much that the King of England was absolutely astonished at the vehement love between them and marveled at what it could mean.[1]

This passage poses the problems of understanding passionate male friendship and the love of kings in dramatic clarity.

At first glance the passage appears unequivocal. What does it leave to interpretation? Richard Lionheart and King Philip Augustus love each other "as their own soul" and share the same bed. Their affection is unapologetic; they make public gestures displaying it. The problem posed by the first glance is to explain how homosexuality could have asserted itself so baldly (and blandly at the same time) at the highest level of power of the two greatest kingdoms of the twelfth-century west without raising comment. But even a short way into the governing discourse, the word "homosexuality" becomes misleading. The text itself contains a few warnings against reading it as the mode of loving we call "homosexual." First, the reaction of two "observers," the king and the chronicler. Henry II, the young prince's father, was absolutely astonished at the vehement love between them and marveled at what it could mean. In order to take future precautions, he postponed his plans of returning to England until he could determine what plots this sudden love portended. (p. 7)

This is the reaction of a betrayed general, not an outraged father. The king's only concern is strategy. His military campaign, not his family honor, is in danger. His sole response to his son's passion is a change in his travel plans. He sees "plots," not a gay love affair, portended by this sudden, vehement love.

Roger of Hovedon narrates the budding love as a morally unencumbered subject. If these emotions and gestures had any power to indict, then he would have given us some nods, winks, or critical comments. The accusation of homosexuality was serious,[2] and it would have injected acrimony alien to the passage's idealizing. The coy gesture of supplying the reader with the material of a charge without making it himself does not fit the writer's *modus scribendi*. He did not hesitate elsewhere to criticize the royal family and Richard personally. But describing the love of Richard and Philip Augustus, he remained silent on the obvious question, and by doing so he validated the king's political hesitations as the appropriate reaction.

It may be possible to read elegantly camouflaged moral disapproval into the king's astonishment, which the narrative stresses. But that is because we are looking for moral disapproval. The text conveys none directly. Astonishment is neutral; it takes its moral coloring from its context. In this case the writer's attitude is clear: the love of the princes is exalting, not immoral; it "honored" the future king of England (. . . *in tantum honoravit . . . quod . . .*). Later in his narrative, the chronicler reported with admiration that the two kings resumed their old love when they met some years later in the holy land:

It seemed that the affection of mutual love between them was so strong that it could not be broken, nor could they ever betray their love.[3]

The tone is awe at a sublime relationship, its value that of lasting fidelity.[4]

Its very public character is also part of this love story. Since the affair knits two opposing princes, and, in effect, their armies and countries at the same time, and since it resolves a siege, it unfolds in the public spotlight. All the participants from grandees to foot soldiers are its witnesses. The "lovers" are on stage, and no indication is given that they reserve intimacy for off stage — just the contrary. Gestures of intimacy are exchanged at meals. There is apparently no fear of scandal at any level of this event, as recorded by Roger of Hovedon.[5]

This same author had a clear and strong conception of scandal and subversion wrought by the "sin of Sodom," and he thought Richard himself capable of that "sin."[6] His idealizing of the love of the princes rules out any intention on the part of the chronicler to "implicate" that love. Whatever the actual relationship between the two may have been, Roger of Hovedon's words do not convey, imply, or suggest homosexuality. In fact their intention may be to rule out suggestions of an illicit love.

Charismatic Love and Friendship

The chronicler had a conception of an exalting, "honoring" love between men that expressed itself in the gestures and language of passionate love. To understand this love without the help of the anachronistic concept, homosexuality, is the greater challenge of the text.

Philip Augustus and Richard are not the only kings in love. To judge from the number of royal love relationships, it seems normal rather than exceptional that a king loved his favorites, and that the courtiers and advisers, clerical and lay, loved each other. There is a language of royal favor which draws on the idiom of mutual love, passion, desire. It asserts itself (and shows its roots in the Roman nobility) in the poetry of Venantius Fortunatus in praise of various potentates in sixth-century Gaul. (See Chapter 2). The Carolingian court spoke an especially extravagant dialect (see Chapter 3). Charlemagne himself cultivated the love and friendship of those around him, and his courtiers addressed the king and each other as lovers. Here we might just note Alcuin's searing verses to his friend, fellow courtier and cleric, Archbishop Arn of Salzburg:

Love has penetrated my breast with its flame . . .
And love always burns with new heat.
Neither sea, nor land, hills nor forests or mountains
May stop or hinder the way of him
Blessed father, who always licks your innards,
Or washes your chest, O beloved, with his tears.[7]

Whatever is expressed in these impassioned lines, it is unlikely that it is what we would call homosexual love. Alcuin was an old man, around sixty five, when he wrote them, and while his age does not exclude sexual passion, his attitude toward male-male sex is fairly clear in other of his writings. At approximately the same period of his life, he and the emperor promulgated laws prescribing harsh punishments for "sodomy" in the realm.[8] Alcuin himself wrote a letter to a former student in England who is rumored to have had homosexual dealings. His condemnation is unequivocal. He warns him away from a practice that threatens both his social standing and his salvation.[9] At the very least that must mean that Alcuin's passionate letters and poems to male friends had no power to suggest or propose or strengthen an illicit relationship. If that were his intention, he would have pursued it in another form than the public one he chose, letters intended for communal reception.

The language of passionate male friendship stretched over various realms of aristocratic life. In the earlier Middle Ages it is documented most abundantly at royal and imperial courts. It is a language that may be called upon to describe favor relationships, peace arrangements, and genuine passionate friendships, and the three are often mixed in proportions that cannot be untangled by reading the documents. I will discuss some of the texts in Chapters 3 and 4.

The other major context is cathedral and monastic communities. Up to the end of the eleventh century I do not see distinct differences between the language of royal love and passionate friendship among monks and clerics. When this language appears in the communities of reformed monks in the twelfth century, it proliferates and infuses an intense Christian spirituality into the language of love. But these communities also share the apparent innocence of erotic language used publicly and unapologetically. A text by Anselm of Bec gives us an example. It is a letter the abbot wrote to two novices welcoming them into the community of Bec:

My eyes eagerly long to see your face, most beloved; my arms stretch out to your embraces. My lips long for your kisses; whatever remains of my life desires your company, so that my soul's joy may be full in time to come. . . . You have come, you have set me on fire; you have melted and fused my soul with yours; this soul of ours can now be rent asunder, it can never be separated.[10]

Is this a man shaken by a violent passion of body and soul? For *two* men at the same time? Not likely. Anselm had probably never set eyes on either of the men.[11] This was just his way of giving two newcomers a warm welcome to the community. His protestations of love and desire show them the atmosphere they can expect from the abbot of their new residence. The thought that he was welcoming them into a den of forbidden male eroticism is preposterous, and scholarly opinion on Anselm, whose letters and meditations push this question into the foreground, agrees.

Problems in Reading the Literature of Nonlibidinous Desire

An odd state of affairs: it is possible for medieval writers to say — in public documents — that a king loved his courtier vehemently, embraced him with the flames of intimate love, kissed him, slept with him, shared the same clothes, and ate from the same dish; it is possible for a cleric/courtier to say that he longs to kiss his archbishop-friend and to sink into his embraces, that he licks his "viscera," bathes his chest with his tears, and longs to fuse their two souls into one—and none of these formulations was received as an indication of an illicit erotic attachment.

These texts are like moral optical illusions. Interpreting them means laboring through a tangle of crossed signals and double-crossed perceptions. We have no vocabulary that can come to terms with the love of Richard and Philip Augustus. "Homosexual," "homoerotic," even "male friendship," are colored by the erotic. Even when the erotic is unstated ("male friendship") the terms still operate in the same force field.[12] Eve Kosofsky Sedgwick's term "homosocial" is useful.[13] It sets sexuality to one side, eliminates its automatic inclusion, while holding it in readiness. The discourse of male-male love displays on its surface sexuality vanquished and banished. Sexual desire and sexual intercourse can infiltrate it secretly, but they do not govern it from their position of hiding. Unquestionably the texts treated here are grounded in male desire; but just as unquestionably there is something in the discourse that screens off or remains oblivious to a sexual element in this desire. It posits nonsexual male-male desire, a contradiction neatly formulated in the richly ironic phrase of Paulinus of Nola, "chaste voluptuousness" (*casta voluptas*).

The peculiar character of homosocial desire in the Middle Ages emerges from a criticism and problematizing of the paradigm which takes sexuality as the grounding of love, desire, and friendship. Michel Foucault described the development of this paradigm in the first volume of his *History of Sexuality*. He asks the question, why do we talk about sex so much? Since the eighteenth century, the subject in the west has experienced a veritable "discursive explosion." Foucault combats the idea that some sort of movement to liberate sexuality from the strictures of a Victorian-Wilhelminian mentality is advancing slowly toward a grand victory over repressive Puritanism, a victory which will at last free us to talk about, teach, indulge without guilt to our heart's and body's content in safe and rational sex, a victory that makes us beneficiaries of a kind of enlightened Dionysianism.

Far from repressing sexuality in any other than the most superficial way, nineteenth-century Europe, says Foucault, organized a discourse on sex that was totally invasive, that sought to leave the subject no peace, to force it out of its hiding places, persuaded with the conviction of an inquisitor, that there is more everywhere than meets the eye. Society becomes the administrator of a "singular imperialism that compels everyone to transform their sexuality into discourse." It requires and facilitates "an immense verbosity" on the subject:

Rather than the uniform concern to hide sex, rather than a general prudishness of language, what distinguishes these last three centuries is the variety and wide dispersion of devices that were invented for speaking about it . . . for inducing it to speak of itself. . . . What is peculiar to modern societies, in fact, is not that they consigned sex to a shadow existence, but that they dedicated themselves to speaking of it *ad infinitum*, while exploiting it as *the* secret. (pp. 33–35)

The superficial repression of sexuality, the token taboos placed on it, were the outer signs of a symbiotic relation between power and the discourse of sex. In their urge to drive sexuality out of the private and into the open, to expose it, the forces of Victorian repression cooperated with the forces of libertinism and perversion. The father confessor wanted—in terms of a discourse on sex—essentially the same thing as the Marquis de Sade. The web of prohibitions grows along with the web of discourse, precisely because the symbiosis of taboo and transgression allowed the mechanisms of power to reestablish dominion over the human body, a dominion which had weakened when monarchy was forced to give up its absolute power over the life and death of the individual. Therefore the apparently daring gesture of trying to liberate the sexual life from its captivity among the forces of prudishness in fact is collaboration with a greater power structure orchestrating both the repression and the revolt against it.

The paradigm at work in this process influences our perceptions of everyday life, of motivations and their relations to the subconscious in a way so pervasive that we are hardly aware of it, like the air we breathe. It has its most prominent formulation in Freudian psychology. It is the major site of the hypertrophy of sexual discourse which is the subject of Foucault's first volume. It grounds a science of the explanation of human psychology in its every aspect on libidinous impulses. The sexual gains an explanatory power uncontested by any other realm or source of motivation; ego, will, reason, intellect, moral and religious values are subordinated to it, are seen as its agents operating from within an illusion of sovereignty. This paradigm makes the level of appearances in human relations—and the literal level of a text—into veils concealing the actual moving forces. It makes the subconscious the ground of explanation and the source of truth.

Unmasking what is masked, penetrating to the final object hidden behind the veils of concealment, exploring that which ultimately grounds the emotional and even rational life and their discourses become major intellectual tasks and obligations. The libido becomes the place of final appeal for arguments admitting of no contradiction, a Supreme Court of the psyche. Signs and signals on the surface of a text or of human actions that point to a hidden sexual motive answer all questions and place the inference of a libidinous source beyond refutation.

That is the force operating when we first read the texts on the love of medieval kings, courtiers, and monks. The governing logic is clear: since all friendship is libidinous, therefore passionate friendship is especially so. And that hermeneutic coercion coincides with a nearly completely absence of non-libidinous male love in our twentieth-century northern European-American culture of the emotions. It follows that the king's love must have been subject to the same psychological law. All the signals are there.

Love Objects

But they lead us in a circle; what starts as an analysis of the medieval mind ends in self-analysis. The lost sensibility at work in the medieval texts remains safely hidden. What we need to do is excavate it, expose its layers, map its structure, reconstruct it archaeologically.

The simple binary oppositions with which we operate — man-woman, man-man, hetero-homosexual, normal-abnormal — fix our understanding at the level of lowest differentiation. They fix it also at a point in time when love is not detachable from sexuality, and that includes, given the Freudian paradigm, friendship, prepuberty love, and the relations of children to parent.

The attachment of love to sexuality has a history; it was not always so firm, or rather the relationship between love and sex was far more variable than at present. To map this complex terrain we can begin by expanding the range of partners in love relationships and objects of desire. The list above presupposes sexuality. Man and woman, woman and woman, man and man, are thought of as bound in a relationship that would be endangered if sexual intimacy were removed from it. The terms "hetero*sexual*" and "homo*sexual*" set the modality of intimate relations.[14]

But within a mode of love that professed indifference to sex, or mastery of it, gender was a matter of indifference, far less important than social ranking. We can expand the list of love relationships to include ruler and courtier, teacher and student, bishop and cleric, abbot and monk, religious woman and spiritual mentor. These are relationships in which passionate love is not just "normal," but an exalting, distinguishing, "honoring" mode of relating lover to beloved.

Love and Politics

The best indication that our texts operate in this mode and not a Freudian one, is their very openness. They contain no subtle signals at all, no double entendres, no "slips," no allusions to *underlying* sexual motivations. They are perfectly direct and open. A precritical glance at them calls up a picture of homosexuality legitimized and fully accepted among the lay and clerical nobility.

But that poses a problem for the Freudian reader, whose interpretive mode lives from thwarting concealment. These texts act as if they had nothing to hide. Any psychological reading would have to explain why their authors did not try in any way to veil tabooed behavior. Far from disguising and masking, all these writers proclaimed openly feelings that would be perceived at any period of the Middle Ages as shameful and damnable, if coupled with libidinous desire and ambition.

To enter the discourse and the mode of feeling at work here, we need to imagine the love of kings as first and foremost a way of behaving. It is a social and political gesture, part of an extensive public discourse expressing aristocratic patterns of behavior. Its ambitions are social and political, not sexual.

But what is love other than individual experience? How can passion be anything else than a deeply intimate and therefore deeply private experience?[15]

Medieval poets and historians were by and large indifferent to what we call private life. We could infer from Georges Duby's introduction to the *History of Private Life* that no such concept existed, that all life was public, and those acts which occurred in privacy were simply unseen public acts.[16] Before the private life was anything in itself, it was the lack of the public. The etymology urges that interpretation: *privatus* means "deprived of," "lacking." Especially striking is the silence of medieval sources on sexuality. Concerned to the point of obsession with love, the medieval aristocracy and intelligentsia discoursed on the subject in the mode of ethical and fictional writings. Courtship and its difficulties were the subject, not sexuality as a screened-off private sphere with its own language and concepts.[17] The same appears to be true of the earlier Middle Ages. Peter Brown compared Augustine's interest in human sexual behavior to one's concern for "the gurgling of the plumbing in the neighbor's apartment." It existed. It was important in some limited realm of experience. But it did not generate a discourse.

In the public realm, however, the discourse of love developed extensively, placing sexuality in a very different position from any modern discourse. To illuminate this development it will help to distinguish experienced emotion and social gesture, two modes in which emotion operates and sensibility responds to it, and to see them in their relation to each other.

Social gesture is the fundamental act of a nonprivate love; it is the public manifestation of a sanctioned, idealized way of feeling. Acting according to a widely idealized pattern — love, compassion, courage — displays the actor's acceptance and embodiment of a society's or a community's ethical values. It makes him or her admirable, gives prestige (what medieval poets would call *pretz*, *valor*, and *werdekeit*). It demonstrates worth, raises status, and coalesces political support. It is public behavior, practiced equally by greats and by hypocrites.

That of course does not mean that social gesture is empty, ceremonial posturing. Just the opposite: in order to have weight and meaning, the gesture must be grounded in experienced emotion. The two relate to each other as sign to thing signified. If you "perform" love without feeling it, if you claim courage without possessing it, it reverses the prestige-giving effect, shows the act as hollow, the actor as hypocritical. Conversely, if you perform the gestures and speak the words of love badly, crudely, awkwardly, the force of the gesture evaporates. The public act has an audience that "reads" carefully and tests the performance for its congruence to lived and experienced emotion. Since all public acts are performances, a social gesture is self-discrediting if it is not performed with the gestures and expressions fitting the posture. The *habitus* of love or courage must be a seamless unit joining the inner virtue with the outward signs of its presence, as the Latin word just quoted fuses inner posture with outward indicator. A general's speech to his troops prior to battle must show forth — in its every aspect, in articulation, gesture, body posture, modulation of voice and facial expression — the emotions from which it purports to arise: commitment to a cause, love of country, willingness to die. Unless the general makes himself in the critical moment into a work of art proclaiming courage and patriotism, the cause to which he rallies his troops will lose legitimacy, his troops will wonder whether the man asking them to put their lives at stake would himself risk the same. The fervor proclaimed must *be seen* as deriving from fervor felt and experienced — and if it actually does derive from it, so much the better.

The congruence of experienced emotion and social gesture is no less critical in declarations of love. Love as a public gesture reverses the relationship of signifying act to signified experience that applies in private life, where the ill-performed gesture does not count so heavily. For public acts, outward gestures are the guarantors of commitment or engagement or fervor; they have quasi-legal force; they are policy made visible. This places a high value on good performance, makes it into an art that must be learned, be it the art of political rhetoric or the art of love. Good intentions are never an excuse for bad performances.

This creates the dreary necessity, for the witness to public performances, of distinguishing between genuine acts and affectation. Performances of courage or compassion or love become a locus for the most high-minded behavior and the worst hypocrisy; heroism and empty boasting alike claim courage as their emotional grounding. While the naive equation of good performance with inner commitment remains in place as a kind of moral imperative, experience shows that ambitious connivers master the art of performance just as well as exemplary public figures.[18]

The performance of public gestures creates a stage scenery of emotions, still usable in contemporary political life. In the 1988 American presidential race Michael Dukakis was accused of lacking compassion, and the charge caused one of the crises on which his campaign eventually foundered. This one was serious enough that he had to go on television and show his capacity for emotion. He declared his sympathy for the suffering and disadvantaged, and at the high point of his speech told his audience, "I love you!" Whether he did or not, his declaration was compliance with a norm of exalting behavior, that is, social gesture.

Social gesture in the realm of politics removes the emotions it signals from the force field of Freudian interpretation. There can be no question of libidinous motives in Dukakis's confession of love, or in the famous kiss planted lovingly by Leonid Brezhnev on the lips of Erich Honecker. Applied to public acts, Freudian psychology becomes a source of bad jokes, not a viable analysis of motives. Social gesture displays policy, based on an art of representing intention, and like any other work of art, it is a product of calculation and planning. It does not have the quality of unreflected execution of impulses bubbling up spontaneously from the libido. Public emotion has force in any political system, monarchy or democracy. In Dukakis's declaration of love there was something at work other than a personal love for Americans, something critically important for government, and something that makes irrelevant or naive the question "Does he really love us?" The question confuses private and public emotion, and the same confusion is at work if we wonder about the sexual preferences of medieval kings passionately in love with their "minions."

Eros and Power

Nonetheless, the erotic has an important role to play both in political and personal relations that draw on the discourse of the king's love. The law is still at work that makes performed love legitimate only if it derives from experienced love. But what sort of love is that? In what sense is the erotic present and functional when the aged Alcuin "dwells constantly in loving thoughts" on the beauty of Charlemagne's face which "fills all the channels of memory with desire and an immense joy," or when he longs to "sink into the embraces" of Arn of Salzburg, lick his breast and press his lips against each of his toes?

Anna Kartsonis said that there are more uses of the erotic than just erotic ones. And there are more conceptions of eros than are contained in our diminished vocabulary of amatory experience. The emotional life and the experiences of love have gradually lost their public face, and at least in this sense have narrowed, not broadened, since antiquity. They have experienced a steady "privatization" since the High Middle Ages. What was a labyrinth has become a one-way street.

"Power is an aphrodisiac": a famous quip of Henry Kissinger.[19] The more one moves away from diffused power (democracy) and into concentrated power (monarchy), the more broadly its implications fan out.

At its most primitive the love of kings is an emotional response to charismatic presence. The aura of the king's body creates a magical circle. Entering it has the effect of enchantment, like coming into the presence of a god and suddenly participating in divinity. The legitimation of rule through deification of the king is not just a ruler's tactic of maintaining power. It is a subject's response to royal charisma, an interpretation of it.[20] The representation of the king — regalia, robes, thrones, ceremony — tries to reinforce in the viewing subject the sense of witnessing a higher being with good connections to the supernatural world.

The king's presence has peculiar effects. It tends to numb the will and efface individuality. It creates something like a single being out of a mass of individuals. It has effects close to what Nietzsche called the Dionysian. Both are phenomena of mass psychology. The king's presence produces the responses of mass meetings even in a private audience. Imagine a single subject waiting with his petition to be ushered into the king's presence, anticipating the comforting distance of an elevated throne and obligatory lowering of the eyes. Unexpectedly the king appears in the same room, near him, looking him in the eye. The result: embarrassment, confusion, loss of will. The king speaks, and — lo and behold — he is a charming, grand gentleman almost flattered by his subject's petition; his affability is so disproportionate to his power, his ability to crush is so humanely muted by his will to please, the terror all prepared and packaged as the subject's emotional response to this audience is replaced by an immense gratitude, as at an act of grace, unexpected, undeserved, inexplicable. Like the thing on the threshold between terror and beauty in Rilke's first Duino Elegy, we admire him so because of his nonchalant refusal to destroy us.[21] Feelings cowed and rendered vulnerable by fear swing in an instant to homage and awe, then to love and devotion, intense enough that one's own life no longer means anything; one would gladly sacrifice it to maintain the life and power of this sweet and sublime king. Weeping and hysteria are common mass reactions to the ruler's presence. A common individual reaction is love, willing self-subjection, and the subject's urge to remake himself in the image and likeness of the monarch. Richard Fanshawe expressed this response in a few lines on Charles I:

. . . the people fix their eye upon
The king; admire, love, honor him alone.
In him, as in a glass, their manners view
And frame, and copy what they see Him do.
That which the murdering cannon cannot force,
Nor plumed squadrons of steel, glittering horse,

Love can . . .[22]

There is an order of experience in which human charisma produces a powerful, obsessive, shattering, transforming emotional response. One aspect of this experience, one among many, is the element of terror transmuted. The person with your life in his hands spares you; this transforms terror into love. Dostoevsky experienced this effect when he was sentenced to death along with a cell of liberal "conspirators" and, facing the firing squad of Tsar Alexander, was unexpectedly pardoned. The tsar was just kidding. And with the irrational force of religious conversion, the beneficiary of imperial grace is changed into a devoted adherent of the tsar and an ardent Russophile, even though there was certainly more malice than grace in the tsar's act.[23]

So, does the kind of love generated by concentrated power and authority have an element of libidinous desire? I think it often does, or can. Certainly the physical expressions of the king's love, embracing, kissing, sleeping together, sharing clothes, are natural gestures of desire. The initial response to the king's presence is awe and reverence, but one of the by-products of charisma is desire. A peculiar observation in the biography of Gerald of Aurillac (d. 909) shows the political object of desire especially clearly. Gerald ruled his vassals in an atmosphere of mutual love (so says his strongly idealizing biographer Odo of Cluny, d. 942).[24] His appeal to his subjects was not entirely paternal. It was in no small part physical. His beauty (not the kind that kindles lust and pride, Odo warns) suffused every part of his body, but his neck "was so radiant [*candidulum*] and shaped to such a norm of perfection that you would think you had never seen anything so beautiful" (1.12, 650C). His vassals were "accustomed to kiss his neck with great delight" and did so without any sense of degradation (1.12, 651A). The love for Gerald arouses the urge to kiss his most beautiful part, but only homage is expressed in the kiss, however much the gesture itself may signal sexual desire. "Enormous reverence" (*Ingens veneratio* — 1.32, 661B) binds Gerald to his vassals and friends, and this stimulates a desire whose ultimate motive is political.

Inseparable from such gestures of love is also the motive of favor and advancement. For the courtier to proclaim fervent love of the king is to claim feelings appropriate to the king's favorite. I think we would misrepresent the mode of feeling and expression at work here if we called such declarations of love self-serving or insisted that favor and advancement were masking themselves in a show of affection. The urge for promotion is no less open than the love of the king. (See the discussion of Smaragd of St. Mihiel's *Via regia* in Chapter 3.) The licit discourse of love between a prominent man and his favorites was a given of social interaction. The language of intense love embraced the economy of giving and receiving favor, the bestowing of rank, the service of the king, bishop, or archbishop; passionate friendship provided the language of favor. It is important to insist that the utilitarian character of the relations described as love does not argue against genuine feelings of intense love as basic to such relationships. The logic at work is that of charisma-inspired love, and when that logic is in effect, there is no good reason for us to think that a purse of gold, accompanied by words and gestures of love, inspires or increases genuine affection in a courtier less than a diamond ring or a dozen red roses might in a loved woman.[25] It is a modern sensibility that makes us suspect the one is buying favor and the other making a genuine gesture of love.

Taking the dynamics of passion into the political sphere integrated them into the dynamics of power, or rather made the two inseparable. The king's court becomes a family, his courtiers bound to him in *familiaritas*, *amicitia*, *amor*, and *caritas*.[26] The system of rewards and punishments operated through a discourse of emotion: love and hate stand for favor and disfavor; the king's frown, his unhappiness or anger, register policy, not only the private mood of the moment. Or rather, emotion and policy become inseparable.[27] The king's "private" persona disappears, submerges in his public persona. His feelings and his policies, his person and the state, become one and the same thing.

Still, we should not reduce the king's love to a play of power and self-interest masking itself in a language of passion displaced from its true object. That reduction would privilege one element of a rich, layered, and highly nuanced mode of feeling and expression. Also tempting is the reduction to rhetoric: "Political love was ceremonial language or gesture, and nothing more." Gerald's vassals lining up to kiss the most beautiful part of his body may be seen as a ritualized feudal obligation, like kissing the hand of the pope or bishop, but Odo's description makes clear that it is more, a response to the person of the count. His beauty arouses admiration and desire. The passage ushers us into the archaic atmosphere of a somatic reverence for the king that commended him in some cultures as a giver of fertility and that gave rise to the belief in a custom called "first night's right," *ius primae noctis*.[28]

The love of Gerald of Aurillac is experienced love (at least in the biographer's imagination), not empty ritualistic gesture. And even if Odo of Cluny made the whole thing up, his mode of imagining suggests the grounding in emotion of rituals of kissing generally.[29] There was something like the desire for the ruler, for both of his bodies, the personal and superpersonal, which originally gave rituals of reception and submission their lightly erotic cast. One of the great puzzles this kind of love poses for us is why the Cluniac monk Odo imagined that the whole cycle of desire and its physical gestures — seeing, admiring, and kissing the beautiful body — hallowed and exalted the relationship expressed, rather than the opposite. It is a shared conviction among Alcuin, Odo of Cluny, Roger of Hovedon, and many others.

But while the element of power is inseparable from the king's love, the form of love that Aelred of Rievaulx would call "sublime" is not grounded exclusively or even centrally in power. We are dealing with a phenomenon that shades off into gradations so subtle as to defy the scholar's, certainly the historian's, ability or wish to follow in all detail. The element of power, charisma, or force of person as an individual quality must in some sense be present in any romantic love. The sense of the transfiguration of the beloved, that she or he is rendered into a higher being by love, that some kind of magic is afoot that clears away the webs of everyday vision from the eyes of the lover and reveals a kind of divinity of the beloved, the language of religion that inevitably accretes around romance: these experiences argue that love as we idealize and practice it is a charismatic experience, an extraordinary state in which an individual responds to the beloved in a way analogous to the crowd's response to the king's presence. The conviction or illusion of the extraordinary character of the beloved is an experience of charisma.

Gender Questions

The aristocracy knew and practiced — with few exceptions up to the twelfth century — one form of love and friendship in its public life: the love of men. It is common enough in warrior societies, where the circumstances of war and military life produce strong bonds between men, where comradeship can shade into love and desire, and partnership become marriage.[30]

But it applies no less to men in public life, especially to those destined to take over the leadership of the state. This form of love develops a social tradition and a body of ethical and philosophical writings in Hellenic, Hellenistic and Roman societies, one which continues into the Middle Ages and Renaissance. Platonic love is an early form of it.[31] Through much of Greek and

Roman antiquity and the earlier Middle Ages, the love of men had the power to exalt the partners in relationships, to cultivate and proclaim virtue, a power that has turned into its opposite in a culture that taboos male love. In the friendship of Richard Lionheart and Philip Augustus love crystallizes at the pinnacle of power, and far from abasing, the public gesture of loving each other and sleeping together "honors" them.

That poses the central problem of this book: to recover the sensibility that sees passionate love relationships as exalting and ennobling, and to watch some of the twists and turns ennobling love takes in its historical development.

Homosexuality

The main texts in the earlier sections of this study are relevant to a history of homosexuality in the Middle Ages. But not at the level of the questions: Was Anselm of Bec gay? Was Aelred of Rievaulx homosexual? Those questions, and a common orientation of gay history and literary theory, are dominated by an assumption that sexuality is constitutive of identity and human dignity.[32] Sexuality becomes a point of conflict because it is claimed by a traditionally persecuted group as exalting and distinguishing, and by its persecutors as degrading and "unnatural." Its position is comparable to religion in the history of the conflicts of Judaism and Christianity, and that means that it is an extremely sensitive issue.

Very few texts of any genre from any milieu in the Middle Ages represent sex between males as ennobling or exalting. They are, however, only slightly fewer than the texts which represent sex between men and women as exalting. But putting aside the virulently antihomosexual literature (like Peter Damian's *Book of Gommorrha* or Alan of Lille's *Complaint of Nature*), the moral hesitations, the taboos, the circumscriptions and proscriptions relate *to sexual intercourse, and not to the choice of gender in friendship and love relationships*.

A representative text is the twelfth-century debate poem between Helen and Ganymede. It is a reasoned debate in which Helen defends the love of men for women, Ganymede that of men for men. Nature, Reason, and an assembly of gods are to be the judges of the debate. It presents — up to a point — a serious and powerful defense of male-male love. The judges hear the positions impartially until at the very end Helen mentions the act of sexual intercourse between men. The mention is enough: Reason stops the debate and gives the victory to Helen without discussion. The gods concur.[33] The poet was arguably "tolerant" of male love, but not of male-male sexuality.

Richard Lionheart may well have included men among his sexual partners. The same chronicler who thought the king of France honored him with his love included a scene in which a hermit confronts him and warns him against unnamed vices which clearly refer to "sodomy."[34] Evidently he did not regard Richard's relation to Philip Augustus as an example of that same vice. Both Augustine and Aelred of Rievaulx confessed that early in life they had not only loved particular men, but also desired to have sex with them — or actually did. But exalting and ennobling as the love and desire were, sexuality polluted and destroyed both.[35]

Love as sexual discipline was a social form as important as courtesy, central to the social and political functioning of many European courts, cathedral, and monastic communities. Of course, like any social form, it was also a mask, and behind it the whole spectrum of sexual practice could play itself out — including heroic renunciation, also including "sodomy." Richard Lionheart received honor, heightened respect, and fame because the king of France "loved him as his own soul." That statement says nothing at all about Richard's sexual orientation. It no more opens Richard's sexual habits to view than the public love declarations of Elizabethan courtiers reveal those of Queen Elizabeth I.

Male lovers are very much an issue in this book, but not homosexuality. Nor is the question whether Aelred, Anselm, and others who loved men were homosexuals. It is a bit like asking whether they were liberals, Jacobites, or Unitarians. The category did not exist and using it thrusts an alien set of values onto a sensibility which is delicate and wants reconstruction on its own terms.

But I hope that this study also contributes to a history of homosexuality in the Middle Ages — by moving the texts on the ennobling love of men beyond the question of sexual practice. The question raised here that, to me at least, is far more interesting and far more challenging to modern sensibilities is why the medieval aristocracy, in a society that at one extreme demonized homosexuality and at the other merely "tolerated" it, took its language of ideal, exalting love from the love of men. Why did it do honor to Alcuin, Anselm, Aelred, Richard Lionheart, and many others to love and to be loved passionately by male friends?

Virtue and Ennobling Love

(I)

Antiquity and Early Christianity

Ennobling love in antiquity had many ideas and customs in common with medieval. Predominant is the idea that love raises the value of lovers, shows forth virtue, increases their social standing. Three passages asserting that point can serve as a bridge from antiquity to the Middle Ages:

Aristotle, *Nicomachean Ethics*:

The friendship of good men is a good thing. It grows constantly through close association. And as experience shows, the friends increase in ethical worth. This is a friendship of actions and of mutual perfecting. For each forms in himself, as it were, the excellent qualities which please him in the other by taking each other as a pattern. Thence the proverb, "You learn to be good from a good man."[1]

Plutarch, *Dialogue on Love*:

Love makes a man clever, even if he was slow-witted before; the coward brave. Every lover becomes generous, single-hearted, high-minded, though miserly before. His meanness and avarice are melted away. . . . Doesn't love change the ill-tempered and sullen and make them more sociable and agreeable. . . . A mean, base, ignoble soul suddenly is invaded by high thoughts, liberality, aspiration, kindness, generosity.[2]

Andreas Capellanus, *De amore*:

The effect of love is that no greed can cheapen the true lover. Love makes the hirsute barbarian as handsome as can be; it can even enrich the lowest-born with nobility of manners; also it customarily endows the arrogant with humility. A person in love learns to perform numerous services becomingly to all. What a remarkable thing is love, for it invests a man with such shining virtues, and there is no one whom it does not instruct to have these great and good habits in plenty![3]

Antiquity and the Middle Ages treated love in any public discourse as an ethical subject.[4] This is perhaps the fundamental distinction between those periods and the modern age. For the aristocracy love was a potential source of distinction. That made it an important social form. It was constantly being fussed over: formulated in philosophical treatises, debated in symposia, invested with rules, moral restrictions, prohibitions, defined, the definitions refined, the distinctions fanning out broadly into taxonomies of the amatory or erotic life.

From this complex skein I am separating out one motif that remained more or less constant in the west from Hellenic times to the thirteenth century and beyond: what constituted the true object of love in its best form and that which conferred love's ability to ennoble was called "virtue." Virtue — Greek *areté*, Latin *virtus* — was the name of clusters of excellent qualities. The object of ennobling love might be strength, courage, wisdom, charisma, sanctity, piety, goodness, mercy, or many others. During that entire time span — and well beyond — the conviction persisted that beauty was one of the external indicators of an inner virtue, since beauty was most able to stimulate love and desire. But so could, in this view, the other virtues: eloquence, bravery, compassion, good actions. Pausanias, in his speech on love in Plato's *Symposium*, distinguished between two kinds of love, one which is "beautiful and worthy of praise," and another which is ugly. The latter seeks to love more the bodies than the souls of lovers. Those who practice this "ugly" love wish for witless lovers and rush toward gratification of the body. Against this, "beautiful" love derives from a heavenly Aphrodite and has as its object boys in the first blossoming of their mind; it is restrained and disciplined; it is love of the soul, not the body, aimed at the education of the young man to courage and greatness of soul. That "ugly" love that seeks only the gratification of the body, so says Pausanias, fades along with physical beauty; but the other is permanent, since it desires and cultivates the noble soul in the beloved. Likewise for the beloved, the only service he may perform for the lover with honor is that which is directed at wisdom and virtue. Only that love is beautiful which is based on education in reason and virtue.[5]

Phaidros in the same dialogue had represented eros as an ethical force that spurs men on to bravery, great deeds, the defense of the country, lends nobility to men who shun disgrace, and raises them in the favor of the gods, who shower honors and preferences on lovers: "In truth there is no sort of valor more respected by the gods than this which comes from love."[6]

Aristotle's treatise on friendship in the *Nichomachean Ethics*, books 8 and 9, is a sober analysis that presents itself as a reflection on social practice. He distinguishes three kinds of friendship, one based on lust and pleasure, the second on self-interest and political advantage, the third on "ethical excellence" (*areté*).[7] This latter kind of friendship distinguishes the best states.

Since friendship is a thing like justice, the level of friendship in a state is an indication of the level of justice; if there is no friendship, the "constitution" is corrupt and the state a tyranny; friendship is a higher form of justice, since if men are friends, they have no need of justice.[8] As with the state, so with the individual, the moral excellence of a man can be measured by the number and quality of his friendships:

[Friendship] is noble in itself. We praise those who love their friends, and it is counted a noble thing to have many friends; and some people think that a true friend must be a good man. And many are persuaded that "good man" and "friend" are equivalent terms.[9]

The connection of friendship with virtue became the theme of Cicero's *Laelius de amicitia*, the handbook of friendship for the European aristocracy into the seventeenth century.[10] While he recognizes its pragmatic side, he restricts the definition of friendship to "love of virtue in another man": "Friendship cannot exist except among good men."[11] When friendship consists in perfect agreement among men on all things human and divine, joined with goodwill and affection, then it is the best gift of the gods to man, apart from wisdom (6.22). Cicero agrees with the "noble" view that virtue is the chief good of man, and claims that virtue alone creates and conserves friendship. Virtue is the highest object of desire, that force in a person most able to generate love:

There is nothing more lovable than virtue, nothing that more allures us to affection, since on account of their virtue and uprightness we in some way love even those whom we have never seen. (8.28)

This is a phrase that was to have a grand future in the Middle Ages and which marks the character of Ciceronian friendship perhaps most clearly: it assumes the chasteness and spirituality of a friendship which does not require the physical presence. A man's goodness and virtue are the common knowledge of his society, passed on in its common report. Hence absence is the test of friendship based on excellence of character: if love originates in the admiration of virtue, then friendship can be generated with no admixture of sensuality, even without the physical presence of the beloved.

Love is inseparable from friendship, Cicero claims; their names show their relatedness: *amor, amicitia*. Love is older and "more beautiful," deriving from Nature. Allied with its "child," friendship, love generates goodwill, *benevolentia*. Friendship is "an inclination of the soul joined with a feeling of love [*sensus amandi*]" (8.26–27).

Cicero's idea of love and friendship is very different from Hellenic and

Hellenistic notions. For Plato and Aristotle love and friendship existed between the three terminals of the erotic, of self-interest, and of virtue. The
Ciceronian idea virtually eliminates the erotic. Lust is not the adversary of
virtue; it plays next to no part. In Plato and Xenophon physical desire is
present in love as a powerful threat to virtue and honor; the disciplined subordination of desire to virtue constitutes the heroism of love. Physical possession
was the last stage in Platonic love, the lowest, and the least able to confer
honor and standing. But from Hellenistic times on it was increasingly tabooed
and banished from the cult of friendship and its practices.[12] It has no place in
Cicero's writings or in the cult of ennobling love in Roman and earlier medieval traditions.[13] Here total forbearance and relations aiming only at refinement of the soul were marks of *askesis*, *disciplina*, self-discipline. Sexual intercourse could only pollute and destroy friendship. Certainly libidinous desire in
the narrower sense was often present in male friendship, but within the post-
Hellenic ethic of this relationship, it could only be regarded as a lurking
danger.

The essential tension in Cicero is between virtue and utility or self-interest,
the latter shaded into need, weakness, ambition, and their allies, cunning and
calculation. The antagonist of virtue is not lust, but baseness and evil. It is an
erotics of the public man, removing any element of physical pleasure from the
surface of discussion. Friendship was available to unite members of a ruling
elite and to show others in their political network, friend or enemy, how good
they are (therefore meriting power) and how firm their alliance is (therefore
inspiring caution or fear in enemies and respect in all).

The force of social ideals in strengthening and legitimizing power is easy
to underestimate or to dismiss as "ideology" masking class privilege. But Cicero's idea that close and real friendship creates firm alliances, and alliance
means power, is an experience of any form of public life in any period. For
antiquity the ability to make and maintain friendships was also made into a
visible sign of moral and class superiority. This connection had an important
influence in shaping social ideals and the exercise of power in the Western
aristocracy.

*   *   *

Friendship played an ambiguous role in early Christianity. Early traditions of monasticism and the writings of the eastern fathers cast doubt on it
and reject it as part of the worldliness that monks abandon when they enter the
religious life.[14] The testimony to friendship in early Christianity in the west is

almost exclusively a derivate of the Roman aristocratic tradition.[15] This tradition continues among secular clergy and reaches into monastic communities, not as a social element philosophically suited to the monastery, but as a Christianized aristocratic practice. This relationship is evident in the treatment of friendship in Ambrose's *De officiis ministrorum*. The work creates an ethic of the public life for "ministers" of the church, an ethic forged above all from Cicero's formulation of the ideal of the Roman statesman in *De officiis*. Ambrose borrows and adapts Cicero, illustrating the obligations of the church minister with biblical testimony. The passages on friendship are likewise confected from Cicero and the Bible:

What is a friend if not a consort of love, to whom you can join and attach your spirit, mingling it so that out of two you would become one? One to whom you are united as to another self, from whom you fear nothing, from whom you yourself seek nothing dishonourable for the sake of advantage—for friendship is not calculating, but full of beauty, full of grace. It is virtue not gain.[16]

The passage is rife with Ciceronian ethical concepts: friendship wards off dishonor (*inhonestum*), flows with beauty (*decor*) and grace (*gratia*). This Ambrosian friendship fits the ethical scheme of *De officiis*, and even outbids Cicero by fully identifying virtue and friendship: *Virtus est enim amicitia*,[17] though it is far more suspicious of advantage gained by friendship than Cicero, who understood its political value.

This dependence on classical traditions for formulations of friendship was still strongly in force in the twelfth century when Christian writers had developed a rich vocabulary of passionate friendship adapted from the Psalms, the Song of Songs, and the New Testament. Aelred's *Spiritual Friendship* is, like the end of Ambrose's *De officiis*, a Christian appropriation of Cicero's *On Friendship*.

Christianity complemented or checked ancient conceptions of friendship with a communal ideal, called in Latin *caritas*, in which love was given from the love of Christ to all alike for the sake of establishing peace and claustral paradise. This is very different from the ancient tradition, which always presupposes intense personal attachments between exceptional men distinguished by virtue and conformity of soul. The latter is not a communal experience. It is important to insist on the distinction. In the major stations of noble life in the Middle Ages two conceptions of love were current: the one a modified Greco-Roman elitism of the emotions, the other a social obligation intended to create harmony in a community; the one charismatic, the other communal. At royal and imperial courts, in cathedral communities, and in Benedictine monasteries, the dominant mode of friendship is Ciceronian, elitist, based on virtue and charisma. This kind of friendship is never formulated prior to the twelfth century as a specifically monastic ideal.[18]

Two important texts will bring the tensions between charismatic and communal friendship into sharp relief.

John Cassian (died 435) wrote one of his *Collationes* (Conferences) on the subject of friendship.[19] It is a useful work, because it is concerned with friendship as a specifically communal experience. But as such, friendship shrivels in comparison with the intense and passionate attachment it was for Augustine and Paulinus of Nola to little more than the control of conflict and maintenance of peace and order among monks.[20] In a significant passage he leaves open more intense personal attachments. By analogy to the particular love of Christ for the apostle John, he describes a hierarchy of love:

This is truly the ordering of love, which hates no one, but loves certain people more because of their merits: although it loves all in a general manner, this love nevertheless chooses some of these whom it ought to embrace with a particular affection.[21]

There is, then, one exception to the rule of loving all equally: the *jus meritorum*, the merit of certain individuals. This is an early Christian relative of the Ciceronian conception, love as a response to the virtue of another man.[22]

The Rule of Benedict was the most influential formulation of the common life in Western monasticism. It has nothing to say about friendship and comes closest in stipulating that virtue should be the sole consideration that might bring the abbot to love one monk more than another.[23]

These are telling witnesses to the nature of friendship in earlier western monastic tradition. Charismatic friendship represents a problematic intrusion of a classical tradition into the monastery, where equality, *equalitas morum*, is an important social ideal—however seldom achieved in largely noble communities.

The adhesion of Christianity to a Roman aristocratic tradition is dramatically evident in Paulinus of Nola's verses to his former teacher Ausonius Autpertus, one of his best known poems.[24] He preludes by rehearsing the metrical schemes he has chosen to harmonize with the various themes of his poem: elegiac for the introductory regret at their slackening correspondence; light iambic for words of praise and gratitude; then heroic for rebuke. It is a highly self-conscious display of a lettered gentleman enjoying and making use of an education reserved for an aristocratic and intellectual elite. It is prelude to a rejection of the traditions of classical learning in favor of Christian spirituality. He invokes the muses and Apollo only to reject them, while keeping them palpably and audibly in the background as informing spirits of his poem;

he conjures the weight of the law and the cleverness of philosophers to reject them as false and empty in favor of Christ, who illumines the whole being and gives truth and goodness. Christ the source of all blessings and the "Master of the virtues" cleanses bodies and minds of all foulness and compensates men thus purified with "chaste voluptuousness" (line 62).

The phrase *casta uoluptas* is intentionally provocative, since *voluptas* is inseparable from sensual pleasure, as is the English "voluptuous." The positing of a sensuality beyond the flesh seems to me typical of the Christian adaptation of Roman social and cultural forms: he rejects sensuality only to return to it in a higher sense. As in the classical intellectual tradition, desire is not abandoned; it remains very much the giver of discourse, but it is cleansed and chastened. The logic of the progression out of Roman culture to a Christianity that offers a higher sensuality, the notion of a licit delight, which appropriates and speaks innocently the language of physical delight, will repeat and entrench itself in the friendship traditions of the medieval nobility.

The poems of Venantius Fortunatus (ca. 530–ca. 600) show both Roman continuities in the expression of fervent friendship and the transformation of Roman traditions into the milieu of medieval kingship and early monastic life.[25] Fortunatus was an Italian who visited the Merovingian potentates of Gaul in the middle of the sixth century, settled in Poitiers, became Bishop of Poitiers and died shortly after 600.[26] The influence of his liturgical writings, hagiography, and of his epistolary verse was considerable. He produced a large body of panegyric poetry commemorating his friends and patrons. His poems speak a fervent language of friendship. He wrote to King Sigibert that not his own, Fortunatus's, talents prompt him to write, but rather it is "love of you which spurs me on."[27] Sigibert has chosen his counselor and favorite, Gogo (perhaps *major domo*) because, "being wise [Sigibert] has chosen a wise man, and being a lover has chosen one who loves" [elegit sapiens sapientem et amator amantem]; "You [Gogo] love [the king] so much that you've won good fortune for him."[28] He praises Conda, another court official of Sigibert, for having won "the singular love of such great kings"; when Conda held power at the "great court" of Chlotharius, the household was "ruled with the same love"; Conda enjoys "the great love of the king," and therefore from love receives lavish gifts.[29] The "sweet name" of Duke Lupus of Champagne is "always inscribed on the page of my heart," which possesses a "wealth of love, a rich affection forging pure gold by its own feelings!"[30] These were a few passages (there are many more) characterizing the love language to members of royal courts.

But the range of recipients in Fortunatus's correspondence to beloved friends is broad. His poems of love and friendship have been well analyzed by

Verena Epp.[31] She shows the extensive network of friendship relations that Fortunatus cultivated, in fact calls him "an artist of personal connections" ("Beziehungskünstler"). His rich body of poetry contains a panorama of the terms of friendship. He regrets the distances that separate him from his friends. He dwells on the beauty of their faces in absence. He hails them as the other half of his soul. He finds in the cultivation of friendship refreshment, even perhaps salvation.[32] The erotic component of his language is strong. The "beautiful shape" of the courtier Gogo "ignites him with love" (7.12). Kisses and embraces were signs of veneration, reverence,[33] and love (*signa amoris*), along with gifts, letters, and poems.[34]

The cultivation of friendship in poetry is not restricted to secular nobles; he writes in a similar vein to clerical friends,[35] and most significantly, to two remarkable noblewomen, Radegund, daughter of a Thuringian king and widow of the Frankish king Chlotharius I, and Agnes, a younger nun whom Radegund installed as abbess of the monastery.[36] The friendship among the three was extraordinarily tender and affectionate. The poems have the quality of private letters and probably were meant as such.[37] Peter Dronke has given a marvelous characterization with a few deft strokes:

a widowed queen, austere, but beautiful in all she thought and did, a young girl who grew up under her care and at twenty became her abbess, and a gentle, Epicurean court poet, capable of piety and of greatness, who made themselves a little haven, bourgeois and at the same time beautiful, in an age of chaos and brutality. (*Medieval Latin and the Rise*, p. 204)

The poems are written as thank-you notes; their subject is often food: he thanks Radegund for a gift of chestnuts (11.13); he admires the graceful, sculpted cut of Agnes's fingers, of which he finds a print in the butter rising to the top of the milk she sent him (11.14); his head still spinning from the rivers of wine that flowed at a feast, his "befuddled Muse" and love compel him to write some verses of thanks "with wavering hand" (11.23).

Verena Epp's analysis of these love relationships questions the connection with love service or courtly love, and Peter Dronke's questions the proximity to mystical reverence of saints and the Virgin Mary. Both show that the language of love is that of ancient *amicitia*, not distinguishable from the language in which Fortunatus addresses his male friends. But Epp also shows that the expressions of love for the women are regularly intensified by adjectives of religious fervor. Love is not just love, but "pious love," "heavenly love," "saintly love." Fortunatus reveres the women, sets them far above him in worth, and elevates the "love service" conventional to the Roman elegy into a spiritual, Christian love service ("Männerfreundschaft," p. 25).

But the distinction Fortunatus makes between women's and men's love has another purpose. Women's love is more open to reproach. This poem to Agnes (11.6) makes it clear:

In honor you are my mother, in love my sweet sister
    whom I worship with devotion, faith, heart and soul
with heavenly affection, without any sin of the body:
    I love what the spirit, not the flesh, seeks.
Christ is my witness, with Peter and Paul at his side,
    and along with this holy company Saint Mary sees
that neither with my eyes nor my soul have you been to me
    anything other than a sister, Titiana, from the same womb,
as if blessed mother Radegund in one birth-giving
    had produced us both in her chaste womb,
and as it were nourished us both
    from her dear breasts with a single stream of milk.
Alas, I weep at my cursed fate that with murmured whispering
    malicious words hinder my feelings.
And yet I am resolved to stay this course,
    as long as you wish me to be cherished with sweet love.

The essential difference between the love service of men and women is not that the one is social and the other spiritual. It is rather that the latter requires justification. His love for the two women may be heavenly, but it is also suspect and vulnerable to malice. That is the reason he has to conjure such a host of holy witnesses to its purity. Fortunatus's poems to Radegund and Agnes do not represent the invention of a new kind of religious reverence for women. He discovered, as Jerome had also discovered, that to love women in the same way one loved men put the "lover" on the defensive, opened him to reproach. Fortunatus's "cursed fate" is an early and all but isolated example of the romantic dilemma that will beset the medieval aristocracy on a much broader scale: male love is justified through virtue; but the love of men for women has to seek justification. Fortunatus justified it by projecting an urbane Roman cult of fervent friendship into heights of sanctity.

3

Love of King and Court

Charismatic Friendship

The experience of love and friendship inherited from ancient Rome was elitist and class-bound in the highest degree. That is clear in its major formulation, Cicero's *De amicitia*, which represents friendship as the prerogative of a social elite:

. . . friendship is cultivated by those who are most abundantly blessed with wealth and power and especially with virtue, which is man's best defence; by those least in need of another's help; and by those most generous and most given to acts of kindness. (14.52)

The alignment of wealth, power, and virtue was built into the system of social and political values of the European aristocracy. It is a means of self-validation but at the same time contains an ethical imperative: aristocracy defines itself as the possessor of virtue, therefore it must make itself virtuous. Its right to power and privilege depends in no small measure on its moral superiority. Its self-definition as the *aristoi*, "the best," imposes the need to assert and prove superiority.[1] To maintain rule by the best people, *aristo*-cracy, the best had to structure society and their own manners so as to reflect their standing and maintain it through exclusivity and various forms of coercion. They also had to display and represent the position at the top of the hierarchy they had created.[2]

The experience of friendship became structured and deployed as a social and political gesture. The admired ideal, the ennobling mode of feeling, gets worn as a badge of distinction. It is too valuable to remain hidden in the private dealings of individuals, nor did it occur to anyone to conceal it there. It was not only a philosophical abstraction or aesthetic ideal, but also a visible sign of moral and class superiority. The urge to self-representation asserted itself strongly in the area of sensibilities. Nobility of blood could justify itself through nobility of mind and soul. External refinements and physical beauty were hollow unless they were visible signs of inner worth. The Beautiful was the outer clothing of the Good. The ideal of *kalos kai agathos* made virtue, *areté*, into the inner motivating force signaled by external refinements. It obligated the aristocracy to certain kinds of behavior: generosity, condescension, kindness, affability. Those wealthy and powerful people who alone were capable of friendship in Cicero's view practiced generosity and acts of kindness as a privilege and mark of their class — at least generosity and kindness were social ideals, which of course they were free to violate, as they were free to refuse hospitality.

The simple equation of friendship and alliance, which was the glue of power and influence, was always present,[3] obviously, also in the philosophical discussions of friendship, but it was relegated to the level of "lower" friendship (Aristotle) and "facile" or "cheap" friendship (Cicero). Elitism of the emotional life and love as a moral selection test ranked far higher in the philosophers' hierarchy of values, and power and influence were among its fringe benefits.

The ideals of courtliness that chivalric literature imputed to the knightly class in the High Middle Ages are also expressions of this elitism. The chivalric idiom and the courtly mode of feeling made common cause in the Renaissance. And the cult of refinement is alive and well into the eighteenth century and beyond, the literary apotheosis reached perhaps in Madame de Lafayette's *Princesse de Clèves*. Balzac's take on the cult of emotion (see the passage quoted in the Introduction) is only exaggerated through the extreme emotions of Lady Arabella. Her conviction that the aristocracy asserts its place "by exceptional feelings" far better than by possessions would have found little contradiction within that class from Hellenic times to Balzac's.

In all its historical settings aristocracy appealed to sentiment as one of the groundings of superiority: the best people have the most refined and exalted feelings. This is the field in which the cult of friendship operated as a social gesture. Nonerotic love ennobled and gave witness to nobility.[4] Good love and passionate friendship were assertions of virtue, value, and quality of person, just as physical beauty and gentle manners were; they were badges of noble refinement.

*   *   *

Charismatic friendship and love based on virtue were preeminently at home in secular society, at least in those social arenas where exceptional character, virtue, charisma were admired. If this included monks and nuns, then it was because of their indwelling virtue, their sanctity and miracle working force, not because of their monastic profession. Clearly it did not respect strictly the social boundary, lay — religious. In the Ottonian period and beyond, it emerged as an important social code and an object of instruction in cathedral communities. When it did appear in monastic communities prior to the late eleventh century, it bore clearly the stamp of imperial forms of behavior.

Love of King and Court

The prince's court is an important locus of ennobling friendship in our period. Smaragd of St. Mihiel called love the "royal virtue" in his *Via regia*, a "Fürstenspiegel" written for Charlemagne: "This truly . . . is the royal virtue: . . . to give sweet kisses to all and to embrace all lovingly with open arms."[5] It is often colored by overtones of Roman senatorial nobility, a connection assured by the popularity of Cicero's *De amicitia*. The purpose of this section is to show love as a modality of interaction at royal courts in the earlier Middle Ages up to the eleventh century.

The "royal virtue" had been practiced in Merovingian times, as we saw in the poems of Venantius Fortunatus (see Chapter 2).

The Carolingian court developed a high culture of love and friendship. Love in its many shadings is the mood music of a large body of poetry[6] and letters.[7] Carolingian court life had a "staged" and "composed" character. The close friends and advisers of the king took on classical and Old Testament epithets: the king was "David," Alcuin was "Flaccus Albinus," Angilbert was "Homer." The language of love so prominent in the court poetry is part of that staging. A style of courtly representation and a scenario of court life are forming based on a mixed neoclassical and Old Testament idiom. Emplotted in this scenario are three of the main themes of Carolingian court verse: learning, poetry, and friendship.

The much quoted poem of Angilbert (Homer) sending greetings to the court in his absence is a good example.[8] The poem is written in a mannered style with strong reminiscences of Virgil's pastoral poetry and fainter ones of the Psalms. It has a ceremonial aspect to its "plot": Angilbert sends his flute to the court as his messenger; he bids it to sing as though, self-activated, it could deliver his messages by its own breath and performing skill. The idea that structures the song is the flute's progress through the court. It moves from one member to the next, greeting with its song all the poet's friends. There are flattering descriptions of each, the verbal counterpart of a court ceremony of receiving and being received, bowing, paying compliments. The structuring imagination at work is not that of a chronicler, or historian, whose genres would favor a series of portraits. The difference between "next in this series is . . ." and "next you will come to . . ." is the difference between the logic of narrative sequence and the logic of ritual progression.

The song's progress through the court is musical both within the metaphorical frame (the poem sings a song to the court) and in the character of the song. The dance-like nature of its progression is underscored by the refrain, repeated in some variant 18 times in 108 lines:

David loves poetry; rise up, my pipe, and make poetry!
David loves poets, David is the poet's glory . . . (2–3)

In its choreographed progression the poem assumes the role of a love messenger. He, or it, calls to the other poets to respond to the king's love by joining him or his flute's song in a chorus:

David loves poets . . .
and so, all you poets, join together in one,
and sing sweet songs for my David! (3–5)

The singers are to draw their inspiration from their love for the king:

May David's sweet love inspire the hearts of singers,
and love for him make poetry in our hearts!
Homer the poet loves David; make poetry, my pipe!
David loves poets . . .
May David's name resound on your lips in poetry,
and love for him fill your heart! (7–13)

Dulcis amor David inspiret corda canentum,
Cordibus in nostris faciat amor ipsius odas!
Vatis Homerus amat David; fac, fistula, versus!
David amat vates . . .
Nomen in ore tuo resonet per carmina David,
Illius atque tuum repleat dilectio pectus!

The song makes audible the love flowing from Charlemagne and circulating through the court. The song is to run along "through the holy palaces of David" and bring greetings "to all his dear ones" (cunctis caris), "embracing" them with its sweet tune (72–78). He bids it to throw itself down before the king and "sweetly kiss the hallowed toes on his feet!" (77). He varies the refrain to repeat the love theme:

David is our love, David is dear above all.
David loves poets, David is the poets' glory.
David loves Christ, Christ is David's glory. (90–92)

David amor noster, David super omnia carus.
David amat vates, vatorum est gloria David.
David amat Christum, Christus est gloria David.

This love language has in Angilbert's poem a particular honeyed sentimentality and preciosity, but it is common in poetry from the court circle.[9]
Paulus Diaconus expresses his love for the king in the conceit of a compulsion:

What need of cells or chains to restrain me. The love of my lord king conquers me. . . .
Just as Saint Peter burned in the immense love of Christ . . . so also the strong love of
you inflames my heart.[10]

Alcuin, like Angilbert, sends a "love song" (*carmen amoris*) to the king as a love
messenger: "May my flute make songs for my beloved David." And again in the
same poem: "As my spirit pursues you, so also does my song of love . . . O
beloved David."[11] In another poem to the king he cites Virgil: "'Love conquers
all'" and wishes, "now let it conquer us also."[12] The poet of the "epic" on
Charlemagne's meeting with Pope Leo, possibly Einhard, speaks of the radiantly happy figure of Charlemagne illumining the nobles of the court "in the
glow of his great love"[13] The poet called "the Irish exile," "Hibernicus Exul,"
addresses Charlemagne: "With these unkempt verses but with the highest love
of spirit, I contrive these things for you, O Caesar."[14] And Theodulf protests to
young Charles, the king's son: "My head's dual lamps thirst for the sight of you
with unquenchable longing, and the lofty love in my breast desires you."[15]

If the language of love were restricted to poetry, we might think it was
determined somehow by the lyrical genre. But it registers in other forms. Here
are some excerpts from the dedication of the *Via regia* of Smaragd of St.
Mihiel, a "Fürstenspiegel" for Charlemagne written around 810:[16]

We were moved to compose this little book not by any spirit of presumption, but rather
by the spirit of love and charity [*dilectionis et caritatis*]. . . . For we dwell in our memory
incessantly on the thought of all your good qualities and of your manifold gifts; those
embraces which your royal arm has sweetly bestowed on us are painted on the secret
surfaces of our mind, your honey-dripping kisses carved on the tablets of our heart,
your words — kingly, honey-flowing, sweet and gentle — we treasure in the innermost
recess of the mind.[17] Happy are those who live with you every day, happy those who
abide with you often, for your mild and beautiful presence brings happiness to all,
exalts and glorifies all, distributes to all gifts, affection and love. Stirred to action by this
royal and sweet love, we, little as we are, have composed this little booklet.[18]

Smaragd was plain in connecting his love for Charlemagne with the gift he had
received from him.[19] The conflict between *honestum* and *utile*, which for Cicero was acute in the relations of friends, seems solved for this writer. The

connection of emotion and political ends in the king's love is an important element of the style of Carolingian rule. Far from being decoration and overlay, the language and gestures of love made up the code in which favor relationships were publicized.

The documents from the Carolingian court give us a consistent picture of a court of love.[20] Love beams from the king like light, engulfs the court, bathes its members in its warmth, compels them with its chains, charms them with its songs. It circulates back and forth between the king and the poets; the king's love inspires their writings. They live, act, and speak in metaphors: they are players in a pastoral idyll, they are ancient sages and Old Testament patriarchs reborn. Love is represented as a force which structures the courtiers' behavior: they are wounded by the king's love, they pine for him and feel immense desire welling through the chambers of memory at the thought of his beautiful face.[21] Love unites the entire community.

Excursus: Court "Scenarios" and Historical Reality

With healthy skepticism historians will ask whether poems of laudation, celebration, and dedicatory statements are of any use to indicate what went on in the lived reality of the court of Charlemagne. (Unhealthy skepticism will reject the possibility out of hand.) It is an important concern of methodology, and we might begin discussing it as a question of the anthropology of monarchic courts. It is a principle still observable today that power tends to generate aesthetic forms in which it represents itself. Concentrated power tends to aesthetic structures; diffused power to functional ones. The symbiosis of art and power is well known.[22] The self-representation of rule produced a wide variety of forms of expression: ceremony and court ritual, the use of liturgical forms in court ceremony, court dramas, dramas and scenarios of performance as ritual staging of political arrangements like reconciliation, peace-making, begging forgiveness.[23] This is the level at which the exercise of power and the art of the court meet. The public exercise of royal power is staged and dramatized in scenarios. The political and social life of the court draws on various fictional idioms. The stagers and masters of ceremony create fictional worlds in which life is sublime, ideal, the monarch and his court godlike, in which the ruler is to his courtier in the place of Christ.[24]

This is the level at which experience and literary models meet and fuse. The exercise of power and any acts that bear on the economy of favor, standing, rank and honor at court require a fictive scenario. Some of the court scenarios from the High and late Middle Ages are well known: Roman history and the Trojan War supplied some of them; the most popular idiom into the Renaissance was King Arthur and his court, chivalry, and courtly love.[25]

It is not always possible to distinguish codes of behavior from fictional scenarios. The two made common cause. There are three codes of behavior so widespread in court life, not just western, as to qualify as social constants of the court: courtliness, refined love, and warrior honor. The courts of the west, like Chinese, Japanese, and Arabic courts, produced a large body of literature celebrating an idealized form of love. They varied widely in style, in attitudes to sexuality and to the relations of the sexes, but in all cases they were the literature that expressed the self-conception of court aristocracies. The courts of kings, emperors, and lesser nobles tend at some point in their development to produce an extensive literature based on these codes. This fictionalizing of court forms and ideals was not somehow an abstract, intellectualized, or aestheticized love of narrative, but rather a practical framing of the values and forms of behavior that one must understand and master in order to appear at court and play in the scenarios of its life. The life of the court tended to be aestheticized, and the production of literature is a secondary response to that fact. The poetry of "courtly love" from European courts was a form of "ceremonial behavior" closely related to court ritual generally. At least that is the belief of a growing scholarly consensus.[26]

If this close connection between court ceremony and court literature in fact existed, then literature becomes a major source of our understanding of the self-conception of individual courts, a testimony to court style. But self-conception and court style are inseparable from policy. The neoclassicism of the Ottonian courts is directly grounded in the political idea of the "renewal of the Roman empire," *renovatio imperii Romanorum*.[27] Court literature tends to be "unreal" and fantastic, tends to draw on mythology and the imagination, tends to create extravagant ideals, and all of this has been a hindrance to understanding its documentary value for court style, to accepting its testimony to the scenarios of court life. The hermeneutic posture needed to overcome a false division of literature and life into incompatible categories is to understand conventional forms of expression as scenarios of social action, to enter into the language of a culture which knit life and literature far more closely than ours does. The stark separation of literature and life, the denial of the event that has a literary form *prior to all interpretation*, is the last stirrings of the romantic divide between art and experience. Topoi may be empty conventional formulae, but they may also be stage directions and scene-settings, the formulae of a style of behavior. They may be tied as closely to the living style of a court as the text of a play is to the stage drama performing it. That is the challenge to "Quellenkritik" in the area of court life: to weigh the power of conventional courtly forms to influence lived fashion.

Dhuoda's Manual

We can confirm the belief in love as a code of behavior at the Carolingian court in the Manual (*Liber manualis*) of Dhuoda, practical advice by a woman of high nobility to her son, written in the middle of the ninth century. In advising him on his debut, education, and service at court, she writes:

If you attain to a position where, along with your companions, you serve within the royal or imperial court . . . then fear, love [*ama*], venerate and cherish [*dilige*] the famous and distinguished parents and retainers of your lord who are close to royal power. . . . Recall how David was his life long a pure, loyal and true servant to Jonathan, son of King Saul, and to the father no less than the son. . . . Upon their passing away, pressed by the sweetness of a boundless love, he sang this grave lamentation, in a flood of tears of mourning: ". . . I mourn for you, o my brother Jonathan, my love for you surpassed love [of women]. . . ." You also, my son William . . . , be loyal to your lord Charlemagne,[28] whoever he may be. . . . There is dignity in such service. . . . For God has selected and elected them, we believe, for the kingdom.[29]

This is an ethic of court service, based on a relationship of loyalty and love, placed against the biblical model of David and Jonathan. It shows that the power and charisma of high court dignitaries legitimize and dignify servitude, partly because of the divinity of kingship and rule that so clearly plays a part in Dhuoda's conception of royal power.

This passage gives us a prescriptive text enjoining personal, charismatic love as a communal ethic. It corroborates the testimony of court poetry indicating that love provided a scenario of court behavior and structured the relations of court to king. The Carolingian cult of friendship is a major factor in court style. It would be quite appropriate to wonder whether the model of David and Jonathan, common though it is in the writings on friendship, were not particularly commended in this case because of the tradition that made Charlemagne into a second David.

Alcuin

Alcuin of York, tutor, adviser, and favorite of Charlemagne, abbot of Tours, is the most important and most prolific figure in the Carolingian cult of friendship. His love songs and letters speak a language fashioned from the Song of Songs and the Psalms, but with little echo of the classical Roman language of friendship.

He brings a startling innovation to the conception of love. In Cicero, Ambrose, Augustine, Paulinus of Nola, loving friendship was represented as chaste, heroic, idealistic, a love of the virtue in another man, held in tight check in the strictures of temperance, decorum, and self-control. In Alcuin love is passionate and sensuous. I would like to call it "romantic," at the risk of irritating readers jealous of the temporal bounds of concepts. I think a reading of some of his poems and letters justifies the provocation.[30]

Alcuin's poem 55 is addressed to an unnamed friend, who is traveling to take up service at a distant court, where he is honored and is vulnerable to the allurements of court life[31] (see Appendix for an English translation). In his absence the beloved friend "shines brighter than all treasures," and the poet desires and seeks with his whole will and his whole mind to restore his presence, "to have, to hold, to love and to worship" (stanza 1, lines 6–8). The poem is a love lament and states as much in the first lines ("Sweet love laments with tears an absent friend . . .").[32] The poet's mind and heart are troubled. He weeps as he writes, his tears well forth as the song ends, and he imagines Christ, his consoler, wiping his tears away:

We shall end this song with the tears welling up while I write,
But the love in our breast is never-ending.
I've written this song weeping, dearest one,
And I believe that merciful Christ will wipe away the streams
Of tears from my eyes . . . (4.1–5)

Carminis hic finem lacrimis faciemus obortis,
Pectore sed numquam finem faciemus amoris.
Flentibus hoc oculis carmen, karissime, scripsi,
Flumina, credo, pius lacrimarum Christus ocellis
Abstergat . . .

There is turbulence outside: "the whirlwinds of activities," the "many thousands of things" (1.4) press in on him; anxiety and longing upset him deeply, and he seeks peace and calm in the thought of his friend:

. . . joined to me in great love,
You are peace to my mind, sweet love to me. (1.9–10)

. . . mihi magno coniunctus amore,
Tu requies mentis, tu mihi dulcis amor.

And he knows he will never find rest until he sees his friend again (4.5–6). As lovers do, he closes the chasm between longing and fulfillment with the vision of reunion:

Oh would that the moment of wished-for love might come.
When will that day be when I may see you,
O beloved of God . . . (2.1–3)

O quando optandi veniat mihi tempus amoris,
Quando erit illa dies, qua [. . .] te cernere possim,
O dilecte deo . . .

And it is also a lover's vision that imagines love, which otherwise fades, as in this one case eternal:

The love in our breast is never-ending. (4.2)

Pectore sed numquam finem faciemus amoris.

The poet is timidly anxious for his friend's well-being: his trip is not without danger, and he equips him for the journey with his poem and his prayers.

This remarkable poem is filled with the tensions of absent love: the turbulence of mind, the longing, the hopes and fears of the lover. The recipient is clearly headed for a court where he will have a high position, probably exercising his learning (cf. 2.3), certainly dependent on the favor of the locals. I suspect that the poem has a practical purpose: to demonstrate the friend's high respect and favor with Alcuin, this powerful, favored member of the royal court, and to assure him honor (twice invoked in the poem) and safety. The language of love must be unmistakable to anyone tuned to the court idiom: it was the language of the imperial court, as validating as a royal seal; it shows the high worth of the man to whom it is directed and commends him to others for similar treatment.[33]

That is not to deny that Alcuin "loves" this man as vehemently as he claims to. The expressions of admiration and respect in modern letters of recommendation are not undermined by the practical purpose of the letter. What is remarkable here is the style, the sentiments and the personal cast of the letter/poem.

Reading Alcuin's poems after the court poetry of Angilbert, Modoin or Theodulf is like moving from the Anacreontic verse of the early eighteenth century, witty but tinny, to Goethe's love poems. Alcuin's poetic language goes well beyond the honeyed and jeweled imagery and the rococo sentimentality of court poems. He uses the trite image of the "flames of love" in many skillful variations. He writes to an unnamed friend:

O that the spirit of prophecy might be in you, . . . so you might perceive with how sweet a savor the love of you fills my breast. . . . I send you these small jottings as signs of great love, so that what surpasses understanding can at least receive partial expression in words. For just as one can see a flame but not touch it, so also one can make love sensibly perceptible in letters, though in the mind of the writer it is not visible. Just as the fire sprays sparks, so love sparks out from letters.[34]

Alcuin particularly likes the image of the wounds of love. His friend Peter of Aquileia, he writes, has received "the sweet lance of love, sweeter than any honeycomb, in his heart" (Epist. 86, 15, p. 129). In Alcuin's own heart the flame of love for Archbishop Ricbod of Trier burns so hot that "my heart could say to me, 'I am wounded by love.'"[35]

Alcuin can represent love as vehement, deeply felt, personal, and genuine. He suffers, he burns, he is sick or wounded, he pines, he dreams of his beloved and of an inseparable friendship in the next world. Love and longing drive him and pursue him. He would have sympathized with the figure of the driven wanderer in Goethe's love poetry. Both live in turmoil, long for rest and the peace that comes through the beloved, and both feel magnified by love, since the soul without love is, not just tinkling and empty, but dead.[36]

Even though the love language is anticipated faintly in York traditions, Alcuin's use of it is striking and original. Out and out startling, however, is the thoroughgoing mixing of the language of erotic and religious love. A comparably consistent mingling of the two must wait for Bernard of Clairvaux's Sermons on the Song of Songs. But Bernard eroticizes the relationship of the soul to God and Alcuin eroticizes his personal relationships to his loved friends; in Bernard's sermons abstractions long for spirits, while in Alcuin human beings long for bodies. Human friendship can found itself on Christ and the image of God within,[37] but Alcuin feels no contradiction in depicting longing for his friends in frankly sensual terms.

Alcuin's Carmen 11, quoted earlier, was probably directed to his friend Archbishop Arn of Salzburg, though the recipient is not named. (For a translation of the poem, see Appendix.) It also deserves to be called "romantic." I doubt that any other court love poems from the Middle Ages speak so distinct an erotic language in a tone of such high seriousness:

Love has penetrated my breast with its flame [. . .]
And love always burns with new heat.
Neither sea, nor land, hills nor forests or mountains
May stop or hinder the way of him
Blessed father, who always licks your innards,[38]
Or washes your chest, O beloved, with his tears.

Pectus amor nostrum penetravit flamma [. . .]
    Atque calore novo semper inardet amor.
Nec mare, nec tellus, montes nec silva vel alpes
    Huic obstare queunt aut inhibere viam,
Quo minus, alme pater, semper tua viscera lingat,
    Vel lacrimis lavet pectus, amate, tuum.

The lament that follows is solid Boethian tradition, but as a love lament, it would not be out of place in the courtly lyric or narrative of the twelfth and thirteenth centuries:

Why, O sweet love, should you bring bitter tears,
And why make bitter draughts flow from sweet honey?
If your sweet delights, O world, are mixed with bitterness,
Then good fortune must quickly give way to adversity.
All joys change, sad to say, to mourning,
Nothing is forever, all things are changeable. (7–12)

Cur tu, dulcis amor, fletus generabis amaros,
    Et de melle pio pocula amara fluunt?
Si tua iam, mundus, miscentur dulcia amaris,
    Adversis variant prospera cuncta cito.
Omnia tristifico mutantur gaudia luctu,
    Nil est perpetuum, cuncta perire queunt.

He imagines a kingdom and a court where friendship remains unchangeable:

Happy is the court of heaven, which never abandons a friend,
The heart which burns with love always possesses the object of its love. (17–18)

Felix aula poli nunquam disiungit amicum;
    Semper habet, quod amat, pectus amore calens.

Friendship is not a human attachment to be shed upon reunion with God;[39] this heaven is a place "where our love will never suffer separation" [Qua noster nunquam dissociatur amor] (20). It is a vision of lovers meeting in the beyond to fulfill a love that was thwarted in earthly life — a deeply romantic idea.[40] Heaven is a kind of paradise of lovers. In other passages Alcuin imagines earthly love fulfilled in the love of Christ, but he never imagines friendship as part of that perishable, unreliable world of the present life,[41] and he is very far from seeing it as sinful. Sinfulness, on the contrary, is a hindrance to deep, intimate love. He writes to Arn,

O would that I could be transported to you, like Habacuc: with what eager embraces I would enfold you, o sweetest son; nor would the heat of the long summer day tire me and diminish my urge to press breast to breast or join mouth to mouth; rather I would kiss all the limbs of your body with the sweetest greetings. But since my sins prevent this from happening in my frail body, I shall do what I can do more urgently: I dip my pen in the tearful abyss of charity, to write sweetest words of salutation on the parchment. . . . O hard cleft of the heavy weight in the body! O sweet conjunction in the viscera of love! . . . May we find unity in Christ without whom there is no perfect charity.[42]

Alcuin speaks this powerful erotic-religious language of romantic love to his few best friends. This includes Charlemagne. There is not a strict distinction to make in Alcuin between one form of love reserved for religious, another for seculars. For Carolingian writers a friend's illness is a particular occasion for reminders of love. Alcuin wrote to an ailing Charlemagne,

My most beloved lord, my sweetest master, most desired of all men, My David, your Flaccus is saddened by your infirmity. I hope and pray to God with all my heart for your quick recovery, so that our joy may be fulfilled in you.[43]

And after the emperor's recovery he writes,

The sweetness of your sacred love abundantly refreshes and soothes the ardor of my breast every hour, every minute; and the beauty of your face, which I constantly dwell upon in loving thoughts, fills all the channels of my memory with desire and an immense joy, and in my heart the beauty of your goodness and your appearance enriches me as with great treasures.[44]

And on receiving news from Angilbert of the king's well-being, he wrote these verses to Charlemagne:

Yes, your servant Homer has arrived
Bearing happy news, O David, from your own lips.
It brought joy to the heart of your Flaccus also,
To hear of your good health and that of your children.
Sweet is this love to me, sweet presence of Christ,
Sweet the thought of your studies and of the sound of your voice.
Both you and yours, my friends always through all ages,
Be well, be strong, wherever you may be, O David farewell!
I have sent this boy again to your kindness
To serve you with heart, with hand, with song.[45]
                    (Carmen 13, Poetae 1, p. 237)

Ad nos quippe tuus famulus veniebat Homerus
    Nuntia laeta ferens, David, ab ore tuo.
Fecerat et Flaccum gaudentem in pectore vestrum,
    Deque salute tua, de sobolisque tuae.
O mihi dulcis amor, dulcis praesentia Christi,
    Dulce tuum studium, et dulcis ab ore sonus.
Tuque tuique simul per saecula semper amici
    Pervaleant, vigeant, David ubique vale!
Hunc iterum puerum vestrae pietate remisi,
    Serviat ut vobis carmine, corde, manu.

This is the love of a courtier for a king. The charismatic effect of royalty is no doubt at work, as in the Carolingian cult of the king's love generally. Even though Alcuin never speaks the language of Cicero's *De amicitia* and leaves the classical tradition of friendship very much in the corners of his writings,[46] the love of king cannot be separated from the love of virtue, strength, power, in the king.

Still, in Alcuin the language is intimate and sensual, and this makes the reader curious about the relationship of language to experience. But the mask of discourse is opaque in Alcuin's poems too; there is no seeing through and behind it. What we are reading here are roles played and scenarios staged. But as with any role played, the best actors assign themselves the roles that correspond best to their sense of self. If the actor writes his own script and plays it consistently, then the more powerful and original expression may well be an indicator of the screened-off world of private emotions now hidden and now revealed behind the veil of role.

If that relation of individual to role is at work in Alcuin's poems and letters to his friends, then we can see him as a man who was able to love other men deeply, to desire his friends' presence passionately. The language of physical love provided the most intimate expression of this passion. It is not possible to "lick the innards" (*tua viscera linga[re]*) of another human being, but as an imagined gesture of love it expresses a longing too intimate and too deep for the body to fulfill. As the language of physical love intensified the expression of friendship, the longing for Christ could stand for the unhappiness of separation and the hope of reunion.

＊   ＊   ＊

Alcuin's cultivation of friendship was not limited to the elitism of emotions. He regarded peacemaking as a special mission, dubbed himself a "seed-sower of peace,"[47] and the seeds he sowed were meant to bear fruit in communal, fraternal friendship. This applies to monastic and clerical communities,[48] but equally to secular.[49]

One of the most interesting documents on Alcuin the sower of friendship is a letter he wrote to Charlemagne, promising to compose a piece of music that will turn warriors gentle:

[Your letter] urged me to add a sweet melody of verse to the horrible din of battle and the raucous blast of trumpets, since the music of sweet melodies softens the fierce emotions of the mind. . . . You wished that the savagery of your boys be mitigated by the sweetness of some song or other. (lines 9–14)[50]

The "royal path" between the extremes of savagery and lassitude is good for men in the battlefield; this golden mean will "compose all things according to the way of peace" (line 19). He is ready and willing, "if the flute of Flaccus can avail to mollify ungentle minds" (line 25).[51] It is no coincidence that the paragraph following that on peace-bringing music is a reflection on friendship:

> a friend is so called as the custodian of the soul.[52] He strives with all his loyalty to keep the soul of his friend harmoniously integrated so that no point of the sacred law of friendship may be violated. Rare are those who understand it. For almost everyone strives to comply with this duty of friendship by attending to the character of his own soul, not that of another who is his friend. And if it is incumbent on a friend and coequal to preserve the integrity of his friend's mind inviolate, how much more so on a lord and on one who loves to raise up and govern his subjects in all honor. (pp. 242–43)

The context of the passage connects the civilizing force of music with friendship, though Alcuin does not make the point directly. He is helping the king in his custody over the "fierce souls" of his "boys" by restoring peace through music.

*   *   *

The Carolingian cult of friendship weakened after the death of Charlemagne. Expressions of fervent friendship in letters from the ninth century take on the character of topos-like salutations. In the poetry of passionate love, the court scenario and the Alcuinian language of spiritual love are in force.[53] But given the wealth of love letters and poems from and around the court of Charlemagne, the sparseness and commonplace character of sources from the later ninth century indicate that the obligation to express love remains as a rhetorical form, but the expressions of love have been emptied out; often they are limited to the salutation. None at all bear comparison with Alcuin's writings. The testimony to passionate friendship is remarkably scant;[54] there is some reason to think there was a rebirth of the early Christian hostility to friendship.[55] Many of the ninth-century letters are of interest as letters of instruction and requests for instruction framed in stereotypical salutations, but the comparisons with other examples of their genre from the eleventh century will bear out the general impression that the cult of friendship degenerated both at court and in the learned centers of the kingdom after the death of Charlemagne.

Ottonian Times and After

Its course did not run either smooth or strong in the early Ottonian period either. Ruotger of Cologne can say of Henry I (ca. 875–936), the father of

Otto the Great, that he gathered his nobles or court members (*domesticos*) around him "in such love that nowhere was any so mighty kingdom so closely wedded."[56] But the references not only to passionate friendship, but also to friendship as a form of peacemaking,[57] virtually dry up in the reigns of Otto I and Otto II.[58]

The letter collection of Gerbert of Aurillac has many letters of friendship, but the tone is cool and the conception of friendship not clearly separable from "alliance."[59] Gerbert professed himself a Ciceronian, but *De amicitia* played next to no role in his letters.[60]

The sources on passionate friendship are somewhat richer under Otto III and his successors. A dedication in Otto III's prayer book reads:

Accept this trifling little book,
O most illustrious of kings, . . .
Which I've written in gold, rich with manifold meanings,
Because my mind seethes with manifold love for you.
             (MGH Poetae 5, lines 1–4, pp. 633–34)

Hunc satis exiguum, rex illustrissime regum,
Accipe . . . libellum,
Auro quem scripsi, signis varriisque paratum,
Multiplici vestro quia mens mea fervet amore.

The royal/imperial court is again the focal point of a new scenario that is forming. Otto "very much loved" Burchard of Worms.[61] He was so fond of his cleric Tammo that they wore the same clothes and at table ate from the same bowl, joining their hands together when they met in the dish.[62] Henry II (973–1024) also received protestations of love from his former tutor, Bebo of Bamberg, who despaired that "mere words" can express, "most beloved emperor, how much I love you" [te caesar dilectissime diligam],[63] and from Meinwerk of Paderborn, who showed the emperor "the flames of his intimate love" and was promoted to bishop of Paderborn.[64]

A courtier bishop named Benzo of Alba, who had served in the chapel of Henry III, includes some extravagant praise of friendship as a virtue of imperial courtiers in his book of instruction for Henry IV. Here also love appears as a high court ideal. He says that the emperor should love the ministers who love him and by his love stir them to more fervent service.[65] He constructs an allegorical "Palace of Virtue," in which *amicicia* is "the very sun in the firmament of worldly life" (p. 674, line 13). The Latin epic-romance *Ruodlieb* was written during the reign of Henry IV and probably commemorates the court of Henry III. It is full of confirmations of a held ideal of friendship and love uniting the king's court. I will discuss the work in later chapters.

Monastery and Cathedral

It is clear that love had a context as scenario and social gesture at secular courts. It is easy to show that it moved from there into clerical and monastic communities.

In the mid-980s the community of St. Remi of Rheims courted a man of Frankish royal lineage named Constantine, schoolmaster at Fleury, either as abbot of their house or as archbishop of Rheims. A monk of St. Remi, probably writing for the whole community, composed a poem in praise of Constantine.[66] Wisdom herself has built her temple in him, since he is a "man magnificent above others and always loveable," and is "ornamented with the excellent light of virtues" (33–40). He beams "nobility of merits" like a light and is famed for his "probity of manners" (70–71). Both his face and his body are beautiful, and this is a sign of his "intellect" displaying itself visibly. Constantine is the poet's dear friend, his "beloved companion" and "sweetest doctor" (52). The recipient of this adulation, Constantine, a poet as well as teacher, has composed "odes" that allude to their "happy love" (106–8). Anyone who, like the writer, had loved him happily for so long must wish to have him as "patron, constant companion, lord" (84–85), and indeed, all the "brothers of the Remigian cottage" are his faithful friends (75).

Both St. Remi and Fleury (and Micy, where Constantine eventually became abbot) were monastic communities, but the relationship described and proposed in this poem of courtship is far from monastic, at least in the sense of a monasticism based on Christian ascetic, world-renouncing values. The poem speaks a highly classicistic language, with references to Parnassus and the "Sophoclean stage," a Ciceronian ethical language, and most strikingly, the language of imperial charisma: he is "magnificent above others" and "ornamented with the excellent light of virtues" (33–40); he "beams nobility of merits"; he is a "mirror of justice" and "hosanna of kings" (90–91).[67] The author and presumably the monks of the Rheims community he represented, were much closer to imperial, neoclassical forms of expression and ethical concepts than to the ideals of the reform movement. It is also clear that loving friendship in the Ciceronian tradition could be held out to a candidate for the abbacy as one of the attractions of the life in that community. Friendship appears as a communal value, but one based on classical, imperial models and on the aura of individual charisma, not communal charity.

The communities of reformed monks in the eleventh century produced next to no documents on friendship.[68] The only friendships claimed by the early Cluniac hagiographers for the founders of Cluny are those with emperors and their wives and with the princes and grandees of the realm. Odilo of Cluny says of Maiolus:

by the friendships, the services, and the imperial gifts of all these [various kings, queens and emperors] he was so raised in stature [*magnificatus*] that he was "one heart and one soul" with them.[69]

Both this passage and the general disposition of sources speak clearly: friendship was worldly, aristocratic, its context was royal service, not the life of reformed monastic communities. It was expressed and rewarded by gifts and services. The above passage bundles the constellation together in unusual brevity and clarity: *amicitiae*, *officia*, *imperialia munera*. Friendship with the emperor and his nobles "magnifies" its recipients.

Many of the major Cathedral communities were in the political sphere of the emperor in the late tenth and earlier eleventh centuries. Their schools prepared young men for administrative positions both at the royal court and in dioceses loyal to the emperor.[70] They produced some of the best sources on the cult of friendship. I will return to them often in later chapters.

4

Love, Friendship, and Virtue
in Pre-Courtly Literature

The "Satyra de amicicia"

"Satire concerning Friendship and the Marriage of a Saxon and a Frank" is the
title of a poem fragment (forty-four lines have survived) from the early eleventh century.[1] Its double occasion is the marriage of the poet's liege lord, a
Count Heidenreich, to a Saxon woman, and the lord's gratuitous release of the
poet from his unfree status for the occasion. The generosity of the act shows
the "lordly virtue" of Heidenreich. Virtue is not easily acquired: it requires
effort striving for "grand things." Virtue constitutes the "shining fame of nobility" in the lord who exercises it. This was preface to the "Satire."[2] The lines
that follow praise music and its ability to create harmony. The beauty of music
calls forth like-mindedness: "Sic etiam similes componit gratia mentes" (line
10). But the real glue of friendship is virtue:

It is fecund virtue which joins together loyal friends,
Virtue always seeks what is good . . . (12–13)

Est virtus fidos generans que comit amicos,
Semper honesta petens . . .

Virtue is like a great circle flowing from the "supreme good" (*summum
bonum*), linking men together, and flowing back into its source:

Since we now rejoice to be called brothers and companions,
Let [virtue] now join our breasts and firm up the bond — that is my wish."
                                                      (lines 18–19)

Ipsa volo societ, volo nostri pectora firmet,
Si dici fratres gaudemus sive sodales.

The pure Ciceronianism of the poem is worth noting. Virtue and friendship
are linked as cause and effect; it joins together men who are good, coming as it

does from "the supreme good," and moves them to seek good and grand ends. It also makes men like-minded, a requirement of friendship in *De amicitia*, and the context of the poem (freeing of a bondman) implies that it also makes men equal, another defining feature of friendship in Cicero. Also of interest in this poem is the connection of music, peace, and friendship. It is the beauty of music which composes minds to likemindedness and removes strife and discord.

The Cambridge Songs

The poems of the collection called the Cambridge Songs were mainly composed prior to the mid-eleventh century.[3] Many of them are from the milieu of the German imperial courts. Several are relevant to the topic of friendship. The story of Lantfrid and Cobbo (Cambridge Song no. 6) tells of two friends and a test of friendship. After a stay in the land of his friend, Cobbo decides to return to his homeland. He makes one request of Lantfrid: hand over his wife. Lantfrid does not hesitate. Cobbo departs with his friend's wife, but returns soon and hands her back untouched. It was just a "test of love," *amoris experimentum*.[4] Real love is what holds the two men together; the woman is chattel; her role is to pose the lesser term in the test of the husband's loyalty. This poem also makes or suggests an interesting connection between music and friendship that we have seen in Carolingian sources, in the "Satyra," and will encounter again. "Lantfrid and Cobbo" begins with musings on the sources of music with no clear connection to the following story other than the relatedness of music and love.[5]

Cambridge Song number 82 rehearses various episodes in the life of King David, and says of his friendship with Jonathan,

He becomes a friend of Jonathan: he commended himself to him through great virtue.[6] (Stanza 2a, line 2)

fit amicus Ionathe: commendabat sibi se magna virtute.

Whatever the content of "great virtue" we are clearly once again in the atmosphere of the ancient and Ciceronian conception of friendship as love of the virtue in another man.

Song 80 is also important for the topic of friendship. It is from a student to his teacher. It draws a religious aura around the activity of the teacher, using the language of imperial charisma, and it shows his student's fervent love.

These few references are the only notice of love and friendship in the Ciceronian tradition in the Cambridge Songs. The sparseness is perhaps significant. For poems written partly for, partly at the German imperial court, they produce remarkably little in the way of friendship references when compared with Carolingian poetry, where love omitted is the exception. No single panegyric poem in the Cambridge collection speaks of the court's love for the king or the king's for his courtier or of the poet's for his master, prominent though that motif was in Carolingian panegyric.

But the compiler of the Cambridge Songs was quite interested in other aspects of love. Most striking is that the love of women for men and of men for women suddenly finds literary testimony — very early in the history of that development. The collection contains some of the earliest Latin love poetry from the Middle Ages.[7] And the Cambridge Songs are not alone: other sources from the period show the emergence of woman in the literature of love (see below, Chapter 6 on the poem "Deus amet puellam").

It also contains a poem of erotic male love remarkable both for its poetic quality and for the character of the love relationship.[8] The poem "O admirabile Veneris idolum" (no. 48) makes it possible to distinguish love in the Ciceronian tradition from male love and desire. The poem is a love lament, possibly by a teacher for a young student who is leaving him. The poet's sophisticated knowledge of classical mythology and the lack of any Christian coloring mark it as a work of a worldly, educated cleric. There is no trace of the Ciceronian brand of male friendship based on virtue. The pain and passion in the poet's voice brings the poem close to the tone of Alcuin's poem to his departing student (above, Chapter 3). The anguish of the teacher at the departure of his beloved friend is common to both. In both the poet prays anxiously to — very different — gods for the protection of his friend. But while Alcuin shows passion and suffering over the loss, the later poet complains of the cruelty of his beloved, who is deaf to his complaints and whom he imagines as going to a rival. Often it is not easy to distinguish the language of erotic physical desire from that of Alcuinian passion, but here it is clearly the former. A reproach to the loved one can only happen within the discourse of the love of kings in the form of moral correction (as in a poem of Baudri, see below, Chapter 5). The poet's jealousy is decisive. The poem is closer to the genre of erotic poems from antiquity known as *paidikon*.[9]

The motif of chastity in the relations of men and women looms large in the collection.[10] "Lantfrid and Cobbo" is one statement of the theme. Lantfrid gives his wife to Cobbo "to freely enjoy her embrace," and Cobbo, having her completely at his will, refuses the "enjoyment" offered him. That ability to refuse is what Cobbo put forward as proof of his friendship.

I do not see a contradiction between this theme and the love songs. The love poems of the Cambridge Songs widen the register of love emotions, but do not represent or even refer to the act of love, whether the relationships are male-female or male-male. The body and sexual intercourse are never mentioned. The love songs are far from the explicit sensuality of much Latin love poetry from the next century. They are poems of longing and suffering in love, and it is not at all unlikely that that mode of feeling was gaining acceptance among the forms of ennobling love, though the Cambridge collection gives no clues either to its acceptance or rejection among the aristocracy. I have avoided a distinction between ennobling love and the passionate emotionality of love poems in the Cambridge Songs. Nothing in the collection suggests that the love of man for woman or man for man does not play in the mode of exalting love. The story of Lantfrid and Cobbo strongly suggests that it does.

Ruodlieb

The Latin epic *Ruodlieb*, probably composed around 1070, returns us fully to the context of the royal court and the king's love, though like the Cambridge Songs, this work extends the register of love relationships that can be depicted. The poet fictionalized the king's love. He created an ideal court and an ideal king.[11] The atmosphere at the court of the "greater king" is marked by love, friendship, good humor, courtly manners (practiced even, or especially, by the animals at court). The king's hunter who introduces the hero, Ruodlieb, to the court speaks to the king "more as to his friend than his lord" ("non ut domino sed ceu respondit amico," 1.131). The early books of the narrative describe how the king (called *rex major*, the greater king), is attacked by one of his vassals (called *rex minor*). The greater king puts down the rebellion, capturing many hostages, and receives the rebel and his ministers for peace negotiations. The scene is made into a showpiece of reconciliation based on the renunciation of revenge, the creation of peace and harmony through love and forgiveness. Ruodlieb, who leads the king's troops in victory, restrains his men from hanging the leaders:

"Our king has given no such command . . .
Be a lion in battle but a lamb in vengeance.
There is no honor for you in avenging acts self-condemned to anguish.
The grand form of revenge is to restrain vindictiveness.
Therefore consent, by that love arising in you,
That this count should accompany us unarmed . . ."[12] (3.7–16)

. . . "rex noster non ita iussit, . . .
Sis leo pugnando, par ulciscendo sed agno!
Non honor est vobis, ulcisci damna doloris.

Magnum vindicte genus est, si parcitis ire.
Hinc, precor, annuite, vestro quo fiat amore,
Solus ut iste comes nobiscum vadat inermis . . ."

The lesser king is humbled at hearing the generous terms of peace, which include an offer, first, of service, then "of heartfelt love" (" . . . Primo servimen post fidi cordis amorem . . . ," 4.92). The ambassadors are released with kisses and "with great love."[13] The great king is a mirror of modesty and good humor.[14] He receives the minor king and his court with kisses and embraces, a ritual that the poet calls "love" (*amor*).[15] The king takes leave of his courtier Ruodlieb with the language of love, calling him "my dear one," "most beloved," "O dearest to me of all."[16]

This work is unique in the eleventh century in revealing through a fictional narrative the contemporary conceptions of an ideal court.[17] It is a showpiece of courtly form, politeness, civilized restraint, piety, and the dominant of this ideal court scene is love and friendship.[18] Also in its later episodes it portrays a refined, ethical conception of love and courtship between a man and woman, the first work in the Middle Ages to do so. Modern commentaries on *Ruodlieb* treat it as if it had no contemporary context. It is seen as a "proto-romance" (Dronke) and assigned a role as pointing ahead to a chivalric culture which found its fuller expression in the vernacular literature of the late twelfth century. In its treatment of love between men and women, this is hard to dispute, since there is nothing to compare with it. But its representation of court life corresponds to the idealizing of a blossoming court culture from the eleventh century. Love at court among king and courtiers was part and parcel of a considerably older noble code of courtly behavior, not a literary invention.

5

Love in Education,
Education in Love

Being a major element of life at court, love also became part of the education of the nobles. Charismatic friendship is a subject of instruction and at the same time a medium, a modality of teaching. It follows that love as an object of education is an important line to follow in the history of charismatic love and friendship. It is an important subject in the history of education, certainly of ancient and medieval education.[1] The love relationship between student and teacher is too long lived and persistent to refer to as a "tradition," which implies recognized values transmitted from one generation to the next. It is more like a primal relation in which the potential for powerful love is inherent as an anthropological constant, as in the relationship of parent and child, lover and beloved.

Love of teacher is also simply good pedagogy, then as now. Quintilian formulated the idea in a passage that would be frequently quoted in some variation in the Middle Ages:

[Students] should love their masters . . . and should think of them as parents of their minds rather than their bodies. This love is a great aid to study, since . . . they listen gladly, believe what they say, and long to be like them . . . and seek to win their master's affection by the devotion with which they pursue their studies.[2]

I suspect that in any situation where one of the main purposes of the private tutor is to form the student's character and initiate him into social values, the development of love between the two is as natural as parental love and love between the sexes. If the teacher's "virtue" is the curriculum, then love is a major factor in learning. Impelled by love, reverence, and awe, the younger strives to make himself into the image and likeness of the older.[3] The pedagogy of love is especially useful to analyze for our purpose, since education is the site of the most intense negotiation between actual behavior on the one hand, and social goals, social and philosophical ideals on the other. The real and the ideal are contiguous in the values and practices of education. Social values come into sharp focus whenever they contest unshaped nature.

There are two important aspects of this love relationship in instruction that antiquity shares with the Middle Ages. The first is love pedagogy as a means of enculturating rulers, princes, governors. The second is love pedagogy as a means of teaching virtue.

Princes and Their Teachers

Aristotle says that the rulers and governors must understand and practice friendship particularly, both because it is a worthier maintainer of harmony in the *polis* than justice and the law, and because it has "something noble" about it, being the guarantor of an inner goodness.[4] The relationships of Socrates and Alcibiades, Aristotle and Alexander, Demosthenes and the unnamed recipient of his "Erotic Essay," Fronto and Marcus Aurelius are representative for antiquity. Likewise much of the testimony to the king's love in the Middle Ages derives from the king's teachers. Some we have observed in Carolingian times: Paulus Diaconus and Charlemagne, Alcuin and Charlemagne; Einhard and Lothar I (?).

One of the teachers of Otto III was Bishop Adalbert of Prague. He formed a close tie to the emperor when they met in Rome in 996. He became the young man's tutor and "sweetest chambermate" (*dulcissimus cubicularius*). Constant companions, they spent day and night in each other's presence, exchanged kisses and embraces, and slept in the same room. Adalbert did this not out of any love of the world (*amor mundi*), but rather because "he loved him" (*dilexit ipsum*) and so that "with his sweet sayings, he could inflame the emperor with love of the celestial fatherland."[5]

Henry II, successor of Otto III, received two long letters from a Bamberg deacon named Bebo, both written in 1021.[6] Bebo had been the tutor of the young emperor. His letters reminisce on their private colloquies on Scripture. They bubble over with nostalgia for the intimate, loving relationship the deacon once enjoyed with his illustrious pupil. Now, says Bebo, in the emperor's absence he longs for their "sweet conversations" "as the doe longs for the flowing spring."[7] Very often they had spoken together the "language of instruction of the heart" (*lingua litterationis cordis*). This happened not in the open hall, but in "some corner" of the palace, because their colloquy could be more intimate the more private it was. In the "solidarity of their love" (*caritas*) they are not reluctant to share a "loyal secret," since it strengthens their intimacy. "Mere words dare not express, most beloved emperor, how much I love you" (*te caesar dilectissime diligam*). Private conversation favors that to which their undivided love moves them: the recognition of their true, sincere love (pp. 486–87).

The letter contains a lengthy sermon on virtue based on the formula of temperance, "nothing in excess," and—Bebo lays his cards on the table—a request for a promotion.

Teaching Virtue

The second point of continuity between ancient and medieval teacher-student relationships is the love relationship as a medium for the acquisition of virtue.[8] Here it is appropriate to talk about the continuity, or renewal, of a tradition from classical antiquity. Ethical discipline became one of the fundamental goals of education in cathedral schools since the mid-tenth century.[9] The learning of *mores* ranked next to *litterae*: "letters" or "literature" and "manners" is the formula of a new kind of study, radically different from the Carolingian educational programs. The new education suited the social and political needs of the "imperial church system," but it spread through cathedral communities beyond the immediate orbit of the emperor. It brought with it a renewal of Roman senatorial ideals and their integration into the program of education.

It also developed a new style of love and friendship based on classical models and on the conception of friendship and love as responses to virtue. Love became inextricably connected with the pedagogy of virtue. The logic of the connection is obvious: Cicero defined friendship as "love of virtue in another man." If the acquisition of virtue is a goal of education, then love and friendship cannot be absent. To teach or learn without love would amount to an admission of the absence of virtue. "I will teach you but I do not love you" would be equivalent to a teacher in a contemporary classroom saying, "I will teach you, but I am ignorant of the subject and indifferent to your intellectual development." The absence of love would discredit the relationship in one of its fundamental purposes.

Accordingly the cathedral schools from the late tenth century to the late eleventh provide some of the best sources on the cult of friendship.

The Worms Letters

The letter collection from Worms, completed by 1036, contains a number of letters of friendship between students and masters.[10] In some cases claims of friendship are a rhetorical strategy; they clothe some kind of request for favor or service. In others friendship itself is the issue, not merely a rhetorical form of address. Epistles 60 and 61 are an interesting case. Both are from a student (who signs himself only with his initial, A.) to his teacher at Worms, named

Wolzo.[11] In the first he complains angrily about Wolzo's disloyalty to him. An enemy has slandered him, he claims, and instead of defending him, the master has not only listened to, but believed and repeated the slander. He gives a string of quotes from the Bible on false friendship and ends by dissolving their friendship:

Up to now I have loved you for your virtue, which makes us love even those we have never seen, as Cicero teaches. Thus have I loved you. I loved you in true love. From now on I love you only out of fear.[12]

A.'s next letter offers a reconciliation. He addresses it "not to his former, but to his future beloved" [*non tam in preterito dilecto quam in futuro diligendo*] (p. 103). He begs his teacher's forgiveness for the harsh words in the previous letter, which "had made bitter the sweetness of our love." Anger was the cause. Again, a series of quotations on friendship from the Bible and Cicero, and finally the plea (here drastically cut):

Let us love each other therefore with that love in which God is, let us love each other mutually. . . . Let us love each other with all the power, all the constancy, all the perfection of love. I will love you for the sake of God and your virtue which deserves love.[13]

The way friendship functioned and was enforced as a social ideal in cathedral school communities is evident in some remarkable sources from Worms and Würzburg in the early eleventh century, included in the Worms letter collection. The two schools carried on some nasty polemics with each other from about 1030–1032.[14] Some students from Worms had provoked the squabble originally by composing a satirical poem, allegedly as a rhetorical exercise, and sending it to their colleagues at Würzburg. But its negative comments on the school and its master moved the Würzburg community to a rousing defense. One or more students composed a poem praising and defending their own school and blasting Worms. It depicts Würzburg as a paradise of scholars, a community of friends, "united by a single vow," enjoying happiness and the joys of "true peace." Their assailant from Worms is "a sower of wrath and destroyer of friendships." His harsh words trouble the "sweet life of Würzburg." The Würzburgers offer peace in a language we will recognize easily:

Now let the discord and cruel anger between us fade. Let us shun war and become joined as twins in our love. A bond like that of David and Jonathan will join us. No cruelty will disturb us now or ever more. Those caught up in unending quarrels will marvel to see such a friendship between us. (lines 127–35)[15]

The posture was an ideal one. It asserted social values of the cathedral community and painted the picture of an ideal school life. It showed an offended party magnanimously offering peace and love to the enemy who has "wronged" him.

These values were affirmed in the outcome of the dispute. Two years after it had begun the perpetrators from Worms are in deep trouble. A trial threatens, which draws in the bishops of both dioceses and local princes, and possibly even the emperor himself (Conrad II). The extent of the proceedings and the fear of those threatened are good testimony to the seriousness of the issues. To form an impression of the stakes one can imagine what kind of student prank at a modern American university might call for the intercession of the chancellors of two universities, the governor of the state, and the president of the United States. The issues in the Würzburg — Worms polemics, we can assume, are serious ones. The poem from Worms violated some sacred principle that high authorities thought worth defending.

In 1032, with serious trouble brewing, the Worms students write to their fellow students at Mainz in quest of information from the imperial center — in quest also of help. In answer they received a letter from a student at Mainz, identified only as "R. of Mainz," who speaks for the whole school.[16] (See Appendix for an English translation.) His letter was cold consolation. Its tone is sugared and honeyed friendliness. The writer's every sentence appeals to the ideal of friendship; he greets the recipients with the offer of "seamless friendship and unshaken fidelity"; he and his colleagues seek the love and affection of all good men, and thus are delighted at the writers' invitation to enter a bond of love and friendship. But the loving tone is undercut by not very subtle irony. The letter brims with barely concealed satisfaction at the predicament of the Worms students. R. of Mainz assures them respect and reverence in the same degree as they have "always cultivated the reverence of friends with such fervent and abundant piety." In other words, they are receiving loving support in the same degree as they have given it — presumably very little in the present case.

The Worms students have gotten themselves off the moral high road, and their colleague from Mainz sprinkles his letter with snide reminders of the great community of peace-loving friends from which they have cut themselves off, all the time appearing to include them in its ranks:

We are grateful to you over and over again for your willingness to receive us with such heart-felt charity and such loving sincerity into the communion of your friendship.

As for their request for advice and counsel, however, he cannot comply with it for fear of forfeiting the friendship of one or the other of the parties to the dispute. He urges them at this late point in the conflict to seek the counsel of those whose counsel led them into it. He assumes such advisers must exist, since wise men like them do nothing without counsel. This response amounts to saying, "You got yourselves into this; now you can get yourselves out." Isolated and with the bishop and local princes breathing down their necks, they received in their colleague's letter a reminder of the intact world of friendship and love from which a satiric poem got them banished. Such was the price paid, in the 1030s, for breaches of the *lex amicitiae*.

Guibert of Nogent

Guibert of Nogent (d. ca. 1125) described his education as a young man in some detail. It is a case that takes us to the periphery of cathedral schools,[17] but is very useful to show the love relationship between student and private tutor.

The mother of Guibert of Nogent had trouble finding a teacher for her son when she went in search of one probably just prior to 1070. Finally she found an older man who might be a candidate for the job. But he was employed at the time at the court of relatives of Guibert, a distinguished noble family, a branch of the lords of Clermont. The man was engaged there as chaplain and tutor, and was reluctant to leave the court where he had been raised and had received at least part of his education.[18] Guibert's mother pleaded. The man's resistance was finally overcome by a dream vision: The aging teacher dreamed that while he lay sleeping one night, an old man with brilliant white hair entered his bedroom leading young Guibert by the hand. "Go to him," the apparition said to the boy, "for he will love you very much." Guibert approached his future master and kissed him repeatedly. Then the old man "conceived such affection" for the boy that he brushed aside all other considerations and accepted him as his student (*De vita sua* ch. 4, p. 28).

The dream represents a kind of contract of love which is the basis for the relationship of teacher to student. It operates in the dual modality of love and fear: "Although he crushed me by his severity . . . he loved me as well as he did himself"; "I conceived much love for him."[19] The master beat Guibert brutally, a technique he found useful to cover over his own ignorance of grammar and literature.[20] But the beatings do nothing to diminish their mutual affection: "Through a kind of love deeply implanted in my heart, I obeyed him in utter forgetfulness of his severity."

Guibert gives us a fairly clear idea of the tutor's areas of competence: he was nearly ignorant of "letters," but he made up for this lack in "modesty," "propriety," and "moral excellence" (*honestum*). The teacher devoted all his efforts to laying a foundation in "good conduct" (*honestas*):

Most faithfully and lovingly [*amanter*] he instilled in me all that was temperate and modest and outwardly elegant.[21]

My argument is not that the love relationship is exclusive to an education in manners (*mores*). We know that Peter Abelard, a teacher in a much different

stamp from Guibert's tutor, was fervently loved by his students. And Wibald of
Stablo in the mid-twelfth century paints a picture of a school scene where love
overrides reason and judgment:

Students study their masters' pronouncements not because they are true, but because
they love the authors. One school is set against another in love or hate of masters.[22]

This relationship is probably institutionally rooted in the schools of the earlier
Middle Ages. Abelard wanted it uprooted. He wrote in the *Carmen ad Astralabium*, a long poem to his son,

Do not put your faith in the words of a master out of love for him, nor let a learned man
hold you in his influence by his love alone.[23]

But instruction in *mores* especially favors the love relationship. It rests on
reverence of teacher and takes place in a shared life (*convictus*). Guibert's tutor
devoted six years of his life to his pupil, was with him night and day, weekends
and holidays. Love would be virtually necessary to make such an intimate
relationship tolerable — and to mitigate its cruelty.

Hildesheim Letters, Number 36

The Hildesheim letter collection (1076–1085) bears out the picture of the
Worms collection, of love rooted in the institution of cathedral schools. It
contains various friendship letters.[24] They show some consistency in basing
the representation of friendship on Cicero's *De amicitia*. One of them complains, like the letter from Worms discussed earlier, about a breach of friendship, and like the Worms letter, it implies that friendship based on virtue, when
broken, indicates the false friend's lack of virtue.[25] In another the writer is
grateful to the recipient for raising him up from his humble position to the
heights which his friend has attained, in formulas well known from Cicero:

The supreme quality of friendship is that it could regularly render superior men, men
exalted by private honors, the equals of lesser men. . . . This clearly holds true in our
case, since friendship by itself could join us in such kind regard, and at the same time, by
that sweetest and memorable intimacy of the life shared with you, render you, so highly
honored, so exalted, the equal and the companion of me, a private, lowly and insignificant person.[26]

The implication that the friendship with the greater man raises the stature of
the lesser is obvious, though not made explicit. The language of friendship
throughout this letter collection is classical. The favored authors are Cicero,

Horace, Sallust, Virgil. Biblical language is rare. This literary style is consistent enough in the letters to suggest it is representative of the style of friendship cultivated among the members of this school and community.

Letter number 36, from a master to a student,[27] is one of the most remarkable letters of the Hildesheim collection, perhaps one of the most peculiar personal letters from the Middle Ages generally.[28] (See Appendix for an English translation.) Reduced to its business, the type of the letter is well-known to most readers of this book, who have either written or received something similar: "Don't worry. I have written the letter of recommendation which you requested, and you will certainly be accepted at some school." He also warns him against studying at Beauvais with a certain Heribert, who, he claims, himself never studied at Beauvais, lured others away from studies, and in any case knows nothing he has not gotten from him, the writer.

But this kernel takes up a few lines, and is all but swallowed up in the declarations of love which go on for several pages. The letter no longer speaks the conventional pitter-patter of pious love declarations, as in late Carolingian letters and Bebo's letters to Henry II. It is a highly original language of love, subordinating Christian scripture and liturgy to the love between the two men.

The writer responds to a letter from his student assuring him of his health and well-being, received just as the Easter celebration is in full swing:

No sooner had I heard what I breathlessly desired, hardly had my ears, wide open and tensed with expectation, taken in the news that your life, which is my own, and your affairs, which I regard as mine, were secure, hardly had I taken in your salutation, when at once my soul was suffused with such joy that the simple and undivided Easter celebration which others were intent upon became for me a double festival.

He compares the joy of the two occasions: news from his student, and Christ's resurrection. Receipt of the letter transforms the Easter celebration into a "double festival":

The one was the gross, palpable and corporal festivity all were celebrating; the other, inspired by your letter, is mine alone, private and unique: the festive and spiritual celebration of your love.

The physical, corporal nature of the Easter celebration is set against the "intellectuality" of their private love festival ("unam . . . crassam palpabilem et corporalem festivitatem, aliam . . . meam . . . et privatam, pro tua dilectione celebrandam unicam festivam et intellectualem celebritatem," p. 76, lines 17–19). The conventional hierarchy of Christian values, which would place Christ's resurrection above a personal friendship, is here reversed, and the exaltation of friendship above Easter is not left to the implication of *corporalis* versus *intellec-*

tualis, or *solus et simplex pasca* versus *unica pro dilectione tua celebritas*, but driven home bluntly by the adjectives *crassam* and *palpabilem*. He uses religious language with mocking playfulness; it glorifies *their relationship*, not religion. Their separation is compared to Egyptian captivity; the receipt of his letter is return to the promised land. The "divine words" of the letter "deify" him. The writing of his return letter is for the writer a "paschal burnt offering," like that of Israel rescued from Egypt. He treats the student's long silence as the anger of the God of the Psalms: "How long will you seem to turn your face away from your servant as though in anger?" echoing Psalm 27.9: "Hide not thy face far from me, put not thy servant away in anger." Some verses he includes to the student end by varying Ruth's words, "Where you go I shall go, / Where you lodge I shall lodge" (Ruth 1.16), but they complete a sophomoric thought: "Whatever you drink, I shall drink; wherever you go, I shall follow" [Tu quodcumque bibis, bibo; quo tu, prosequar, ibis] (p. 78, 18). He reduces Scripture to a supplier of a cheap rhyme (*bibis/ibis*) to show devotion to his friend. The writer is facile with language and metaphor, clearly, and treats their sources — institutions and the faith — with an irreverence that is better known in the Latin satire of the twelfth century than in the epistolary — or any — literature of the eleventh. But it is not the big irreverence of the Goliard, but the smaller mischief of a man who drops a mask of reverence when he thinks he is not overheard.

He stretches language and imagery for effect. He likes startling dichotomies and inversions: physical versus intellectual festival; exterior versus interior Egypt. In a gesture on the borderline between extreme devotion and silly wordplay, he reverses the authority relationships between them. Following the allusion to "the Lord" of Psalm 27 turning his face from "his servant," he makes himself into the servant, his student the master:

I have played the loyal servant to you, my lord (let me speak thus, though it is not especially appropriate). (p. 77, lines 17–19)[29]

As his love transforms the student into the master, so also it turns those other masters, to whom he recommends his student, into servants:

I have made of those who were merely masters most humble servitors for my faithful lord. I have praised you so much to so many Frenchmen, Normans, and Germans as so good and glorious that even without having seen you, from report alone, they would kindly promise their loyal services. (p. 77, lines 19–23)

The reversal of master-servant roles of course has a place in formulas of humility and deference, but his willingness to extend the mode to his colleagues speaks clearly. Again the flamboyant disregard of a reverence jealously protected in the schools[30] is at work: he talks as though he has done "mere masters" (*simpliciter magistri*) a great favor by "promoting" them to his student's servants. His pleasure in speaking in a mode which is "not especially appropriate" is evident.

It may be that the social standing of the student is above that of the master. But it is also interesting that the same kind of role reversal occurs in the lyric of courtly love, where the poet turns the woman courted into his *domna* and himself into her vassal, servant, slave.

The erotic language and imagery of the letter is as original as the rest of it. It needs a careful analysis. The language of desire is so overdrawn as to raise the question whether it is meant seriously. Virtuosity can be cold and passionless, and if its subject is passion, the tension between emotion and rhetorical display is acute. One of the most striking statements in a letter that otherwise speaks a variant of the language of ennobling love comes toward the end. It gives us some clues for reading the erotic language:

Although I may desire many things, I will never persuade you to come if it is contrary to your well-being and honor; far be from me any motive of lechery. (p. 78, lines 26–28)

It gives us something we never find in earlier letters and poems: a statement of the potential connection between love declarations and sexual ambition. In fact the letter gives various signals for reading the discourse at work, looking behind the stage setting of a conventional scenario, a kind of meta-commentary by a highly self-conscious, self-aware writer. Assuring the beloved that his intentions do not include lechery shows, for one thing, that it is possible to claim innocence for the extravagant declarations of love and longing. But it also shows an awareness of hidden motives behind a scenario of "pure" love. It confirms what we have assumed until now: an implicit claim of discursive innocence.

But the disclaimer also implies that the discourse is losing its innocence. It is unimaginable that Alcuin or Anselm of Bec might explain that in spite of their heated declarations of love and longing they have no lecherous motives. The Hildesheim letter speaks a language that in its non-ironic form "honors" and exalts writer and recipient. And yet its writer was aware of his letter's power to suggest dishonorable motives. Also the teacher's distinction between "all the things he might desire" and his overriding concern for his beloved's honor speaks fairly clearly: what he might desire includes things contrary to the student's honor and well-being.

The letter ends with a double cautioning, another of the meta-comments: "Regard these things as spoken to you alone and this as said in all seriousness" (p. 79, lines 2–3).[31] The statement is useful for warding off a reading of the

entire letter as ironic.[32] Also the *tibi soli . . . dictum* shows his awareness of the
questionable character of his comments.

One of the provoking erotic allusions comes in the form of an apology for
the stylistic plainness and spontaneous character of what he writes:

[My letters] rush on their way to you unkempt like barefoot country girls to their boy
friends, having hastened in the middle of the night on their way to you their lover,
frivolously uncomposed, forgetting their cosmetics. And so much the worse on this
most sacred of nights [i.e., Easter]. (p. 78, lines 20–23)

Is the charming metaphor to be understood as framing the teacher's relationship to the student? It has the non-committal referentiality of metaphor, and as
in any statement of open, multiple reference, it is possible to press out its
narrowest allusion and read it as strictly personal: "I love you as impetuously
(and physically?) as country girls their lovers." Since it presents itself as a
comment on style and not substance, that would be pressing claims on the
language that it cannot support. But also, the style of the letter is in fact not
rude and rustic, but brilliant and virtuoso, the imagery worked out with great
pains. There is plenty of "cosmetic" in the makeup of this very well-kempt
letter,[33] and so the comment has the character also of a modesty formula.

It is another example of his penchant for inversions. Here gender is in-
verted. His letters and by extension he himself are like rash, silly country girls
in love. He submits them to the judgment of his friend and requests appropriate "punishment" for their "flaws":

they deserve great and severe punishment. Castigate them well and as befits foolish
women; and return them to me chastened. (p. 78, lines 24–26)

The pain of separation is expressed in terms that could come from Alcuin.
He contrasts the joy at receiving his letter with the joy of his physical presence:

how much fuller when you will enrich me with your bodily presence, and I rejoice
to embrace you and speak with you, exult in this joy, and my whole body dances
inwardly! How long shall I be deprived of your presence with no consolation? (p. 77,
lines 1–4)

Alongside its erotic elements, the letter contains Ciceronian strains that
connect it with many others of its type. In commending his student to other
masters, he calls on the idea of "distant love" and the dynamics of virtue
inspiring admiration even for those we have never seen:

. . . even without having seen you, from report alone, they kindly promise their loyal
services. (p. 77, lines 21–23)[34]

The turn of thought that his praise makes the masters into servants implies that it generates in them the kind of love he feels for the student, whose love has turned him, the master, into the servant.

Since the master has praised his student so, it now behooves the recipient to make himself in the image of his praise. This logic produces exhortations to virtue:

Now you, who have received as a gift of nature the highest nobility, an impressive beauty of bodily shape, see to it, keep on your guard, and be ever vigilant that your noble humility should make you beloved of all, approved of all, the intimate friend of all, and that your probity of holy manners should win you favor. (p. 77, lines 26–29)

The opening turn of thought is conventional in the *cultus virtutum* of the schools: your outer gifts received from nature should prod you to develop the inner virtue appropriate to beauty, nobility, and so on.[35] Unusual in this case is the character and motive of that virtue; it should make him "beloved of all, approved of all, the intimate friend of all," and his "most holy" behavior should endear him. We could hardly ask for a more explicit statement of the practical context of love, friendship, and virtue. A student seeking admission to studies with the goal of high office (*culmen honorum* — p. 77, line 25) is advised to make himself beloved of all, the "intimate friend" of all. There is no element of sentiment implied; this brand of intimate friendship is an instrument of ambition. The cultivation of virtue, one of the main goals of cathedral school education in the period, still arouses friendship and love, as in Cicero, but it is expressed here as a kind of prerequisite course of studies leading to high office. In the Ciceronianism of this writer the pragmatic and the ideal, *utile* and *honestum*, are completely reconcilable.

There are, then, elements of ennobling love in the traditions of ancient Rome and contemporary courts and cathedral schools in the Hildesheim letter, and there are elements that set this passionate friendship decidedly apart. It is as though the curtain of the discourse parts momentarily — as it does when amateur actors peek through the stage curtain before it rises at a play — and we see something of what can move behind the conventional language. The discourse provides gestures and scenarios of virtuous, ennobling, royal, Roman senatorial love. But behind the masks and the stagings, the whole range of desires and sexual relations could take place, from chastity and renunciation to lechery. We can be equally grateful to this author for his brilliance and for his eccentricities. Without the combination of silliness and rhetorical skill the letter would be less interesting and have less documentary value. As is, this private letter made public shows some of the fundamental tensions in the discourse of ennobling male love.

Baudri of Bourgueil

In the first years of the twelfth century Baudri of Bourgueil wrote a poem similar in its love pedagogy to the Hildesheim letter.[36] Baudri writes as a teacher chastising a young student for his arrogance and conceitedness. (See Appendix for English translation.) Baudri begins by praising him for possessing every gift of nature: high nobility, physical beauty, a voice "as sweet as honey." He lingers with pleasure over the excellence of his body:

Your appearance pleases, because it is both decent and beautiful:
Your downy cheeks, your blond hair and modest lips please;
Your voice is honey and balm to my ears,
Since it sings as sweetly as the sweet nightingale,
Not yet fixed between girl's and boy's voice;
You will be a second Orpheus, unless age spoils your voice,
Age, which draws the line between girls and boys
When the cheek is clothed with the first down of youth
And the curve of the nose lends beauty to the face.
Your bright eyes touch me to the heart and core;
For I take these luminous orbs to be the constellation Gemini.
Your white skin and ivory breast suit these well.
A touch from this snowy body gives the hands sportive pleasure. (7–19)

The pleasure is not disinterested, not pure aesthetic satisfaction; the boy's body arouses eros in the observer's eye and hand. But this is one of many texts in which the erotic is invoked as a goad to learning. The teacher/poet, stirred by the student's beauty, moves from the language of courtship to that of moral instruction:

These are the things that properly should please me and others.
Especially since the lusts of youth do not stimulate you
Nor turn the divine art of your body into a reproach.
All this pleases me, all this I commend to my care. (20–23)

The outer instruments of the erotic are divine gifts, good and "decorous" — hence the stress on "propriety," aligned with beauty and chastity.[37]

But the erotic pleasure aroused by the viewing of his body, the urge to allow hands to play along the lines of this "divine work of art," are set clearly apart from sexual gratification. The boy deserves praise because he "refuses to be Ganymede to Jove" (24); his teacher begs him not to be corrupted by love and commends him for resisting corruption (25). The courtship in progress here is subtle and complex. It is certainly not what we would call "homosexual," since it rejects the sexual as corrupting. In fact the passage gets us out of the coercive field of the word "homosexual" because the force and momentum of desire in the teacher is consciously and purposefully transferred from its natural object, sexual gratification, to moral instruction. Physical beauty is "proper" (*decet*), but the "lasciviousness of youth" and the love of Jove for Ganymede is not. The sharp distinction is of fundamental importance for understanding the teacher's "love" of the student. Beauty is erotic, but the desire aroused cycles back and forth between the aesthetic and the erotic, without ending in lust. The value affirmed is physical beauty coupled with the control and restraint of desire. The source of his pride is not only his beauty, but his chastity: "Nor are you the only one on earth who is both chaste and beautiful" (39). Beauty is decorous because it is allied with chastity.

What is the point of the erotic blandishments that begin the poem, if not to win the boy's love? It is to chastise him and correct his manners. It is courtship indeed, but the courtship aims at improvement of *mores*, not at debauchery. The boy's awareness of his own gifts and talents makes him arrogant:

. . . I have no praise for your rude manners:
It is crude to sport such haughtiness
That you'll hardly honor anyone with a sideways glance,
That with pursed lips and nose in the air you'll hardly ever deign to greet anyone,
Until at long last he has greeted you first.
Perhaps you think you alone rule on earth. (26–31)

The teacher is not suing for the boy's love; but vice versa:

If you wish, boy, to please me,
Then you must strip off these arrogant manners. (56–57)

It is a poem of moral correction, not homosexual courtship. The boy is threatened with the loss of the teacher's love and support if he does not correct his arrogant ways. The boy's desire and practical need of the man fuels the correction of his manners:

My complaint is certainly just, as is my lament.
You can satisfy it by correcting yourself. (79–80)

The teacher's love is made the reward of good manners. He refuses his love until the boy behaves. The lesson in virtue is close to that of the Hildesheim letter discussed in the previous section: "deserve the love I have for you; make yourself lovable so that all will love you."

The eroticism of the poem has a pedagogic function: it becomes an instrument of correcting manners. The erotic is stimulated, properly so; the boy needs to be aware of the power of his beauty to arouse admiration, love, service ("Si tibi vis ut agam," line 76), as he is aware of its power to arouse lust.

He has learned to manage the lust of his fellows, but not to cultivate their affection.

Baudri's posture to the boy is the paradigm of the love relationship between teacher and student since antiquity: based on moral correction through love and desire, it presupposes the banishment, at least the control, of lust. There is a distinct parallel to Socrates receiving the passionate advances of Alcibiades with reserve[38] and to Fronto correcting the passion of the young Marcus Aurelius for his teacher.[39] Adalbert of Prague had given young Otto III lessons in the perishability of beauty and power while they lived, ate, and slept together, because "he loved" the emperor. Of course, the teacher courts the student and wins his love with praise, admiration, affection, but the first purpose is to husband that love and praise in order to fashion the boy's manners to virtue. Baudri himself would provide the most lucid commentary on this love pedagogy in a letter-poem to his friend Galo. Having entrusted a poem (clearly of love) to his friend, he says, after all it does not matter what the fate of his work is

If while I seem to teach you, love is the real teacher.[40]

Si quasi te doceo plus amor id doceat.

Love hovers behind the teacher's lesson, part muse and part sergeant-at-arms. I have to stress this point, since the presentation of sublime love in the twelfth century depends on it: love inspired, felt, then mastered is a fundamental course of *moral philosophy*, of teaching manners in the eleventh and twelfth centuries. John of Salisbury states the principle paradigmatically in making Socrates into its embodiment:

Socrates, we are told, was naturally wanton and overly susceptible to women. . . . But he subdued and controlled his passionate nature, which he corrected *by philosophy and the exercise of virtue*.[41]

The cultivation of virtue dominated instruction at cathedral schools in the eleventh and twelfth centuries and was prominent at worldly courts into the twelfth century and beyond. It is inseparable from love in its scale of experience from "wantonness" to "virtue." One of the central goals of that study was the taming and governing of passion.

Rodulfus Tortarius: "Amelius and Amicus"

A little-known Latin poet writing around the same time as Baudri, Rodulfus Tortarius, composed a series of verse epistles, one of them on friendship.[42] It tells the story of the two friends, Amelius and Amicus, which became extremely popular, adapted in many versions including saints legends.[43] The author introduces the work by explaining its purpose to his friend Bernardus: to define the nature of true friendship. Then follows the story of unshakable friendship and self-sacrifice of one friend for the other. Rodulfus ends by explaining the lesson of the story: "I have related this story, my dear, so that you will strive to be loved [Haec retuli tibi, care mihi, studeas ut amari].

*　　*　　*

In the various texts treated in this chapter, love appears as a pedagogic medium and at the same time a mode of behaving and feeling that can be learned. It is based on the Ciceronian idea that friendship is the love of virtue in another man. In this sense love is a central element in the "cultivation of virtue" (*cultus virtutum*). This curriculum of cathedral schools prepares for service at secular and ecclesiastical courts. Prominent among the virtues cultivated are *affabilitas* and *amabilitas*.[44] The goal is a man whom all love and who loves all men, whose *amabilitas* is the guarantor of his own virtue and that of his friends. This goal of education had a practical role to play for courtiers: never to cause trouble, never to show anger and to soften that of the prince as soon as it arises, never to arouse envy, to be affable to all and loved by all. These are courtier virtues from Carolingian times to the Renaissance and beyond. They become spiritualized in the formulations of spiritual friendship from the twelfth century. Aelred makes these qualities into the means of cultivating spiritual love, which include

jocundity in speech, cheerfulness of countenance, suavity in manners, serenity in the expression of the eyes, matters in which there is to be found no slight relish to friendship.[45]

Learning to love and to be loved, it is clear, fits into a broader education in virtue. The connection is a given not only of the Ciceronian tradition, but of the conditions of school life, which required love of virtue leading to friendship no less than modesty, self-control, moderation, temperance, decorum, greatness of soul, humanity, and the other virtues.

The "Regensburg Love Songs"

The "Regensburg Love Songs" are a series of poems composed in a Bavarian convent around 1106. They are remarkable documents, perched between the ennobling, virtue-giving love of previous centuries and the "courtly love" of the twelfth and beyond. They show us love and poetry as dual and joined objects of instruction, and they show us instruction in virtue based on love between student and master.

Wilhelm Wattenbach drew attention to the manuscript, and Peter Dronke produced an edition and English translation.[46] A new edition appeared in 1979.[47] Dronke stressed the importance of these texts for the beginnings of courtly love, but as far as I can see no one has shown any interest in this connection.[48]

Dronke describes the twelfth-century manuscript that transmits them as "magnificent chaos." It appears to contain a jumble of papers of a schoolmaster, written out without any sorting or ordering probably several decades after his death. Alongside and in between excerpts from classical and patristic texts, fragments of commentaries, the paraphernalia and flotsam and jetsam of a grammar teacher, are love poems, love letters in verse, brief love messages. Most of them are written in Leonine hexameters. Some of them are fragments; some are polished, fully developed poems.

Dronke reconstructs the circumstances of composition:[49] a master from Liège comes to Bavaria (possibly with teaching assistants), and he takes over teaching duties in a convent in Regensburg. Its residents include young ladies of high nobility. They receive male visitors. A certain "Count Hugo" and his friends are mentioned as potential love rivals of the Liège master.[50] So are an unnamed king and his comrades. But such august company does not make the nuns indifferent to the charms of their guest professor. Several of them fall in love with him. Envy and competition for his favors complicate the situation. But not too much. It seems that the women for the most part manage the complexities of loving the same man very well. The teacher also shows skill in juggling a number of lovers at the same time. Love poems are exchanged. Many of them seem tossed off, jotted down as quick greetings or breathless summonses. This spontaneous character is the best guarantor of their "genuineness." This is not only a discourse about love, but also a poetic reflection of experience.[51] At least it is hard to imagine how lines like the following could constitute a stylized, conventionalized love relationship or a school exercise presented to a teacher (less likely yet, composed by the teacher):

You should be called monkey, or sphinx — you are like them
In your ill-shaped face and unkempt hair!
(Carmen 4 [Paravicini 5], ed. Dronke, p. 424)

Simia dicaris,   vel spinx, quibus assimularis
Vultu deformi,   nullo moderamine comi!

or this one:

It is your lover who writes—do not betray him! I implore you to come to the old chapel at dawn. Knock softly on the door, for the sacristan lives there. Then the bed will reveal to you all that my heart now keeps hidden. (Carmen 14 [Paravicini 16], p. 426)

En ego quem nosti,   sed amantem prodere noli!
Deprecor ad vetulam   te mane venire capellam.
Pulsato leviter,   quoniam manet inde minister.
Quod celat pectus   modo, tunc retegit tibi lectus.

Spontaneous they may be, but it is evident that many of the poems are in fact school lessons. The girls hand over their poems like composition exercises, class assignments in which the pedagogic and the erotic are hard to separate. For instance this one:

Correct the brief verses I am sending you, master, for to me your words are like the light of The Word. But I am very sad, because you prefer Bertha to me. (Carmen 6 [Paravicini 7], p. 424)

Corrige versiculos tibi quos presento, magister,
Nam tua verba mihi reputo pro lumine Verbi.
Sed nimium doleo, quia preponas mihi Bertham.

The teacher answers with declarations of longing and with high praise of her compositions. The quality of their poetry is a constant topic of the poems.[52] The girls downplay their accomplishments and praise the master to the skies; he insists that he cannot compete with them in poetic skill. In this way love and instruction in composition are woven together into a single event.[53]

Another prominent subject of instruction is *mores*, behavior or manners, synonomous with "virtue" in the language of the poems. Remarkable is that the girls and not the master are the teachers of virtue. They regard it as their duty to maintain and administer virtue and chastity:

The vestal chorus sends you gifts of friendship [poems presumably], granting your company rights of dominion, but in such a way that virtue exacts an honest price.[54]

In another poem the girls speak as a band sworn to preserving virtue by holding their suitors at arm's length until the men can learn proper and decorous manners:

The shrewd god Mercury gave me this flower [eloquence] that I might resist unworthy frailties and entreaties. (Carmen 17 [Paravicini 22], p. 426)

Hunc mihi Mercurius   florem dedit ingeniosus
Quo possim viciis   precibusque resistere fedis—

Any man with dishonorable thoughts in mind is banished from their circle; it is barely possible even for those who have been tested in a thousand ways to gain admission. If there should be some whom Virtue selects as worthy of their attention, then she (Virtue)

takes care to mould them well, when the moon is at its end, so that secretly they grow in excellence and courtesy of speech, that they are duly refined in every way with manners of distinction. (lines 9–12)

The joy the girls have to give can only fall to the lot of a man "who has acquired a reputation for courtesy equal to ours" (16–17).

   These lines and many others in the Regensburg Songs are situated just on the line between the cathedral school curriculum of *mores* and the *fin amor*, *hôhe minne* of the worldly courts. As in the poem of Baudri to the arrogant boy, a false love is rejected in favor of a love based on virtue and fine, winning, chaste manners. In both cases the party seeking love is urged to virtue and held at a cool distance until he learns decorous manners: humility, courtesy, amiability. Love in the Regensburg Songs develops in the same context as the texts cited earlier in this chapter: instruction in how to behave. Eloquence, acquired in the study of "letters" and poetry, is exercised in instructing lovers in the manners requisite to winning honorable love. Love is a medium of moral instruction and the reward of the successful student. The Regensburg nuns practice — among other forms obviously — also an art of virtuous, courtly loving, an *ars honeste amandi*.

   What starkly distinguishes the Regensburg Songs from the curriculum in virtue of cathedral schools is that the women teach the subject. This new role is especially evident in one of the poems in which a girl rebuffs her pushy lover. He has fed himself full on foolish hopes, she writes, tricked by Cupid and his mother. He is very wrong if he thinks he is dealing with girls who yield at once:

We love only those whom prudent Virtue has moulded, whom Gentleness has trained to look on her with deference. (Carmen 31 [Paravicini 40], p. 433, lines 9–10)

Illos diligimus   quos sculpsit provida Virtus,
Quosque Modestia se   monuit spectare modeste.

Put aside the deceptive lessons of the lascivious Ovid, she cautions; he has seduced you without refining you. She forgives his rude courting in the end, because he seems restored by the "antidote of reason." She ends by laying down the law of courteous courtship:

The grace of Ladies [*gratia domnarum*] will always grant whatever is honourable — to one who always asks with due deference. (24–25)

Here again virtue is the condition of loving. The lady wards off the unrefined lover driven by "false hopes" (*spes mendosa*) of fast, easy conquest. She does not reject him outright, but returns him to reason and promises him future favors, once he gets his act together and behaves like a gentleman. We are breathing the air of *fin amor*; the woman is that haughty and virtuous lady who reproaches the "vain hopes" of lovers and sends them out for testing in the school of good manners.

The Regensburg Songs show a highly refined mode of loving flourishing in a Bavarian convent in the first years of the twelfth century. By 1106 William IX of Aquitaine had probably just begun writing lyric, and if the traditional sequence of poems in his oeuvre is correct, the poems of courtly love are later rather than earlier.[55] Chrétien de Troyes and the authors of the romances of antiquity were probably not yet born. Nonetheless, the phenomenon is not at all new. Love letters and poems had been exchanged in the context of teaching for over a century at the schools, and the love relationship invariably involved instruction in manners and virtue. The gesture of Baudri of Bourgueil denying his love to an undisciplined pupil is fully the counterpart — in terms of love pedagogy — of the nun who refuses an impetuous lover until he learns decorous behavior.

Many social boundaries are crossed in the picture that emerges from the Regensburg Songs. Nuns, used to the company of high secular nobles, are in love with teachers from the secular clergy; the women teach the men / man the same virtue they dispense to kings and counts and learn poetic composition from them or him. The most important ranks of the social hierarchy are interconnected in the love constellations of the Regensburg Songs: monastic, high nobility, worldly clergy. Love based on virtue appears here as an aristocratic preoccupation that crosses institutional lines.

Distinctions like "monastic" friendship and "courtly" love have relevance only when the sources are isolated in narrow categories of genre and national language. It is an artificial isolation that creates the appearance of kinds of love institutionally determined (court and monastery). This guarantees the concealment of (and the indifference of scholarship to) the existence of ennobling, virtue-giving love as a shared value of the nobility. True, there are fundamental differences in the regulation of life and the style of life in these various communities, but there are also shared forms, and love and friendship are among them. It may have been a force that leveled the forms of aristocratic life in worldly monasteries, cathedral communities, and worldly courts, rather than demarcating and distinguishing them. The ladies of the Regensburg Songs with their eclectic tastes in men are an argument for just that force.

The circumstances of worldly convents and monasteries are clearly as ripe for the flourishing of love instruction as are courts and cathedral schools in the eleventh and twelfth centuries.[56]

Ovid as a Teacher of Good Love

The major authority on love prior to the twelfth century is Cicero, not Ovid.[57] But in the transition from the eleventh to the twelfth century, Ovid experiences a renaissance, and along with the reemergence of the sensualist Ovid, he also assumes incongruously the position of an authority on chaste and "moral" love.

The commentaries on the *Ars amatoria* and *Heroides* make clear that love had a position in the curriculum of the schools in the period.[58] Ovid's works are regularly classified within instruction in *mores*. The writer of an *accessus* to the *Heroides* writes:

We assign this work to *moralitas* because it is a teacher of good manners. . . . Its ultimate purpose is to commend chaste love by showing its value.[59]

And in a later passage: "The intention of the work is to commend the virtues and ward off the vices" (Hexter, p. 158).

The *Ars amatoria*, a far more frivolous and provocative work than the *Heroides*, was for the glossators a thoroughly useful and edifying work of morals and manners. The author of the Copenhagen glosses writes:

Here Ovid intends to instruct boys and girls in love. . . . For by observing that love poses dangers for boys and girls because of their lack of experience . . . his aim is to enlighten them on the nature of love. (Hexter, p. 219)

The *Ars amatoria*, filled with cynical advice on seduction and the carrying-on of love affairs, becomes a high-minded authority in a delicate area of morals.[60] A reader and poet as sophisticated as Baudri of Bourgueil had seen him as such. Baudri wrote a verse epistle in which the exiled Ovid defends himself against the charges of immorality leveled at him. The fictional frame of the dramatic monologue is that Ovid writes to his friend Florus in Rome and refutes the false accusations of Augustus Caesar:[61]

I have not taught the youths to love, but rather how and what to love in licit love, and it was my constant concern to teach every citizen of Rome to love in an urbane and civil manner, thereby eliminating the boorishness of my city. (Carmen 98, p. 109, 67–70)

Nec docui iuvenes, ut amarent, sed magis illud:
   Si quid amare libet, qualiter aut quid ament,
Curans, ut civis civiliter omnis amaret
   Urbis seducta rusticitate mee.

Baudri's Ovid has a sweeping program of love instruction: "every citizen" of Rome should learn sophisticated love from him. But also striking is the program itself: *civiliter amare*. The words *civilis* and *civiliter* had for Baudri in the eleventh/twelfth century a different meaning than for Ovid in the first. The vocabularies of the period associate *civilis* with "urbane" and "courtly."[62] That quality which Ovid hopes to eliminate from "his" city, "boorishness" (*rusticitas*) is the opposite of "urbane," "civil," and "courtly" in the language of courtliness. Ovid presents himself in Baudri's lines as a teacher of "civil love," and the medieval poet's contemporaries will have read that formulation as closely related if not identical with "courtly love."

The glossators also recognize Ovid as a teacher of civil, courtly love. The Copenhagen glosses on *Ars amatoria* explain a historical distinction Ovid himself makes in the work: love in the early history of Rome was very different from the golden age of his present; the uncivilized past had known only rustic simplicity (*simplicitas*) in loving. But a more refined manner is appropriate to the splendid age of Augustus. The twelfth century gloss comments on this distinction: Ovid, living in a courtly age, had taught women to be courtly (*curiales docet esse in tam curiali tempore*). The glossator places love in a courtly context, a context which had not existed for Ovid, whose vocabulary of refinement drew on words for the city: *urbanus* and *civilis*.

The glosses on Ovid are school texts, sober, practical documents in the discipline called *mores*. They have the character of lecture notes and are not suspect of literary stylization. What sense would it have to warn young people against the dangers of love by recommending as a remedy nonexistent postures, a purely literary discourse on love? And the glosses are certainly not dubious texts, handed about under the table in frivolous competition with serious ones. Ovid and his works could, of course, be understood as frivolous (as in the Regensburg Songs), but they became useful and practical where love itself was the object of instruction.

What I was able to present in this chapter is a brief outline of a subject that deserves much more detailed treatment. It may at least serve to encourage further study and to give a framework to accommodate such seemingly anomalous texts as the *Questio* on "the art of love" prepared by Peter the Chanter from classroom notes, but not included in his *Verbum abbreviatum*. It argues that the art of love is good in itself, but can be corrupted by misuse. The precept of Ovid that we should seek out a woman to love, says Peter, has to do not with crass seduction (its misuse), but with "the choice of a mode of life."[63]

A final text suggests a historical curve of Ovid as teacher of chaste love—downward. This poem from the *Carmina Burana* (no. 105) is a complaint about the decline of love.[64] It dates from the end of the twelfth or early thirteenth century. In a dream vision the god Cupid appears to the sleeping poet. The god of love is shabby and sad. He speaks to the dreamer and reveals the present state of the art of love. It is in decline. "My ancient vigor is gone, my virtue has vanished" (6.3). The main symptom of decline is that instruction in love is no longer offered, and the lessons of Ovid are everywhere being misunderstood and perverted:

Artes amatorie   iam non instruuntur
   a Nasone tradite,   passim pervertuntur. (7.1–2)

Cupid's monologue contains a lament about the demise of the great teacher of love:

Ovid was so well instructed in my arts, and he shunned the allurements of worldly delights. He sought to convert the world from its errors. Anyone who possessed self knowledge learned [from him] to love with wisdom. (8, 1–4)

Naso, meis artibus   feliciter instructus
mundique voluptatibus   et regulis subductus,
ab errore studuit   mundum revocare;
Qui sibi notus erat,   docuit sapienter amare.

This Ovid clearly taught the art of loving wisely. His students were not frivolous seducers, since the prerequisite of this vanishing course of study was Delphic wisdom, self-knowledge. In the present, however, men seek only sensual pleasure, and wise love is neglected.

The irony is charming, at least for us: the god of love blames lust for the decline of true love and regrets the passing of that prudent teacher, the ascetic and morally severe Ovid.

*   *   *

Instruction in love was fundamental to the schools of the earlier Middle Ages. A student's love for a teacher may always be useful in teaching, but it is not always built into the curriculum and it is not licit in the social customs of modern schools and universities. But from the eighth to the twelfth century, it was an instrument of a program of education in *mores*. The dethroned god of moral love in *Carmina Burana* 105 can stand as an emblem of this love pedagogy and its weakening in the course of the twelfth century.

6

Women

Ennobling love created a Camelot world of erotic discourse, which survived for a long time with its innocence untroubled. Until the twelfth century it had been an exclusive club for gentlemen.[1] Of course there had been a few ripples on the surface: Jerome's letters to Paula and Eustochium, Venantius Fortunatus's letters to Radegund and Agnes, Boniface's to and from various Anglo-Saxon abbesses.[2] But these were insignificant waivings of the rules, or individual acts of condescension, not a welcoming of noblewomen generally into this discourse.

The essential and traumatic change in the amatory customs of the nobility was the inclusion of women as major players in ennobling love relationships, a game that had long been the exclusive preserve of men. Ennobling love turned on virtue, and inscribed in the word itself is gender exclusivity: *virtus* is strictly for *viri*, who also are the sole possessors of **vir**ility.[3] The cult of the high noble courtly woman has always seemed a startling feature of the literature of the twelfth century. But scholarship on the subject, instead of asking about the social function of the cult of women, has asked, what are its formal literary conventions, what other literary conventions do they come from, and what is the "system" of love they imply. This has led to the impasse it is now in.[4]

Part of the problem is that the traditional scholarship has seen "courtly love" as something radically new, "an entirely new mode of feeling" (C. S. Lewis), a "discovery" that took place in the twelfth century (Peter Dinzelbacher). This may be true for some aspects of the love relations of men and women, but equally true is that there is a strain of high courtly love, *fin amor*, *hôhe minne*, that continues an older mode of ennobling love, transforming it in a wide variety of ways. Our purpose is to hold on to that older strain, watch it transferred from men to women, and, in a later chapter, observe it taken over into the literature of courtly love. Two features are central to that continuity: love as a school of manners and virtue; and love as a "magnifying," exalting, and prestige-giving force.

Bad and Dangerous Women

Alcuin wrote to his female correspondents with officious respect and with love that is lukewarm in comparison with any he expressed to his male correspondents. The reasons for this cooling in Alcuin's letters to women elude interpretation, and we are left with the intuitive sense that greater caution might be appropriate when declaring love to women. The love that played like a flute song through the king's court in the court poetry did not select men above women. But other poems did. Alongside the passionate love for men, there was a darker mode for representing women. Theodulf wrote a poem warning against the dangers of women's love:

Watch out for your own wife,
let her not corrupt your mind with temptations!
On your knees, hands, neck and cheeks
she will press sweet kisses mingled with soft words,
practised at spiking her prayers in the poison
with which the archer tirelessly equips his shafts.
If you are protected by a helmet of strongmindedness
which makes her see that her weapons bounce off it,
she will then retreat groaning and heave feigned sighs,
grieving that her prayers have no weight.
Soon a servant boy or a nurse or perhaps her lying little maid
will say: "Why do you spurn my lady's requests?"
She will cast down her gaze and say with a muted sigh:
"He whom I now see is the one I always honour,
whatever *other* women ask for, they get, for good or for ill,
but *I* am the one who gains none of her wishes."
They will tell her to make her request and run to kiss you,
and to you they will say: "How can you bear to be horrid to her?"
But may your mind fight back as it would resist the return of an enemy;
be careful that a fresh onslaught does not see you beaten![5]

This generic wife shows no capacity for love. Her desires are sexual, and they have the trivial pestering quality of women whose destiny and mental capacities are exhaustively fulfilled in the bedroom. The man, however, is a moral warrior, who meets his wife's simpering with "weapons," "arms," "helmets." The man's mind is a mighty fortress against temptations. Woman's love does no honor to woman, and it honors the man only because it gives him an enemy against whom to brandish his weapons and show his courage. To succumb to woman's love, even that of a wife, would be — within the implicit values of the poem — itself womanish. It is a danger that threatens to "contaminate" or "corrupt" (*maculare*) man's mind.

Lantfrid and Cobbo

The wife of Lantfrid had neither personality, individuality, nor soul in the story of Lantfrid and Cobbo (Cambridge Song no. 6). She was a piece of property exchanged between the two friends, distinguished from a cow or a horse only in that her use is sexual gratification. Cobbo's refusal to put it to this use is his sublime gesture of friendship. Theodulf of Orleans might have regarded that gesture as virile restraint added to friendship. The idea that the woman may have had something to say about the friend's request, the husband's compliance, and the duty it implied for her seem not to have entered the poet's mind. But given the scant vocabulary of praise and the abundant vocabulary of blame in midcentury, silence may have been the best Lantfrid's wife could hope for.

Managing Female Carnality (the Loire Circle of Poets)

In the second half of the eleventh century it seems that the same members of the clergy who were writing poems of praise and spiritual love to women of the nobility (we will look at some of them later in this chapter) also took on the pastoral duty of rescuing these and other women from an inherent carnality that threatens their entire sex.

The poets of the so-called Loire circle, Marbod of Rennes, Baudri of Bourgueil, Hildebert of Lavardin, still can speak the language of fierce antifeminism. Hildebert wrote a poem on the three major vices by which "sacred manners," "holy morals," are subverted, the first of which is woman:

A frail thing is woman, constant only in crime,
never on her own does she desist from harm.
Woman is an insatiable flame, extreme madness, unmitigated catastrophe . . .
Woman's intimacy is the worse the closer it is,
She invites crime by her attentions, her voice, her hand.
Consuming all things, she is consumed by every vice,
and preying on men, she makes herself the prey . . .
A woman deprived Paris of his sense and Uriah of his life,
David of his virtue, Solomon of his faith . . .[6]

But the image of the dangerous woman is muted in the poems of praise, the complaint of licentiousness turned to a commendation of chastity.

The praise of virginity is a leitmotif in their poetry. The theme is prominent in Marbod. His poem to Countess Ermengard begins by praising her as the glory of all Gaul, beautiful, modest, well-mannered, but then veers in an oddly unflattering direction:

Had you not suffered the marriage bed and the pains of childbirth,
You could in my judgment be Cynthia [the goddess Diana].
But since woman man-bound can't compare to woman chaste,
The greater honor is still virginity.[7]

The praise is not only ungallant (what she has lost) but backhanded (what she will lose). He enumerates her many praiseworthy qualities, but only to remind her that they along with all the delights of this life will soon fade and she would do best to love Christ, hate the world, and do good works. The essence of such two-faced praise is pithily bundled in Hildebert's line, placed in the mouth of Queen Mathilda,

"Part of me lies in the grave, the other part governs the English realms." (Carm 35, ed. Scott, p. 22)

It is worthwhile to stress the *memento mori* theme that undercuts the praise of feminine excellence, since these poets are often spoken of as the originators of a culture of female praise that was to find its highpoint in vernacular love lyric. Students of the lyric of Marbod and Hildebert who (like the present one) quote impressive phrases such as "glory of the female sex" should remind their readers of the full context:

snow-like will melt the glory of the female sex.

neve simul caderet muliebris gloria sexus.

Woman emerges from the lower depths of antifeminism not a glowing antithesis but acutely in danger of recidivism. The chaste, beautiful paragon of a woman rescued from the vice of carnality operates fully within the strategy of moralizing polemicists in the Middle Ages. Medieval social criticism in general operates within a two-pronged discourse: the one prong skewers the objects of attack on their gross abuses, the other fixes them into codes and norms; the first finds or invents inflated wrongs, the second fashions sublime ideals.[8] The Loire circle exalts noble women to goddesses not only to deify, but also to manage, take control of and rein in their vices.[9]

Anselm on the Bride of Christ and the Bride of Worms

Two letters from Anselm of Canterbury to the nun Gunhild, daughter of the Saxon king Harold, who died at the battle of Hastings, illustrate the rhetoric of this pastoral mission against female carnality.[10] It seems that Gunhild had either fled or been abducted from the Abbey of Wilton some time in 1093 by

Count Alan Rufus, lord of Richmond and one of the most powerful men in northern England. Gunhild, around thirty at the time, must have been a charming and beautiful woman. It is probable that at the sight of Gunhild Count Alan's head was turned and his loyalties alienated from his fiancée, Matilda, daughter of King Malcolm of Scotland (later wife of Henry I of England and a recipient of poems of praise from Hildebert), also a resident of Wilton at the time. Whatever the exact circumstances of this turning, Alan dropped Matilda and took Gunhild. After her lover's / husband's death in the same year, she remained in the world, and this is the occasion of Anselm's two letters.

The tone of these letters is as severe as any Anselm wrote.[11] The purpose is to bring Gunhild back to the monastery, and the rhetorical frame is two loves: the love she owes to God, the love she has given unjustly to her lover. Anselm speaks as the voice of the former. He assumes without qualification one motive behind Gunhild's love for Alan — carnality — and so his duty becomes demonizing and opposing it with spiritual rewards:

Consider now, dearest daughter, how far apart are the embraces of men and the pleasure of the flesh from the embraces of Christ and from the pleasure of chastity and purity of heart. To be sure, I do not call the embraces of Christ physical; they are such that a soul makes itself his friend through love and desire for him through a good conscience. (trans. Fröhlich, 2.65; ed. Schmitt, 4.44)

Nothing positive — loving companionship, mutual help, conjugal affection, offspring or the hope of them — is among the motives which Anselm imputes to Gunhild. He directs his weapons against one target only, the uncontrollable sexuality driving Gunhild. It is unlikely that this *reductio ad carnalitatem* is just rhetoric; it probably is Anselm's earnest conviction that he has diagnosed the cancer on the soul of woman.

What follows is a courtship for the love and affection of Gunhild, where Anselm is the spokesman of the one suitor, Christ. He promises "delightful anticipation" against the "carnal pleasure" of the other. There is of course dowry, as in any marriage arrangements: the one offers the kingdom of heaven, the other "corruption and contemptible things." She is already betrothed to Christ who is waiting for her to become his lawful bride, and "if not a virgin, at least chaste." He refers to holy women whose penitence and chaste life made them closer to God than many holy virgins. He depicts the attractions of the life of the *sponsa Christi* with the rich imagery of the Song of Songs.

In the next letter, written after the death of Count Alan, he paints with equal vividness the grizzly inheritance of the fleshly bridegroom:

Your loved one who loved you, Count Alan Rufus, where is he now? Where has that beloved lover of yours gone? Go now, sister, lie down with him on the bed in which he now lies; gather his worms to your bosom; embrace his corpse; press your lips to his naked teeth, for his lips have already been consumed by putrefaction. Certainly he does not now care for your love, in which he delighted while alive, and you shrink from his rotting flesh, which you longed to possess. This assuredly is what you loved in him. (trans. Fröhlich, p. 70; ed. Schmitt, 4. 47–48)

The macabre atmosphere of the ballads of dead bridegrooms claiming their living brides wafts from the lines, as the twice repeated "Where . . . ?" evokes or rather already is a sounding of the memento mori motif, "where are the greats of bygone years?" or "where are the snows of yesteryear?" Putrefaction as a rebuke to worldly love proved useful to contemporaries,[12] and would prove useful to ascetic critics of courtly love later in the next century. Heinrich of Melk, writing around 1170, called up a scene of a courtly damsel at the grave of her husband:

Come, woman, see your dear [dead] husband, his face . . . , discover whether he still has those merry manners which he showed to you in public when he exchanged those private glances of love with you. Where are his frivolous words with which he praised and narrated the things in which women take pride? Look at that tongue, with which he sang songs of love. Now neither words nor breath issue from it.[13]

The attitude of a cleric to an apostate nun may well be more fierce than to a worldly woman,[14] but the two letters to Gunhild speak an only slightly heated version of the stark dualism of carnal woman versus chaste woman that inhabited the rhetoric of this generation.

Virtuous Women

A tradition of the praise of high noblewomen continued strong from antiquity to the end of the reign of Charlemagne. Then it ends abruptly.[15] From the mid-eighth century to the end of the Middle Ages it is possible to find literature vilifying women,[16] but one must wait until the second half of the eleventh century to find literature idealizing them.[17] Only then do poetry and narrative in Germany and France begin to include praise and a positive image of women.[18] The works treated in what follows in part continue earlier panegyric traditions, but they are enriched by a new courtly social ethos and, most strikingly, a conception of woman as a moral force, an idea which earlier ages had not known. This new literature appears simultaneously with a transformation of the position and stature of women in the political and social realities of life in the period, and there is general agreement that the emergence of a literature of high courtly love at the beginning of the twelfth century is closely connected.[19]

It is important to note that at the same time woman becomes virtuous, she also becomes a poet. The image of the virtuous woman is coupled with learning virtue, but also with learning and practicing poetry.

Laurels for Eurydice

A good witness to the crossing of this threshold is an anonymous poet who wrote an allegory of education around 1080 called, like the work which was its model, "De nuptiis Philologiae et Mercurii."[20] He probably belonged to the circle of poets including Godfrey of Reims and Marbod of Rennes; at least he was familiar with their poems. At the end of his complex allegory he retells the story of Orpheus and Eurydice. Both Orpheus and Eurydice sing for the assembled gods and muses. That the bard sings is obvious; remarkable is that his wife does also. It is the only time in the tradition to my knowledge that Eurydice sings.[21] When she finishes her song, the gods reward her with the laurel wreath, gems, gold, and an interesting laudation:

The happy court of the gods unanimously award Eurydice their acclamations, *thereby approving the praise of women*, and she is crowned with the laurel, with gems and gold, as was appropriate.

Leta cohors superum *laudes probans mulierum*
Euridicis totis referunt preconia votis,
Utque decet lauro, gemmis redimitur et auro.
(ed. Boutemy, lines 398–400; emphasis added)

The passage suggests a new role for women in the culture of poetry in central France in the late eleventh century,[22] but it also sounds very much as if some general taboo on the praise of women were lifted here.

We want to study the main features of a new image of the noblewoman in letters, narrative, and lyric poetry.

Ruodlieb

The Latin epic *Ruodlieb* (ca. 1070) doubles the cast of female characters. There is still the dangerous temptress governed by her sexuality. She is the beautiful young wife of an older man. She succumbs to the seduction of the redheaded adventurer, causes the death of her husband, and, crushed by the realization of her foolishness, imposes horrible mutilation of the offending female parts on herself: hanging by her hair, cutting off her nose and lips, branding Xs on her cheeks. The judge and jury dealing with the old man's death show mercy in the face of such penitence, but the woman does not accept it: she punishes herself by shaving her head, tying off her breasts until they wither, and other acts of extreme penitence (8.35–102). Lips and cheeks, breasts and long hair—female beauty in general—are dangerous instruments of crime and immorality, and self-mutilation of the woman who has misused them looked to the poet like understandable retribution. The swing from casual lasciviousness to deep penitence will have reprised a theme in the air, the glorifying of the penitent sexual sinner. The clearest testimony to the theme is the rise of the cult of the *sancta meretrix* Mary Magdalene at just this time.[23]

Alongside the foolish, dangerous woman ruled by her sexuality, there are in the *Ruodlieb* also noblewomen loving nobly. One is a landowning widow; the other her daughter, who is introduced weaving gold bands for her future bridegroom, whoever he might be. She enters the scene "glowing bright like the moon" (10.51–55). The widow has a harp that belonged to her husband. When she hears it played, she becomes "sick with love": "Cuius clangore mea mens languescit amore" (11.32).[24] So both of them are women nobly and admirably in love, the widow sending her love to the lost husband, the daughter sending hers to the future husband. Ruodlieb's nephew dances with the widow's daughter, "like a falcon and a swallow," they "burn in love" for each other, become engaged, and exchange rings in a playful game whose object is to lose the ring to the other (11.55–72). Vows of loyalty are exchanged, the young man promises not to go "whoring," and gives his young wife a sword, with which she may cut off his head if he breaks this vow. He reveals during the ceremony that he had earlier been in the clutches of a "witch," from whom the love of the young girl has rescued him. Love is legitimized by marriage here. It also has the double moral force of holding him, at sword's point so to speak, to monogamy, and rescuing him from an immoral love. We are not far from the view of Andreas Capellanus and others that love makes a man chaste and virtuous. The alternative represented to the romantic and licit love leading to marriage is enslavement to a dishonoring passion. Honor comes to a man through love and marriage; dishonor through illicit love.[25]

Women are capable of giving and receiving honor in this work. Ruodlieb's mother urges him to seek a wife "whose lineage is the equal of your own, and whose manners [*mores*] do not diminish your honors."[26] He asks his counselors to find a woman for him, "who would not be indecorous [*non indecor*] to our lineage, but rather would gild it with her good manners and the inborn nobility of her conduct [*moribus ingenita vel vitae nobilitate*]" (16.55–57). The counselors realize that Ruodlieb needs an heir who will inherit the "manner, virtues, and worldly goods" [heredem morum, virtutum sive bonorum] with which God has honored him (16.60–61). One of the advisors commends a woman who is the equal of Ruodlieb in "goodness of behavior, virtue [*moris honestate virtute*] and nobility" (16.64–65). He is sure that Ruodlieb will find her "a little lady who practices every virtue so diligently that she would be a proper wife for any man" [dominellam, / Omnem virtutum tam strennuiter facientem, / . . . ut quemque virum decuisset] (16.68–70).

These prerequisites of marriage to a landowning noble are very different from those among the high nobility of a previous generation elsewhere in Europe. Queen Emma, great-aunt of William the Conqueror, was attractive to her second husband King Cnute (the Great) of Denmark (d. 1035), so her encomiast (writing in the 1040s) tells us, because of her nobility, wealth, beauty, and wisdom:

> In view of her distinguished qualities of this kind, she was much desired by the king, and especially because she derived her origin from a victorious people, who had appropriated for themselves part of Gaul, in despite of the French and their prince.[27]

A desirable wife for Ruodlieb, however, must have "manners" and "virtues." The prerequisites are ethical rather than martial: *virtus, mores, morum honestas*; she must be *non indecora* and *decens* (*ut quemque virum decuisset*). The vocabulary is easily locatable; it is the Ciceronian ethical vocabulary taken over by the cathedral schools and made into a central part of a curriculum of *litterae et mores*,[28] the staples of *cultus virtutum*. As Queen Emma offered "conqueror" qualities to a warrior husband, so the bride of a courtly noble a generation or two later must excel in virtues and manners.

Women are introduced into the exclusive male preserve of moral improvement, instruction in virtue, *decorum*. This view of good women as a positive moral force is to my knowledge new in the Middle Ages.[29]

Women also enjoy both respect and power in the work. Ruodlieb entrusts his land to his mother to administer when he sets out to seek his fortune (1.16).[30] Later he reaps general praise for seating his mother at a banquet alone on a dais "so that she could oversee all the guests and be recognized as mistress of the house" (16.30–31). Because he honors her thus and recognizes her as *domina*, he earns not only praise from the guests, but also the crown of eternal life (16.32–34). This is a radical rise in the moral stature of women: a single act of honoring and recognizing their authority earns redemption!

The young woman betrothed to Ruodlieb's nephew extracts vows of fidelity and service from her bridegroom in a playfully joking speech. She refs to him as a slave or servant (*servum*) whom she has won in a game of dice, and demands service from him:

I want him to serve me diligently night and day,
The better he does this, the dearer he will be to me. (14.55–56)

Her "audacious" but "friendly" jest (*praesumptive, tam vel amice*) makes the courted woman into the *domina* over her future husband, setting playfully harsh terms of service for the lover courting her. It seems to me quite right to see a connection of the passage with a later cult of "love service" in courtly romance.[31]

Marbod on Whores and Matrons

Marbod of Rennes (ca. 1035–1123) wrote a number of love poems to both men and women.[32] His early poems have nothing to do with ennobling love. They are love poems pure and simple, wooing, lamenting, complaining.[33] Alongside these is a series of poems rejecting and warning against "Venereal" or "intemperate" love.[34] Also included among Marbod's poems is a series of tediously repetitive lines enumerating the evils of women,[35] and others praising chastity and virginity.[36]

This parataxis of woman condemned and woman celebrated occurs in a late work of Marbod, the *Liber decem capitulorum*.[37] Two of its ten chapters are devoted to female types, the whore and the matron (*meretrix, matrona*),[38] the bad and good woman, the one an abyss of temptation and deception, the other an embodiment and disseminator of virtue — essentially the same two types we encountered in *Ruodlieb*. Here the portraits are so vivid and the thinking in a reductive dichotomy so evident, it is worthwhile looking at them in some detail, at least the matron.[39]

The portrait of the evil woman is predictably fierce. She spreads scandals, causes strife, turns old friends into enemies, stirs children against parents, and so on. The crimes escalate until the seducing woman is a major threat to political stability, the source of all evils, and embodiment of all vices. She will stop at nothing to get her way, regarding nothing sweet as forbidden (lines 19–20). She burns with uncontrollable passions — and generally uncontrollability is her dominant vice; she governs neither her speech, her lusts, nor her ambitions. With her arsenal of bad qualities she overturns the world: "His armata malis subvertit femina mundum" (25). A predator, her special weapon is *amor*: simulating a noble face, she consumes those captured by her beauty in the flames of love (52–53). Marbod invokes the heroism of manly resistance, close to Theodulf's lines on a wife's wiles, full of the vocabulary of combat and warfare (73–79). Ulysses tied to the mast, as a type of Christ on the cross, is made the paradigm of virile self-defense.

The ninety lines of this tirade amount to an attack on woman generally. Though the titles seem to restrict it to a single type, the evil woman or prostitute, the word *meretrix* never appears in the body of the text, only *femina*. The undeceivable deceiver, "woman" (1–4), is the embodiment of the devil's plans. The poem has some features in common with Theodulf's satire against wives, but the trivial, pestering sexuality of the Carolingian bad wife has metastasized into the most hideous of all evils. Threats unspeakable loom over man from female sexuality.

The portrait of the good woman in stark contrast raises the married woman to a paragon. (For an English translation, see Appendix.) The remarkable turnabout is not only the reversal of the moral valence on woman, but the insistence on the equality of man and woman:

For, being the same creature, we live under the same condition,
And there is nothing which we do not bear in common,
Being in all things alike except for the distinction of sex.
We are conceived in the same way, we eat the same foods,
Dress alike, our sadness and tears are moved
By the same feelings, we judge with like intelligence
What is good what is evil, what is just, what is sinful,
And our mutual sentiments flow with equal eloquence . . .
All these things man and woman can do in common. (7–18)

These lines have the forced and condescending argument of a "defense" based not on love and respect but on diminished contempt. It has some striking resemblances to Shakespeare's defense of the Jews. Compare Shylock's

Hath not a Jew . . . senses, affections, passions; fed with the same food . . . subject to the same diseases, heal'd by the same means, warm'd and cool'd by the same winter and summer, as a Christian is? (*Merchant of Venice* 3.1.61–66)

with Marbod's

We are conceived in the same way, we eat the same foods,
Dress alike, our sadness and tears are moved
By the same feelings, we judge with like intelligence . . .

And for the sharper classification of woman (20–38), Marbod distinguishes her from other things living which act (animals and plants), or nonliving which give pleasure (jewelry and precious metals).

But also behind the condescending there is a sense of genuine admiration:

Therefore since the dignity of woman is greater than all these things,
More beautiful than silver, more precious than gold,
More precious than gems, which lack the light of reason,
We think it abundantly proven that she is
More to be wondered at and more to be cherished. (34–38)

However, the issue is not Marbod's sincerity, but the image of woman that emerges from the poem. And his comparisons "upward" to man produce a striking laudation. Woman's intelligence in judging good and evil, right and wrong, is the equal of man's as are her powers of eloquence. The comparison with Portia briefly evoked in the post-Shakespearean reader fades as Marbod praises motherhood, the pains endured in childbirth, the procreation of the race — these are debts man owes to woman that should inspire a fitting love (*digno amore*). Woman also is superior in domestic activities: spinning, weaving — minor things, but without them "the level of culture would be lowered" (*si deficiant vitae minuatur honestas*, 61). She has a gentle touch in caring for the sick, and she assists with greater skill at the bedside, she prepares food and drink more diligently.

The important realms of female superiority are love and learning:

Woman loves more and is better able to adapt precepts
And to be shaped into the image of the Good like soft wax.
The hard mind and stiff neck of man rebels against
And hardly will take the yoke,
Denying all the time his inferiority.
And furthermore the pursuit of virtue
Is more laudable in the more frail sex. (67–73)

This is high praise, and it rises well above the condescension of the previous lines. The capacity to judge the Good, to love more and to learn virtue more readily places woman solidly in the game of ennobling love, which grants love as recognition of virtue. Marbod does not say in so many words that woman is therefore better able to make stiff-necked men virtuous by her love, but it is implied in the logic of this praise, and that logic would unfold in the next generation. Woman by her nature is peculiarly able to learn virtue, and the pursuit of it is more laudable because the sex is physically more frail. It is an idea that Abelard will repeat a few years later in his writings for the Paraclete and for Heloise,[40] but not so generously formulated as in Marbod. For Abelard female is more admirable than male virtue — when it happens to appear. For Marbod, woman's nature suits the entire sex as the learner and bearer of virtue, and of love. So, behind the rough edges of this praise in a man known for preaching contempt and mistrust of women is a fairly extravagant rehabilitation of the sex. Woman is equal in many ways to man, and in moral and emotional value his superior. The poem ends,

. . . woman deserves no blame for her womanhood alone,
Nor does man deserve praise for his manhood,
But rather vice is blameworthy in both sexes,
And virtue is equally praiseworthy in both. (122–25)

Moral value, not sex, is the measure of worth, and woman is declared better able to learn virtue than man. This is an important moment in the reshaping of the image of woman, not only for ruling out the automatic superiority of man by virtue of his manhood, but above all because it formulates (perhaps creates) the enabling logic of woman participating in the public discourse of a love that arises from virtue and responds to virtue. It makes woman into the giver of prestige, standing, goodness, value, a role previously restricted to man.

The *Book of Ten Chapters* gives two starkly opposed images of woman. The unresolved contradiction is a provocation. Which is it? Is woman the tool of the serpent or of virtue? In both poems the judgments apply to "woman." Even the married state of the good woman plays no role in the poem.

The double optic is not a contradiction, but rather the two-pronged discourse of the polemicist, inflating potential wrongs to make them hideous and demoniacal, at the same time fashioning sublime ideals.[41] The one extreme works through extravagant vilifying, the other through extravagant glorifying. Womanhood, placed between these two poles is meant to be repelled by the negative and attracted by the positive, and extreme exaggeration at both ends turns up the pressure.

The point is that the positive pole here introduces into the public forum of poetry a differentiated view of woman, an awareness of the virtuousness and honor potentially present, maybe even inherent, in women, a sensitivity to the "glory of the female sex."[42] The wholesale condemnation of woman is overcome.

Baudri of Bourgueil

Baudri of Bourgueil, talkative and self-revealing like few medieval poets, says outright that at some point in his writing he lifted the exclusivity that had limited it to men. The passage is in a poem to the English nun Muriel, a skilled poetess praised also by Hildebert:

There is one thing that blunts the sharpness of my pen:
That is that it does not know the way to the homes of girls.
No virgin has until now received my songs except you,
None has heard my letter bid her farewell.
We wrote to buddies, we joked a lot with friends,
And any girl was excluded from this game.[43]

Porro mei calami res una retundit acumen:
 Quippe puellarum nescit adire domos.
Nulla recepit adhuc nisi tu mea carmina, virgo,
 Nulli dixit adhuc cartula nostra vale.
Scripsimus ad socios, sat lusimus inter amicos,
 Expers ludendi queque puella michi.

The "game" and the "joke" is about love;[44] the above lines mark the
threshhold point when women become players in it.

If Marbod's reflections on love still turned on the dualism of bad woman/
good woman, Baudri finds the beginnings of a synthesis in a subtle and provocative mingling of the two loves. Baudri speaks the language of ennobling
love which responds to personal distinction and cultivates virtue, a language
spoken among men for centuries. The immediately noticeable change produced by woman's emergence is the prominence of chastity and virginity as
sources of that lovable excellence. These virtues of course had no role in the all-
male discourse, which appeared to know nothing of unchaste behavior. Writing a "love song" (*carmen amoris*, line 7) to Lady Constance, a young nun of
high nobility, living probably at the monastery of Le Ronceray near Angers, he
proposes a love relationship based on chastity and mutual cultivation of virtue.[45] Young and beautiful though she is, his wish is not to be her husband
(42–43), but her chaste lover:

Let our hearts be joined, but our bodies remain apart,
Our acts be pure though our words be jesting. (45–46)

Pectora iungantur, sed corpora semoveantur;
 Sit pudor in facto, sit iocus in calamo.

It is passion without sex, love beyond the flesh:

It's clear, then, that this kind of love
Savors of the special, not of the common.
This is a special love: the flesh does not taint it
Nor does illicit desire mar it.
I am always a lover of your virginity,
I long for the purity of your flesh. (77–82)

Ergo patet liquido, quoniam genus istud amoris
   Non commune aliquid, sed spetiale sapit.
Est spetialis amor, quem nec caro subcomitatur
   Nec desiderium sauciat illicitum.
Ipse tue semper sum virginitatis amator,
   Ipse tue carnis diligo mundiciam.

He also loves her wisdom and her writing. Virtue and poetry, not lascivious desire, stir his love (49–52). Indifferent to her flesh, except its purity, he depicts her beautiful body (55–70) with only one end in mind:

I have described your beauty in my song
So that the outer beauty will mark your beauty of character. (85–86)

Propter id ergo tuam depinxi carmine formam,
   Ut morum formam extima forma notet.

The "flowered" virgin puts forth "florid manners" so that she may flourish inwardly more than outwardly (87–88). Their pact of love, their shared learning, their exchange of poems, has one purpose, to cultivate the "thirst for lofty things" (120). It is a love alliance based on the pursuit of virtue,

Let us tread the path of virtues, let us rise to the stars. (113)

Virtutum gradiamur iter, gradiamur ad astra

and of literature.[46]

   He wrote to another nun, "Domina Emma," in a loving but less flirtatious tone (Emma was presumably older and higher in rank), with the same subordination of love to cultivation of virtue:

Pattern of decorum and beauty for the nuns, Emma . . .
Let your special virtue [goodness] join you ever to me
And let the law of good behavior perpetuate the bond.[47]

Cenobitarum decus et decor, Emma, sororum . . .
Te michi contiguet semper specialis honestas;
   Lex bene vivendi te michi perpetuet.

The language of virtuous love does not vary with the gender of the recipient. He writes to Galo (male):

I love you vehemently, more than I let you know.
I love you vehemently, because you are so vehemently lovable.[48]

   Plus, quam significo, te vehementer amo.
Te vehementer amo, cum sis vehementer amandus

And to the nun Constance:

... I love you vehemently and without deceit;
I love you vehemently and will love you completely,
I enfold you and you alone in the depths of my being. (74–76)

... absque dolo te vehementer amo.
Te vehementer amo, te totam totus amabo,
    Te solam nostris implico visceribus.

The cause of love in both cases is poetry. He writes to Galo:

The reason for this vehement love is your muse. (18)

Ut vehementer amem te, tua Musa facit.

and to Constance:

Your writings have aroused my feelings for you,
and your Muse joined me to you deep within. (51–52)

In te sed nostrum movit tua littera sensum
    Et penitus iunxit me tua Musa tibi.

The flirtatious, provoking game with carnal love is common to both
genders. He had "played" with the physical in writing his friend Galo.[49] But
this escalates in the letter to Constance. He declares his vehement love for her,
sets her worth as far above that of Venus for Mars, Helen for Paris, Eurydice
for Orpheus, as true love (*verus amor*, 27) is set above false. He wishes that
nature had joined them in a "bond of love" (*foedus amoris*, 34). The constant
foil and sounding board of this chaste, special love, is carnal love:

Jupiter still ravishes today and beckons for a session with you . . .
Many youths pursue the godless ways of Jove . . .
The realms of chaste restraint swarm with them . . .
Let us follow another path:
The path of virtues . . . (cf. 97–113)

The double image of woman, temptress and chaste mediatrix of virtue, is
present, but it unites in the same woman; the face of the whore is playfully
morphed into that of the virgin. Seduction metamorphoses into cultivation of
chastity. The dynamics of the game are a teasing reversal of the valences on the
flesh: the beautiful body arouses admiration of inner harmony; passion is
fulfilled in chastity.[50]

Baudri may be abbot of a Benedictine monastery, but he is also faun-like
in his love-posturing.[51] How else can we understand his provoking act of

writing to a young, beautiful nun, whose commitment to her vow of chastity may not yet have firmed up, playing the strains of romantic, passionate love, however muted into the spiritual?[52]

But Constance's answer allays that concern.[53] She plays the nymph to his faun, takes up the challenge to dance on the sword's edge of sensual/spiritual love, and outdoes the master at his own game. To summarize the relevant points of her letter-poem: She has touched his manuscript *nuda manu*, folded and unfolded it repeatedly with joy. During the sleepless night that "troubled love" caused her, she placed the letter by turns "in her lap" (*gremio*) and on her breasts, nearest to her heart, and she wishes that her beloved himself would take its place:

Hoc iacet in gremio dilecti scedula nostri;
    Ecce locata meis subiacet uberibus.
O utinam noster nunc hic dilectus adesset . . . (67–69)

Her talent for playing at Baudri's game is confirmed here and especially in the following line: [would that our lover were here] "who could explain the meaning of his own letter." Having placed him imaginatively in the very position of sexual intercourse, she teasingly switches to intellectual intercourse. She praises his beauty and sounds very much like Heloise[54] in thanking her lucky stars for so excellent a man: "Every girl envies my hopes; no girl could be more fortunate than I, if I had safe love and sure arrangements" (92–94). While conjuring him to fidelity, she declares, "I love you watchfully"! [te vigilanter amo] (120). Her *vigilanter* answers his *vehementer*. This is not what a lover wants to hear; he wants vigilance overwhelmed. Constance is no lamb, clearly, but a clever girl! That she is playing is perfectly clear, but here and throughout she leaves wide open whether she is playing Isolde to Tristan, or Dorine to Tartuffe. She appoints the law of chastity as the warden of their love (121–22), but ends by summoning him to come to her, on any pretense. She even suggests contrived excuses he might make for his absence. She needs him because she is sick with love and torn with desire (173–74). If he does not come, she will assume he cares nothing for her (169).

Baudri's poem to Constance has elements of love that we have found in other works from clerics educated in the classical tradition. Behind the playful, off-color urbanity of the discourse,[55] we see the clear contours of ennobling love. Its "game" is still played by the rules of *cultus virtutum*: it lives and thrives in a culture combining love with poetry and eloquence; its end is the cultivation of virtue. The interplay of virtue, poetry, and seduction, the virtuoso gesture of snatching chastity from the jaws or the haunches of seduction, brings it close to the Regensburg Songs. The husbanding of love for the sake of poetry and virtue places it solidly in the traditions of the cathedral schools. Love transmuted into virtue places it in the Ciceronian tradition. The pedagogic intention recalls the Hildesheim letter analyzed earlier and Baudri's poem to his haughty young student, though the counterpoint of love and discipline there is set in a very different key.

What distinguishes Baudri's letter to Constance sharply from his love letters to male friends and from any document in the history of ennobling love prior to the twelfth century is the continual warding off of suspicions of seduction and lechery. "I am sincere; trust me; my motives are chaste, not lascivious"—this was not a message that any writer of love letters prior to Baudri needed to convey. It entered the discourse of exalting love as a brief anxious tremor in Hildesheim letter 36, which ended with the assurance that the student passionately summoned should not fear dishonorable motives (above, Chapter 5). It is repeated tediously in Baudri's poem to Constance.[56] He has not only to assure her personally that lechery is not his intention, but also to impress on her the damage to his reputation that a "false" construction of his poem might bring. The silence on sexuality in Alcuin, Anselm of Bec, Aelred of Rievaulx confirms the innocence of the discourse, at least its claim of innocence. Innocence is oblivious of guilt, and that obliviousness must be instilled in a language intended to put forth the virtue of its speakers. Adam and Eve did not protest their innocence before the fall.

The threshold between guilt denied by silence and acknowledged by denial is crossed in Baudri. Along with a sense of guilt and shame as potential threats in chaste love, ambiguity enters the discourse in a big way in his poetry. Baudri is a man of layered meanings, a man of interpretations, a man of words more than deeds. Could there be a small but sharp barb in Constance's wish that her beloved, Baudri himself, not his letter, might lie in her lap during her night of troubled love, so that he "could explain the meaning of his own letter"? Of course, it projects their virtue and self-control into the sublime. But it also suggests a male sexuality weakened to the point where overcoming nature is no problem and hermeneutic intercourse effortlessly supplants sexual. Self-control is a virtue when self-imposed against strong desire, but taken for granted by the partner, it becomes the stuff of taunts: "Come sleep with me, my love, spend the night in my arms, and you can explain your poems to me."

And Baudri himself takes pleasure in masking experience in fictional postures. Writing to Godfrey of Reims he states a principle that may well extend to much of the discourse of ennobling love:

I have written a few things on love,
And my songs have given pleasure to both sexes.

I wanted to explore the limits of expression
Rather than to capture in verses what I truly might have loved.
For if I desired something really, if I vehemently loved,
My love would never turn up in my writing.
I'm not making confession when I write songs.
Confession of misdeeds should be a private matter.
A true love of someone is not to be sung out at the crossroads;
Anyone in love carefully hides the act of love . . .
The ironic Muse inspired me, and my actions were pure.[57]

Baudri the poet has something of the chameleonlike irony of the artist figure in Nietzsche and the young Thomas Mann. He is infinitely capable of — often willful — self-contradiction, hence, it seems, without (to use his own word) integrity. He wrote an admonishing letter to a boy, forbidding him to speak of love in ambiguous terms. Leave ambiguity to conniving wolves, he warns. "A frank love should have frank trust" [Nudus amor nudam debet habere fidem]; "friends do not use ambiguous words" [Utendum non est ambagibus inter amicos]. But he adds, obviously feeling that he is the pot calling the kettle black, "If occasionally ironic jests creep into my writings, my integrity is preserved because I am a jovial man by nature."[58]

    To end this section on Baudri, we look at another poem which shows us a kind of ennobling courtship of man for woman with many affinities to courtly love, practiced within the context of court society. Hennig Brinkmann points out Baudri's long poem to Countess Adela of Blois as a bridge between learned Latin poetry (there is an elaborate allegory of learning in the description of the countess's bedchamber) and courtly love.[59] The ennobling power of both love and poetry are themes that Baudri plays through:

The grand subject matter ennobles my songs,
My songs do not ennoble the subject.
Her probity of manners, her chastity do her honor,
Her child and the love of her husband enhance her. (59–62)

The chaste, honorable countess has many suitors distinguished for their *probitas*. But those who have tried to tempt her have found their efforts fruitless, since her marriage bed is protected by an inviolable pact. Baudri understands the efforts of her suitors:

Her unusual beauty and incomparable loveliness
Commend her, as does her pleasant conversation.
But who could soften her flinty resolve?
Their gazing on her is pointless, though delightful.
Nourished by empty hopes, they dream of grand rewards,
And strain their eyes with gawking. (67–72)

So here we have the distant *domna* drawing the men of court to her by her virtue and beauty but thwarting their vain hopes by her chastity and loyalty. He does not say that she sends them out to polish their manners and accomplish bold feats before granting them any hope. It is the framework of courtly love, without, for the moment, its educating aspect and without love service.[60] But it also has the structure of chaste, ennobling love, where the bearer of virtue and chastity (Adela) is placed between a noble lover (her husband) and seducers (the young men nursing false hopes). Baudri says to his haughty student: I praise you for refusing to be Ganymede to Jove. Baudri says to Constance: "Jupiter still ravishes today and beckons for a session with you . . . [but] let us tread . . . the path of virtues." And Baudri praises Adela for resisting tempters and founding her probity on marriage. In each case the wooed one is placed between high and low, chaste and unchaste love; sexual advances resisted are the source of virtue and probity.

But here sexual promise is part and parcel of the mechanism of recognizing virtue and giving honor. The "grand rewards" (*praemia magna*) of which the suitors dream are those given in the marriage bed (*pacta sui thori*), from which her fidelity banishes them to gawk and hope in vain. That means that sex is now part and parcel of the discourse of ennobling love, and it is one of the elements that entered necessarily with women.

Finally, the poem to Adela returns us to a major theme of this study: the interchangeability of court, cathedral, convent, and monastery as a location of ennobling love. In Baudri as in the Regensburg Songs, chaste love, however earnestly or jestingly proposed, crosses most of the social bounds into which the aristocracy divided. The tone and posture of the poems to the Countess Adela and the nun Constance are very different. But both turn on a chaste love sought by many men and held firm by the partners to a contract of special, chaste, virtue-giving love.

The Regensburg Songs

But the love songs from Regensburg suggest that women were not only the passive tools of this strategy, but its willing instruments. The active role of woman as man's instructor in virtue and refined manners emerges strongly in the Regensburg Songs (see Chapter 5). Female sexuality is the antagonist to vestal virginity, and sexual pleasure denied is the pedagogic instrument of men's moral improvement. As with Baudri's love poems to men and women, here also the cultivation of love and poetry are closely bound together. As with Baudri writing to Adela and "playing" with Constance, female sexuality is the

testing ground of virtue for the resisting woman and its inspiring force for the
seducing male.

The entire collection is illustrative of a new role of women in the joint
cultivation of love and virtue. Here we can limit the discussion to one poem
not previously analyzed.[61] (See Appendix for English translation.)

A group of women send "gifts" to the Liège master. The gifts are consistent with their sense of duty and their flaming love. The gifts they send are the
three Graces, the daughters of Philology and Mercury. They are gifts fashioned
from reason, not physical matter. The one is named Euprophore; she receives
good friends (or lovers? [*bonos amicos*]) with affable and courteous speech.[62]
The second is Eugiale, who serves the guests thus received and attends to their
needs. The third is Basilea (or Basithea), the epitome of virtues, who enhances
all she does through her chaste and decorous behavior. Though they embody
intellectual gifts, coming from Mercury, the "father of genius" (line 8), they
are presented as a courtly welcoming team consisting of eloquence, courtesy,
and virtue.

These three have until now served the nuns at the Regensburg monastery,
who received them as tutors from Mercury. But now their schoolmaster needs
them, and they graciously give them to him. It seems that another group of
women is luring him. These competitors, whose "bodies are as vagrant as their
minds," are called "hostesses" (*hospitibus*), presumably because they also welcome *amicos*. And so the function of the loose women answers to that of the
three Graces. Translated out of the allegory, the passage opposes prostitutes to
courtly ladies. To ward off the danger of seduction, the virtuous ladies send
their personal serving women to their teacher "for your intimate use" (*in
contiguum usum*). The slightly salacious hint in this phrase suggests that those
desires aroused by vagrant female bodies can more loftily be satisfied by the
products of eloquence and wisdom. It intensifies more than it dissipates the
erotic interplay of poetry and desire. They send these mind and body servants
on the condition that he lead a "special way of life" (*vitam specialem* — a close
relative, clearly, of the *specialis amor* Baudri offered to Constance and other
friends). He should avoid loose women and learn the lessons of the three
allegorical serving girls, who represent progressive stages in an ethical, courtly
education: from eloquence to courtesy to virtue. Virtue is what the Liège
master needs: "It is decorous for you serenely to venerate these three loyal
maidens." The waters of the hot springs of his home, Liège, ought to warm
him with "that wholesome fire by which love of virtue should be kindled"
(cf. 18–20).

Here again, a lover is placed between sexual and virtuous love, and is urged in the direction of virtue. The sexual lure is imposed in a playful meta-phor on the Graces. "We send you these women for your intimate use" is a line that Baudri or Constance might have written. It functionalizes woman's sex-uality as a lure to chastity and virtue. And that means the crude dualism of whorelike, corrupting desire and virginal/matronly chastity is overcome.

Thisbe's Wall: Passionate and Chaste Love in "Parce continuis"

A poem from the late eleventh century, "Parce continuis,"[63] brings together a number of strands in this discussion. It is a poem of love consolation.

The poet consoles a friend suffering the torments of a passionate love. It is cruel (*saevus amor*, line 59), related to the tragic love which destroyed Hero and Leander (59–71), and ended Orpheus's happiness (71–123). The poet, who presents himself as a simple, unlearned lutenist,[64] opposes destructive passion with good love and friendship. The latter gives pleasure through *hon-estas* and passion through *utilitas*. It is a gesture well known in Baudri, the lover of virginity, who longed for the purity of Constance's body — the transfer from the physical to the ethical. There is a form of love based on *honestas*, which he proposes as an alternative to the storm-tossed passion of Ovidian love. Turning from "lofty words," like *honestas*, he names famous friends and lovers who illustrate this kind of love: Nisus and Euryalus, Pirithous and Theseus, Polynices and Tydeus, David and Jonathan, Pyramus and Thisbe. The last couple seems a double breach in the logic of the list. It is male-female friendship, and it ends tragically; killed by ill-fated love, they seem to fit better with Hero and Leander than David and Jonathan.[65] But this poet remodels them into the representatives of chaste, virtuous love. They spoke with each other, shared their "intimate colloquies," through Thisbe's wall. The wall transmitted their conversations but not their kisses; it separated their bodies but allowed their souls to pass through (47–58).

The poet makes the wall into a symbol of that which a generation of poet/moralizers sought: the transformation of sexual into virtuous love. Thisbe's wall is virtue's filter. It filters the body out and leaves only soul passion. It is the magic threshold that turns Ovidian into Ciceronian lovers. Powerful alchemy, it makes possible the inclusion of woman's love in the all-male lineup of virtu-ous lovers. It applies specifically to woman's love. A passion of the soul was an unquestioned given of male-male virtuous friendship. The conceptual tour de force of the poets we read in this chapter — or of whoever was thinking the thoughts they formulated — is the rehabilitation of the female and her incorporation into the cult of ennobling love. Using the logic of this poem, we could say that what we have observed in Constance, Adela of Blois, and the virtuous women of the Regensburg convent, is the internalization of Thisbe's wall, an ethical posture that filters out carnal love and leaves only virtuous passion.

Constance of Brittany Woos Louis VII

A remarkable document shows us the love of women integrated fully into that representative function that the all-male love of kings had had into the twelfth century. It is a "love letter" written in 1160 by a Breton noblewoman, Constance, sister of Duke Conan of Brittany, to the king of France, Louis VII. It contains a proposal of love, of an exchange of love tokens, and of a love tryst. The letter reads (in excerpt):

I wish your highness to know that I have long dwelt on the thought of you, and that while many men have offered me many gifts of love, I have never accepted any. But if it should please your generosity to send any token of love to me, who loves you beyond what words can convey, be it a ring or anything at all, I would hold that more precious than the whole world. . . . I swear to you that if fortune forsook me, I would rather wed the least of your servants than become Queen of Scotland. I will prove this by my actions. As soon as my brother, Count Conan, returns from England, I will come to St. Denis to pray and to enjoy [*uti*] your presence. Fare well. Your welfare is mine.[66]

The letter was included in the official correspondence of the king in the collection of his chancellor, Hugh of Champfleury. Neither the king nor his chancellor nor contemporaries presumably read it as indiscreet or even as sensitive. It took its public, official character from its political purpose: it is a proposal of a political alliance masking as a declaration of passion.[67] What is important in the letter for our purposes is the style of noble self-representation. Passionate love is the idiom in which political goals cloak and proclaim themselves, a structuring fiction within which a power- or favor-seeker can maneuver.

    The discursive giver in this letter is courtly love (Peters and Köhn). But the social practice it is based on is the king's love. Courtiers had desired, wooed, and declared their love for their lords at least since Carolingian times. In Constance's letter the language and the motifs are new, but the custom is not. For the first time in historical documentation a woman is cast in the role of king's wooer, passionate love is the proposed relationship, and the important business of forging a political alliance is entrusted to the medium of a woman's love letter. This would have been impossible a generation earlier.

Woman is now a public figure, her love can ennoble. In this letter, the love of kings has become courtly love.

*   *   *

In the second half of the eleventh century we see the resolution of woman as vessel of evil into woman the vessel of virtue. The temptress and seducer is joined by the virtuous, decorous, ethically educated virgin, nun, matron, and this pair is joined by the woman whose love and sexuality makes men virtuous. The deficit of education and the burden of vice shifts from woman to man; man recedes from the virile warrior armed against sexuality to the one in need of moral instruction; woman advances from the ruin of man to his tutor in ethics.

The progress from temptress/whore to virgin/matron to passionate soul-lover might suggest a structure of development of thesis, antithesis, synthesis. But in fact the far cruder view of woman does not lose strength in the course of the twelfth and early thirteenth centuries. The unresolved dichotomy of incorrigible seductress and embodiment of courtly virtue remains common; we find it in Peter Abelard[68] and in architects of noble love as sophisticated as Andreas Capellanus and Gottfried von Strassburg.[69] The important point is not that the negative is dragged along with the new positive image, but that there is an entirely new and unique image of woman created in the years between 1050 and 1100: woman the vessel of virtue, soft wax to Goodness, sensitive, loving and learning more intensely than hard-necked man.

What is discovered then is that the moral training common to cathedral schools and spreading fast to the lay nobles is the instrument of taming and controlling female "riotousness." Training in *mores* not only produces A+ students in women, but raises them into the master's chair.

So love follows a development well known elsewhere in the society of the late eleventh, early twelfth century: the behavior of the laity comes under fierce attack,[70] and it is reined in by extending moral training from clerics to laymen; women's love is declared out of control and moral training is deployed to control it, transferred from its original context, clerics, to laywomen. Discipline (*moralis disciplina, mores, moralitas*) becomes a form of crisis control in situations perceived as social crisis. The dynamics which account for the spread of courtliness outward from the humanistically educated court clerics also account for the rise of the image of woman as giver of virtue through love.

We know that lay noblewomen insert themselves into the game of courtship and create the social circumstances in which "virtue" and social rank become interchangeable concepts, so that the old Ciceronian notion of friendship as love of virtue translated into "love raises the worth of lovers." Baudri could make the virtue and chastity of Adela of Blois into the force holding those many virtuous young men courting her in their place — and in place at the same time. Guibert of Nogent early in the twelfth century says that noblewomen "rest their claims to nobility and courtly pride" on their "crowds of suitors."[71] Clearly there is an affinity between the cultivation of virtue, the dynamics of virtuous friendship/love, and the all-important establishment of rank, prestige, and "worth" at worldly courts.

Monastic reformers and worldly clerics are at least in agreement on the need to find curbs on the frivolity of the lay nobles, and the clerical humanists at court, in cathedral or monastic communities, cast the great net of moral discipline over men's and women's manners, modes of dress, sexual habits. The catch of these fishers of frivolity is an ideal of the courtly gentleman and the courtly lady. Whatever it may represent in the society which produced it, in its literature the infusion of virtue into woman's love is the construction of the ethics of courtly love and of the noble damsel of courtly romance and love lyric.

PART II

SUBLIME LOVE

7

Sublime Love

The charm of a love hedged in by all sorts of restrictions on the physical is a peculiar mystery of the western erotic tradition.[1] To renounce what appears essential to love gives love special allure. One strain of Western erotic poetry made a virtue of refusal, restriction, sublimation, restraint, turned amorous desire into the first step of a process of moral education. Leo Spitzer described the sublime love of the troubadours with his usual elegance:

I had always believed that this love ["distant love"], wrapped in the mists of a dream, was the most moving assertion of what I call the "amorous paradox" at the basis of all troubadour poetry: love which does not want possession but rather pleasure in the state of non-possession, *amour-Minne* moved both by the sensual desire to caress the truly feminine woman and by chaste distancing.[2]

The passage describes an exclusive ideal of love, so refined as to place it on the borderline of the quixotic. Love that renounces the main object of desire overcomes a human nature regarded as vulgar at best and sinful at worst, but it projects love into the superhuman and the unnatural at the same time.[3]

The experience of the dreamer in Guillaume de Lorris's *Romance of the Rose* (ca. 1236) is a metaphor for a stage in the history of a sensibility: welcomed into an enclosed garden peopled with charming, gentle, and courteous nobles, excluding any with vices, he is stricken with love's arrows at the sight of a marvelous red rose. As he reaches to kiss and take possession of it, a figure springs up to defend the rose and send the lover onto a path of education and refinement of manners with some vague promise of fulfillment at the end, a promise wrapped twice in layers of mist (to borrow Spitzer's phrase): once the dream character of the vision and once the fragmentary state of the poem. It ends with the infinite openness of the incomplete.

A love with an endlessly receding goal, which finds fulfillment only in longing, striving, aspiration: however complex and unsystematic courtly love may have been either in representation or practice, this was a prominent aspect. The purpose of this chapter is to show that the elitist sensibility that governs the experience and its discourse is not restricted to the literature of courtly love.

Aelred of Rievaulx

Aelred of Rievaulx was born into a Scottish noble family. As a young man he served at the court of King David of Scotland from 1124 to 1133. He had a remarkable career at the king's court, rising to become steward of the court and personal adviser of the king, who placed him in charge of all the business of the court, internal and external. The king placed many officials under his charge. He became "as it were a second lord, an alternate prince."[4] Aelred had the qualities appropriate to a courtier: he pleased all men in all things; never showed rancor or resentment against any man, and though in a position to do harm to many, he did good to all. Such an abundance of affability and benevolence (*benignitas*) met in him that no abuse, no slander could provoke him to anger or revenge. He was "faithful in all things, friendly and welcome to good men." And as a result he was loved by all. The king "loved him vehemently" and "embraced him in love."[5]

To show Aelred's gentle, conciliatory personality, the biographer tells an incident where Aelred is slandered before the king's court by a boorish knight. He suffers the abuse patiently, shows no resentment, seeks no revenge, and in the end makes friends with the knight, for which the king loves and favors him still more.[6] The biographer says that Aelred behaved himself like a monk while living in the world. But his qualities as courtier are those of a "second lord and future prince."[7] He fits the mold of the beloved courtier who inspires the king's love, as do many others we have observed. But Aelred's court service makes it clear also that the love he was to formulate in his tract on *Spiritual Friendship* was not exclusive to the monastery. Just the opposite: he brought with him to Rievaulx from the royal court the capacity to love all without resentment and to make friends out of enemies. This sensibility grew out of his renunciation of early sexual misbehavior, which we now understand much better from Brian McGuire's study of Aelred.[8]

He also brought the major inspiration for *Spiritual Friendship* with him from his worldly period. Cicero's *De amicitia* was the great discovery of his youth. He tells of the genesis of his work in the prologue:

When I was still just a lad at school, and the charm of my companions pleased me very much, I gave my whole soul to affection and devoted myself to love amid the ways and vices with which that age is wont to be threatened, so that nothing seemed to me more sweet, nothing more agreeable, nothing more practical, than to love.[9]

Then he found Cicero's treatise on friendship, and was won over by its eloquence, profundity and charm. It opened to him a kind of friendship of
which — like the speakers in *Spiritual Friendship* — he did not think himself
capable. Its "law of friendship" brought some stability into loves which had
been vacillating, puerile, full of conflicts and driven by an ill-controlled sexuality. When Aelred discovered Scripture Cicero's work paled. He wished to
love spiritually and now brought his readings of the Bible and church fathers
to bear to shape a doctrine of "chaste and holy love" (Prol. 6). As in Ambrose's
De officiis, the classical tradition and Cicero are the foundation upon which a
superstructure of biblical and patristic texts is erected, with claims of the
typological superseding of classical through Christian. Alongside the many
Christian elements, quotations from Scriptures, from Augustine, from John
Cassian, Cicero remains the major inspirer of *Spiritual Friendship*.[10]

"Sublime love" and "sublime friendship" are Aelred's phrases. One of the
speakers in his dialogue on spiritual friendship confesses himself "terrified
by the admirable sublimity" of true friendship, but Aelred urges its pursuit
nonetheless:

it is the mark of a virtuous mind to reflect continually upon sublime and noble
thoughts.[11]

We should hold firm to that last phrase in a critical study of the ideal: both
Aelred and his dialogue partners recognize the ideal and its difficulty of attainment, but they do not consign it to the realm of the unreal. Pondering and
setting unattainable goals is the "mark of a virtuous mind," and "virtue" constructs and pilots noble behavior.

Aelred defines spiritual friendship by setting it in contrast to carnal and
worldly friendship. Spiritual is based on similarity of manners, character, and
goals of good men (1.38). It seeks no reward other than friendship itself
(1.45); the "dignity of its nature" and the feelings it inspires in the human
heart are its fruits. Friendship is the most valuable of human experiences. By its
charm it cultivates and nurtures all the virtues and repels vice. It is the source of
happiness for human beings (2.9–10). No deceit is possible either in charity or
friendship, but friendship is unique in that those bound by this special tie
experience all joys, all security, all sweetness, all charms (2.19). Friendship is
possible among good men and comes to full fruition in the best, since it
"springs from an esteem for virtue." It excludes those who prefer sensuality to
purity (2.38).

Spiritual friendship matures out of a boyish affection which is "always
mixed with impure loves," and which "obscures and corrupts the true character of friendship" by drawing it to the desires of the flesh (2.58). "Wanton

affection" (*affectionis lascivia*) must be governed by "the foresight of reason" (3.130). Friendship begins in love (3.2), in "purity of intention, the guidance of reason, and restraint through moderation" (2.59, trans. Laker, p. 84). It responds to excellence and charm of character (3.4), and it is cultivated by courteous and agreeable manners (3.88).

Aelred ended his work with a reminiscence on two of his most intimate friends.[12] It is an emotional passage illustrating "all the stages of friendship" (3.120). The first of his close friends died young. He gave his affection to the other when he realized what virtue he possessed.[13] They became lifelong friends. His self-discipline was admired by many and served as an example to many. He became the "master" or "conqueror of his body" (*victor corporis*). His heroic self-mastery was to Aelred "a source of honor and delight."[14] His humility, gentleness, restraint, graciousness, and obedience bound Aelred to him so intimately that he raised him from his inferior to his companion, from companion to friend, from friend to "most cherished of friends" ("de amico amicissimum facerem," 3.122, ed. Hoste, p. 346). In another passage on cultivating friendship, he tells in more detail what qualities inspire it: "affability in speech, cheerfulness of countenance, suavity in manners, serenity even in the expression of the eyes."[15] The admiration and the proof of virtue are followed by a period of testing. The friend shows his frankness, honesty, loyalty, and his willingness to criticize Aelred. Aelred reveals to him the "secrets of my inmost heart," and he guards them well:

In this way love increased between us, affection glowed the warmer and charity was strengthened. (3.124)

Seeing him advance so in "virtue and grace," Aelred promoted him to subprior. That is, having started in mutual affection, the friendship bears fruit in *utilitas*, just what Cicero had claimed for true friendship. The friend both receives and gives the benefits of *utilitas*. He wards off scandals and exposes himself to dangers to protect Aelred (3.125). He was "like my own hand, like my own eye . . . the refuge of my spirit, the sweet solace of my griefs" (3.126).

When virtue, discipline, *honestas*, and *utilitas* coalesce, the highest stage of human friendship is reached. Aelred perorates:

Was it not a foretaste of blessedness thus to love and thus to be loved; thus to help and thus to be helped; and in this way from the sweetness of fraternal charity to wing one's flight aloft to that more sublime splendor of divine love, and by the ladder of charity now to mount to the embrace of Christ himself. (3.127)

The affection of the beloved friend as a foretaste of the love of Christ — we have seen the idea in Alcuin. That foretaste is savored at the end of a long process of discipline and acquisition of virtue. The rise along the "ladder of charity" passes from "fraternal charity" to a "more sublime splendor." The ascent is not only hierarchical, but elitist. It advances from less to more selective friendship, "to which here we admit but few" (3.134).

This distinction between fraternal charity and a "sublime" form of love that will be realized fully in heaven, is fundamental to the work. Sublime friendship is something different from monastic charity — and higher:

in the perfection of charity we love very many who are a source of burden and grief to us, for whose interest we concern ourselves honorably . . . sincerely and voluntarily, but yet we do not admit these to the intimacy of our friendship.[16]

At another point Aelred recalls a recent walk through the cloister, where he saw the brothers sitting together "in a loving circle" as if among the amenities of paradise. He was filled with joy at the thought that there is not one among them whom he does not love or by whom he is not loved (*diligerem*, *diligi*). And yet, asked by Gratian whether he has taken them all into his friendship (*amicitia*), he denies it; they are not his "friends" in the higher sense:

We embrace very many with every affection, but yet in such a way that we do not admit them to the secrets of friendship.[17]

The distinction is significant: *dilectio*, *omnis affectus*, embraces all, but *amicitia* excludes most. Again, after this comment, his interlocutors despair of attaining that higher, more sublime kind of friendship:

Walter: "This friendship is so sublime and so perfect that I dare not aspire to it."[18]

Aelred faces the problem that all writers on friendship faced: love and friendship have two faces, one social, practical, looking to community interest, utility, self-interest; the other "pure," disinterested, rooted in the inexplicable attractions and affinities that draw and join one person to another. The affection that Aelred feels when he looks at all his assembled brothers, is practical; it is the "glue" that holds the community together and assures a peaceful life, and while it is close to the pleasures of paradise, it is different from that exalting friendship based on virtue and giving virtue, from which also ultimately "usefulness" comes; the latter is personal and special.[19]

Sublime friendship rises above the social setting. Aelred is far from seeing it as a communal characteristic of monastic life. On the contrary, intense personal friends are chosen by virtue, not social order: "You see, therefore, that friendship cannot exist except among the good."[20] This formulation may even have been read by Aelred's fellow Cistercians as creating an elitism set above the spiritual elite of membership in the claustral community.[21] The dialogue stresses how rare and nearly unattainable spiritual and sublime friendship is.[22]

A "sublime" ideal of love and friendship with many common features emerged in the various orders of the nobility, lay, clerical, and monastic. The more general term, "sublime love," seems preferable to "spiritual," which modern readers associate with "monastic" friendship. A comparative approach to the various representations of friendship in the twelfth century would be useful. Restricting the discussion to a single social order one can easily lose sight of the forest for the trees. Of course, monks loved each other differently than knights and poets loved ladies. But there were also broad, shared conceptions, which tend to get lost to view because of the methodologically sound wish for sharp and narrow focus. The Regensburg Songs make clear that it can in some cases be bad methodology to make assumptions about the rigorous maintenance of boundaries between ideals of the nobles in monasteries and worldly communities.[23] The defining point is not a unilinear social order, but a single conception of love based on virtue branching into various orders that gives coherence to ennobling love.[24]

Andreas Capellanus

Andreas Capellanus served at the same level of society as the young Aelred. Both were kings' chaplains. Andreas was in the service of the king of France. A few years after Aelred completed his work on spiritual friendship, Andreas wrote a tract called *De amore*.[25] It is a peculiar and difficult work, so shot through with contradictions that it is tempting to read the whole thing as ironic.[26] One of the strangest of these contradictions is the general structure of the work: in the first two books he instructs a young man named Walther in the art of love, and in the third book he tells him to renounce the entire wicked and dangerous doctrine of the first two, reject women, and remain chaste.[27] This kind of dissonance repeats well into the fabric of the "lessons" of books 1 and 2, and makes it impossible to speak of "Andreas's" conception of love, or to derive a consistent doctrine of "courtly love" from this work. It is a jumble of sentiments explaining, defining, arguing about the refined love of the nobles.

But self-contradiction is something different from self-cancellation. The sentiments expressed in *De amore* stand as part of a conceptual arsenal at the disposal of men courting women and of women warding off seduction. It is of immense value in the study of courtly love. It shows us the panoply of sentiments and concepts that clustered around it, including the stark, ascetic rejection of it.

In a dialogue between lovers at the end of book 1, a cleric (whose standing is *nobilissimus*) distinguishes between "pure love" and "mixed love":

Pure love is that which joins the hearts of two lovers with universal feelings of affection. It embraces the contemplation of the mind and the feeling of the heart. It goes as far as kissing on the mouth, embracing with the arms, and chaste contact with the nude lover, but the final consolation is avoided, for this practice is not permitted for those who wish to love chastely. This is the love which anyone whose way of life is loving ought to embrace with all his strength. For this love always experiences growth in itself constantly. . . . The more one draws on it, the more one tries to obtain. This love is recognised as having such virtue that the source of all moral worth derives from it. . . . God sees in it only a minor offence.[28]

Mixed love is essentially the same, he goes on, except that it "allows outlet to every pleasure of the flesh" and wanes soon after indulged. This was the voice of the wooer.[29] The woman courted responds first with amazement at the idea of pure love:

You utter words strange and unknown, words which one can scarcely account credible. I am startled that in any person such abstinence of the flesh has been observed, that a man was ever able to curb the onset of pleasure, and repress the urges of his body . . .

then ends by approving it strongly (and mixed love along with it):

But if a man were found to practice chaste love . . . I praise and support his resolve and account him most worthy of every distinction. (1.477, pp. 181–83)

I have highlighted chaste love because of its clear resonance with expressions of chaste love, special love, sublime love, passionate friendship in works discussed earlier. It requires a self-mastery of which few are capable and creates a category of noble victors over the flesh alongside the *victor corporis* Aelred admired, his friend Geoffrey. It is the source of merit, it marks a man or woman as especially virtuous and stretches virtue to that point where it seems unattainable to some and absurd to others.[30] But even the gesture of mocking rejection operates within a structure that creates an elite of the spirit. In court society no less than in Aelred's view of friendship, "it is the mark of a virtuous mind to reflect continually upon sublime and noble thoughts."

I do not mean to suggest that it is a dominant conception or a paradigm of good love in *De amore*. A romantic love based on renunciation of the flesh is highlighted in a few passages, and in each Andreas or his speakers also approve physical love, setting it only slightly lower in value.

The mainstream of amorous customs through all the orders of the nobility was ennobling love. For all the difficulties of reading Andreas's work, it is easy to show that traces of an older paradigm remain present in it. Those traces are especially evident in chaste love and love based on virtue, arising from virtue, and conferring virtue. Love, says Andreas, banishes greed and confers "nobility of manners" even on the lowborn. It "invests a man with shining virtues" (1.4.1, p. 39). Love is the source of all virtue and goodness:

No good or courtly deed on earth is performed unless love is the source from which it springs. Thus love will be the beginning and fount of every good . . . no man will be able to perform good deeds except under the compulsion of love's persuasion. (1.6.49–50, p. 53)

The idea persists throughout the work.[31] It was worth quoting the above passage because even given its apparent extreme exaggeration, it points backward to Ciceronian friendship, sideways to sublime friendship, and forward to what I will call the "grand amatory mode" of noble behavior in the late Middle Ages and beyond (see Chapter 15). It is one of those "unattainable" notions and "sublime and noble thoughts" of which Aelred said that it is "the mark of a virtuous mind to reflect continually upon."

Love derives from virtue, creates virtue and noble manners, and accordingly, it "raises the worth" of the lover:[32]

Though all good things manifestly derive from women. . . . To men who perform good deeds they must show themselves in such a light that the worth of such men seems to grow in every way from virtue to virtue under their gaze. (1.6.403, p. 159)

The phrase, "the worth of men grows" in virtue through love, is important — long recognized as such — and we will look at it in its broader context in the following chapters.

*   *   *

Aelred and Andreas are prominent formulators of aristocratic ideals of sublime love and friendship. The common features of their ideals, their grounding in virtue, their source in Cicero, are clear. The transmission and assimilation of a classical tradition within two strains of noble culture is a given of the social situation of their authors: both were trained and educated as royal servants, and they brought a classical education to bear in defining the shared concept of sublime love in different ways for different social settings.

8

Love Beyond the Body

It seemed useful to juxtapose Aelred and Andreas as two formulators of love in different social settings with a common social background and many common points of what both of them call "doctrine." The resonances between *De spiritali amicitia* and *De amore* are evident. But the comparisons can be drawn more broadly, and in mapping the extent of "sublime love" it seems appropriate to follow some of its central conceptions and try to illuminate points of commonality where they have not been seen. One of the most broadly shared characteristics is the idealizing of a love that overcomes the reliance on the body.

Chaste Love, Pure Love

The capacity to love and remain chaste is one of the sources of "value," "virtue," "worth" in ennobling love. Abelard argues that the virtue in chastity varies directly with the strength of the desire it resists. Chastity in a cold and frigid person has no value.[1]

Against this there is a form of "virtuous" chastity in Christianity that takes its strength from demonizing desire: the chastity of the desert saints. Ascetic chastity renounces love and stifles emotions. It also denies humanity. Richness of experience, affirmation of humanity, and ambiguity result when chastity intensifies love, longing, passion. "I am chaste; therefore I do not love" is something very different from "I love, but chastely." The greater the affirmation of Eros, by Abelard's logic, the greater the act of self-mastery. Eros easily stifled is a trivial force. A daunting opponent makes the conquest of the body admirable. John of Salisbury admires Socrates because he was wanton by nature, but he subdued and controlled his lust, correcting it by "philosophy and the exercise of virtue."[2]

The denial or demonizing of Eros is common prior to the twelfth century. That denial is implicit in the letters and poems speaking the language of the erotic without crediting Eros. It is implicit in the marginalizing of human erotic experience in the reading of the Song of Songs in earlier medieval exegetic traditions, which made that love song into an allegory of the relations of the church and Christ. Bernard of Clairvaux framed it differently, declaring it "a marriage song of chaste souls in loving embrace."[3] Without Eros the matter of the song remains matter; but its activation transforms the matter into energy. That key interpretive phrase ("chaste souls, loving embrace") takes its tension from an *agon* in progress between love, desire, embraces, marriage and their natural ends, and a spirituality that wants to appropriate the natural, raise it up into the spiritual, take its sufferings, passions, and delights into a higher realm where the erotic regains — not only innocence — but heroism and sanctity.[4]

That is, I believe, one of the most powerful attractions and moving forces of sublime love: the higher return to innocence, sexuality transformed into strength and spirit, shedding the body but retaining all its tensions and dynamics. Sublime love allows the staging of relationships in what appears a prelapsarian world of passion unencumbered by sexuality, or rather, including a sexuality "purified" of the physical by some act of moral conquest that creates complete freedom, openness and frankness in the realm of desire — as conquest in battle creates peace — eliminates guilt, humiliation, degradation, all the dangers of earthly passion.

I do not find the formulation "chaste love" commonly in the early medieval sources on ennobling love. This may have to do with the silence on sexuality in all male love. The stress on chaste love in the Cambridge Songs refers exclusively to female-male love (see Chapter 4).

Around 1125 a learned German cleric named Ulrich of Bamberg wrote a work he called *Ars dictaminis*. It is a letter-poem-tract written to a friend named Godeschalk in the tone of Ciceronian loving friendship common to cathedral communities.[5] He frames one of his many declarations of love in some verses drawing on the language of love poetry (p. 155, lines 21–22):

. . . Chaste love [for you] always tended to grow within me just as the green leaves grow on the elm tree in springtime.

. . . michi . . . castus amor tantum consuevit crescere, quantum
Vernis temporibus viridis se subicit alnus

"In spring when the trees turn green, chaste love awakens in me": that is not exactly what the lines say, but it renders the tension on which they are built: the "Natureingang" introduces songs of love, as it does here, just a different kind of love. Chaste love appropriates the language (and, here, genre) of romantic love, wraps itself in its poetry. It is an assertion of a higher form of romantic love, and a provocation.

Whatever the social practices were behind its expression, chaste love was admired in poetry and letters from the eleventh century on. The "Thisbe's wall" effect is at work filtering out the "savage" elements of passion. Baudri is a good example of the tensions between passion and restraint. He likes to titillate the recipients of his letter-poems with suggestions of physical love, then recede into the ambiguous language of "special" or "chaste" love. He writes to his friend Galo in this teasing mode and explains,

> While I joke and jest to keep myself busy,
> My pen and my joking have exceeded moderation.
> I write to boys and girls as well
> As if a young man's love were torturing me.

The ironic muse made him do it, in effect, or rather made him *say* it; what he *did* was innocent:

> But life played as a game shuns the acts of the game . . .
> It's the ironic muse for me, but the chaste life for this ironic man.
>   (no. 193, lines 97–107, ed. Hilbert, pp. 257–58)

> Dum iocor et nugor, dum taliter otia vito,
>   Excessit calamus et iocus iste modum.
> Ad pueros scribo nec pretermitto puellas,
>   Tamquam torruerit me iuvenilis amor . . .
>   Sed mihi iocundo Musa iocosa placet . . .
> Musa iocosa michi, set vita pudica iocoso.

He talks the talk of love, but lives chastely — this is essentially the relationship he offers to Lady Constance:

> Let our hearts be joined but our bodies remain apart,
> Our deeds be chaste though our words be lewd. (no. 200, lines 45–46)

Their "special love" has no traffic with the flesh nor with illicit desire; Baudri calls himself the "lover of her virginity" (*amator virginitatis*), using an ironic formulation that neatly joins an illicit agent to a licit object (lines 79–81). And Constance's answer asserts her past and present commitment to chastity and takes up Baudri's formulation, "May chaste behavior commend our playfulness" (no. 201, line 122).

The women of the Regensburg Songs played the same game, sending (allegorical) womenservants to their teacher for his "intimate use" who "shed lustre on their actions by their chaste and upright behavior."[6]

Two poems in the *Carmina Burana* (= CB) treat the theme of chaste love. CB 59 is set in springtime with a group of virgins sitting beneath a grove of linden trees on a splendid day while the birds sing and the flowers bloom.

They debate "the secrets of Venus" with such decorum that Dido herself might explain her demise without expecting abuse from them. The poet wanders through this vale and at the sight of the beautiful women is struck with an arrow from Cupid's bow. In their discussions of love the question arises, which kind of love has greater propriety and dignity, chaste or unchaste.[7] Flora, the friend of Phyllis, answers, "There is no comparing a woman who has loved lasciviously to a chaste woman." The goddesses Juno, Pallas Athene, and Diana affirm her judgment: "He who loves a chaste woman is more happily inflamed with that honeyed nectar than one who loves insatiably." The poet joins in to acclaim the judgment. Unchaste love has no proponents. The tensions of passion and chastity are clearly in place in the structure of thought and expression: "flagrabit felicius castam amans"; the flames of passion can be directed at a chaste woman with the result of greater happiness.

Carmina Burana 88 is close in form, style, and theme to the poem just discussed. Its refrain runs, "I take love's consolation coupling with a virgin; I plough without seed, I sin without fault."[8] The poet begins by telling how great the power of love is, which enchains even the gods. He himself is inflamed with love for a virgin named Cecilia. He "plays" with her, but as the ward of her innocence; the "lily of her chastity" remains fresh. He shuns the voluptuous ways of corrupt women and prostitutes. He calls for a "delicate" and decorous game appropriate to the delicacy of their age. Not that he wants to forgo love:

I want only to play this game,
    that is, to contemplate,
to speak, to touch,
    at last to kiss;
but the fifth stage, the act —
    don't even think it.[9]

Chaste love is fairly common in vernacular literature.[10] It is, like most themes of courtly love, a disputed point. Courtly love is not a doctrine, but a large grid crisscrossed with conflicting opinions.[11] The lady of Aimeric de Peguilhan promised him a night together if he would content himself with a kiss.[12] An Old French debate poem discusses a case where a lady promises her lover to reward his loyal services by sleeping with him naked for a whole night, but to restrict her lovemaking to kisses and embraces.[13] The debated question is, who serves the other more by this restraint, the man or the woman? The "Breviary of Love," a kind of Summa of love by a Franciscan "Master" Ermengau (1288), mentions chaste love as a force that improves a man who knows how to master his desires, turning "carnal impulses" to the service of God and moral improvement.[14]

Andreas Capellanus claimed that chastity is one of the benefits of love.[15] The commentary on the *Echecs amoureux* explains "true love":

[true love] makes true lovers live as if they were chaste; for he who loves truly and faithfully has fixed his heart and mind so intently on the loved one that he could not wish for another, no matter how beautiful she might be. . . . Thus do worthy lovers incline to a number of fine qualities, and they abound in good conduct, as lovers themselves frequently assert.[16]

In chaste love, it is clear, the point is not to renounce desire, but to stoke it and inflame the lovers, to maximize desire so that the victory over it will appear all the greater. This could only appear quixotic to a culture that had lost the sense of the many uses of the erotic and of love as a means of moral perfection. Of course it is natural to consummate desire brought to the border of consummation. But in a society that saw the contest against nature as an essential part of moral training, what is natural is vulgar.[17] To succumb to nature was common — peasants and animals did it regularly — to overcome it rare, and that meant, admired and valued. It is probable that chaste love itself was on the curriculum of *moralitas*. We noted earlier the passage in an *accessus* to Ovid's *Heroides*:

We assign this work to *moralitas* because it is a teacher of good manners. . . . Its ultimate purpose is to commend chaste love by showing its value.[18]

The value of chaste love was honor, virtue, good conduct. Christine de Pizan argues in her polemic against Jean de Meun's version of the *Romance of the Rose*:

You [Jean de Meun] presume that all in love seek happiness in striving to lie with their ladies. Not so. . . . A goodly number have loved faithfully and wholly who never lay with them . . . and whose principal purpose in loving was to render their conduct more worthy. And for that love they became valiant and renowned.[19]

Practices of chastity became common among medieval nobles in the context of marriage.[20] But these practices belong only on the periphery of this discussion, since they do not operate on the dynamic of chastity stimulating passion, passion enhancing chastity. Women who take vows of chastity in marriage are no longer in love in the same way as courtly lovers practicing "pure love." But one historical figure who (along with Christine de Pizan) seems to confirm the conception of chaste love as a courtly form is Thomas Becket.[21] As a young courtier at the court of Henry II and Eleanor of Aquitaine, he practiced many "courtly frivolities," court manners, games and pastimes, hunting and chess. He was "proud and vain," John of Salisbury notes, and "on occasion, he foolishly took on the appearance and spoke the words of lovers, though for chastity of body he was admirable, indeed a model":

etsi superbus esset et vanus, et interdum faciem praetenderet insipienter amantium et verba proferret, admirandus tamen et imitandus erat in corporis castitate.[22]

This is a good passage to note in the discussions of courtly love. It is not imaginative literature and it does not glorify and idealize love at court; just the contrary: Becket's behavior is "foolish." It is critical of the ways of lovers at court — and so has a high documentary value for an argument that lovers' ways were practiced at court. It shows us the possibility of combining lovers' ways with chastity. John also says that Becket "assumed the face" of lovers. He may want to stress the shallowness of the game in Becket's case, but just as possible is that John recognizes the staged, ritualized, public performance aspect of love customs at court.

Distant Love (*Amour lointain*)

THE DISTANT LOVE OF THE TROUBADOURS, ROMANCIERS, AND MINNESINGER

A thirteenth-century biographer of the troubadour Jaufré Rudel wove a romantic legend out of the matter of Jaufré's poems. The poet fell in love with a distant lady, the countess of Tripoli, so the story runs, without ever setting eyes on her. Pilgrims from Antioch spoke so well of her that he loved her just from these reports. He began to compose songs to her and conceived such a desire for her that he took the cross. On board the ship to the holy land a sickness overwhelmed him, whether from love or another cause the biographer does not say. When the countess heard that the poet was near death for love of her, she came to his side in an inn in Tripoli, embraced the dying poet, who expired in her arms. She had him buried with great honor, and then herself took the veil, so moved was she by grief at his death.[23]

It is the legend-making mode of a powerfully romantic imagination. The biographer had his inspiration in Jaufré's poems of "distant love."[24] Three of his seven extant songs tell of his love for a woman in a distant land. In their power to suggest connections, to set up resonances and associations between elements of the poem not obviously related, they are highly evocative. In the poem "Lanquan li jorn son lonc en may" bird song from afar enchants the poet and stirs the memory of his distant love.[25] He wanders over the meadow, but is so bent by melancholy that neither poetry nor the hawthorn flower brings more joy than winter's ice. No love will ever give him joy again, unless it is this distant love; there is none better or more noble. So true and pure is her worth (*sos pretz*) that he would seek her out even if he had to live in exile in the kingdom of the Saracens. But how can he? The roads are so long and the ports so many. God, having created distant love, now should also give the poet the strength to seek and find her. But the barriers, both inner and outer, are great. A prophecy has it that Jaufré's fate is to love and not be loved.

The woman's indistinctness is ghostly. She has no face, no body, no identity. There is not even that report from pilgrims about her goodness that gave her some moral contours in the *Vida* of Jaufré. He knows that her worth is high, and this draws him. But since distance and fate thwart him, the love, good and noble in itself, is circular; the desire diffuses — without evaporating. "Love from afar" turns back on itself and takes on qualities appropriate to the lady: it, this kind of love, is good and noble; God has created it and administers it. As the lost joy of the bird song hallows melancholy, so the lost love of the woman hallows desire. Love ends and is perfected in desire. "I cannot love the lady I desire," the poet's resignation implies, "but the thought of her worth makes me love desire itself." That states the paradox of the troubadour love that Spitzer referred to in the passage quoted earlier.

"Distant love" is a widespread motif in Western literature,[26] particularly popular in courtly literature of the twelfth and thirteenth centuries. Marie de France's Lay of Lanval begins when a mysterious damsel summons him and declares she has come from a distant land seeking him out because, without ever seeing him, knowing only his reputation, she has been seized by love for him, and she offers him her love on condition that he be brave and courteous.[27] Likewise in the anonymous Old French "Lay of Melion" the hero meets a damsel in the forest who has come from Ireland to seek him out, having fallen in love with him upon hearing him strongly praised.[28]

The motif is very common in vernacular literature, French and German.[29] Significant in the German sources is that the motif is pre-courtly. The bride-quest epic *König Rother* (ca. 1160) employs it. A queen hears tell of the "virtue" of Rother and begins to love him before ever seeing him:

The maid heard so much of him that she began to love this virtuous man in her heart with all her senses. Still at that time he was a stranger to her.[30]

The early date of the work means that the motif of distant love did not enter German courtly literature along with the other elements of courtly love. In Konrad von Würzburg's adaptation of the romance of Partonopeus de Blois (mid-thirteenth century), the fairy Meliur tells Partonopier how she was seized with longing for him at the report of his excellence:

"They reported that your pure virtue is so refined and so famed that you would suit me as husband both in public and private. . . . This kindled a fire of longing in my heart. And so I would not let up whatever might become of me until I had seen you with my own eyes and admired this paragon they described to me.[31]

The motif is common in Minnesang. A few lines of a poem by Meinloh von Sevelingen strip it to the essentials: When I heard you praised, I would like very much to have met you.

Because of your many virtues I set out wandering until I found you.[32]

Reinmar of Hagenau likewise falls in love upon hearing a lady's reputation:

A tale that I heard of her has conquered me. I heard that she is a woman who knows how to bear herself beautifully.[33]

Walther von der Vogelweide sings to his lady, "I hear so much of your virtues that I will always be prepared to serve you" (43, 9–10).

The Distant Love of Clerics and Monks

The poems and narratives of distant love give a literary setting to a conception that was as widespread as the idea of ennobling love. The stance of love of virtue, love of reputation, love before first sight, had been widely appropriated by aristocratic society as a scenario of amical and amorous self-presentation.

The extravagant spirituality of Ciceronian friendship formulated and regularly provided the conceptual language of a distant love. Friendship that springs from "an inclination of the soul joined with a feeling of love" (*De amicitia* 8.27) can be completely divorced from physical presence. Since it aims at virtue, reputation alone can inspire it:

there is nothing more lovable than virtue, nothing that more allures us to affection, since on account of their virtue and uprightness we in some sense love even those whom we have never seen. (8.28)

Since the soul can love over a distance, how much more powerfully it is stirred in the presence of virtuous and good men "with whom a close intimacy is possible?" (9.29). For Cicero presence is not necessary, though it can intensify a distant friendship. This is different from the exorbitant idealism of Jaufré Rudel that envisions no "more noble or better" form than distant love. But Cicero certainly competes for extravagance on the score of spiritualizing friendship and removing it from dependence on presence. Real friendships, he claims, are eternal (9.32). Love of true virtue creates a life after death:

For me, indeed . . . Scipio still lives and will always live; for it was his virtue that caused my love and that is not dead. Nor is it only in my sight and for me, who had it constantly within my reach, that his virtue lives; it will even shed its light and splendour on men unborn. (27.102)

This spiritualized love from afar loomed as a motif in Latin letters and poems from late antiquity.[34] Alcuin played around the idea of love from afar without quoting Cicero directly.[35] His poem to an absent friend lamented that "A distant land denies him to my sight" (see Alcuin's Carmen 55 in Appendix). To Arn of Salzburg he wrote that "Neither sea, nor land, hills nor forests or mountains / May stop or hinder the way of him" whose love overcomes such barriers (see Appendix). Even in his absence he "shines brighter than treasures," and the poet seeks with his whole mind and will to restore his presence. Though he cannot have him present, the love that joins them "is neverending" (see Chapter 3).

Cicero's claim that love of virtue makes us love those we have never seen was available to structure that emotion in the Middle Ages. The student A. of Worms had broken off friendship with his teacher Wolzo in the 1030s referring to Cicero:

Up to now I have loved you for your virtue, which makes us love even those we have never seen, as Cicero teaches. (Worms Letter Collection, no. 60. See Chapter 5)

It is probably inherent in the medium of the letter that it favors the expression of "love from afar" in a culture of friendship. Alcuin stated it:

For this purpose letters are written . . . so that presence may arise in the love of souls, where there is absence of bodies because of the distance of places. (Epistola 113, to Arn, p. 166, 17ff.)

Anselm of Bec wrote (ca. 1074) to a high noble lady named Frodelina:

Ever since I became aware of the odor of your good reputation which has spread far and wide like a sweet perfume, I have longed to make myself known to you . . . that I might deserve . . . to gain your friendship.[36]

He proposes a "mutual love" and calls her "most beloved lady" because [you are] "most outstanding in the merits of your life." Anselm's love is clearly detachable from physical presence; he sent expressions of love to people he did not know: "I see you as the sort of person I must love. . . . I hear about you as the sort of person I must long for. . . . Wherever you go, my love follows you; and wherever I stay, my desire embraces you."[37]

Baudri of Bourgueil wrote to a certain Odo:

A brother has reported . . . that you love me ardently, and that having seen me once, you carry me in your heart."[38]

To a young man who sent him a poem of praise he wrote, "Though I have never seen your face, I gather you into my whole mind and I frequently imagine your ruddy face" (Carm. 10, ed. Hilbert, p. 41, lines 13–14).

Hildebert of Lavardin while bishop of Tours introduced himself to Bernard of Clairvaux and asked for his friendship:

Though we are separated by some distance in space, still the news has reached us . . . how entirely you have shown yourself a cultivator of virtue and enemy of the flesh. . . . In your life the prize of virtue is evident. . . . We have desired with great desire to be ushered into the sanctuary of your friendship.[39]

Bernard himself wrote of a monk named Godwin:

Can the necessities of place and physical presence curb the freedom of those who love one another? I know that neither space nor distance, neither death nor absence can separate those moved by one spirit and joined by one love.[40]

He declares to Abbot Robert of St. Aubin:

Though your face is not known to me, your reputation is. . . . By your reputation, I confess, you have crept into my heart . . . so that . . . the most soothing memory of you, my sweetest brother, so lures me away from my other occupations that I wish to rest sweetly there. And yet the more I give myself to your memory, the more avidly I long for your presence. (Epist. 204, *Opera* 8. 63)

Nicholas of Clairvaux, once the secretary of Bernard, wrote to Peter of Celle:

Before I ever saw you, I loved you, and the beginning of my love was the report of your piety and the things I heard of you from others. (Bk. 2, epist. 62, PL 202, 490)

The phrases that these writers use to introduce and ingratiate themselves would not be out of place, with a few appellations appropriately changed, in the speeches of wooers in in Andreas's *De amore*, the work in which the Latin and the vernacular traditions of ennobling love meet most closely. The man of higher nobility speaks to a noble lady:

What I longed in my soul to see before all else I am now allowed to gaze upon with my eyes . . . Nor is it any wonder that I was moved by so powerful an urge to see you and tortured by so strong a desire, since the whole world sings the praises of your virtue and wisdom. And in parts of the world beyond numbering there are courts which feast on reports of your virtuous character as if on some physical food. (1.6.322–23, p. 133)[41]

* * *

"Distant love" provided a scenario as distinct as any we have seen yet. It was at the disposal of wooers of men and women, be they monks, clerics, bishops, or lay nobles. It was part of a widely diffused inheritance from ancient friendship, memorably formulated by Cicero, which raises the experience of friendship into the spiritual by making it a response to virtue in another. But the medieval nobles, with a particular admiration for "sublime and noble thoughts" and the vernacular poets with an increasingly hectic romantic imagination gave the scenario a cast of longing, suffering, even dying in deprivation of the never glimpsed beloved that it had not had in antiquity or clerical culture. But it is also clear from contemporary wonderment at the motif that its use was highly restricted. It represented a claim to especially sharp moral eyesight in the vision of the heart. Many may have wished for it, but few will have claimed it. Therefore we find it in the letters of men who have in fact acquired a reputation for virtue and in a legend-making literature that fashioned its heroes and heroines into paragons.

The "distant love" of the troubadours is an element of courtly love poetry that appears most removed from "reality," most fairy-tale-like, most impenetrably "wrapped in the mists of a dream." But in a noble society whose forms of social intercourse were set in part by Ciceronian ideals of friendship, and whose modalities of communication were those of an epistolary culture, it is also a widespread mode of conceptualizing and formulating the first approach to an admired person.[42]

9

Sleeping and Eating Together

Chaste and virtuous love were performed or performable gestures. There was an articulated vocabulary of acts publicly proclaiming love. Some of them can still be seen, for instance in the iconography of Christ and St. John.[1] The gestures conventional in secular society constituted rituals of peace-making and made their way by this route into historical documents. Prominent among them are sleeping and eating together.

Gregory of Tours (d. 595) tells of the conflict between two nobles in Tours, Sichar and Chramnesind, who were reconciled after a blood feud and made public show of the *magna amicitia* they formed: "They loved each other [*diligerent*] in mutual charity so much that they frequently ate together and slept in the same bed."[2] Nithard (d. 845) refers in his *Historiae* to two kings who enjoyed such *unanimitas* and *concordia* that they took their meals together and slept in the same house.[3] The story retains the representative force of the gesture, sleeping together, even though it does not place them in the same bed. The intent is to show profound concord. We already referred to Otto III, who loved his cleric Tammo so much that they "wore the same clothes and at table ate from the same bowl, joining their hands together when they met in the dish."[4] Adalbert of Prague became Otto III's "sweetest chambermate"; they were together day and night and slept in the same room, because "he loved him."[5]

The practice of sleeping and eating together, it is clear, goes back to the early Middle Ages.[6] It probably was widespread as a gesture of reconciliation or simply of favor.[7] At least it is presented in the above texts with the lack of highlight of a gesture that is perhaps admirable but not unique, certainly not open to criticism. None of the writers who observed it felt any need to ward off suspicion of any kind. It was presented in that same wrapping of innocence as Carolingian passionate friendship: a meaningful gesture, but not sexual. It retains this character in the love of Richard Lionheart and Philip Augustus, who sealed a peace treaty by loving each other, eating and sleeping together, and the gestures did not provoke disapproval or apology, at least not from the chronicler Roger of Hovedon. It was still something like a royal prerogative, a grand gesture to a favorite or a former enemy.[8]

But a sense of shame and potential blame does emerge in other witnesses from the twelfth century. John of Salisbury was still speaking the language of the archaic gestures of favor when he described his relation to Pope Hadrian IV:

I was closer to his heart [than either his mother or his half brother]. Indeed he used to declare, both in public and in private, that he loved me more dearly than any other mortal. So great was his esteem for me that as often as he had the opportunity he took pleasure in revealing to me his innermost conscience. Even after he became Roman pontiff it was his delight to have me eat with him at his very own table, where, against my protestations, he willed and ordered that we use together a common cup and plate.[9]

Chaste though the joining of lips and hands via the shared cup and bowl may be, John is embarrassed, it is clear, by the proposed gesture of intimacy, or claims to be. There is no mention of a shared bed.

By the twelfth century sleeping together had become, in clerical communities, a charged gesture, requiring explanation. Marbod of Rennes writes a poem "dissuading those of the same sex from sleeping together," "Dissuasio concubitus in uno tantum sexu":[10]

Therefore sleeping together with a member of the same sex
Is no minor crime, nor is it punished less than others.
Therefore he who fears punishment will not release the reins of turpitude . . .
Therefore this fetid scandal of goat chasing lamb
Is punished no less than any other . . . [11]

It may be that this fierce condemnation is a monastic attitude. The gestures of love and friendship were more carefully regulated in the monastery than in secular society or worldly clergy.[12] But more likely it represents the crossing of that threshold of shame clearly located somewhere at the boundary of the eleventh and twelfth centuries.

Marbod also responded to the sleeping arrangements at Fontevrault of the religious leader Robert of Arbrissel (ca. 1045–1116), which he and others of his milieu took to be a daring and shocking innovation.[13] Men and women slept alongside each other. The custom provoked two letters of correction, one from Marbod, who was Robert's former teacher:

It is reported that you deem them [the women in the community] worthy not only of a common table during the day, but also of a common bed at night,[14]

and another, more interesting, from Abbot Geoffrey of Vendôme.[15] He criticizes Robert for having "too close a familiarity" with certain women, speaking with them privately, even sleeping with them and among them. Geoffrey gives Robert's justification of the practice, by way of criticizing it: "you claim . . . you are attempting to extinguish the flames of desire ignited in this evil way." If this is true, then Robert has "invented a new and unheard of, but fruitless form of martyrdom." It must stop, the abbot commands; Robert should not speak privately with women; he must not show himself "charming in his speech and eager in his service"; the many kindnesses (*omne genus humanitatis*) he shows them should be reined in with strictness, and above all "this new martyrdom of sleeping together, with which you afflict yourself," is a test for "angelic perfection"; applied to humans it turns to "diabolic presumption."

This passage is important, even if the rumors Geoffrey reports are false. Removing the kernel of this exchange from the question of rumor / truth, we find in its core a scenario of rousing desire to thwart it, a dramatic staging of the victory over the body won by exposing it to the greatest temptation. It was thinkable to an abbot that a man might sleep with favored women in order to stimulate desire, so that the martyrdom of the flesh would be the more glorious. Geoffrey doubts that any human is capable of such restraint, but he does believe Robert capable of staging such a scenario. The drama would be intensified, of course, if rumor had it that this new martyrdom involved sleeping together nude. But so would the scandal, and Geoffrey gives us no further details of the sleeping arrangement. But we can see the outlines of a practice, however different in its ultimate intention, comparable to the "pure love" of Andreas Capellanus, the purpose of the one being to overcome, of the other, to stimulate, desire. Both are scenarios of heroic self-control. The parallel is reinforced by the nearly identical reaction of Geoffrey (a "new and unheard of" practice, PL 157, 182A) and of the noble lady of Andreas's dialogue ("You utter strange and unheard of words," *De amore* 1.6.476, p. 181), who goes on to articulate doubts like Geoffrey's that humans are capable of the perfection of angels:

I am startled that in any person such abstinence of the flesh has been observed, that a man was ever able to curb the onset of pleasure, and repress the urges of his body.

This states very clearly the intended "audience reaction" to the staging of chaste love.

From the turn of the century on instances of sleeping together as an assertion of love and friendship tend to be ambiguous and the reports are sensitive to a need to ward off reproaches. (Roger of Hovedon on Richard and Philip Augustus is a big exception.)

An odd incident in the early life of Bernard of Clairvaux poses some intricate problems of interpretation. Entering the Cistercian order in 1113 he did not go alone but gathered friends about him and persuaded them to join — the opposite of the admonition to leave all family and worldly ties behind. One of his friends, a wealthy cleric of noble birth, Hugh of Vitry, resisted. He tried to dissuade Bernard from converting, using words and tears:

Upon seeing Bernard, Hugh wept and threw himself into his embrace. But the man of God paid no attention to his tears. After Hugh became calmer, Bernard revealed his intention to him, and so Hugh's sorrow returned and the flood of tears flowed all the more, so that during that entire day his eyes did not rest. On the following night they slept together in a bed so narrow it could scarcely hold one of them. Nor did Hugh's tears cease then, so that the saintly man [Bernard] complained that he would not allow him to sleep. But he replied to Bernard: "The reason why I cry is not the same today as it was yesterday. Yesterday I wept for you, today I weep for myself. For I know your way of life and am aware that a conversion to the monastic life is more necessary for me than for you."[16]

This is truly strange persuasion. There is a language of the emotions that altogether replaces that of the tongue. There are few indications that they talk; what they do is weep, embrace, and sleep together. What persuades Hugh to convert? What brings home to him his greater need for a new life? The only instrument of conversion is Bernard's body, which he applies to his blubbering friend. In fact the body, physical persuasion, and emotional high tension are the clear focus of this scene, not words.[17] It continues. Hugh and Bernard walk about holding hands, now inseparably bound to each other. But Hugh's worldly friends, learning his plans to convert, resist. They place themselves bodily between the two. Bernard struggles against the defense ring of bodies and can get just close enough to shed tears down his friend's neck. Separated again by Hugh's scrimmaging advocates, Bernard calls up a rainstorm that drives them to shelter, and, after "confirming a bond of spiritual union," the two friends return hand in hand.

The guiding idea in this curious scene must surely be body magic and body rhetoric. On center stage is the dramatic act of sleeping together. Why in a bed too narrow to hold both of them? Why not in a saint-size bed, or at least rich-cleric-size — the biographer stresses Hugh's wealth and possessions? Of course: the bed too small for one requires that their bodies be pressed close, and they need to be pressed close in order to transmit the silent messages that "explain" to Hugh Bernard's "way of life." The idea at work must be that the will and intent of the saint suffused Bernard, like an aura, and Hugh, being difficult to persuade, required a direct laying on of the body. No reference is made to any sexual aspect of their joining. It is of course evoked by the very act. Neither St. Benedict nor the two stern clerics who bawled out Robert of Arbrissel would have approved of the sleeping arrangement. Probably Bernard had to call on a sexual act, or sexual-like act, for this conversion, because the sexual is the highest level of somatic persuasion. This is one of those uses of the erotic that is not limited to the erotic. Body magic creates enchantment and fascination; why not also religious sentiment? Bernard performs an erotic miracle, which makes the more common one of calling down a rainstorm on his opponents seem ordinary.[18]

The scene is a great affirmation of erotic force. Something so precious is not squandered on a brief and tabooed physical pleasure — thus the logic of the event described — but is put to the highest use thinkable to the biographer, entry into the religious life. Here as in other scenes in the life of Bernard, the body becomes a fount of charismatic force.[19]

But the scene did not make it into the final version of Geoffrey's biography, and there is no reference to it in William of St. Thierry's report on the same events.[20] It may be that the "laying on of the body" was open to taunts. A scurrilous anecdote by Walter Map indicates as much. It connects Bernard and somatic healing: Map tells that he was present when a group of abbots were discussing Bernard's miracles in the house of the Archbishop of Canterbury one day. One of them commented that his miracles did not always work. He tried unsuccessfully to revive a dead boy by laying his body on the boy's (after the model of Elisha reviving the son of the Shunamite woman, 2 Kings, 4.18–37). Map quips that he has heard of various monks throwing themselves upon a boy, "but always, when the monk got up, the boy promptly got up too."[21]

Aelred described a scene of loving friendship that has nearly the erotic force of the scene just discussed. He elaborates on the advantages of intimate friendship:

It is a great consolation in this life to have someone to whom you can be united in the intimate embrace of the most sacred love; in whom your spirit can rest; to whom you can pour out your soul; in whose delightful company, as in a sweet consoling song, you can take comfort in the midst of sadness; in whose most welcome friendly bosom you can find peace in so many worldly setbacks; to whose loving heart you can open as freely as you would to yourself your innermost thoughts; through whose spiritual kisses you are cured, as if by medicine, of the sickness of care and worry; who weeps with you in sorrow, rejoices with you in joy, and wonders with you in doubt; whom you draw by the fetters of love into that inner room of your soul, so that though the body is absent, the spirit is there, and you can confer all along, the more secretly, the more delightfully; with whom you can rest, just the two of you, in the sleep of peace away from the noise of the world, in the embrace of love, in the kiss of unity, with the sweetness of the Holy Spirit flowing over you; to whom you so join and unite yourself that you mix soul with soul, and the two become one.[22]

It was worth quoting this long passage to show the vision of sleeping together as the culminating act of a rise in erotic intimacy ending in a climax:

united in intimate embrace . . . [finding] peace in the friend's bosom . . . kisses . . . whom you draw by the fetters of love into that inner room . . . just the two of you . . . in the embrace of love, in the kiss of unity, with sweetness . . . flowing over you; to whom you so join and unite yourself that you mix . . . and the two become one.

Remove the language and syntax of intimate spiritual friendship and you have a progress through the act of love. Aelred knew perfectly well what a daring game he was playing and warned against this kind of reduced reading by citing the loving friendship of Christ and St. John, "lest this sort of sacred love should seem improper to anyone."

Finally we return to Roger of Hoveden's description of the truce between Philip Augustus and Richard Lionheart that ended the campaign of 1187:

[the king of France] so honored him for so long that they ate every day at the same table and from the same dish, and at night their bed did not separate them. And the king of France loved him as his own soul.

This brings us full circle, but I hope not without spiraling upward. The circular trek back to our point of departure also should enrich our understanding of the field of tensions within which this text operates. So serene, so unapologetic on the surface, the text's silence bares its breast to fears that Geoffrey of Clairvaux, William of St. Thierry, Aelred of Rievaulx had shrunk from. Again, it may be that the monastic clergy were more sensitive to the possible reproaches. But the reasons for the apparent return to a positively Carolingian innocence of erotic gesture are more complex. The next chapter analyzes them.

10

Eros Denied, Eros Defied

King Pentheus underestimated the power of Dionysus and was torn apart by the Bacchantes. Chaucer's Troilus scorned love, and was brought to ruin by Cressida. The "Duke of True Lovers" and his lady in Christine de Pizan's story maintain a strictly chaste and spiritual love, and they lose honor and reputation in spite of their innocence. It is no small matter claiming to master Eros, boasting of victories over the body. Robert of Arbrissel was playing with fire, and Geoffrey of Vendôme was understandably skeptical of his claim that he was not burned. But Geoffrey's admiration for anyone who could face the fire and not be burned was widely shared.

It is now time to face a critical problem this whole discourse of ennobling and innocent love poses: why does it defy Eros, seeking out and situating itself right at the border of the illicit, even while claiming virtue, exaltation, chastity, saintliness as both its causes and its results? Why does the elitism of sentiment seek the idiom of passion and forbidden love, now homosexual, now adulterous, to give it expression.

Religious Experience

The question is not *whether* religious experience was eroticized. That is clear from previous examples and from simple observation of the literature.[1] But *why*? Aelred could have spoken a much more moderated language of friendship instead of evoking a sweet overflowing union of two men joined and becoming one in a loving embrace. Bernard of Clairvaux was the most eloquent orator and the most persuasive proselytizer in Europe, and yet when it came to converting Hugh of Vitry his ultimate persuader was not words but his body laid in bed next to his friend at closest quarters. Rupert of Deutz describes a vision of embracing Christ, who has stepped down from an altar crucifix and hastened to his arms; Rupert kisses Christ only to experience how pleasing the kiss was to Christ when Christ opened his mouth, "so that I could kiss more deeply" [ut profundius oscularer].[2]

There is also the sublime drama of Christina of Markyate's underwear. Her spiritual lover, Abbot Geoffrey of St. Albans, about to set out on a trip to Rome, requested two of her undergarments (*interulas*), "not for pleasure," the biographer assures us, "but to mitigate the hardship" of the journey. Christina hesitated, and finally deflected the request by giving the desired garments to the poor, when this line was approved by a voice from heaven, which evidently did not consider the issue beneath its dignity.[3] The talismanic garment could not have been a sleeve or scarf; its "comforting" force grew greater the more intimate, more private it was, the closer it had touched Christina's breasts and *pudenda*.

It is worth recalling that Geoffrey of Clairvaux decided not to include the bed episode in the biography of Bernard; that Aelred expected that "this sort of sacred love" might "seem improper," and that Christina turned aside Geoffrey of St. Alban's request. Each of these episodes (except Rupert's unapologetic vision) participates in an awareness of the tightrope-like acrobatics at work. They move back and forth precariously between exaltation and shame.

Why did the elderly abbot of St. Albans want Christina's undergarment? And why did Rupert of Deutz not feel that Christ's divinity was profaned by the fleshiness of their imagined kiss? Dualities and ambiguities clustered around the eroticizing of religious experience. Geoffrey of Vendôme expressed its unstable character very sharply in warning Robert of Arbrissel that aspirations to angelic perfection can easily plummet into diabolic presumption. There is exaltation to be gotten from sleeping with a woman chastely, but also disgrace. The act is "sublime." Its two faces could hardly be better expressed than in that word: what is sublime is *sub limine*, beneath the threshold, hidden, and tabooed. But some invisible dynamics transformed sub-lime into trans-lime.[4] While the dynamics of sublimation in the sense of Freudian psychology may well be present and at work, it is not the source of exaltation in the discourse — precisely because it eliminates the ambiguity of "sub-lime" by locating the moving forces beneath the threshold. Love exalts more, the more physically present, the more visible and palpable Eros is in its representation.

It will help understand this dynamic of exaltation through abasement to look critically at the concept of "Nature." It has now almost exclusively a positive valence. We admire the twelfth century for "discovering man and nature,"[5] and the goddess Natura is therefore of special interest. But while that concept did indeed come into its own,[6] along with the Stoic morality of "following nature," an earlier ideal of "overcoming nature" that had been something like the foundation and final goal of moral training in eleventh-century cathedral schools survived alongside of it. A school poem from the eleventh century made Orpheus into the model of moral and artistic development because his music "overcame nature" (meaning death, in the particular context of the Orpheus myth) and so showed that "art, with the mediation of fervent effort, conquers nature, proving that all things yield to Lady Virtue."[7] The eleventh century set virtue in an adversarial role to nature. The idea retains a place in the twelfth century in the discourses of ennobling love, both religious and secular.

That is, I believe, an important element in the exalting force of the erotic. Eros is a force like Nature. Gestures and acts like the ones that introduced this section assert the overcoming of that great force and demonstrate that its realm "yields to [Lady] Virtue." It asserts the "super-natural" character of the man or woman who can win that victory. The physical conquered is not denied, not forced under the threshold. It remains in place as visible, sensible proof of the battle and its ground; it reminds the reader/observer of the heroics of sexuality mastered. Eros in the discourse of ennobling love is like those lions or dwarfs or monkeys at the feet of kings, queens or nobles in sarcophagus statues, present as the representative of the great foes vanquished. In this commingling of victor and vanquished more than anywhere the claim to nobility of sentiment and mastery of passion is staked.

Ennobling love lived from the peculiar brand of self-discipline and self-control inherent in the traditions and practice of aristocratic friendship since antiquity, enriched by Christian disciplining of the flesh. The flesh was the testing ground (hence also the showcase) of virtue. Ennobling love makes no sense if the sexual is accommodated by sublimation, hence hidden. Love had the power to project and represent virtue and "angelic perfection" especially when it showed both sides of the threshold, the *limen*, separating love from lust. Love had to have lust as its adversary, as Virtue needed Nature. The opposition of equal forces within the soul, psychomachia, is the psychic model within which this love operated, not a cooperation of repressed and repressing forces, as in a Freudian model. The erotic frankness typical of the discourse on ennobling love makes lust into a visible antagonist, not a hidden accomplice. It is constantly provoking exercises in double-optics, like ours of a previous chapter, stripping Aelred's hymn to true friendship of its syntax of spirituality, seeing the description of a sex act, returning to the language of spirit, straddling the *limen* in this way and turning our head from one direction to the other.

The double force transmutes flesh into spirit. It remains flesh, of course, since otherwise "angelic perfection" would also be angelic sterility. But it is not only flesh. The extent to which all fleshly can legitimately be transubstantiated and appropriated for the spiritual is a measure of goodness, virtue, piety. Or rather let's say—since that list speaks what has become the language of a milky congregational piety—that transubstantiation of flesh into spirit creates aura and charisma. Eros dominated is like heat in a boiler that drives only if not released.

This peculiar commingling and cohabiting of the moral with the erotic imagination produces offspring:

For instance, intensity of experience. The suppressed scene of the conversion of Hugh of Vitry is positively hectic with emotion.

For instance, a soaring intensity of expression sensible in Aelred's description of true friendship and in virtually all of Bernard's sermons on the Song of Songs. The "sublime" is a mode of expression as well as of experience.

For instance, freedom of expression in word and gesture. Desire and its physical objects became the legitimate exalting language of friendship. That language "sweetened" (*dulcis*, the most common adjective for friendship) the experience of friendship once it was secured in sexless or parasexual innocence. The ability to maintain the tension between self-control and desire established a freedom of erotic expression not available to men and women in the grips of Eros. Those who had wrestled with Eros and won were warriors and heroes whose moral will had faced and conquered the great antagonist — and as in any battle, the honor, reputation, and prerogatives of the conquered fall to the conqueror. Eros was defied, but far from being denied, it handed over its rights to erotic language to its captor and great adversary, spiritual purity, chastity. Rupert's kiss of Christ and Geoffrey of St. Albans's request for his beloved's undergarments are gestures that assert the flesh made spirit. They indicate the intimacy, sweetness, delicacy of the love relationship, and the dynamic at work is: the more sensual the gesture, the purer the intent and the greater the innocence.

And for the final instance, it neutralized the taboo on the love of the same sex, held it in limbo — without overcoming it.

Courtly Experience

Recall that our question is not, what is the exalting power of love? — the subject of the next chapter — but rather why exalting love uses the language, imagery, and gestures of sexual love? and what holds the debasing power of illicit sexuality in check? While the two questions of course are closely related, the creation of virtue through love will be more approachable if the suppression of shame is clarified.

Court society admired and sought again and again representatives of refined love successfully deflecting shame and turning debasement into exaltation. Chrétien's romance of Lancelot turns on the theme of shame and dishonor warded off through love. The mechanism in that case is the will of the lady, Guinevere. Love service and the lady's rewarding it turn dishonor into honor.

But that does not give us a general principle for understanding the relationship of shame and honor in love. (It might have if Chrétien had finished the story.)

Lancelot actually did suffer humiliation. Sir Gawain shows the avoidance of shame in a more positive light. It became one of the major roles of Gawain in Arthurian romance to face the dangers of passion, expose himself to them, and come away unharmed, or nearly so.[8] The landscape of Wolfram von Eschenbach's *Parzival* romance is littered with the bodies of men and women who have succumbed to the dangers of love. Most of them fall prey to the seductive Orgeluse, who uses up the men in her service and leaves them either dead or disgraced. The same fate threatens Gawân, but he snatches exaltation from disgrace, transforms the cruel avenger into a loving woman, and lives with her as lord and lady of the Castle of Wonders. Wolfram states the role of this virtuoso of love paradigmatically:

He is without disgrace,
though caught in the bonds of love. (532, 23–24)

er ist doch âne schande,
lît er in minnen bande.

The admiration for Gawain does not just aim at his success as a courteous lover, but at this tightrope act of balancing between destroying passion and virtuous, courteous loving. And in one of the best of the Gawain romances, *Sir Gawain and the Green Knight*, admiration extends even to his humiliation through a woman.

Lancelot and Gawain overcome shame, but not by the double operation of exalting/debasing — but rather a progress from debasement to exaltation.

A widespread, fashionable erotic language teeming with potential indictments, opposed by a fierce ascetic/clerical will to indict and "correct," sharpened by the jealousy and malice of secular courtiers and the perennial vulnerability of their victims to charges of lechery and whoredom, makes for an unstable and dangerous situation; it maximizes the potential for humiliation and disgrace through love.

But the idiom of ennobling love could reach and maintain a sovereign position in the aristocracy because it also contained a mechanism that restrained criticism, a rhetorical strategy that held blame in check and challenged the reader or observer to join the speaker in ignoring any suggestion of the illicit. Humiliation and disgrace are always barking at its gates, so to speak. Baudri of Bourgueil compared Adela of Blois with a chaste Diana and pointed to the crowds of suitors she kept — at arm's length — neither satisfying nor dismissing them. There is a much nastier construction that could be placed on those crowds and the countess's apparent restraint. Courts are dangerous places, where the urge to ruin reputations is always alive and at work and even the appearance of wrongdoing can serve it. Noblewomen who practice or are rumored to practice courtly love, from Eleanor of Aquitaine to Elizabeth I of England, are also regularly rumored to be whores.[9]

Courtly love shielded its speakers from the nasty constructions that suitors writing letters and poems of allegedly "innocent" or unrequited love might invite. The public performance of the rituals of courtly love, including love poetry, imply that the illicit is near at hand, but either shunned or ignored. It is managed, controlled, held in its place. The public performance of love implies, "Such people are we, above base desiring, immune to its dangers. The lewd and the forbidden only have power over weaker minds. Our lust is chastity and our passion is virtue." The texts of ennobling love, from earliest to latest, from monasteries to royal courts, assert dominance over the erotic; and the performance of love scenarios represents public displays of strong passion governed. The mode of feeling defines itself and establishes its superiority by its casual obliviousness to the dangers it first conjures, then manages. The pose implies the "overcoming of nature," moral heroism, governance of an economy of virtue and passion in the soul. The group of "nobly bred" young men and women who retreat to the countryside to escape the plague in Boccaccio's *Decameron* stand on a non-chalant footing with the lewd, their virtue freeing them from the fear of taint:

Although the tales related here have been . . . of a sort to stimulate carnal desire, and we have continually partaken of excellent food and drink, played music, and sung many songs, all of which things may encourage unseemly behavior among those who are feeble of mind, neither in word nor in deed nor in any other respect have I known either you or ourselves to be worthy of censure. . . . It surely redounds to our communal honour and credit.[10]

Honor is not gotten by living like monks and nuns, but by facing temptation. That test divides nobles into those with honor and those with feeble minds. Virtue is not gotten from rejecting the matter of vice, but from living in it virtuously — at least appearing to do so.

The scenarios of ennobling love put forward sublime models of behavior and patterns of relationships, Platonic archetypes working socially, and they invite the court, the kingdom, the reader to enter into them. They show kings, counts, ladies, and courtiers as masters over nature, behaving as gods (the Socratic, not the Homeric ones) behave, with a degree of control beyond the lot of mortals. If the reader or viewer accepts the claim of lofty refinement in the relationships expressed, he shows his capacity for such feelings. If he criticizes, he denies it and excludes himself from the elite of sentiment. This strategy divides the audience into noble hearts and vulgarians.

The discourse also defended its speakers by posing a challenging gesture. Claims of superiority put forward in the language of the illicit invite the listener to commit a form of insult of majesty. As with any challenge, to accept it and defy the terms it sets is to provoke a response and put into operation the mechanism of enforcement that backs it up. If a member of court society "unmasks" the king's love, he runs the risk of exclusion, or in extreme cases, a duel, imprisonment, execution. No one dependent on the king's favor will do it, and that includes a lot of people.[11]

The story of the founding of the Order of the Garter illustrates the entire discursive mode and its defense mechanisms. The Order of the Garter is the highest honor the English king can confer. The story of its origins is compounded of gossip, actual events, and legend in proportions that are no longer measurable. A public embarrassment boldly faced down is said to account for its beginning. The story has it that King Edward III (1312–1377) was dancing with either his queen or his mistress (another report says it was Joan, countess of Kent and Salisbury), when a blue garter slipped from her leg and fell to the floor. Some courtiers made mocking comments, but the king picked up the garter and put it on his own leg, with a prediction that they would soon revere the object they now mock, and with a warning that is the motto of the order and could be that of the discourse we are dealing with: "Honi soit qui mal y pense," "Shame be on whoever thinks evil of it."

It is an odd reversal of the mythmaking tendency to elevate origins. By putting a woman's garter on his leg, the king abases himself and suggests or proclaims intimacy with her. But the same gesture exalts him: it is a sublime act of gallantry, Lancelot or Tristan performing some act of self-abasement to shield his lady. He checks criticism by multiplying the cause for embarrassment and taking it on himself; and this brings the act into the structure of an ennobling chivalric deed. The private and the intimate lose their power to embarrass, because the king's act rescues them and transports them, like a knight a damsel in distress, into the realm of invulnerability reserved for the king, where the gross, the bawdy and the illicit are illusions and even seemingly tabooed acts turn sublime.

It is also a challenging gesture, which places the observing courtiers before two realms of perception — the base and the sublime. They see in double-optic, and are free to interpret the gesture as effeminate, to chuckle knowingly about the implied liaison between the (married) king and his dancing partner. Or they can regard it as an act of chivalry, courtliness in a heroic mode. The one is vulgar and insulting; the other exalting. The one brings down on them the shame and embarrassment of evil thoughts — not to mention the king's anger. The other raises them up to membership in a chivalric elite. Backed by those incentives, the sublime intimidates the base and silences it.

The only primary evidence contemporary with Edward III is the order itself, its symbol, the blue garter, and its motto. There is virtually no support for the story of the dropped garter in contemporary historiography.[12] The thrust of historical scholarship for some time has been to discount the legend and explain the garter and motto in terms of Edward's political ambitions in France.[13] This connection is at least as questionable as the story of the lost garter, and the position Richard Barber and Juliet Vale defend seems to me accordingly a weak one. The English invasion of France had to be seen and represented as a heroic undertaking, especially when confronting the enemy's invective. A woman's undergarment worn by a man is a sign of shame. Barber argues that garters in the mid-fourteenth century were men's garb, and that the order's garter is probably the belt received in the knighting ceremony (*Edward*, p. 87), and not a sign of shame at all.

The parallels to one of the most famous of medieval romances, the Middle English *Sir Gawain and the Green Knight*, throw light on this question, though I find no reference to the work in recent historical writings on the Order of the Garter. The scholarship on *Sir Gawain* generally accepts some connection between the romance and the order.[14] Sir Gawain accepted a *girdel* or belt from a married woman as a talisman and a token of their flirtation, in which Gawain resisted seduction. Accepting the *girdel* saves and disgraces him at the same time. But when he reproached himself for cowardice and betrayal before Arthur's court, the king turned the shame to honor by royal proclamation and declared that all the knights and ladies of his court from that time on will wear a green ribbon.

Here also the intimate garment is an erotic token that shames the recipient, but that turns into a sign of honor when the king elevates it by making it into what amounts to a symbol of membership in his court.

The Gawain poet lived during the years of the order's founding. The exact date of the poem is uncertain, generally placed in the last quarter of the fourteenth century. The only manuscript which preserves it dates from around 1400. It ends with the words "Hony soyt qui mal pence," added in a hand different from that of the scribe. This entry, no matter who made it, gives us an interpretation of the order's motto within a century of its founding. The scribe or reader or manuscript owner connected the events of the romance with the Order of the Garter. He used its motto to ward off the shame symbolized by a woman's undergarment. It is unlikely he would have done that if the order's traditions only connected the motto with Edward III's wars in France. The garter had to be understandable as a sign of disgrace, like the green girdle.

The first full version of the order's founding is in Polydore Vergil's *Historia Anglica* (1534).[15] Vergil was an Italian living in England. He was more debunker than mythmaker. He mistrusted legend and imagined that, in bringing the story of the order's founding to the light of day, he was writing as a clear-eyed skeptic, intolerant of the pious silence of earlier historians.[16] His narrative of events is especially interesting for us because it is also a metanarrative defining the discourse that concerns us. He considered the order's garter a woman's undergarment,[17] not the belt of knighting, and he considered the origins of the order, as he reported them, "trivial and sordid" (*parva sordidaque*, p. 374). But he also chides the English historians who have passed over the "true" story in silence, fearing insult of majesty, because they do not comprehend how disgrace can turn into honor, especially when it comes from love:

Therefore the true origin of the Order of the Garter ought not to be hidden in silence, even if it arose from love, than which nothing is more noble, as Ovid says: "Nobility lies hidden beneath love." (*Angl. Hist.*, p. 374)

The writer is instructing the reader in how to read the events he narrates. He does to English historians what Edward III supposedly had done to the courtiers snickering at the dropped garter: turns the shame of their thoughts back on them and commands veneration for what they took to be a base object.

This is good testimony to the transubstantiation that worldly love can effect: Polydore Vergil states it, and the existence of the order to the present day is testimony to the power of ennobling love to transform disgrace into exaltation—whether the story of its origins happened as Vergil reports or not.

For the purpose of analyzing a discourse and the social code it conveys, the historicity of the events reported does not matter. The legend, fully formed—at least fully revealed—only two centuries after those events, is what matters. Its late emergence shows how a social code "corrects" events and brings them into compliance with its laws. The corrected version conveys the discursive laws at work much better than the eyewitness report of some observer not charged with memorializing that code. The logic connecting the garter and the motto required an act of shame on which the founding of the order rested, and if the historical sources did not furnish it, it had to be invented. The motto makes no sense if it does not deflect the shame of a potentially disgraceful act. An embarrassing event that made public a hidden liaison, or even one that simply revealed the underwear of a court lady or queen, gave content to the inherent logic of garter and motto and provided a model in which the contention of the base and the sublime ends in the victory of the latter.

The event creates an order that is much broader than a club of English gentlemen. It can stand for an elite discourse community which nurtures all the necessary idealizing visions and condemns their unmasking. The symbol of the discursive contract that joins them is the exposed undergarment. They venerate a sign of shame granted immunity from its symbolic valence when the king takes it over from the private into the public sphere. The garter, like Gawain's *girdel*, is made into a talisman good against disgrace by a wave of the royal wand. The blue garter asserts the order's mastery of shame and its causes.

This discursive arrangement—"perceive the ennobling force of things that base men see as shameful, and show your sublime vision"—was at work in Western aristocratic society at least since the earlier Middle Ages. Anyone at all was free to call Charlemagne and his whole court a pack of sodomites, or even just to suggest delicately that men ought not to feel such passionate love for each other, since it is open to misunderstanding. But no sources record such a reproach. Both an unstated assertion that this is the way great and true nobles behave and an unstated warning, "Disgrace be on whoever thinks ill of it," guarded the king and his court. The king had to be regarded as morally invulnerable and had to represent himself as such. The narrower circle of the court had to accommodate itself. Certain visions of his greatness had to be nurtured. Sometimes his personal qualities gave them substance; probably more often than not they were ennobling illusions and fictions. But they were not pure lies. They were partly the results of the enchantment that emanated from his presence. By its effects everything base seemed to grow noble. He had only to pass through the land and it spread from him like warmth from the sun. Numbed and transformed by his charisma, his subjects saw reality as a chivalric, neoplatonic dream vision. If they did not and said so, they faced the terrifying specter of loss of stature.

* * *

In love, base acts turn noble when they are performed by kings and saints. Robert of Arbrissel sleeping with noblewomen and Bernard of Clairvaux with Hugh of Vitry, Geoffrey of St. Albans asking for Christina's undergarments, and Edward III transforming a garter into the symbol of an order of chivalry were bathed in the charisma of the sublime. The suspicions of snickering courtiers were more easily suppressed than the moral concerns of abbots, bishops, and monks. But in spite of them, the feats of defying Eros were recorded, along with the moral ambition that justified them. Two of those instances involve women's undergarments, articles not common as symbols of either ethical or martial heroism and normally tightly sealed off in the private realm, but useful in this case to show the sanctification and exaltation of the private and intimate. The more private and intimate, the greater the force transforming matter into spirit. The exaltation is all the more intense, the more it lends itself to ridicule.

The potential for guilt, shame, and disgrace in love is very high given western traditions of sexual morality, and it is high in any courtly culture even without a morality that puts tight restrictions on physical pleasure. And yet the European Middle Ages developed a powerful ideal of spiritualized love. This required a mechanism built into the entire culture of sublime love that silenced criticism and neutralized the dangers of guilt, shame, disgrace. So successful was the creation of the double-optic that the very language and symbols of shame took on the capacity to exalt.

Virtue and Ennobling Love

(2)

Value, Worth, Reputation

"Love increases the worth of lovers": this common motif of the lyric and narrative of courtly love can get us into an analysis of the mechanisms of exaltation through love.

Philip Augustus "honored" Richard Lionheart by loving him as his own soul (*in tantum honoravit . . . quod*). The public conferring of honor was staged when the two princes ate with each other at the same table and from the same bowl, shared the same clothes and the same bed. For the chronicler it was completely unproblematic that the gestures of love express honor conferred rather than the pinning on of orders or the raising of rank. Love honored, the king's love especially. This was one of the shared conceptions of the nobility, monastic, clerical, secular, and it is central to understanding the social function of love. It is also a case where a restricted view of the custom produces distortions. The king's love gives honor to his favored vassal or conquered adversary as part of a ritual of reconciliation. Likewise the love of a queen or court lady "raises the worth / worthiness / reputation" of the man she loves; the love of a religious leader "exalts," "magnifies," "elevates" the recipient and the giver of that love.

A few references can show the spread of this conception and give us a panorama of its social contexts and its language. The Würzburg student who responded to the satirist of Worms offered him love and friendship:

A bond like that of David and Jonathan will join us. No cruelty will disturb us now or ever more. Those caught up in unending quarrels will marvel to see such a friendship between us.[1]

The suggestion is that the love and friendship are exemplary and a reproach to the norm of conflict. Hence the "wonderment" directed to it. It also can work more pragmatically. Maiolus of Cluny, praised with "wonderment" by his biographer Odilo for his friendships with grandees of the realm, was "magnified" and made "one heart and one soul" with them (Chapter 3 above).

Anselm of Bec writes to Henry, prior of Christchurch Canterbury, thanking him for a gift of gold and for his kindness to his friend, Maurice:

I hear from those coming from him that you treat him with such great honor and love that it appears you love me, his loving friend, not a little.[2]

To Maurice himself Anselm writes, rejoicing in receiving his letter,

On receiving the letter of your love, I admit, the joy that enlarged your friend's spirit was greater than the sorrow that constricted it when you left us.[3]

To Frodelina, a lady of high nobility, he writes affirming their "mutual love" but apologizes because, lacking in merits as he, Anselm, is, she cannot hope to "increase her sanctity" through this friendship as Anselm hopes to benefit from the "communion of merits" he begs of her.[4]

Bernard of Clairvaux also establishes a competition with Countess Ermengard of Britanny, not in merits, but in love:

Enter into your heart and look there for mine and judge that the love I feel for you is as great as the love you feel for me. Nor should you presume to judge that I love you less and you love me more, thereby placing yourself higher than me as the victor in love.[5]

Love creates a scale of worth, the passage implies, and the one who loves more stands higher on it.

Baudri of Bourgueil wrote to a nun named Agnes, urging her to maintain her vow of virginity:

This letter I send you is not for the community . . .
It has a savor of the special to it, because it sings a song of love,
However, it is a love created in Christ.
A love created in the lord exalts the lovers [amor sublimat amantes],
And any love without God debases them.
              (Baudri, *Carmina* no. 138, lines 3–8, ed. Hilbert, p. 191)

Turning to the secular nobility,[6] the troubadour Peire Vidal boasted that he receives a thousand or so love letters each day from Catalonia and Lombardy, and that as a result his "worth" or "price" or "praise" grows and increases each day (*pueja mos pretz e creis*); the king himself may die of envy. Therefore (or perhaps, even without that proof),

It's well-proven and commonly known
How worthy and outstanding I am;
And since God has so well endowed me,
It's not right that my price be low.[7]

Since love is the "source and origin of all good," it is clear that moral worth is part of the benefit of loving.[8] In a very different tone, the Austrian Minnesinger Dietmar von Aist reminds his lady of his long service for her, says that she has "made my spirit more precious [or more valuable or more refined]" [du hâst getiuret mir den muot], and hopes now that having improved him so, she will also reward him appropriately.[9] Similarly Albrecht von Johansdorf depicts a lover courting his lady with good service for years, finally begging for his reward, only to hear:

"Your service will be well requited,
   You will not remain unrewarded."
"How do you mean that, good lady?"
   "That you will be all the more worthy and high-spirited as well."[10]

Heinrich von Veldeke says that love "makes the spirit pure" [diu minne machet reinen muot] (Veldeke 12.1.6; MF 62, 2). Walther von der Vogelweide requests a lady to teach him moderation, because he wishes always to become more worthy ("ich wil immer deste tiurer sîn"); it would have lowered his "worth/worthiness", had he never met her (43, 9–18). He distinguishes between a "low love," which makes a man strive for cheap rewards, and "high love" which goads the spirit to soar upwards to "high worthiness" (47, 5–9).

Narrative literature is useful because of its richer contexts and its more discursive treatment of the character of love. Wolfram has Gurnemanz, Parzival's teacher in courtesy, tell the young knight, "Let women be dear to you, for that enhances a young man's worth" (172, 9–10). The hero of the *Romance of Yder* decides that love is the way to find "glory and reputation" (*pris e valur*).[11]

Andreas Capellanus salts his tract *On Love* generously with references to these effects of love. Once made public, love loses this power: "Love revealed does not serve the lover's reputation" (1.6.5, p. 42). In his first dialogue, the *plebeius* says to *plebeia*,

you must bestow the love I seek, so that it may appear that . . . through you I may be invested with good manners . . . I am convinced that your glory will be enhanced more if you grant me your love . . . out of kindness . . . (1.6.50–51, p. 53)

His argument is that since he is of lower status than the nobles, her feat in educating him to "moral worth" is so much the greater and her honor will be increased so much the more:

just as God obtains a greater gain through the conversion of one sinner than through the improvement of the ninety-nine just men, so society obtains a greater gain if a man without goodness is made honourable than if the moral worth of some good man is enhanced. (1.6.58, p. 57)

The "nobleman" answers the "noblewoman's" argument against love:

Only the women known to have enlisted in Love's service are reckoned worthy of true praise before men, and deserve to have their names mentioned for their probity in the court of mankind. (1.6.211, p. 101)

The Countess of Champagne states that love cannot exist in marriage because

how is the distinction of a husband increased [*crescit honori*] if he enjoys the embraces of his wife as if they were lovers, when neither of them can in that way increase their moral stature [*inde possit probitas augmentari*] . . . (1.6.398, p. 157)

The "man of higher nobility" develops an extensive argument on the duty of women to educate men, imbue them with goodness, inspire them to do good deeds:

To men who perform good deeds they must show themselves in such a light that the worth of such men seems to grow in every way from virtue to virtue under their gaze. (1.6.403, p. 159)

He warns later on that a virgin will not deserve a praiseworthy husband, if she is "unwilling to advance her fame under the impulse of love" (1.6.468, p. 179).[12] A judgment of the courts of love tells of a case where a woman educates a worthless knight:

[she] so strengthened her lover in worthy manners . . . that through her he attained the highest worth of character, and deserved praise for general honesty. (2.7.28, p. 261)

When the man leaves her for another, the judgment of the court sends him back to the first, because

by her wisdom and sedulous toil she made a man formerly devoid of moral character into one more honest and adorned with thoughtful manners. (2.7.30, p. 263)

Finally, it is important to note that there are voices critical of love "raising the value" of lovers. Guibert of Nogent commented early in the twelfth century that noblewomen "rest their claims to nobility and courtly pride" on their "crowds of suitors."[13] And Abelard gave as an example of consent to evil deeds the many men who desire the wives of the mighty "for their own glory."[14] These are important voices because of the suspicion that the discourse of ennobling love is nothing other than discourse, that no social practice attached to them.[15] If that were the case, then the critical sentiments just quoted would have no object. They corroborate the social content of the literary motifs, since it would be absurd for clerical critics of worldly society to write polemical comments against a purely literary discourse.

This panorama of expressions of exalting love shows that a conception of the ability of love to magnify, exalt, ennoble, increase value, worth, prestige and enhance reputation was widely shared and widespread, though its particular expressions vary greatly from one social center to another. But what every one of them shares is the conception of an inner core of selfhood that both nature and nurture determine, the moral core of the person: it can sink to bestiality or rise to sanctity. Its secular middle ground is "honor," "glory," "praise." This aspect reaches bottom at sheer utility: the minstrel is "useful" to the lady because he praises her, thus "raising her value." There will have been an invisible hedge at court against drawing the implication "whether she has virtue or not," but the socially sanctioned presupposition within which the giving and receiving of praise worked was the perception and recognition of inner worth.

From monasteries to secular courts the belief existed that loving and being loved both recognized and gave worth. Anselm knew that true merits in friendship "increased sanctity" (*ad augmentum sanctitatis*), as Andreas Capellanus knew that love "increased probity" (*possit probitas augmentari*) and made "honor grow" (*crescit honori*), as Baudri knew that shared love of Christ "exalts lovers" (*amor sublimat amantes*). The Ciceronian tradition saw loving friendship as a response to virtue and a symptom of it, and it is a variant of this tradition that places human value in the center of a discourse of love and friendship, that determines "value" and "worth" according to the quality of love they receive and give. To love and to be loved was a measure of both inner worth and prestige.

The passages quoted from Anselm and Bernard showed only the inner, spiritual value, but an important element of this discourse of "raising worth" of the person is the public recognition of virtue and sanctity, by which reputation is increased. I quoted earlier Hildebert's letter introducing himself to Bernard of Clairvaux, praising him, and seeking his friendship. Bernard responded.[16] He says that what Hildebert had written "to your glory and to mine as well" justifies both Bernard's praising him in return, and praising himself: "Indeed our [my] glory is this, that your sublimity deigns to recognize it, that someone of your repute credits our unworthiness." He makes Hildebert's letter an example of "visible deeds" establishing reputation, not just "unreliable opinion." It is an "indubitable argument of your fame"; with its grace of style and humility, it is "pleasing and laudable." Unfortunately, what Hildebert admires in Bernard, so says Bernard, is not what he is, but what he wants to be: "non quod sum, sed quod esse vellem."

The letters establishing the friendship of the two men are showpieces of giving and receiving "face." They are a mirror of the Latin vocabulary of praise, glory, reputation, standing, prestige. The "inwardness" of the Christian, monastic conceptualizing of virtue, merit, sanctity, and the love that responds to them should not be stressed to the detriment of these external aspects, nearly always present in a medium so public as the medieval letter. The exchange of these two letters, no doubt read openly in the respective communities, was a public praisefest; their new-formed friendship testimony to virtue and exaltation.

Likewise, the voices from courtly love literature show the exalting effect of love ranging from increasing moral worth to increasing reputation. It is true that virtually all of the testimonies cited from secular love literature are in some sense posed, ironic, subject to a deconstructive reading that calls into question the real existence of social beliefs on which the literary postures depend and to which they refer.

But the broader view, both backward in time to Roman ideals and sideways in a cross section of noble society of the twelfth century, shows a belief in a love that increases worth and prestige *imbedded in a traditional structure of aristocratic beliefs and mores*. Unquestionably the king's love set rank and standing. Those clerical advisers he "vehemently loved" had good reason to expect "exaltation" and "sublimation" to the rank of bishop or archbishop. To share the king's bed was a badge of honor and a token of high favor. It is a short step from the social and political reality of favor among humanistically educated clerical advisers to the incorporation of a humanistic, neoclassical ideology of friendship and love into the structures of rank and standing at worldly and episcopal courts.

The skeptical position on the reality of courtly love in the past few years seems to assume that if sufficient violations can be found to the "rules" of courtly love in historical documentation and if sufficient contradictions can be shown up in a supposed "system" of courtly love, then the love ideals must be ruled as unreal. There is also a tendency to invoke the irony of texts, especially of Andreas Capellanus's *De amore*, to rule out the sentiments expressed as having any documentary value for aristocratic mores.[17] This logic seems to me not to recognize the social issues at stake in exalting love.[18]

The decisive question is not whether nonliterary testimony to wide acceptance in practice of an ideal of exalting love exists, but whether exalting love has a social function, whether it served the members of a society, promoted their interests, conformed to their values in an unstable and conflicted structure of values. "Refined love," "high love," and "sublime love or friendship" have the role of social ideals resisting social ills that develop in a male-dominated warrior society: misogyny, rape, contempt of women, boorish, warriorlike manners. The civil values of the court can be a force reshaping social practice by reward and punishment.[19] It may well be one of the most genial ideas of any social reformer in history that he or she developed an ideology of courtly behavior within which "worth," "price," "value," prestige, and standing in noble society are set by the individual's ability to learn courtesy, restraint, civility, to acquire virtue *as a prerequisite to loving* — hence also as a result of loving.

Both clerical and lay nobility establish a scale of rank and standing and develop elites, and this dynamic is one of the major forces that move the society's members to act as they do. Nobles must master noble behavior, just as they must learn to dress, speak, and fight as is appropriate to their class. To fail to learn is to suffer degradation — at court at least. The boorish knight who attacked Aelred of Rievaulx in front of the king's court learned this lesson the hard way; Aelred's reaction, being a model of self-mastery, gentleness, discipline, gave him "face" and raised his standing; the king took him, as a response to this incident, into the narrow circle of his *familiares*, whereas the boorish knight lost respect. This kind of structure of reward and punishment existed as a real hedge on certain kinds of behavior at courts. Their force will have lessened the farther the members of the class moved from the courts which practiced courtly manners. Factions of the warrior class will have maintained their right to behave in a brutish way, which they called "the customs of our ancient ancestors," or even at some point in the late eleventh century, "French manners."[20] But eventually civility gets set in place in this hierarchical system and becomes a mode of behavior which determines rank and standing. Those knights who had not learned to behave like Lancelot, Perceval, or Gawain, will have felt a strong force of disapproval brought to bear on their bad manners in court society. Things they want badly will be denied them: among those things, the king's and court's favor, reputation, glory, standing, and at some point, the love of high courtly ladies.

The values of love, friendship, and courtly behavior were as real in courts from the twelfth century on as truthfulness and honesty in our universities or as racial tolerance in our civil service. They were probably just as much violated also.

Those sentiments of the literature of courtly love which indicate the idealized love of a courtly lady, love service, the teaching and learning of courtesy, goodness, probity, good manners and good deeds, are testimony to social forces at work shaping or trying to shape a rough cut warrior society into a civil society.

Fundamental to this argument is the notion of "virtue," *virtus*. It has recurred from the earliest to the latest texts treated here, from Plato and Aristotle to Castiglione. Virtue was the foundation of the cult of aristocratic love and friendship: "Friendship is the love of virtue in another man." It is easy to observe it at work in establishing standing and rank both in monasteries, cathedrals, and courts. Anselm wrote to a fellow monk,

Dearly beloved, the more I hear it reported how your behavior towards everybody is daily increasing in honesty of manners [*ad morum honestatem*] and the strict observance of holiness, the more is your friend's heart inflamed by the desire of seeing what he hears by loving, and of enjoying what he loves by hearing about it. (epist. 5, trans. Fröhlich, p. 83; ed. Schmitt, 1.106)

The prior of Bec is following a dynamic of virtue generating love similar and related to Meliur's falling in love with Partonopeus in the romance:

They reported that your pure virtue is so refined and so famed that you would suit me as husband both in public and private . . . . This kindled a fire of longing in my heart.[21]

And both the monk and the courtly damsel (supernatural though she is), are still behaving, or feeling, in structures set long since and formulated most influentially by Cicero:

there is nothing more lovable than virtue, nothing that more allures us to affection . . . (*De amicitia* 8.28)

"Virtue" was a pliable concept, and it will have meant something very different to Raoul de Cambrai and his admirers than to Sir Gawain and his. It was basically rooted in beliefs in a charismatic, indwelling force in the body of people of particular distinction. Bernard was exercising this force in healing and converting by his body. It was a quality that was useful for masters at cathedral schools, where *cultus virtutum* dominated the curriculum and the master's "virtue" could imbue the student through its charismatic force. The personal aura is the locus of pedagogy, and the language of the body is its medium.[22] It is a force exercised by saints. Bernard of Clairvaux is praised for transforming others by charismatic force, in a nearly miraculous way: "The mere sight of him educates you; the mere sound of his voice refines you; merely following him perfects you."[23] This quality transferred to charismatic damsels in romance and courtly love lyric who shape and educate knights into models of chivalrous conduct, whose mere presence infuses virtue.[24] Gottfried says of Blancheflur,

It is said of her beauty that no man of flesh and blood had ever gazed at her with enamoured eyes and not loved woman and noble qualities better ever after,[25]

and of Isolde,

Whoever gazes at Isolde, his heart and soul are refined like gold in the white-hot flame; his life becomes a joy to live . . . Her beauty makes others beautiful.[26]

From this point of view also those miraculous effects Andreas Capellanus ascribes to love are seen to have a much broader context: Love makes an ugly man handsome, gives virtue and nobility of character even to the base-born (cf. *On Love* 1.4.1–5, p. 39). Noblewomen, according to Andreas's *vir nobilior*, have the duty to inspire men to good deeds and increase their worth:

To men who perform good deeds [women] must show themselves in such a light that the worth of such men seems to grow in every way from virtue to virtue under their gaze. (1.6.403–404, p. 158)

This passage opens to view the crux at which the literature of courtly love joins with that ancient and early medieval tradition of ennobling love and friendship. The worth of men increases when women they love and court shine the beam of their gaze on them and thus infuse them with virtue.

That connection is vital to my argument: the motif of love "raising the worth" of men is both central to courtly love literature, vernacular and Latin, and to the Ciceronian tradition of ennobling friendship.[27] The connection is made explicitly in the Old French romance of *Graelent*. The knight Graelent rejects an offer of love made him by the wife of his liege lord, and holds a speech instructing her in "good love." It is only for a man of "very great worth" (*de molt haut pris*); "love requires chastity in deed, in word, and in thought"; the lovers must be "companions" joined "from heart to heart, from body to body"; only with such unity is the love noble (*prouz*):

Tullius, who spoke of friendship,
Said it very well in his work:
What the lover desires, so should the mistress;
Then the companionship will be close.[28]

In the Middle High German romance of *Flore and Blancheflur* Konrad Fleck perorates on virtue in the prologue to this tale of love overcoming great obstacles. There are three means by which men seek it, he says: God, fame, and "noble love" (*hôhe minne*). Virtue pursued for the sake of God is praiseworthy and wise, but "there is nothing that so incites a noble heart to virtue as true high love" (*rehte hohiu minne*).[29]

*   *   *

It has proven difficult to write the history of the ethical component of courtly love. The difficulty is well illustrated in the debate among Germanists on the "chivalric system of virtues."[30] This chapter tried to shed some light on the question by showing the Ciceronian/early medieval provenance of a conception of ennobling, virtue-giving love and its broad applicability to the nobility, lay, clerical, and monastic. The argument is not that this *constitutes*, or is the foundation of, or is the keystone in a system of courtly love, but rather that it is one strand in a complex and rich picture of attitudes toward love among the nobility. But it is the strand that is charged with the morally refining, purifying, educating purpose of aristocratic love and that is inseparably connected with the social concerns that loom large in clerical circles and are the *primum mobile* of court society: rank, standing, reputation, prestige.

PART III

UNSOLVABLE PROBLEMS —
ROMANTIC SOLUTIONS

The Romantic Dilemma

12

The *Epistolae duorum amantium*, Heloise, and Her Orbit

Creating the Threshold of Innocence:
Guilt, Conscience, Disgrace

In the course of the twelfth century, the discourse of ennobling love lost its innocence. Or at least it came under fire and was forced to find new ways of asserting it. Explaining the sudden self-consciousness, the protestations of sincerity, the defensiveness against guilt and shame seems to me one of the most important problems in the study of love, not only in court circles but also in clerical culture and its literature.

The reasons are complex and cannot be reduced to a single line of explanation. The proliferation of a humanistic, classical education in the milieu of the learned clergy, steeped in the witty, allusive poetry of Horace and the sensuous love poems of Ovid, is certainly among the reasons. The development of a larger student class, of urban cultures and "subcultures" is also a factor.[1] The emergence of a counterdiscourse to noble love, a literature of love that was Ovidian, sensual, not licit, helped press ennobling love to justify and explain itself, to set itself apart, to distance itself, and at the same time to establish itself as the single licit provider of stature, prestige, and honor.

But the most visible reason was the inclusion of women in a social code that until then had been almost exclusively the preserve of men. This was the Big Bang of amatory ideals among the European nobility. Admit women to the gentlemen's club of love-as-a-public-phenomenon, love-as-a-source-of-virtue, love-as-an-exalting-and-prestige-giving-force, and the smooth surface of innocent erotic discourse shattered. It was invaded by irony, double entendre, ambiguity, and shame. Its magic cloak of invulnerability lost its powers, and gentlemen in love with women had to ward off dishonor and suspicion in the ordinary ways, something they were spared when their only object of desire was some quintessence of male virtue. Love and its expression were free to rise

to ecstasy, as long as chastity was their grounding. Sexuality conquered—
smothered, in reality by prudence and in poetry and letters by silence—was a
plausible, even an ideal, posture in love among men.

But sexuality between man and woman had a level of legitimacy that it did
not have between men. That meant that suspicions were stronger. And at the
same time, for whatever reasons, the thresholds of inhibition and of shame in
the discourse of love diminished at the same rate.[2] The double discourse of an
exalting and a debasing power of woman followed logically.

From the twelfth century on the ideal of ennobling love was more prominent and widespread than before. But it leaked at all its edges. The realm of the
private seeped in. Early in the century Baudri of Bourgueil can still insist that
his love songs are not private confession and that if he were truly in love, his
"public" poems would say nothing about it.[3] And the hermetic seal on experienced love that Baudri posited as a law ("Quisquis amat, cautus celet amoris
opus . . .") is broken at every point with the seepage, or inflooding, of the
private.

The private experience of love emerged as an area with its own rights
and privileges, insisting both on its privacy and its virtuousness, its expression accompanied by qualifications and warnings against its dangers. The age
needed the image of the two Venuses; it required distinctions between a "pure
love" aimed only at perfecting the lover and "mixed love" that permits sexual
union (Andreas); between "fin'amors" and "fals'amors"; between "minne"
and "liebe" (Wolfram); between "high love" that raises a man to esteem and
worthiness, and "low love" that reduces him to bestiality (Walther). These
were necessary forkings and shatter lines of a previously intact discourse of
innocent passion.

At the far ends of this scale of opposites sat the embracing extremes of a
discourse that glorified woman and another that vilified her.

The tortured disquisitions of Andreas Capellanus show us the problems of
integrating the love of women into the discourse of ennobling love. They become so painful for this faint-hearted voyager in new land that after two books
he turned tail and headed for the safety of the unequivocal, hissing defiance and
showing the flip side of exalted love for women, an ugly antifeminism.[4]

Ennobling Sexuality

The conceptual tour de force of twelfth century learned culture, courtly and
clerical, was the incorporation of the *opus amoris*[5] into the idealism of love. No

philosophy of love in the West had ever tried this. The fulfillment of love had occurred not in the sexual act, but in the development of character, virtue, courage, self-control — and the management of sexuality consequent on moral victory. For Hellenic ethics the sexual act itself was a satisfaction of a low order, regularly assigned to the same level with eating and defecating.[6] Cicero paid no attention to it whatsoever. Indifference rose to taboo in late antiquity and the early Middle Ages.[7] In male friendships sexual intercourse had been a factor that polluted love and destroyed its ability to confer dignity and honor.[8] Its exaltation in the twelfth century required an unheard of feat of reconciling opposites. Andreas Capellanus can open his treatise on love with the words, "Amor est passio quaedam innata," "Love is a certain inward suffering," claim the goal of this "passion" is the complete fulfillment of "all the commands of love" in the embrace of the lover/beloved, and yet insist that love is also the only source of virtue, of courtesy, of prudence and probity. The definition attaches love to the sexual act, and so gives to a sentiment in the air in the earlier twelfth century the cachet of a formal definition.

This is the unsolvable problem to which the medieval aristocracy created highly inventive romantic solutions. The lay nobility wanted and needed love to be noble, refined, and aristocratic; yet at the same time it wanted the fulfillment of "all the commands of love" somehow to supply that need. The clerical nobility had the Song of Songs and traditions of passionate friendship, and they wanted the sexuality latent in those traditions to become activated and energized.

Taking sexuality into the idealism of ennobling love meant forcing a union of eros and agapé, of the earthly and the heavenly Venus. The great challenge that project posed was to maintain love's ability to ennoble even while declaring the sexual act and its fulfillment a quasi-legitimate element.

But what would be the source of honor? Its source for ennobling love had been precisely the sovereign managing of sexuality. That had shown strength, given innocence, allure, freedom of erotic gesture and expression, and granted the ability to confer aura. Robert of Arbrissel was a hero of the erotic agon because temptation maximized was countered with "angelic" restraint. But how can passionate love confer aura, prestige, rank? How can it claim virtue, while admitting virtue's old enemy, the sexual act, as the natural end of love and full partner in the exalting process?

The twelfth century put forward an array of creative and original solutions to this unsolvable problem. These solutions are the subject of the next chapters. We turn first to a series of founding moments in non-literary sources, clerical and monastic.

The Letters of two Lovers (*Epistolae duorum amantium*)

A set of love letters from the early twelfth century, which we can now accept as letters exchanged between Abelard and Heloise in the early days of their love affair, not literary exercises, shows the integrating of Ciceronian love idealism with sexuality.[9]

The writers are a learned and famous teacher in a French school and a beautiful and exceptionally learned young woman. The tone of the letters is hectic and impassioned. Many are incoherent, outcries rather than sentences. There is none of the playful, ironic tone of the Regensburg Songs, though breathlessness is a feature of both collections. Desire and longing are strong. There is exhilaration and eager anticipation of each other's presence after forced separations. A powerful sexuality drives both the lovers.[10] Circumstances force long separations, and their joys are mixed with suffering and persecution.[11]

Abelard speaks as lover and philosopher. He both professes and defines love for his beloved. The following passage shares ideas of the opening chapter of Andreas's *De amore*:

You often ask me, sweet soul of mine, what love is, nor can I excuse myself through ignorance, as if you were asking me something about which I know nothing. Now love has subjected me so completely to its reign that it is no longer a thing outside of me, but rather a member of my family and my household, or rather residing inside me. Love then is a certain power of the soul which has no existence in itself nor is self-contained, but rather constantly flows out with a strong appetite and desire into another, and constantly longs to become identical with that other, so that of two separate wills one new being without distinction may be created.[12]

This was for the early twelfth century a modern approach to explaining love. It wants to naturalize it, understand it not spiritually or magically, but empirically, nominalistically (it has no existence in itself, is not self-contained), wants to determine its nature and assert its rules.[13] It has existence as a power of the soul. The definition sets love apart from those things other philosophers would call Universals, which do purportedly have existence in themselves, outside of human will and thought. Love is inward, innate, not a force breaking in from the outside, not a woman carrying a torch or a child with bow and arrow. The "familial" character is a metaphor, not part of a mythology of love. Love is consuming and obsessive, but there is also a restraint and tactfulness in the definition, a reluctance to speak openly of the *occulta Veneris*, although its object might be inferred from the sources which drive it, *appetitus* and *desiderium*.[14]

It is important to recognize the singular character of these letters. They are not run-of-the-mill love letters like the Tegernsee collection, nor do they have the slightly stiff conventionality and wooden spontaneity of the Regensburg Songs, which come from a comparable milieu. The passion in these letters is sensible to the modern reader. For instance the immediacy of the following lines of Abelard:

All that is charming in nature has flowed over into you, because wherever I turn I find no pleasure unless I find you alone. And so when you are in my mind's eye, I am alive, I feel, I think, I am happy, I forget all hardships, I am strengthened for all tasks. (Epist. 43, p. 22)

to which Heloise answers (incoherently),

You my full joy, without whom I stray an exile abandoned by fortune — live happy, enjoy to the heights, if it is possible, so that you may have joy [also when you are] without me. Farewell. God is my witness that that "farewell" brought tears to my eyes. (Epist. 44, pp. 22–23)

Abelard's line about Nature giving Heloise all its gifts may have a source in Hildebert of Lavardin's poem to Abbess Cecilia.[15] But Hildebert's lines turn on the cold image of Nature as a sculptor using the patterns of goddesses to carve Abbess Cecilia, and this contrasts starkly with Abelard's passionate reaction to his beloved's coopting of all pleasure in life. What was in Hildebert a frigid allegory is in the *Epistola* an experience: the exclusive concentration of all vitality in the beloved.

The language of these letters can be fully conventional, comparable to Alcuin's love poetry and letters, but as in Alcuin's there is a heartbeat and a pulsing in them that is distinctive.

The letters are purely private, in fact secret. They have no public aspect. Even where the lovers talk about their public personae, the context is the need to protect it by separating off the private. And yet they use the language of ennobling, virtue-bound love, a language and ethic that in general is a public one. They are rich in the language of love in the ancient and Christian traditions,[16] but the main givers are the two major ancient sources on love, Cicero and Ovid. The conceptual core, if the term applies for such highly emotional letters, is Ciceronian. Heloise ponders the causes of her love:

You know, o greater part of my soul, that many love for many reasons. But none creates so firm a friendship as that which flows from probity, virtue and intimate love. . . . It happens that when wealth and the lust for it fade, love also fades in those who do not love possessions because they love each other, but who love each other because they love possessions. . . . My love is fixed on you for very different reasons . . . : your most excellent virtue, the cause of all decorum and prosperity . . . I have found in you the reason why I love you. (Epist. 49, pp. 25–26)

Abelard's reply (Epist. 50, see Appendix) is an enthusiastic encomium of those virtues which made him love her. She is the vessel in which Fortune has placed "the gifts of manifold virtues." She is "the only disciple of philosophy among all the girls of our age." He admires her genius, since she explains the "laws of friendship" not as if she had read Cicero, but as if she had given to Cicero those precepts which he wrote down. Her virtue likewise made him love her:

I have chosen you from among many thousands[17] for your innumerable virtues. The sole advantage I sought was to repose in you, to find consolation for all suffering in you, to seek of all worldly goods in your beauty alone refreshment and release from sorrows. (Epist. 50, p. 29)

He praises her genius, her eloquence, her humility, affability, restraint, and great dignity. The admired virtues of the other form a common motif of the letters, which constantly infuses the sensuality of the letters with a moral seriousness and creates what I take to be peculiarly and individually the remarkable tone of these letters, a combining of the sublime and the sexual. Heloise writes, "Farewell my bright star, my golden star, jewel of virtues, sweet medicine for my body" (Epist. 76, p. 44). The moral aspect of the Regensburg Songs was one-sided; the women "trained" the man. The same is true of Andreas Capellanus and generally of troubadour lyric and Minnesang: its moral aspects have to do with the tempering of ill-considered or unwelcome courtship on the man's part. Here both partners long eagerly for the other, both give themselves eagerly, and restraint is self-imposed:

    Nothing will I give you, my life, but what is sweet,
I'll neither say nor do but what I know pleases you;
    I shall restrain myself at my lady's pleasure;
Never may we ever disagree on anything.
        (Epist. 87, p. 51, lines 26–29)

The sense of delicate restraint out of respect for the other which is the theme of the poem (by Abelard) just quoted is consistent with a quality of considerate respect, which she shares and requites. The sensibilities in these letters are all the more refined in that the love and the urge for fulfillment are so perfectly mutual. They find a balance between the strongest desire and caring concern for the body, soul, and reputation of the partner. This perfect mutuality is based on a fusion of identities. Abelard writes,

You fill me inwardly. I embrace you with arms of the spirit. The more I drink in your sweetness, the more I thirst for it. All the wealth I possess has coalesced in you alone.

All that I can is yours. To share our burdens, then: you are me and I am you. (Epist. 77, p. 44)

The formulation (*tu es ego et ego sum tu*) changes the trite "I am yours" from a statement of possession to a statement of the interchange of identity.

This is very far from "courtly love." And insofar as it is ennobling it is so purely privately. The lovers delight in extravagant compliments that "give face" to the other.[18] The Ciceronianism fundamental to ennobling love is clearly present here, but it is turned inward, privatized. The honor, rank, standing to be gotten from this ennobling love is conferred in the intimate sphere of the two lovers.

Reconciling sublime and passionate love is not a problem in these letters. It happens by the alchemy of experienced passion fusing the two lovers body and soul. They are convinced that their attachment is pleasing to God and never express any uncertainty on that score. On the contrary, God is regularly invoked as the protecting spirit of their love.[19]

We might ask what has become of that clerical taboo on the flesh. Why is there not so much as a token or even a mocking recognition of a value widely accepted *in their milieu*? They give each other their bodies eagerly and with the sense of the fusion into one that the "rules of love and friendship" enjoin in both classical and Christian traditions. And they seem to think that God agrees with them rather than with tradition in the incorporation of physical pleasure into ennobling love.

Their love does have enemies. They are in danger and forced separation because the "envy of malicious men" will not let them be joined as they wish.[20] Their renown and reputation require that they be cautious in their love.[21] This is the form which the taboo against nonmarital sexual pleasure takes in the *Epistolae duorum amantium*. It is reduced to motives of malice and the evil will to hurt and hinder good and virtuous lovers.

A private, passionate love based on virtue and mutual respect, pleasing to God, is endangered by envy. Clandestinity is forced on the lovers not by the marriage of one of them, but by the man's career. The scaffolding of the Tristan romance is in place here. Also the substance of its conceptual problems is present here but unobserved, not acknowledged by the lovers: if their society disapproves of their love and their station in life prohibits it, how is it possible to claim morality and virtue for it? Here, as in the romance of Tristan and Isolde, this happens by relegating the demands of society to moral inferiority (envy and malice motivate them) and creating a private world of the lovers which is elite and superior, but also highly threatened and charged with potential destruction.

Here is a founding moment in the idealizing of romantic love in the West:

passion is idealized against logic and in blindness of the destruction it can cause.[22] The "two lovers" of the letters experience the same conceptual blindness as Madame Bovary and Anna Karenina. And as we know from the life of Abelard, they share something like their tragedy also. They glorify their passion, forbidden or dangerous though it may be, only to find disgrace, humiliation, tragic death are its result. A later step in the logic of sublime sexuality is to incorporate even destruction and tragic death into its idealism. The West created a new kind of ennobling love which accommodates destructive passion. Sexuality comes to constitute, or to be a major constituent of, identity, and the cult of sexual passion generates its own idealism and heroism, its own virtues.

In stark contrast to earlier ennobling love, passionate love is self-affirming. The heroism of love required constant acts of self-mastery; passionate love found its affirmation beyond the rational, in some elemental constituent of the soul, especially of loving women, loving desperately, outside the law and the social code, placing love above those things, rising to idolatrous worship of the lover. The great pioneers of passionate love discover some irrefutable ground of affirmation in love beyond law and society, love that insists on its dignity and exalting character in full awareness and acceptance of society's will and power to crush it. The great, fateful, dangerous discovery of these pathfinders is that reason, the law, and social norms are not the only sources of affirmation of human conduct, that in fact they are a rather low form of it.

We are dealing with a culture which largely demonized passion, made it into the foil of moral heroism, regarded the act of love itself as squalid, beastly, polluting, and sinful. The cult of high, ennobling, spiritual love was at least in part a response to clerical fear and mistrust of passionate love and human sexuality, and that fear was generated far more by love between man and woman than between man and man. An elaborate strategy of moralizing was set in place. It ranged from fierce, ascetic rejection of sexuality, to high courtly love. At all levels, moralizing took charge, cast the net of discipline and restraint over sexuality, clapped it in the manacles of civility and courtesy, reeled it back into the orbit of clerical control of morals and mores.

Imagine now the boldness of action and of conceptualizing, the personal and intellectual daring of rushing through the minefield of taboos, prohibitions, restraints — and glorifying the union of body and soul in romantic passion — within a culture that provides no models for doing so. The boldness of course borders on self-destructive foolishness. The "man's" bravado shows in spiting the "envy" and "malice" that surrounds them with the cry, "Let's really give them something to envy!"[23] It is so much the bolder when it appears in a woman.

Heloise

That is the boldness of Heloise. She also regarded her passionate love for Abelard as pure, good, unselfish, unmotivated by any ambition other than the love of the man.[24] Years after her fatal affair with her teacher, as abbess of the monastery of the Paraclete, responsible for the discipline of her abbey, she wrote:

Men call me chaste; they do not know the hypocrite I am. They consider purity of the flesh a virtue, though virtue belongs not to the body but to the soul. I can win praise in the eyes of men but deserve none before God, who . . . sees in our darkness.[25]

The phrase "virtue belongs not to the body but to the soul," is dynamite.[26] If the body acts and derives its moral character only from the soul and the intention of its user, then it is excused, liberated, no longer an object of moral scrutiny. It is the logic of Augustine's "Love and do what you want."[27] Heloise can condemn herself, using the language of society and its disapproval of physical love (sin, hypocrisy, lewdness, wantonness), but she reserves an inner core of privacy and subjectivity, the *animus*, where ultimate judgment of the self occurs. And in that inner core she finds only affirmation of the love of Abelard:

The pleasures of lovers which we shared have been too sweet — they can never displease me, and can scarcely be banished from my thoughts. Wherever I turn they are always there before my eyes, bringing with them awakened longings and fantasies which will not even let me sleep. Even during the celebration of the Mass, when our prayers should be purer, lewd visions of those pleasures take such a hold upon my unhappy soul that my thoughts are on their wantonness instead of on prayers. I should be groaning over the sins I have committed, but I can only sigh for what I have lost. Everything we did and also the times and places are stamped on my heart along with your image, so that I live through it all again with you. Even in sleep I know no respite. Sometimes my thoughts are betrayed in a movement of my body, or they break out in an unguarded word. (Radice, p. 133; Muckle, p. 81)

She describes it as a kind of torture, but around her sufferings she has maintained, it is clear, defiantly to some extent, the scaffolding of affirmation, of soul-morality, of half-religious devotion, that justified such pleasures to her in the first place. She wants to confess and repent, but finds this urge shouted down and silenced by the inner voice that is still dominant:

If I truthfully admit to the weakness of my unhappy soul, I can find no penitence whereby to appease God, whom I always accuse of the greatest cruelty in regard to this outrage. (Radice, p. 132; Muckle, p. 80)

This "weakness" is also a willful clinging to the past. She has set herself against God's law (*eius dispensationi contraria*; trans. Radice: "By rebelling against his ordinance . . ."). She stops short of saying she is unrepentant, but it is clear. She seeks the means to cure her of her obsession, and does not find it within. What is tenacity she calls weakness.[28] Her mind "retains the will to sin."[29] Some fifteen years after the end of their love affair, she longs for what his castration made impossible. Impossibility is no hindrance to her longing.

Heloise both condemns and glorifies her love for Abelard. It is a double gesture neatly formulated in her phrase "Wholly guilty though I am, I am also, as you know, wholly innocent" (Radice, p. 115; Muckle, p. 72). But the condemnation is weak and conventional, and the glorification calls on a powerful language of romantic love with a poetic appeal in it that only underscores the affirmation of "immoderate" passion even in its most destructive, tragic aspects. She invokes the double bond between them, marriage and love:

you are the deeper in my debt because of the love I have always borne you . . . a love which is beyond all bounds.[30]

I found strength at your command to destroy myself. I did more, strange to say — my love rose to such heights of madness that it robbed itself of what it most desired beyond hope of recovery.[31]

The romanticizing of passion saturates Heloise's thoughts — it is not merely in Betty Radice's fine translation.[32] This is apparent in the remarkable intensification: to destroy oneself, *or even more, strange to say*, to "rob [oneself] of what [one] most desired beyond hope of recovery," by taking the veil at Abelard's command. Abelard himself, I believe, had an eye for Heloise's tragic self-conception. In the *Historia calamitatum* he described her capitulation to his demand that they marry as follows:

amidst deep sighs and tears she ended with these words: "We shall both be destroyed. All that is left us is suffering as great as our love has been."[33]

It seems likely that it was Heloise herself who invested the scene, and the affair generally, with a sense of tragic passion.[34]

But she also places it distinctly under the sign of a willed renunciation of desire: she found the strength to destroy herself, nay more, to "rob [herself] of what [she] most desired beyond hope of recovery." A double logic is at work here: first, that of ennobling love, which glorifies by renouncing desire; second, that of a passionate love which ennobles through half-mad, destructive acts of self-denial and devotion to the beloved. The uniqueness and originality of Heloise are evident in the passage just quoted, because in it the dynamics of sublime love lift passionate love onto a level *beyond the conventionally sublime*, beyond Robert of Arbrissel, Aelred of Rievaulx, and Bernard of Clairvaux. It had become more or less conventional among the heroes of chaste eroticism to deny "what one most desired." But to "rob oneself" of the greatest desire by an act of will and submission to the beloved "beyond the hope of recovery" creates a yet nobler stage of renunciation. Love-despair and love-madness appear more heroic in the scale of loving than the comparatively dry, rational heroism of resisting desire.

By her virtuosity in passion Heloise consciously renders the conventionally legitimate threadbare and ordinary. For instance the conventional idea of chastity. "Men call me chaste. . . . They consider purity of the flesh a virtue, though virtue belongs not to the body but to the soul."[35] It is a thought as startling as any her lover was to think. It places the "use" of the body outside of morality. It eliminates the easy and automatic condemnation of the carnal element in passion, in fact implies the shallowness of any view of love that looks only to the body rather than to the soul alone as the locus of moral judgment. Conventional morality is and cooperates with hypocrisy. God—Heloise would argue—agrees with her, not with the standard ethic of actions and behavior. God rendered a clear judgment in their case, she argues, on the question of "fornication" versus marriage:

While we enjoyed the pleasures of an uneasy love and abandoned ourselves to fornication . . . we were spared God's severity. But when we . . . atoned for the shame of fornication by an honourable marriage, then the Lord in his anger laid his hand heavily upon us, and would not permit a chaste union though he had long tolerated one which was unchaste.[36]

God "tolerated an unchaste union" presumably because he judges not the body but the heart. This revalues chastity.

Marriage accordingly is another of those legalized forms of sanctioned conventional behavior which is revalued and subordinated to passion. Marriage in Heloise's thinking and feeling is potentially much more sinful than the pure love of a woman for a man. In fact that institution, having the element of material interest so thoroughly built into it, makes a "sacramental" union necessarily mercenary.[37] Mercenary marriage is a form of sanctioned prostitution. Therefore it is consistent with this reversal of conventional values that Heloise would prefer to be the whore of Abelard than the wife of an emperor:

God is my witness that if Augustus, Emperor of the whole world, thought fit to honour me with marriage and conferred all the earth on me to possess for ever, it would be dearer and more honourable to me to be called not his Empress but your whore.[38]

It is precisely the ethical monstrosity of a married woman giving her body to her husband for "pay" and for benefits that elicits Heloise's most enthusiastic rejection of marriage and defense of "love freely given":

It is a holy error and a blessed delusion between man and wife [to believe that] perfect love can keep the ties of marriage unbroken not so much through bodily continence as chastity of spirit.[39]

It is a difficult passage, but the idea is that "chastity of spirit" (*animorum pudicitia*) is hardly possible in marriage, since the utility will always contaminate the purity and make licit carnality into prostitution. Heloise anticipates the quip by George Bernard Shaw that "marriage is the most lascivious of institutions." For Heloise the *sanctus error* is actually sanctified error, and the *beata fallacia* is a delusion over which men have spoken their blessing; they bless and sanctify corruption by making marriage the measure of purity.

Heloise appropriates the language and the dynamics of virtuous, ennobling love and in bold conceptualizing — or just formulating of experience — creates an entirely new form of sublime passion: devotion so complete that it includes tragic renunciation and self-destruction as acts of love. Heloise had done something similar in the early letters to Abelard (*Epistolae duorum amantium*) by rooting a passionate and carnal-spiritual love in virtue. It employed the terms of Ciceronian friendship in a context to which they were alien. She does the same by arguing the "purity" of her love in her later letters.[40] Pure love is established in the conscience of the lover by an awareness of intention. Heloise knows only one motive of her love for Abelard, the man himself:

God knows I never sought anything in you except yourself; I wanted simply you, nothing of yours. I looked for no marriage-bond, no marriage portion, and it was not my own pleasures and wishes I sought to gratify, as you well know, but yours.[41]

Etienne Gilson has shown the Ciceronianism of the language, and notes that the concept of pure — that is unmotivated — friendship was not unique to Heloise and Abelard.[42] The ardent Ciceronian Petrarch, reading the passage just quoted, could not suppress an outcry to Heloise herself. In his own manuscript of the letters, next to that passage, he wrote in the margin, "Everything you do is sweet through and through and very charming!"[43]

Heloise's confession is well placed alongside Montaigne's famous explanation of his friendship for Etienne de La Boétie:

If one presses me to say why I loved him, I feel that that cannot be expressed, except in saying: because it was he, because it was I.[44]

It is a stark and insistent reduction to person, eliminating all other concerns. But Montaigne was writing to a man whom he loved for the virtues of his soul; Heloise is writing to a man whom she loves for mind, soul, and the pleasures of the body. The point is that Heloise extends the ideal of perfect *amicitia* outside its conventional realm, appropriating it for a powerfully sexual and passionate relation to a man. The same appropriation is at work in what follows. She explains her love of him alone:

A man's worth does not depend on his wealth or power; these depend on fortune, but worth on his merits. (Radice, p. 114)

That means that Heloise's love for Abelard is a love of personal merit, of virtue. The condemnation of "fornication" is resolved in the appeal to personal merit of the beloved, pure intention of the lover. Purity of mind exalts and purifies the state of whore and it elevates the "wretched, obscene pleasures"[45] of the body to outward tokens of virtuous devotion. Heloise does not claim that status for the pleasures of the body, but neither does she renounce or repent of them, and it is consistent with the logic of her defense of love to infer the magnification of the flesh in pure love. Abelard cast her — and she cast herself — as a lily of the valley, not of the heights. Her "tribulations" give her a modesty and humility set against the hypocrisy of "those foolish virgins who pride themselves on purity of the flesh or an outward show of self denial, and then wither in the fire of temptation" (Abelard, Epist. 4, Radice, p. 139; Muckle, p. 84). And the dynamics of exaltation through humiliation are invoked to exalt Heloise.

*   *   *

The defense of passionate love is a creation of Heloise. Her sensibilities are guided by sublime ideals, her passionate nature appreciates and defines the exalting character of passionate love. She constructed a virtuous sexual passion of the elements of ennobling love: selflessness, purity of intention, love of merit, purity of love, mutuality, complete self-abandonment. She is the architect of a higher law of pure love sanctioning sexuality, a kind of carnal *agapé*, set above the shallow morality of marriage and external, bodily purity. Gilson pointed to the couple's self-conception as "heroes of the spiritual life" (*Heloise and Abelard*, p. 51). But Heloise genuinely became a heroine of the amatory life. For Abelard the story is a crass drama of seduction shading off into an idyll of lustfulness; his explanation for the tragedy is simply sin punished.

But what is the exalting character of passionate love constructed and lived by Heloise? It certainly has to do with willing self-abandonment, sacrifice of everything for the beloved, salvation included. It has to do with the refusal to repent pleasures too sweet to forget, with her maintaining of a shallow social role (abbess, nun) while inwardly cultivating the memory of love. Her unrepentance is not the buffoonish defiance of Don Giovanni. Heloise fades into silence with the insistent conviction that her love is worth her destruction, not with a defiant "My will be done."

Ultimately I think it is the structure of tragedy that produces the sense of affirmation of passion in the story of Heloise.[46] It is a dramatic structure (but also an experience) in which the self is set in conflict with certain values. Either the values or the self is broken in the conflict, and tragedy occurs when the self willingly accepts destruction *in order to preserve the values*. Tragedy is the most radical confrontation and conflict of individual with idea; it is resolved in a willing surrender of self to idea. The individual wills to be broken, crushed and destroyed because the alternative is abandoning the idea. Nothing forced Oedipus to blind himself and cancel himself out as citizen and human being — other than his knowledge that he had violated the laws of Thebes and humanity. But he destroyed himself because the alternative is legitimizing betrayal of the laws. The act of sacrifice has the force of powerfully affirming the law, because a distinguished man preferred to cancel himself rather than the laws.

Heloise's act of sacrifice likewise powerfully affirms passionate love by abandoning self rather than passion. In terms of tragic structure, Heloise as abbess of the Paraclete is in the position of blind Oedipus wandering for years in exile; both are still living testimony to the strength of the force to which they sacrificed their lives. The shell of the bride of Christ is Heloise's form of self-mutilation.

In the Wake of Heloise

Peter Dronke published a courageous study some years ago called "Abelard and Heloise in Medieval Testimonies." He argued that the emotions expressed in the *Historia* and personal letters were not only plausible as the lived experience of Abelard and Heloise, but consistent with a medieval sensibility that approved and idealized the passionate relationship of the two. In arguing this Dronke was swimming against the stream. A tradition of scholarship, coming to a highpoint in the 1960s, resisted admitting historical value in these texts until they were drained of all or most of their passion. To make Abelard and Heloise safe for historians, their love had to be removed to the comfortable and irrelevant realm of fiction, forgery, and romance. If the love could be judged also "sordid" and Heloise as "tortured by sensuality," so much the more plausible and manageable. What Dronke showed was that the lived romance of Abelard and Heloise found an approving audience both in its immediate wake and on to the end of the Middle Ages. Medieval testimonies show an audience "convinced of the uniqueness and stature of Abelard's and Heloise's love, [regarding] their tragedy with wonderment and compassion."[47]

I want to look at a passage in one of those testimonies that Dronke did not analyze. It is the anonymous poem "Metamorphosis Goliae," written possibly by a student of Abelard's, probably in the early 1140s after Abelard's condemnation at Sens in 1140 or possibly after his death in 1142.[48] (See Appendix for an English translation.)

The poem is a dream vision. The dreamer wanders in an idyllic landscape and moves into a shrine, which turns out to be the "temple of the Universe."[49] A king and queen sit on thrones, regaled by music that the muses themselves might have produced. Pallas Athene emerges from the king's head. Mercury is present, dressed as a bridegroom, and at his side is his bride, not named but obviously Philologia. The Muses are present, as are the three Graces and the Virtues, Prudence and Largess, bestowing gifts on the couple. The scene is redolent of celestial harmony, concord, beauty, and it states an ideal of education symbolized in the marriage of Mercury and Philology. But the idyllic scene is shattered by a shrill intrusion: Sylenus leads a band of satyrs in, drunk and staggering, their flutes and tambourines drowning out the Muses. Venus and Cupid are the lady and lord of this group. Pallas Athene steps forward to do battle with her ancient enemy. And now the adherents of both sides join the battle, which turns into an allegory for a debate on the question "whether Pallas or Aphrodite is the more worthy" (st. 40). We can infer that Venus, the satyrs and their followers win the day, at least they dominate the rest of the poem:

Psyche is held captive by the embraces of Cupid; Mars burns in fire for spouse Nerina; Janus shudders to part from his Argyo . . .

Psyche is spellbound in the delights of the flesh; fate fluctuates in Mars; Nereus strays aimlessly; the artificer delights in his handiwork; what will happen afterward, God only knows. (sts. 41 and 42)

Now actual philosophers and poets are introduced in the company of loved and loving woman:

Hysopullus brought his lady Ceta with him, Propertius brings Cynthia, Tibullus Delia, Tullius Terencia, Catullus Lesbia. The poets convened here, each with his beloved.

Each lady is fire and flame for her lover. The spark inflames Pliny for Calpurnia, Apuleius burns for his Prudentilla, everywhere the lover holds her beloved in her embraces. (sts. 45 and 46)

An odd state for poets in an allegory of education, but obviously they are under the spell of Venus, and in fact the effects of the sparks, flames and fires of love is that the poets compose:

They begin to create verses, modulating their meters variously. . . . All they sing is elegant, nothing is rustic. (st. 47)

Now the dreamer observes other contemporary philosophers and teachers, many of them students of Abelard, and the sequence of philosophers ends with an absence. A "bride" (*nupta*) seeks her bridegroom:

But now the bride seeks her courtier, her man of Pallet; where is he whose divine spirit altogether outshone all others; she longs to know why he withdraws and journeys about in other realms, whom she had nurtured at her own breast and bosom. (st. 54)

Nupta querit ubi sit suus Palatinus,
cuius totus extitit spiritus divinus,
querit cur se subtrahat quasi peregrinus,
quem ad sua ubera foverat et sinus.

The missing "man of Pallet" could only be Peter Abelard. The poet leaves it unclear whether the *nupta* is the aforementioned bride, Philologia, or Abelard's own bride, Heloise.[50] The structure of the poem, however, requires that the bride be Heloise, at least that she be Heloise in the persona of the mythological-allegorical bride. The structure of the survey of philosophers is two-tiered: first, mythological representatives of an ideal education culminating in a wedding of Mercury and his bride; second, historical and contemporary philosophers and poets culminating in the failed reunion of Abelard and his bride. That structure places the second "Nupta" in the position of Abelard's bride, that is Heloise.

In the "Metamorphosis Goliae" sensual passion has gained a place in the temple of learning itself. True, Venus charges in and introduces disorder, but she has a large following ("For the most part Venus reigns supreme in this crowd," st. 36). And she divides the citizens of the temple, who take seriously the question, "whether Pallas or Aphrodite is the more worthy" (st. 40). The human soul, Psyche, is captive in the embraces of Cupid (st. 41), and she is "spellbound in the delights of the flesh" (st. 42). The poets and their women are likewise captivated by passion, with the result that they compose excellent poetry. The poet shows both his wit and his advocacy of the turbulent effects of Venus in the eccentric lines: "the artificer delights in his handiwork; what will happen afterward, God only knows" (st. 42). In other words God seems perfectly pleased, perhaps even amused, with the coupling in the temple of harmony, prudence, and wisdom.

It is hard to imagine that this poem is not a tribute to the effects of the love of Heloise for Abelard. Its frank approbation of passionate love is not without parallel in Goliardic poetry, but the remarkable aspect is that passionate love is integrated into an educational ideal. Given the role of Abelard and his missing bride elsewhere in the poem, that has to be in part homage to Heloise.

The Loves of
Christina of Markyate

It would be wrong to imagine that the sanctioning/sanctifying of passion was only a result of the frank sensuality that is part of the student milieu in Paris in the twelfth century, helped along by the admiration of Heloise and the loyalty of students to Abelard.

Christina of Markyate was from a very different milieu. She was an English visionary and recluse who lived in the first half of the twelfth century. A monk of St. Albans wrote a *Life* in the 1160s, which remained incomplete. Her story has played a marginal role in discussions of marriage and spiritual friendship in the period,[1] although the marriage theme organizes a single episode of the *Life*, while love is the overarching theme.[2] I would like to call particular attention to this remarkable personality and to stress what we can learn from her about the conceptualizing of passionate love in an ascetic, monastic context.

Christina's *Life*[3] is rich, for what it teaches us about marriage law and practice,[4] spiritual friendship, visions and miracles, but also about sex, rape, desire, love, passion, and a woman's psychological response to them. It is still chaste love, but passion and sexual desire, male and female, are the big forces placed in opposition to chaste love, which remains chaste by the skin of its teeth.

The unfinished *Life of Christina* is structured as a series of love relationships. They involve five men. Ralph, bishop of Durham, tries unsuccessfully to seduce and then to rape her (*Life*, pp. 40–45). A young nobleman named Burthred, egged on by the vengeful bishop, then by Christina's own family, marries her, but never consummates the marriage and after intricate plots and counterplots agrees to an annulment (pp. 44–77). She then lives for several years with a hermit, Roger of Flamstead, in a secret spiritual love relationship (pp. 80–113). After his death she is in the care of a "certain cleric," a man so powerful in both religious and secular life that the writer cannot divulge his name. He loves her and is loved by her passionately (pp. 114–19). Finally she forms a loving friendship with Abbot Geoffrey of St. Albans and becomes his spiritual guide and educator (pp. 134–93).

The writer's intention was clearly to narrate a series of "love stories," all in some sense controversial, problematic, and troubled, but of rising spiritual value.[5] More than Christina, who remains constant in her vow of virginity and more or less constant in her exclusive espousal to Christ, it is her "lovers" who illustrate stages of love. But Christina herself has a powerful capacity to experience human passion.[6] The conflict between spiritual and carnal passion is at the core of the work, and her commitment to virginity must maintain itself against a character and psyche strongly oriented to the erotic.[7] She deserves a place alongside the representative figures of the amatory life in the twelfth century as a transitional figure between the hero of the erotic agon, Robert of Arbrissel, and the heroines of passionate love like Heloise and Isolde.

The narrative art of the writer is our point of departure. The romance-making imagination is powerfully at work in the *Life of Christina*, especially evident in the dramaturgy and staging of some of the scenes. There is for instance the striking episode of Christina and Roger, the hermit of Flamstead, "falling in love" with each other. After long refusing to become her spiritual adviser, Roger is gradually won over by Christina's good reputation, though he still resists seeing and talking to her. But one day they meet by chance:

It happened in this way. The virgin of God lay prostrate in the old man's chapel, with her face turned to the ground. The man of God stepped over her with his face averted in order not to see her. But as he passed by he looked over his shoulder to see how modestly the handmaid of Christ had composed herself for prayer. . . . Yet she, at the same instant, glanced upwards to appraise the bearing and deportment of the old man, for in these she considered that some trace of his great holiness was apparent. And so they saw each other, not by design and yet not by chance. (p. 101)

The half-licit meeting "kindles a fire" in their spirit, which "burned in each one of them" and "cast its sparks into their hearts by the grace of the mutual glance"; it stimulates "heavenly desire" which creates a new life together in the very close quarters of Roger's hermitage (p. 103).

The scene has elements of the beginnings of romantic love: a half-intentional, furtive glance of lovers in some sense meant for each other, is the beginning of a fiery love — but all of it is transferred above human passion into ethereal.

The physical posturing, the composition and staging, are remarkable: Christina, supine in prayer, arches her back as the old man steps over her, himself looking back as he does so. In both the reluctance is visually realized by directing the momentarily ungoverned glance over the shoulder. The double-arching — the man higher, the woman lower — creates both harmonic, symmetrical composition, and tension — the forced posture of the heads. The unnatural physical pose is answered by the moral posturing: the old man's glance seeks only "to see how modestly the handmaid of Christ had composed herself for prayer," and the maiden's glance intends "to appraise the bearing and deportment of the old man," in which his holiness is visible. Furtive lovers' glances, the stuff of romantic first meetings, are moralized. The scene is perhaps best described as "exquisite"; it wants to appear spontaneous, but is obviously "thought out" (*exquisitus*), concocted for a narrative and moral purpose. The emotions and motivations are good and pure beyond human nature, but the artifice is so evident that "sublime" overstates it. They are like actors in some Enlightenment drama of virtue; Watteau could have made good use of the composition, with costumes and scenery appropriately changed, to depict a flirtation between some courtly shepherd and a coy shepherdess.

The romance-making imagination is also at work in a scene in which Christina flees her parents' house, where she is virtually held prisoner. They want to force her to have sex with her husband, Burthred, and so legitimize the marriage by consummating it. She has steadfastly refused and prefers to flee than to face further coercion. The escape is the result of careful intriguing and planning on the part of the archbishop of Canterbury, the hermit Eadwin, and Eadwin's servant, who conspire to rescue Christina and to provide refuge in Roger's hermitage. The servant gets a chance to speak to the closely guarded Christina, and the words he whispers to her are, "Would that I might have you outside the city."[8] Christina "blushed and was embarrassed" at these words, but not for the obvious reason that they sound like the prelude to a love confession and the invitation to a tryst ("I need to talk to you privately" would have served the practical purpose better), but rather for "exquisite" reasons: the narrator explains that she blushed because the servant was non-noble and she feared detection. Nonetheless she gives him elaborate instructions for a meeting:

"Go and tell your master to prepare two horses, one for me and one for you, at a precise time," and she fixed the day of the week. "As soon as Aurora appears,[9] wait for me with the horses in that field over there": and she pointed to the spot with her finger. "I will come to you there. . . . When the horse is ready you will recognize me by this sign. I will place my right hand to my forehead with only the forefinger raised" (p. 89).

Christina comes on the appointed day at dawn, and strides "toward the river, carefully scanning the meadow to see if her companion[10] were there" (p. 89). No companion, no horses, and Christina must wait out a whole day, hidden in her aunt's house. She is anxious, fears detection, and holds a nervous vigil: she "scanned the meadow"; she waited anxiously "with her eyes fixed all the time on the meadow beyond the river"; "scanning the meadow beyond the river once more and not seeing the man she longed for, she turned her steps homeward . . ." (pp. 89–91). The next morning she disguises herself as a man and heads for the assigned spot "swathed in a long cloak that reached to her heels" (p. 91), and after a final leave-taking from her sister, she "turned her steps toward the meadow" (p. 93), where at long last she meets her companion with the horses. She puts on "manly courage" to match her garb, and "jumping on the horse as if she were a youth and setting spurs to his flanks, she said to the servant: 'Follow me at a distance: for I fear that if you ride with me and we are caught, they will kill you'" (p. 93).

The scene is swashbuckling and romantic: a furtively arranged meeting, horses at dawn, a secret sign of recognition, a disguise, a dramatic, unexplained delay, an agile leap into the saddle, a desperate race to safety where the "beloved" waits, life, love, and freedom hanging in the balance. This scene also wants a painter from the eighteenth or early nineteenth century to do justice to its romantic staging, and no doubt the long cape streaming out behind the disguised fleeing maiden would provide a good effect.

Besides being swashbuckling and romantic, the scene is also completely superfluous. It adds nothing to the story of Christina's sanctity, miracles, visions, or of her close relations with Christ. It could have been replaced by a brief, sober report ("Christina escaped her parents with the help of Eadwin's servant"). And yet it is one of the longest sustained scenes in the work, taking up five pages in the printed version. It was included as far as I can see because the writer had a conception of Christina's life that he wanted to dramatize. This is not to exclude the possibility that the scene actually happened very much as described, but much of it and of the *Life* in general shows literary modeling, is formulated by a writer with a keen sense of romance, of drama, and of narrative staging. Especially striking (besides the formulations discussed in notes 8 and 9 above) is the dramatic and sentimental framing of anxiety in the landscape, "her eyes scanned the meadow beyond the river," thrice repeated like a fairy-tale motif.

I have, again, used the term "romantic" loosely to describe a certain atmosphere of love stories more common in the nineteenth than in the twelfth century. But in the very years when Christina's biographer wrote, a new form of narrative, called for the first time *roman*, was in its youth and was highly popular in England and France. There are elements in the *Life of Christina* that bear comparison with "Romance" in the stricter sense. For instance, the motif of trickery and cunning. Christina escapes the wooing of Ralph of Durham by a

clever ruse. The lascivious bishop has trapped her in his bedchamber and will
not take no for an answer. Christina faces an intricate dilemma, like Lancelot
compelled against his will to sleep with the *damsel avenant*,[11] like Sir Gawain
beset by Madame Bertilak, and like Lancelot and Gawain, Christina reacts with
a series of questions that have the character of a narrated inner monologue:

What was the poor girl to do in such straits? Should she call her parents? They had
already gone to bed. To consent was out of the question: but openly resist she dared not
because if she openly resisted him, she would certainly be overcome by force. (p. 43)

She quickly conceives a ruse. Seeing that the door is not bolted, she asks
permission to bolt it, pretending to give in to him: "we should take precautions that no man should catch us in this act" (p. 43). He agrees, after receiving an oath that she will not deceive him. She flees, bolts the door from
outside, and runs home, leaving the bishop to seethe in revenge plots. The girl
is "prudent" and the seducer "deceived" (*illusus*).

Deceit becomes a standard defense of her virginity. The escape from her
parents' house with horses at dawn is the culmination of her counterplots, and
the scene ends a series of ruses in which she matches wits with her persecutors
to protect her vow and her virginal "marriage" to Christ. Of course, Christina
is aided also by moral will and divine help, but clearly the narrator structured
the early episodes of the defense of her vow against seduction and marriage as a
series of clever deceptions thwarted by yet more clever ones.[12]

The scenes bear comparison with the romance of Tristan and Isolde,
where the episodes after the onset of love involve holding the husband at bay
through a series of clever deceptions and thwarting attempts at exposing them
by cunning. As in the Tristan romance, the issue is not whether or not to
marry, — she marries Burthred — but how to maintain a higher obligation to
love in spite of the forces opposing it, among them marriage.

Christina is also aided throughout by her true lover and spouse, Christ,
and this division of life into spiritual, exalting love and degrading physical/
social attachment is one of the basic tensions the *Life* shares with the Tristan
romance. Marriage, the husband, the parents and their helpers are powerfully
in conflict with the wishes of the protagonist, which take on in the eyes of the
antagonists the aspect of secret and forbidden alliances. The private and personal attachment to Christ is set above the worldly plans and ambitions of the
family, and so the story divides into a corporal and a spiritual level of amatory
and erotic attachment. Both the *Life* and the Tristan romance have in common
the subordinating of the marriage tie to higher spiritual obligations. In both,
the "lover" or lovers are aided by Christ in thwarting the claims of the worldly
attachment. And in both there is a radical reversal of the values on public and

private. Christina's public relations — with her family, husband, with various advisers, bishops, and archbishops — are negative, inimical to her spiritual vow. The legal rights of parents and marriage are invoked against the heroine with accurate use of contemporary legal practice.[13] But marriage, the law, the arrangements that structure civil society are relegated to a lower order of experience; their representatives are dubious, immoral, their claim to legitimacy so undermined that Christina has license to deceive — by way of protecting her higher, spiritual obligations. Again the nearness to the Tristan romance is evident. Christina is admirable for the false oath she swears to Bishop Ralph that she will return and slake his lust, as is Isolde in her false oaths made to her husband, King Mark.

Christina's true "loves" all have the character of private, personal, individual arrangements made in secret, maintained secretly (except Geoffrey), all of them threatened by the evil tongues who want to force the private realm into public scrutiny and paint it in the worst light.

As in many courtly romances, the "lovers" are beset by envious detractors eager to blame, discredit and bring disgrace upon the protagonists. From the very outset the men who love Christina spiritually are accused by unnamed malicious persons of carnal motives. The first thing we learn about her early spiritual adviser, the cleric Sueno, is that he is accused of vile sexual practices. "Someone" claims that he "was still so stimulated by lust that unless he were prevented by the greater power of God he would without any shame lie with any ugly and mis-shapen leper" (p. 39). And so it goes throughout. The narrative is infected with the threat and the awareness of shame and disgrace.[14]

All this warding off of lies, gossip, and suspicions places the narrator's consciousness well beyond the threshold of innocence. Christina's mode of feeling and loving is highly open to misunderstanding and attack; otherwise it would not need such justification. She herself is touched by the infection. Before she makes her monastic profession, she has to examine her own conscience, and it is not clear:

Inwardly she was much troubled, not knowing what she should do, nor what she should say, when the bishop inquired during the ceremony of consecration about her virginity. For she was mindful of the thoughts and stings of the flesh with which she had been troubled, and even though she was not conscious of having fallen either in deed or in desire, she was chary of asserting that she had escaped unscathed. (p. 127)

It would take some intricate defining to eliminate her nearly ungovernable desire for the unnamed cleric (see below) from the category "fallen in desire." But the point is, the hagiographer always has the trump card of Christ the judge of innocence, but he does not play it. He allows the uncertainty to hover

over a life troubled by inner and outer accusations of sexual fault — and only in the end rescues her sanctity. The narrative suggests — wants to suggest — that the awareness of sensuality and the successful facing of malice and misunderstanding in spiritual love are part of the pattern of sanctity.

*   *   *

The *Life of Christina* is a defining moment in passionate love. Its treatment of erotic desire is unique and problematic within the conventions of hagiography.[15] In the center of the work and central to the theme of passionate desire is the episode of the mutual love of Christina and the unnamed wealthy and powerful cleric. After the death of Roger, she is placed in the charge of this man, and at first the love they feel for each other is strictly "chaste and spiritual" (*castum et spiritualem amorem*, p. 114). But then the man's resistance is overwhelmed by the devil who attacks him with "fiery darts." Christina herself is assailed with "incitements to pleasure" and with "impure thoughts," but resists for the time being. "Insane with desire," he even appeared before her naked and "behaved in so scandalous a manner that I cannot make it known, lest I pollute the wax by writing it" (p. 115). Christina's reproaches and admonishing can recall him temporarily to his senses. But even while she does so, she conceals the same fierce desire that is tearing at her:

> though she herself was struggling with this wretched passion [*incendio miserabili*], she wisely pretended that she was untouched by it. . . . She used to be so inwardly inflamed that she thought the clothes which clung to her body might be set on fire. Had this occurred while she was in his presence, the maiden might well have been unable to control herself. (pp. 115–17)

She can control the "desires of her flesh" only by extraordinary asceticism, fasting, waking, scourging, and "trials which tore and tamed her lascivious body" (p. 115). She falls seriously ill after receiving a vision of her lover as a monstrous bear blocking her way into the monastery. The man himself is cooled by a warning visitation from three saints: John the evangelist, Benedict, the founder of his order, and Mary Magdalene. Their threats and warnings prevail over his passion. But Christina herself is still tortured and nothing could cool the "fever" (*estus*) of her longing. Finally, she retreats to the wilderness, where, still lashed by desire, she receives an "unheard of act of grace" which frees her from this torment. Christ himself came to her in the guise of a small child. He was taken into the arms of his "sorely tried spouse" who for an entire day not only saw but also felt his presence. The redeeming moment and the rise to a higher stage of loving comes in an ecstatic embrace of Christina and Christ:

So the maiden . . . pressed him to her bosom. And with immeasurable delight she held him at one moment to her virginal breast, at another she felt his presence within her even through the barrier of her flesh. Who shall describe the abounding sweetness with which the servant was filled by this condescension of her creator? From that moment on the fire of lust [*libidinis ardor*] was so completely extinguished that never afterwards could it be revived. (p. 119)

This is fighting fire with fire, clearly. Christ's presence in her body provides the cleansing flame.[16] But did the cure of carnality need to be so carnal? She can feel Christ, man and child, bridegroom and fetus, within her body, and this combines the two high points of female sexual experience, intercourse and childbirth. The writer clearly had a purpose in extinguishing his heroine's physical passion by a higher ecstasy also experienced as physical. The idea is not to reject passion and intercourse, but to posit a passion so deeply, inwardly, and ultimately satisfying that it ends the demon-inspired, earthly kind.

This strange drama of passion exorcised by passion is a pure example of the fundamental paradox and mystery of passionate love affirmed: the sexual is incorporated into a higher, purer kind of love by the deifying of human desires. One may wonder whether this "solution" is anything other than mystification and conceptual sleight of hand, whether there is any psychology of the overcoming of tormenting desire through spiritual-carnal ecstasy. Garden variety ascetic discipline is real, empirically realizable, and effective in the economy of self-control. But Christina's sexual experience to end all sexual experiences is a confection of a romantic imagination that solves real human problems by flights into the fanciful, and the fanciful in this case involves a radical upgrading of sexual experience, its translation into the spiritual.

The mutual love of Christina and Abbot Geoffrey is the high point of the narrative, as received (it breaks off while describing their relations). But to understand its place in the structure of the narrative, it is important to see the development which preceded. The quality of love relations rises in a steady curve throughout the narrative. The rises mark stages in a process of spiritual development, of education if you will. Christina has a series of spiritual mentors, beginning with her early friend Sueno, who encourages her vow of virginity and instructs her in the virtues and trials it will bring her (p. 37).

Her relations with the hermit Roger are characterized by mutual love and mutual instruction and guidance, and the two go together:

Through their dwelling together and encouraging each other to strive after higher things their holy affection grew day by day. . . . And so their great progress induced them to dwell together. (p. 103)

The teaching is not one-sided, but mutual, as is the love.

It is different with Geoffrey of St. Albans. Christina is his spiritual mentor. He is a "noble and powerful person," "a man of great spirit" (*magnanimus*, p. 134–35). But no sooner does he appear on the scene than his judgment as abbot is called in question. Christina receives a vision admonishing her to correct a plan that the abbot is considering — before he has confided it to anyone. With the help of supernatural visitations, Christina bends his arrogance and persuades him to abandon his "evil course" (we never find out what it was). And from this time on, Geoffrey "heard her admonitions, accepted her advice, consulted her in doubts, avoided evil, bore her reproaches" (p. 139). Seeing him so improved and now "bent on doing good," Christina "cherished him with great affection and loved him with a wonderful but pure love."[17] This marks the course of their love: Christina is the warden of his behavior. She "reproves him harshly" when he has sinned (p. 141). She cures him when sick and wards off dangers and temptations. She prays for him when she sees "that he was making every effort to become more spiritual" (*ad superna tendere*, pp. 142–43). A major thread of the narrative until the end is the spiritual development of Geoffrey with Christina's guidance. "She strove to enrich [Geoffrey] in virtue."[18] The drama of Christina's underwear (see Chapter 10) fits in this context: a man of unfixed character requests a dubious love token from his spiritual guide. The turning aside of his request by divine intervention is another sign of the abbot's shortness of judgment and Christina's scrupulousness. In fear of another impending journey, Christina prays so intensely for Geoffrey's safety that she has an ecstatic vision. She stands before Christ, embracing Geoffrey: "she saw him, whom she loved above all others, encircled with her arms and held closely to her breast" (p. 169). Later she receives word from heaven that Geoffrey will be "enlightened with eternal light," as she had prayed, and this brings her "to examine more closely in the depths of her heart whether anyone can love another more than herself" (p. 181).

The high point of the scenes of intensifying devotion is a kind of spiritual love-death, at least the positing of it. God himself asks Christina if she would like Geoffrey to die for his sake. Her answer: yes, she would; in fact she would be more than willing to do the deed herself. Her love for Geoffrey is more spiritual than Abraham's for Isaac, she argues, therefore she can "sacrifice" her friend in the name of higher love: "the kind of love that binds me to him, Thou alone understandest. For what death is more glorious than that which is accepted out of love for the Creator?" (p. 181). The episode is perplexing and mysterious, but it seems as if the writer wanted to represent an extravagant act of spiritual love, a kind of "amor fol" or a spiritual "Liebestod" inflicted on the lover by the beloved once the highest level of loving is attained. There is a peculiar play on the love great enough to lay down your life for a friend. Possibly the scene suggests there is after all one love greater: the willingness to take the life of the beloved.

The structuring idea of this friendship is that the love reaches ever higher stages, consistent with the abbot's rise in spirituality through Christina's efforts to improve him. It is rich in reverberations with courtly love themes. The reward of love is given in accordance with the man's improvement. The woman becomes the moral force which "educates" him and assures him God's favor.

*   *   *

The *Life of Christina* is a kind of summa of erotic-spiritual love; it might be justly called *scala amoris* or *de gradibus amoris*. It shows the rise from earthly to spiritual, a progression from lowest to highest forms of loving. Each love relationship has the character of a *speculum* of a certain kind of love. Like Bernard's *Steps of Pride and Humility* it begins with negative examples and ends with positive. The lovers move from carnality (Bishop Ralph) to utility (Burthred) to two stages in the conquest of the body (Roger, fierce asceticism; the unnamed cleric, sensual overcome by spiritual desire) to a purely spiritual love based on moral improvement (Geoffrey).

Seen in terms of its narrative structure, the hard question the *Life* poses is, what idea justified the placement of the unnamed cleric so high in this hierarchy of loving? The episode represents a love so sensual that the desire-torn woman fears her clothes will catch fire! a hunger so intense that only the experience of Christ pressed "to her bosom" and the "immeasurable delight" of "feeling his presence within her even through the barrier of the flesh" can quench it. This love experience is placed between Roger, the ascetic hermit, and Geoffrey, the abbot. Important is the transitional moment, the rise from earthly to heavenly love. It is mediated still by the body, whose experience of desire and fulfillment provides the dynamics of rise. It is an extraordinarily bold affirmation of human erotic experience, at least as bold as Bernard's eroticizing the reading of the Song of Songs. It anticipates the moment in the *Divine Comedy* when Dante's earthly beloved Beatrice guides him from Purgatory into Paradise, but the comparison only shows how much more powerful the erotic side of love was for the English recluse-saint than for the Florentine poet.

*   *   *

By the middle of the twelfth century, passionate love has a voice. It is by and large a female voice. It was reconcilable with older traditions of ennobling love because it borrowed its ideology largely from Ciceronian ideas (virtue inspires noble, pure passion; noble passion educates). It has a home in the "temple of the university," where it inspires poets. It has its mysticism; it has its saints, its visionaries, and its martyrs.

Virtuous Chastity, Virtuous Passion — Romantic Solutions in Two Courtly Epics

By the decade 1150–1160 virtue-giving love has become far more complex, far more difficult either to understand or to accomplish than the male love that had been its nurturing context. And it starts its march away from life and experience and into fairy tale, myth, romance. It also accordingly generates a body of imaginative literature.

It is an odd fact that love emerges in the literature of "courtly love" as an object not just of adulation but of irony and satire. It is not clear that Chrétien de Troyes takes entirely seriously the harsh demands of loving women or men on which the plots of his romances *Erec et Enide*, *Yvain*, and *Lancelot* turn. Wolfram von Eschenbach out and out criticizes and rejects the practice (real or imaginary) of courtly ladies sending men out to learn lessons in good conduct or to perform extravagant deeds before receiving the reward of love.[1] It is worthwhile asking about the real referent of statements like Chrétien's toward the beginning of *Yvain* that "people don't fall in love nowadays, nor do they love as they used to."[2] Or that of Gottfried von Strassburg:

They are right who say that "Love is hounded to the ends of the earth." All that we have is the bare word, only the name remains to us; and this we have so hackneyed, so abused, and so debased, that the poor, tired thing is ashamed of her own name.[3]

Of course, these statements may be mere topos, golden-age thinking, and *laudatio temporis acti*. But it does seem early in the history of romance to be sounding that particular motif, and given that the originator of Arthurian romance himself tended to irony and satire of love it may be a statement of a real sense of loss.[4] Dealing with an age that supposedly conceived of itself as a period of renewal, one ought to hesitate to give a quick and easy answer to the question, why early poets of courtly love represent love as in a state of decline. Not one courtly poet to my knowledge shares C. S. Lewis's sense that what they depicted was "an entirely new way of feeling,"[5] or Peter Dinzelbacher's that they were among the discoverers of love in the West.[6] On the contrary, Chrétien and Gottfried thought of themselves as trying to breathe new life into a dying ideal. Gottfried blames the decline of love on the lack of "steadfast friendship" in love in the present day (*der staete vriundes muot*) (*Tristan*, 12269; Hatto, p. 203).[7]

A sense of the decline of love and friendship does not just register in literary sources. Cicero had said that true friendships are rare, but the twelfth century took the comment seriously and personally, and created or at least stoked a nostalgia for a kind of friendship that had passed from the earth:

That love which Pylades felt for Orestes
And Laelius for Scipio does not exist today.
Confidence and loyalty in either partner is rare.[8]

Aelred puts a particular spin on this motif by turning it into an indictment of the Christian era:

[there never were many friends, but] in this age of Christianity, friends are so few, it seems to me that I am exerting myself uselessly in striving after the virtue which I, terrified by its admirable sublimity, now almost despair of ever acquiring.[9]

Heloise laments the loss of love and "natural vigor" in men because the world is old. She calls for a new rule of the religious life, one which would take into account male frigidity over against the rule of St. Benedict, written in a time when men could still love:

We see that the world has now grown old, and that with all other living creatures men too have lost their former natural vigour; and . . . amongst many or indeed almost all men love itself has grown cold.[10]

She is of course generalizing from her own castrated husband and measuring the difference that separates the passion of their early days from the cold, frigid consolations of philosophy, theology, and the religious life.

But the god of love himself would make a similar complaint in a poem from the *Carmina Burana*: "The ancient vigor has passed away [from love], its virtue has vanished; my strength has failed me and Cupid's bow shoots no more!"[11] Bernard of Clairvaux recalls the days when the patriarchs "burned with desire for the presence of Christ in the flesh," and weeps "for the luke-warmness and frigid unconcern of these times."[12]

For a period that modern scholars take as the birthplace and birthdate of refined, courteous, romantic love, it is strange that these major figures in the "invention" of love, clerical or courtly, voice such laments. Whatever it may say about the experience of love in the period, it does indicate that the new paradigm of love was perceived as a response to a decline of good love and friendship in the twelfth century.

The literature of courtly love is from the outset a vehicle for dealing with love-trouble, for posing and resolving thorny problems caused by love: the disputations in Andreas's dialogues and courts of love, the debate form *partimen*, the inner monologue, the dilemma are some of the techniques of problem solving it made use of. It is very different from the older epic, which is a vehicle for moving toward the necessary ends to which unquestioned presuppositions guide it.

Courtly literature was never anything other than a literature of questioned presuppositions. It has not been possible to define a "system" of courtly love, or to reduce it to a definition or series of definitions. Gaston Paris set up Chrétien's most ironic and overdrawn work, *Lancelot*, as a paradigm of courtly love, and so directed medieval studies onto one of its oddest and longest detours. The minimum of explanatory power met with the maximum of scholarly consensus.

Regarding love as a public experience of the nobility with a history prior to the twelfth century shows that the paradigm that frames courtly love has been — not recently established — but recently shattered, and the literature of courtly love represents, not a "system" or a widely recognized and accepted social ethic, but rather fidgeting attempts at solutions to the problems that that shattering created.

In the great jumble of attitudes, often contradictory, represented in the literature of courtly love, I want to separate out the strand that joins love before and after the twelfth century: the development and transformation of ennobling love.

From this perspective the major project of courtly literature is the reconciliation of ennobling love with physical love, what I called earlier the romantic dilemma: the insoluble problem to which the twelfth and thirteenth centuries offered romantic solutions in great virtuoso acts of synthesizing. We have seen this conceptual tour de force performed in clerical and monastic culture in the previous chapters. Now we turn to the imaginative literature of secular culture. Hardly a text from narrative or lyrical poetry does not build on the tensions of sublime and passionate love. Common is the stark dualism of good versus bad love. The anonymous Old French *Roman d'Eneas* and Veldeke's *Eneit* both set the destructive passion of Dido for Aeneas against the virtuous love of Aeneas for Lavinia. But our subject is the transformation of passion and desire into virtue, not their separation.

Two tendencies develop in courtly narrative that transform the representation of ennobling love. The first domesticizes sexual passion and the second mystifies it.

Love Domesticized: Wolfram von Eschenbach

The first is represented in the marriage romances, especially those of Chrétien and Wolfram, which managed the problems of sexuality by putting them to one side, either ignoring them or assigning them to negative minor characters, holding them in their place — until they could be brought under the sheltering roof of marriage.

Wolfram is one of the great romanciers of love, but he has stood in the background on that score partly because of his bad match with the "paradigm" established by the Lancelot romance, troubadour lyric, and the antimarriage line of love ideology in Andreas. Also partly because of his obvious dependence on Chrétien, whose Perceval romance of the Grail remained a fragment.

From the point of view of the traditions of ennobling love, Wolfram is important because he dismantles or discredits the didacticism of love — the idea that love is a process of education. He also removes it from the role of ceremonial act and decisively redefines its ennobling character. The ceremony called "love service," "service of ladies," set out in Lancelot, Andreas, and in many courtly love lyrics is Wolfram's great enemy. His antagonism is embodied in various members of the Grail family, most strikingly in Sigune, Parzival's cousin. She turns up mysteriously as a forest recluse at three critical moments in the story. In the second two she is doing penance over the corpse of her dead lover, Schionatulander. She had sent him out on a senseless mission of love service in search of a magical chain/dog collar, in quest of which he died. She realizes the foolishness of "testing" her man before giving her love, and devotes her life to expunging her sin.

The king of the Grail, Anfortas, suffers an unhealable wound in his genitals in the service of Orgeluse, a femme fatale who uses up men in her service. The wound is punishment for a sexual transgression of the Grail king, to whom love service, but not marriage is forbidden. Anfortas's father, Frimutel, had died in love service. So had Isenhart and the three sons of Gurnemanz. The magician Clinschor, once duke of Capua, had served a married woman, but when her angry husband found the two in bed together, he castrated Clinschor.

In short, the landscape of *Parzival* is littered with the dead or mutilated bodies of men who have served women to win fame and love. Sir Gawain (Gawân) has a close call with that destiny. A major part of his role in the romance, as mentioned above in Chapter 10, is to face the dangers of destructive passion and come away with life and honor unscathed. In the one instance of Gawân serving women innocently his woman is the prepubescent maiden Obilot. Her cruel and selfish older sister Obie has brought a senseless and destructive war down on her family by demanding excessive love service from

her wooer and fiancé, Meljanz. The eight-year-old Obilot invites a perplexed
Gawân to serve her for love and end the war. Used to more sexually aware
women, Gawân hesitates, then finally agrees. He ends the war and paves the
way for a reconciliation. He also declines the "reward of love" that Obilot
offers him, but tells her to renew the offer in five years or so. The success
of Gawân and Obilot in rescuing the family confers status on the "lovers";
Gawân transfers all the honor and praise (*prîs*) of his victory onto his young
ladylove. It is a rare moment in *Parzival* in which love service ends happily. But
the episode implies that love service brings good ends when cleansed of any
sexual ambitions. For Wolfram the point would be that an escape from the true
nature of love into childish innocence averts the disasters that otherwise attend
a romance based on winning love and fame through postponed reward. Passion in itself does not ennoble in *Parzival*; sexuality plays no part or only a
negative one in the cosmos of this work.

Wolfram knows a form of love heroism that is close to the warrior sexual
ethic of "strong-mindedness" promulgated by Theodulf (see Chapter 6) that
holds passionate love in control. Gawân may have experienced passion, but he
retained control:

If passionate love stirs him, which undermines even the strongest resistance, yet he was
always so firm, a firmness equal to that of the worthiest, that no woman was destined to
overthrow him. (*Parzival* 532, 25–30)

Wolfram understands the distinction between loving a woman and "being
overthrown" by her, which Theodulf did not understand, at least did not
express.

If sexuality cannot be removed from love altogether, so Wolfram seems to
think, it can at least be managed by "virile" or innocent lovers. Sexuality
strictly subordinated to affection or devotion is a formula for good love in
Wolfram, represented in the love of Parzival and his wife, Condwiramurs.
Parzival wins her love in dire battle with a knight who has besieged her land to
force her to marry him: the classic form of love service, rescuing a damsel in
distress. She had enlisted Parzival's help by coming to him alone in his bedchamber late at night, dressed only in a shift, climbing into bed with him and
explaining her problems. It is a scene that in Chrétien's version had played
piquantly on seduction and sexual bribery. Wolfram transforms Chrétien's
charming bedroom comedy into a showpiece of innocent love. He runs out
ahead of the reader's expectations by explaining, "She did not violate the
bounds of proper womanhood; she was not just loyal, but chaste as well. . . .
The queen was not in pursuit of that love that turns maids to madames" (192,
2–12). Upon entering his bedroom she kneels down on the floor next to him
and wakes him with a rain of tears. Embarrassed to find her kneeling as if in

prayer, he invites her into his bed. She accepts on the condition that he not "wrestle" with her. Why would he? "Neither he nor the queen understood the kind of love made in bed" (193, 2–4). When they lay down together, their arms and legs, though "prone to reconciliation," stayed apart and had no thought of intertwining. She wins the knight's support; he conquers her assailant, marries the woman he has saved, and becomes lord of her lands and castles. On their first night in bed together as man and wife they remain chaste, also their second and third. Then finally the lessons of his educators and of his blood make them "weave together arms and legs" in "the ancient rite that is always in fashion" (203, 6–10). The three chaste nights in bed together are the occasion for Wolfram's praise of chaste love:

He lay next to her with such propriety as would not satisfy many a woman nowadays. Shame on them for betraying good upbringing with all sorts of airs! . . . The loyal, constant man of proven moderation practices restraint with his beloved. He thinks . . . "I have served this woman year in year out in the hope of the reward of love; now she has offered me solace and here I lie. Earlier I'd have been satisfied just to touch the hem of her dress with my bare hand. Now if I craved my fill it would be betrayal." (201,21– 202,14)

The three nights of restraint show mastery of the flesh, and that creates a morality of the act of love; it is assigned a subordinate place in the economy of love service, love's virtues, desire. In Wolfram the act of love itself has a bawdy, burlesque quality to it.[13] It is far from the sensual work of art that Tristan and Isolde form in each other's arms in the work of Wolfram's great rival, Gottfried von Strassburg.[14] When Gawân and Queen Antikonie in *Parzival* are so seized with desire that they set to gratifying it at the dinner table, they are interrupted by an assault of townspeople who imagine the knight is raping their queen. The two have to retreat and defend themselves by throwing chess pieces at the attackers (cf. 406, 28ff.). Unchaste love humiliates and forces great knights and ladies into the roles of fabliau characters.[15]

Only chaste, innocent, or moderated love in *Parzival* has exalting force. Parzival and his wife Condwiramurs embody it. Parzival leaves his young wife shortly after their marriage and wanders for years. He fails in the test of compassion at the Grail castle and is denounced for this failing before Arthur's court. Embittered against God, whom he accuses of disloyalty to him, he declares his hate for God, and wanders for years in search of the Grail, serving his wife — not God — by fighting. He receives many offers of love from many women, Orgeluse included, but turns them all down to remain loyal to his wife. In a climactic scene toward the end of the work, shortly before his return to the Grail castle, Parzival, alone in his tent while a great festival goes on outside, resists temptation:

Now Parzival thought of his radiantly beautiful wife and of her chaste, sweet love.
Should he speak to another, offer her his service in return for love, and go the way of
betrayal? He rejects this kind of love. Great loyalty had so preserved his manly heart and
his body that no other woman ever won his love except the queen Condwîr âmûrs,
lovely as a flower. He thought, "Ever since I learned what love is, how has love treated
me? I am born of love; how have I lost love so? If I am to strive for the Grail, her chaste
embrace must drive me on." (732, 1–21)

The last line creates a new category of exalting love. The chaste love of husband
for wife, of knight for lady, is the fuel that drives him to seek the Grail. This
makes love part of a scheme of salvation and redemption, as the attainment of
the Grail means salvation for Parzival. Good love is a mediator in a rise from
sinfulness to redemption. Wolfram, here and elsewhere bent on outbidding his
contemporaries, wanted love to exalt more than the conventions of *fin amor*
and *hôhe minne* allow: ethical improvement is not enough for this poet. He
wants love to have religious, redemptive force. Parzival had told Gawân not to
put his faith in God but in women, and women, as it turns out, loyally and
chastely loved, function like God.

But parallel to the love of Parzival and Condwiramurs is that of Gawân
and Orgeluse. Orgeluse is the antithesis of Condwiramurs. She demands mur-
derous tasks of Gawân, places him intentionally in dangerous predicaments, as
she had the other lovers who perished in her service. Gawân survives them all.
Her motive is revealed in the end: it was grief for her dead husband, Cidegast,
whom she loved very deeply. When he was killed by King Gramoflanz, she was
seized with an obsession for revenge. That was the compulsion driving her
which spelled the death and ruin of the many who served her. Now she has
Gawân in her service; he has passed her tests, is in a position to take revenge on
her archfoe, Gramoflanz, a knight so bold that he will never fight against less
than two knights at a time. But instead of revenge, the Gawân episodes flow
into a kind of love festival. Orgeluse's plans for revenge melt in the love of
Gawân, whom she learns to love so much and so well that her love teaches her
forgiveness even for Gramoflanz. He himself falls in love with Gawân's sister,
Itonje (before he has ever seen her, just from reputation); everybody loves
everybody, and they wind up literally as one happy family.

And so a woman's obsessive revenge for her murdered husband, a situation that caused the death of thousands in *Nibelungenlied*, dissolves in love in
Parzival. Love perverted into revenge turns into a force of reconciliation that
offers an answer to one of the great social problems of any warrior society, how
to end cycles of revenge.

In the High and later Middle Ages love experiences a process of accretion
of qualities: it moves from a ceremonial form of behavior to a private experience, to a redemptive force in both social and religious experience; in the

theology of Bonaventure and others it is the force that holds the three members of the Trinity together; for Dante and others it is a cosmic force that "moves the sun and other stars."[16] Wolfram's *Parzival* participates in love's expansion into the cosmic and religious. "Condwîr âmûrs," the "guide of love", or the "guiding love," plays a part in *Parzival* that anticipates the role of Beatrice in the *Divine Comedy*, of Laura in Petrarch's lyrics, of Gretchen in Goethe's *Faust*.

Esotericism and Elitism of Love: Tristan and Isolde

I mentioned two solutions to the conflict of sexuality and ennobling love. Wolfram's was the first, sexuality domesticated. A second solution took the opposite tack: it tried to integrate sexual passion fully into the idealism of love, not only give it its due place, but enthrone it as one of the ruling forces in ennobling love relationships. This really took a virtuoso act of conceptualizing. Passionate love with its natural culmination in the act of love ennobling? No philosophy of love had attempted this prior to the twelfth century. To exalt sexual passion in and of itself was no less difficult in the Middle Ages than in Hellenic Greece. It inevitably founded itself on contempt for the values of society, as we saw in the cases of Heloise and Christina of Markyate.

The strain of courtly literature that exalts sexuality did so by removing love into a realm beyond reason, and so solved the problem by declaring the solution attainable, but beyond comprehension. Yes, love is complete, perfect, and exquisite only in its fulfillment in the act of love. Yes, this kind of love, tragic and destructive though it is, also raises status, confers virtue, and recognizes inner worth. But how this happens, and how these benefits accrue in tragic sexual passion, is inexpressible, so exquisite as to defy understanding. The morality of adulterous love is likewise ineffable, its explanation lost in some mysticism of personal election. The ennobling force of passion is like a product that you can't afford if you have to ask about the price.

Ennobling love of any variety has to occupy moral high ground, it has to supply the "sublime and noble thoughts" on which it is the mark of a virtuous mind constantly to reflect (Aelred's claim). Finding or co-opting it when facing the irresolvable dilemma of reconciling ethical and sexual love is a process like the continual redefinition and refinement of the terms of membership in the elite, which Norbert Elias has defined for the process of civilizing: as soon as a custom established itself as entry to the elite, it was doomed to be supplanted by another, because membership had to stay just beyond the reach of the many.

This direction, upgrading passion through receding accessibility, generated a cult of idealized secret love. Esotericism was part of its public face. The amorous nobility forms an elite with common secrets to keep. In open concealment they filter through the court; all become privy to them; all honor the mask because it conceals the secret that is perfectly kept by everybody. Unmasking becomes an offense more serious than what the mask conceals, because all the elite has its own mask, and disrespect for the license to mask the private would create chaos. The husband knows, but the costs of exposing the hidden are greater than the shame of tolerating it. Clandestine love gains its own status, its own rights and privileges. The private aspects of love come to saturate the public without overwhelming them, an accommodation made possible because illicit sexual passion occupies a space long since prepared by an earlier mode of ennobling love.

No one who understood the code of passionate friendship in antiquity and the early Middle Ages would have found fault with the logic that said, "Better people deserve better lovers." But from the late twelfth century on, courtly literature regularly set that code in conflict with marriage, a legal-social practice that both religion and dynastic political interests sanctioned. The conviction that better people deserve better lovers virtually sought out marriage as its testing ground and favored opponent. The conflict of love and marriage created a dilemma where the legal bond could be subordinated to the romantic, and so give strong profile to the esotericism of love. The more power charged the marriage bond, the greater the accomplishment of lovers who violated it successfully. Therefore the king's wife was the natural figure to cast in the role of romantic beloved and courtly adulteress. Ennobling love still finds high expression at the center of power, but the king's love takes a dismal second to that of the superior courtier or knight, and the illicit love bond takes precedence over legal and political interests. Far from losing its power to exalt, it is enriched by the mysticism of personal superiority that can claim precedence even over state concerns. Here again we see that radical reversal of the values placed on public and private, which the Tristan romance shares with the letters of Heloise and the *Life* of Christina of Markyate.

The courtly Tristan romances had their classical formulation in the work of Gottfried von Strassburg, one of the most elegant, skillful, and notorious pieces of poetry in Western literature. Gottfried broke off the poem in approximately 1210 when it was about three-fourths finished. In his prologue he offers his reader the work with the assurance that

It will make love lovable, ennoble the mind, fortify constancy, and enrich their lives. This it can do well. For wherever one hears or reads of such perfect loyalty, loyalty and other virtues commend themselves to loyal people accordingly. (lines 175–80; trans. Hatto, p. 43)

The ethical code that the love of Tristan and Isolde claims to serve and strengthen here is not esoteric. It is a collection of widely shared and sought values, values of a system of education based on the teaching of virtue. The transposing of these values into fiction is a process I have called the "enfabulation of virtue." Gottfried locates virtue in the nature of love itself, as he conceives it:

Love is so blissful a thing, so blessed an endeavour, that apart from its teaching none attains worth or reputation. In view of the many noble lives that love inspires and the many virtues that come from it, oh! that every living thing does not strive for sweet love. (187–94; trans. Hatto, p. 43)

Worth, reputation, honor are conferred solely by love. Its lessons are exclusive. The many who do not make love the source of virtue are lamentable.

But the love of Tristan and Isolde is starkly at odds with such an exclusive claim of virtue and honor. Isolde is the wife of King Mark of England. Tristan has won her in a wooing contest and brought her to his king and uncle. But on the ship from Ireland, Tristan and Isolde drink a magic potion that sealed and bound them together in love. The body of the story is the trickery that protects the lovers' private world from exposure. The dangers of humiliation, disgrace, death are acute, but they ward them off by a virtuosity in deceit that is part and parcel of their intellectual superiority to King Mark and his court. Mark is represented as a man foolish in politics, mercantile in friendship, and coarse in love. But in his gentleness and weakness he develops a tolerance for the love affair that comes from his genuine affection for both Tristan and Isolde. The story insists on arranging the characters in a hierarchy, on creating elites. The two lovers are "noble hearts," and their story is directed at noble hearts in the audience. Others are excluded, those from the great mass whose highest goal in life is pleasure. The mark of the "noble heart" is the acceptance of suffering along with joy in love:

In love, joy and sorrow ever went hand in hand! With them we must win praise and honour or come to nothing without them! (206–10; trans. Hatto, p. 44)

The motive of the rhetoric is clear: the elitism of hero and heroine is available to the audience. Those who accept its terms, who accept the difficult philosophy of love-suffering, love-passion, align themselves with nobility of mind and soul.

It is good rhetorical strategy. If I had a book with a deeply obscure message that many readers might regard as morally dubious, I could not do better rhetorically than to dedicate it to those noble hearts and souls who understand the exquisite profundity of the unintelligible. I would send those trivial minds who seek only reason's pale light and shun the incomprehensible to seek enlightenment in shallower waters.

In the same way, a love with high potential for disgrace and for the destabilizing of states is declared the source of all worth and reputation, and you, reader, will just have to deal with that mystery. There may be the profundity of some primal alliance of love and death, Eros and Thanatos, in this championing of the tragedy of adulterous love, but there is also the illogic of elite formation and of fashion behind it. We attach ourselves with passionate devotion to the object of fashion because, because . . . never mind. If you don't understand it, no one can explain it to you, and anyway no one is interested in making explanations. Justification through esotericism has a powerful hold over aristocratic societies, which feed their self-conception on exclusivity.

In a curious and important passage of his *Tristan* Gottfried reflects on the morality of love. It is an excursus on "surveillance" (*huote*) that comes toward the end of the fragmentary work, just before King Mark discovers the two lovers in bed together and banishes Tristan for good.[17] The king has laid such a close watch on the two lovers that they have to keep their distance. Isolde is tormented by desire and — against all prudence — arranges a tryst in full daylight. Gottfried interrupts the narrative at that point to complain about the surveillance that foolish husbands place on their wives. It is an incentive for women to be disloyal, he says. Unmade prohibitions cannot be broken. The best surveillance is none at all. Certain women, the argument runs, are daughters of Eve, and when something is forbidden them, like Eve, they want it. When a woman succeeds in abstaining by overcoming her natural curiosity and cupidity, then she deserves praise and honor. She grows in virtue, against the urge of her inherited instincts. And having overcome the cupidity of Eve, "she is only a woman in name, but in spirit she is a man!":

What can ever be so perfect in a woman as when, in alliance with honour at her side, she does battle with her body for the rights of both body and honour? (17986–991; trans. Hatto, p. 278)

The poet develops a remarkable argument that "moderation" consists in balancing the rights and demands of the body with the demands of honor:

She is no worthy woman who forsakes her honour for her body, or her body for her honour . . . Let her deny neither the one nor the other. (17997–18002; trans. Hatto, p. 278)

The rights of the female body? What rights? Sexual appetite, clearly, since that is the context of Isolde's tryst. The excursus funnels into a lesson on the discipline of female sexuality. All sympathy, status, respect are lost when a woman "quenches desire as soon as [she] feels the urge" (cf. 18033ff.). That is not love but lust, which brings dishonor.

This little didactic insertion is so clearly directed against the heroine, who in the very next scene will destroy her own happiness and that of her lover by surrendering to lust, it forces the question where Gottfried stands. Is Isolde's love justifiable into its most dubious elements? Is she the administrator of that virtue inherent in higher love and its suffering? She appears in this episode as a woman who abandons moderation with tragic results: the two lovers are discovered by King Mark *in flagrante* and the resulting separation lasts until their deaths.

I want to suggest that two strands in the representation of aristocratic love meet in Gottfried's work, informing its paradoxical conception of love generally, but they roil about in the work like oil and water; they don't mix, they don't produce a consistent conception of love, and their conflict is most evident in the episode just discussed.

Strand 1 is love subjected to reason and discipline, love as a source of virtue, love as a learnable discipline that one can put into practice like any other ethic of behavior. This is the character of ennobling love since antiquity, in which reason ideally dominates emotion, sensation, desire; it takes its moral force from sensuality harnessed and held in check, an idea memorably formulated in Plato's image of the soul as a charioteer reining in, guiding, controlling an ungovernable black horse and a strong and steady white horse. For anyone who shares and believes in the metaphysics of this rationalized love, it is a powerful, admirable force and a major instrument of the Good and of virtue in human life. But it was always also a social form, not just an idea, and as a social form, released from its metaphysics, love subjected to reason can appear as a trivial, ceremonial kind of behavior, emotion reduced to social convention. It appears as such in Andreas Capellanus, so that one is not certain whether to read the work straight or as irony; the author himself seems uncertain whether he wants that conception of love to be taken seriously or not. To reduce love to social gesture is to hold it up to ridicule.

To have loved, then see people enacting and performing love as a social gesture, or to see others prescribing such performance, is to feel revulsion at the debasing of an almost sacred experience. This is, I believe, the experience, or insight, that produced a conception of love like that of Gottfried or the courtly Tristan romance generally.

Strand 2 answers and confronts the rationalizing and trivializing of love. It asserts the essentially irrational character of love, of desire, of emotion—

assuming always the elitist elevation of this experience into the realm of noble hearts or saintlike mystics. This love higher than reason and stronger than discipline takes by storm, overwhelms, devastates and destroys. It is indifferent to law and to social convention. It is not predictable or governable, except that it selects its saints and martyrs by that mysticism of election that pairs "noble hearts." The love of Tristan and Isolde is catalyzed not by the recognition of inner virtue, but by a magical love potion that they drink together by pre-destined chance. The lady-in-waiting, Brangaene, tells them that it spells their death. They fall in love the way birds settle onto the hunter's glue-traps on trees; the more they struggle against it, the stronger the snare grips them. Tristan is wounded, suffers pain and disorientation, as does Isolde: "She found this life unbearable" (11791; trans. Hatto, p. 196). She struggled and strove, "twisted and turned with hands and feet, and immersed them ever deeper in the blind sweetness of Love and of the man" (11803–9; trans. Hatto, p. 196). They drank eternal love and their death at the same time, and the story serves up this brew vicariously and eucharistically to the noble hearts of the audience, who "win praise and honor" by this kind of love "or come to nothing without it." Their tragic love "gives us life" because it is "bread" to all noble hearts:

Their life, their death are our bread. Thus lives their life, thus lives their death. Thus they live still and yet are dead, and their death is the bread of the living. (237–240; trans. Hatto, p. 44)

Unfailing devotion to a love given in full knowledge that the love destroys the lovers is the formula that links Tristan and Isolde with Heloise. It revalues the idea of virtue. It premises virtue and ennoblement on willing self-sacrifice in love. "Honor" and "praise" are attainable in tragic love through the magic of predestination, not through discipline and education.

The romance of Tristan and Isolde turns on an ennobling love completely revalued and redefined. Its claims to superiority, virtue, aristocracy are no longer validated by public acts and performed scenarios. They are removed to an inner realm, and public acts and performances aim at concealing, not reveal-ing the love sheltered within.

*   *   *

Following ennobling love first as public and ritualized form at royal courts, branching into clerical and monastic communities and filtering into lesser secular courts, then increasingly privatized and fictionalized, led us to the insight that in *Tristan* ennobling love makes its peace with sexual passion. I am very aware how much the wealth of courtly literature is diminished by the reduction to that perspective. But it is the perspective that most clearly shows how that phenomenon which appears as a new paradigm of love actually represents the problematizing of an old paradigm. At least this discussion and all that has preceded give us terms to discuss love in courtly literature on a firmer historical foundation than those of a tradition grounded on Chrétien's Lancelot romance.

The Grand Amatory Mode of the Noble Life

Ennobling love rescued itself from its conceptual crises in grand fashion. Out of the agonies of this new literature of romantic problems arose a code of behavior I will call the grand amatory mode. As a scenario of noble action, this creation of the High Middle Ages had a great future, like chivalry, from which it is not easily separable. In the later Middle Ages and earlier modern period ennobling love maintained itself as social gesture and public behavior mainly within this mode. It became a stylized, ritualized code of action, projected in its expression into the far reaches of the sublime, often to the point where it touched the ridiculous.

The literature of the grand amatory mode is vast, and in a coda to a study of love in the earlier and high Middle Ages I can do no more than scan a few of the high points in its history from the late Middle Ages to the nineteenth century. But it is important to stress its survival as one of the codes exercising a strong influence on aristocratic life.

The literature of love proliferated in the high and later Middle Ages. Courtly romance and love lyric remained vital forms. A vast didactic literature on love sprang up.[1] Virtually every book of chivalry will include a section on love and prescriptions connecting it with true chivalry.[2] For instance, Geoffrey de Charny prescribed, in his *Livre de Chevalerie* (mid-fourteenth century), that a knight ought to be in love *par amours*. It will raise the renown of himself and his lady, inspire him to bold deeds, and give him courage.[3] The chivalric orders that grew in the fourteenth century incorporated love into the idealism of the order. The statutes of the Burgundian Order of the Golden Fleece obligated each member "to have a good and loyal love."[4] The English Order of the Garter (see Chapter 10) and the Bavarian Order of the Tress have amorous legends which explain the orders' origins. The chains that bound the members of Jean de Bourbon's Order of the *Fer de Prisonnier* were the bonds of love. Its members were obligated to protect noble ladies and defend their honor at all times.[5] The institution of the tournament lent itself especially to staging pageants of chivalric love. Examples abound from the late Middle Ages. Maurice Keen refers to the great tournament at Valladolid in 1434, "where the presiding judge spoke as the God of Love as he awarded the prizes, and graciously besought the ladies and sweethearts of those who had shown prowess 'to embrace them and give them good cheer as their recompense and reward for their labours'" ("Chivalry and Courtly Love," p. 30).

Entry into the grand amatory mode is regularly seen and represented as initiation into a code of gentlemanly obligations. The knight Jacques de Lalaing, setting out on his career in the service of Philip the Good, received the following advice from his father:

Know that few gentlemen come to high estate of prowess and good renown, save if they have some lady or damsel of whom they are amorous.[6]

Christine de Pisan begins her *Book of the Duke of True Lovers* with the confession of a young man, its hero, who sets out to fall in love:

I desired to become a lover. I'd heard that a lover is courteous above others and better esteemed. Hence I went to where I could find a lady to serve.[7]

The amatory life shows itself especially clearly here as a script to which aspiring gentlemen can subscribe and a role into which they can enter. First the lover chooses the life of love as the form of ennoblement proper to him, then sets out to find the appropriate partner. This love is even more "cleansed" of an object than distant love and chaste love. It is as far from the onset of romantic love as "some lady or damsel" is from "the one true love." Romantic love is unthinkable without an individual who uniquely inspires it; chivalric/ennobling love clearly is not. The Duke of True Lovers chooses the amatory life as though he were making a career decision, more like joining an order or a club than like falling in love. As such it was ripe for parody.

Don Quixote's entry into the chivalric life is in the same vein:

Now that his armour was clean, his helmet made into a complete head-piece, a name found for his horse, and he confirmed in his new title, it struck him that there was only one more thing to do: to find a lady to be enamoured of. (bk. 1, chap. 10)

He mainly wants someone to send conquered giants to, but his instinct is right. He knows the scenario; his lines have been cut for comic effect.

*   *   *

Maurice Keen began his study "Chivalry and Courtly Love" with the question, "How seriously are we to take the idea of courtly love outside the narrow limits of medieval literature and literary convention, with reference to the world of actuality?" He shows its prevalence in nonliterary documents of chivalry and concludes cautiously that it must indeed be taken seriously as a force in the real life of the European warrior class. As an incentive to valor, love must have had, or must have been perceived as having, a powerful influence on behavior. Still, he cannot relieve his historian's conscience of the nagging sense that there is something fine-spun and literary about warriors actually fighting for love and serving ladies and pretending to be King Arthur and his knights, especially since the sources on the phenomenon themselves have a strong literary cast. He sees the crux of the problem as the indefinable impact of emotion on action (p. 37). The problem is alleviated somewhat if we regard courtly love as a code of behavior parallel to warrior honor and courtesy—as I have argued throughout this study. Ennobling love had always been primarily a way of acting and behaving, and only secondarily a way of feeling. It was a mode into which the courtier or knight or lady entered as the dancer enters the dance. The gestures, scripts, and stage settings of the amatory mode relate to the private experience and the individual feelings of love as singing the liturgy relates to religious devotion.

If Keen's answer is right, then those who sang the liturgy of ennobling love derived from it a benefit vital to any warrior society—valor, prowess, virtue, and honor; if I am right, then the benefit derived is one of vital importance to any court society: rank, standing, prestige, virtue. But Georges Duby addresses essentially the same question ("How important was courtly love in the reality of medieval life?"), and his answer makes Keen and me look timid:

Courtly love proved an extremely effective means of strengthening the State. In fact, it was so influential that no study of the progressive rationalization of power can afford to ignore it, although at this period it is only documented in literary works, often centered on the theme of "fine amours," or refined love.[8]

This bold claim sets an important agenda for the next generations of students of courtly love and courtly literature. Whereas my generation and the previous denied the "reality" of courtly love and placed it in the realm of the fantastic, Duby makes a trenchant claim for the opposite and challenges us to understand how the fantastic, the "unreal" and the literary ideal, operated centrally and vitally in the very core of power, of politics, and of society.

*   *   *

The amatory mode was not only courtly and northern. It spread to Italy and found expression in the poetry of the "dolce stil nuovo." Dante's near deification of Beatrice and Petrarch's glorification of Laura play in this mode. As bourgeois heir to the *stilnovisti* Giovanni Boccaccio declared in the prologue to his *Decameron* (ca. 1352):

From my earliest youth until the present day, I have been inflamed beyond measure with a most lofty and noble love, far loftier and nobler than might perhaps be thought proper, were I to describe it, in a person of my humble condition. And although people of good judgment, to whose notice it had come, praised me for it and rated me higher in their esteem, nevertheless it was exceedingly difficult for me to endure. (Prologue, p. 1)

The banker's son recognizes the amatory mode as reserved for high nobility, but benefits from the ennobling effects of loving futilely above his station.

It is still at home among high nobility in the society of Castiglione's *Book of the Courtier* (1525). The participants in the dialogue propose as a requirement of the perfect courtier that he "should be in love." One of the speakers makes some comments on this stipulation which distinguish sharply between love as ceremonial behavior and love as private experience. The noble cavalier, he says, uses dress, manners, and speech to win the favor of ladies, and not only when he is constrained by passion, but often also to honor the lady with whom he speaks, thinking that to show her that he loves her proves that she is worthy of it and that her beauty and her merits are so great that they oblige every man to serve her (bk. 3, chap. 53). It is a remarkable glimpse at love as pure social gesture operating apart from experienced emotion. But there is that other love alongside of it, its antithesis: love out of the constraint of passion, which the discussants reject as a form of seduction. The only ennobling form of love is superpersonal, the extravagant Platonic love that Pietro Bembo describes in his long speech in book 4.

The idiom of ennobling chivalric love appears to have been virtually institutionalized at the court of Elizabeth of England. Representation, pageantry, acts of homage drew on it, even the business of the court could be conducted in the amatory mode.[9] But it is archaic alongside an individualistic conception of love with which it now competes. In the muffled criticism of this mode by Elizabethan courtiers we see signs of the Cordelian turn — and we see it especially in the inwardness and individualized character of Shakespeare's conception of nobility, courtesy, love.

*   *   *

A trend that gave privilege to intense and sincerely felt private emotions ("I have that within which passeth show") and saw external display as the staging ground of hypocrisy, set ennobling love in a competition with romantic love, a competition which the old mode was bound to lose. I have already argued that courtly love begins as a shattered paradigm, not a fresh, new creation. That mode could only survive as an uncontested social ideal prior to the romantic dilemma that the twelfth century faced. Its conceptual foundation was cracked from the outset, as the contradictory teachings of Andreas Capellanus show. In literature the romance of Tristan and Isolde pries ennobling love apart from its nurturing base in the service of kings, sets it in fact against the king, while still idealizing love grounded in virtue. Neither medieval nor Renaissance culture, nor the western aristocracy generally succeeded in rationally justifying a reconciliation of virtue and passion. A history of ennobling love after the twelfth century might proceed by feeling its way along the cracks and fault lines in that phenomenon that extend into the nineteenth century. It is a history of romantic catastrophe generated by the illusion of a truly ennobling passion.

Christine de Pizan's novel/romance *The Book of the Duke of True Lovers* (ca. 1405) exposes the inherent impossibility of noble love. It begins by idealizing and ends by indicting it. The narrative purports to be a tale told to Christine by a man identified only as the "Duke of True Lovers." Resolving on a life of virtuous love, he sets out to find a woman worthy of his aspirations. After long questing, with parallels to the beginning of Guillaume de Lorris's *Romance of the Rose*, the "Duke" finds and falls in love with a Duchess (not otherwise identified), unhappily married, who requites his love. After long and elaborate preluding a tryst is arranged amidst extraordinary precautions: disguises, subterfuges, servants strategically dismissed. The two spend the night together in the Duchess's bedchamber, but under terms that are strictly spelled out from the first moment.

They pledge mutual love that will never end, but the lady places conditions on it:[10]

"Whatever love you see in me — no matter what secret thing, sweetness, or pleasure in love, word, or appearance I give, and even though I may embrace you and kiss you — do not believe that ever, any day of my life, I have the will or desire to commit a base act that might leave me open to every kind of reproach."

All that is dishonorable is ruled out, but

"as for all the other pleasures that a lover may take from a Lady, I wish to refuse you none and you may dispose of them at will. I give you my heart entirely, and abandon to you everything that I have, short of committing a folly or doing wrong."

The reply of the lover is straight out of the textbook of courtly love service:

"I accept, promise, and swear to you, under pain of perjury, never to be honored, but entirely dishonored, if ever a day in my life, in deed, in word, or in intention, I do or think anything in my power, either in secret or in public, which might displease you . . . So command me from now on, for I am your liegeman . . . in everything I will obey your will without contradiction."

He promises himself "noble joy" and "the lover's crown" as the rewards of pursuing good love. Love thus contracted will make him a brave and "worthy man," free of any blemish.

Having set these limits to their love, the two spend the night together in the lady's bedchamber. The lady "embraced me very sweetly and kissed me more than one hundred times." They dedicate themselves from that time on to the other's honor and "worth." The man is her servant; he has no will but hers, and he performs valorous deeds in her service. They conceal their love with great caution. It is the very model of a love beyond the body, confined to the mind, the soul and spirit, confined to desire. The man seeks only honor for both of them.

For some time they are happy in this mutual service, but it eventually goes sour. The Duchess tries to engage the help of an aged confidante, the nurse and friend of her youth, who writes her a long letter to the effect that her love, so carefully concealed, is well known, rumored abroad, gossiped about, surmised from the unmistakable signals lovers necessarily send. Her honor, that of her husband and her family are in the balance; the ruin of their reputation threatens, which will last much longer than the brief pleasure gotten from adulterous love however innocent. The letter contains lessons in good conduct, a kind of "miroir des dames mariées," and a trenchant attack on the premises of an "innocent" chivalric love:

Do not place your confidence in those vain thoughts that many young women have who bring themselves to believe that there is no harm in loving in true love provided that it leads to no wrongful act . . . and that one lives more happily because of it, and in doing this one makes a man become more valorous and renowned forevermore. Ah! my dear lady, it is quite otherwise! (p. 114)

Actual innocence is no defense against rumor, and the greatest ladies who have practiced "honorable" love have destroyed their reputations and dishonored their families under the delusion that it is. Malice feeds on the appearance of wrongdoing: "Such foolish love is dishonorable."

This argument dismantles the whole construct of ennobling love, sees and exposes the impossibility of romantic solutions to insoluble problems, allows neither the solution through separation of love and sex nor the mystifying of the grand passion. It sees and represents only the personal tragedy of

Eros defied; its heroism is fully denied. It does not matter if you separate love from sex and dishonor; it only matters that people do not recognize and credit that as possible. Neither the defense through virtue nor the defense through passion stands intact at the end of this speech, only the defense through marriage. It concedes to women no right to happiness outside of their marriage, places decorum and familial integrity far above any rights of the woman to personal gratification — and insists on it no matter how awful the woman's marriage.

But in spite of these solemn warnings, the lover and the lady continue their distant love. While they hold strictly to the terms of their love, the warnings prove only too true. The lady's reputation is destroyed, and the man's worthiness sinks, in crass contrast to the promises of ennoblement and exaltation in their first anticipations. The "Duke's" last words are "I saw her receive dishonor because of me, since everyone was whispering about the situation, for which I came to despise my long life" (p. 131).

The destruction of this grand illusion of "true lovers" practicing noble love is "romantic" irony in more ways than one. It declares the impossibility of courtly love while casting paragons in ideal scenarios. It shows ennobling love leading only to disgrace. The modern translator's reading of the work's ethos: "Thus the Duke's story, which Christine rendered with great tact, became a vehicle unique in the medieval period: the answer of a flesh-and-blood medieval woman to a literary model that was invoked to justify real-life behavior, one that Christine saw as utterly ruinous for women" (Fenster, p. 10).

This harsh rejection of ennobling love is not explainable as a new perspective that arises with the passing of the medieval world and the rise of a critical, modern mentality. The insight that ennobling love between men and women does not work had been in place and available since its beginnings. Christine's novel is not the voice of a "Renaissance woman"; it is one more rumbling along the same conceptual fault line occupied by Andreas's *De amore*. Andreas and Christine might both have written the solemn warning of *De amore* 3.25:

No one will be able to keep his fame shining or unblemished, or preserve a good reputation amongst men, unless he is clothed in the adornment of virtues. But none can preserve the adornments of virtues if he is soiled with the stain of even the slightest wickedness . . . A woman however noble, wise, and beautiful, is accounted despicable by everyone once she is known to be involved however slightly in love with someone . . . (pp. 295–97)

The remarkable novel by Madame de Lafayette, *La Princesse de Clèves* (1678), has much in common with Christine's work. The criticism of courtly love in a narrative of love by a woman is an especially striking common feature. The princess of Clèves faces the same dilemma as Christine de Pizan's heroine, but she solves the conflict of virtue and passion radically in favor of virtue, and the romantic confusion that deludes both the Duke of True Lovers and his Duchess, does not exist in the mind of the princess: virtue and passionate love are not reconcilable.

The princess, a woman married to a man of high virtue for whom she feels only respect and affection, conquers her attraction to the Duc de Nemours, whom she loves passionately. The duke loves her to distraction, but she never gratifies or encourages his love. Her unexampled act of declaring her love for Nemours to her husband — by way of defusing that love — leads to her husband's jealousy, suspicion, ultimately his death. He dies of disappointed love for his own wife. She is then free to love her lover, but instead she renounces the man she loves in favor of her duty to her dead husband. By a sublime act of self-denial, she resists inclination and follows virtue and duty, a posture ingrained in her from youth by her wise mother:

She showed her how much tranquillity attached to the life of a respectable woman, and how much brilliance and grandeur might accrue to one who already possessed both beauty and birth, by the addition of virtue; but she also showed her how difficult it was to preserve that virtue, other than through extreme self-discipline and scrupulous dedication to that which, alone, can make for the happiness of a woman: namely, to love her husband and to be loved by him. (p. 30)

So here as in many cases cited earlier, virtue is tested in the love relationship and requires a severe discipline and scrupulous dedication, an overcoming of nature, and again the ennobling and exalting force of love derives from the renunciation of passion. The passions and the motivations are sublime and exquisite. The princess is an "inimitable example" of virtue,[11] indeed she reaches nearly the stature of a saint, widely revered and frequenting the convent more often than the court in the end of her short life. She dies young, a martyr to marriage, honor, and duty. The ennobling power of her love derives from its denial. Imagine Isolde renouncing Tristan out of a sense of duty to her husband King Mark while admitting her passionate attachment to her lover. Imagine King Mark dying of jealousy and disappointment. Imagine Isolde as an ex officio nun, burning candles and singing chants to the memory of her lost husband. Goethe was to imagine this kind of heroism and inversion of the passionate love relationship in his *Elective Affinities*. His heroine Ottilie renounced the love of a married man (who dies of his love for her) and seals her renunciation by a refusal to eat, which leads to her death. Miracles occur during her funeral, and a cult arises at her gravesite.

But the princess as a martyr to wedded love is only the foreground of Madame de Lafayette's novel. As interesting for the amatory mode is that which she resists: the atmosphere of the court, saturated with love and gallantry. The main characters receive portraitlike introductions with catalogs of their virtues, of which their style of loving is an element. The king, Henry II, was "courteous, handsome, and fervent in love" (p. 23). The Duc de Nemours, for whom Madame de Clèves contracts her passion, was

nature's masterpiece; his least striking attribute was to be the most handsome and comely of men . . . His whole being had a presence which ensured that wherever he appeared, all eyes were drawn to him. There was no lady in the court whose pride would not have been flattered, were he to feel some attachment for her; few of those to whom he had become attached could boast that they had resisted him; and there were even several for whom he had shown no tender feelings who had not relented in their passion for him. He had such gentleness and such a gallant nature that he was unable to deny some consideration to those who sought his regard. Consequently he had many mistresses, but it was hard to discern which of them he truly loved. (p. 26)

Love penetrates even the exercise of power:

Ambition and gallantry were the heart and soul of the court, preoccupying men and women equally. There were so many different factions and parties, and the women played so great a role in them, that love was always allied to politics and politics to love. (pp. 33–34)

The princess's uncle, the Vidame de Chartres, balances three mistresses at the same time, two of them powerful, influential, and jealous, and since the third of them is the queen herself, his disloyalty revealed leads to his ruin. The author sees, at least represents, no evil in this court of love, and negative strains come only from a conflict of competing superlatives. But the princess's education in virtue steels her against the dangers of gallantry, and makes possible her role as martyr to passion resisted.

The melodrama of virtue either triumphant (Pamela) or tragically crushed (Emilia Galotti) would find expression in novels and plays of the Enlightenment. And in the course of the late eighteenth and nineteenth centuries, a literary consensus formed that the glory of adulterous passion is a delusion which can only have negative, destructive force. This idea informs Goethe's *Elective Affinities*, Flaubert's *Madame Bovary*, Tolstoy's *Anna Karenina*, and Fontane's *Effi Briest* and *Frau Jenny Treibel*. Stendhal's *The Red and the Black* and *The Charterhouse of Parma* are prominent exceptions. While the one ends in tragedy and the other in renunciation for the lovers, both works posit a heroism of the passionate life. Tragedy exalts more than it lowers the romantic love of noble souls.

A spiritual, ennobling love remains in the air in the Romantic and post-Romantic period, but as a vestige of an earlier age, a relic, a mode of behavior perhaps grand, lofty, and elegant, but unrealistic and unattainable, or as an overinflated vision of the aristocratic life whose real functioning is rendered impossible by an age of disenchantment. Courtly love was for much of Romanticism what more generally the Middle Ages themselves were: a lost ideal.

An exception to this trend is a revival of male love and passionate friendship among German intellectuals in the eighteenth and early nineteenth century. The main inspiration of this trend is a rediscovery of ancient Greek, not early medieval, mores. J. J. Winckelmann's fervent advocacy of Greek art gave a strong impulse to passionate male friendship, but it was rooted in an erotic admiration of the male body, and its elitism was intellectual and aesthetic, not class-determined.[12] It gave a public face and a controversial respectability to a strongly tabooed kind of love and sexuality, but without the "discursive innocence" of earlier medieval male love.[13]

The dominant trend is the descent of the sublime mode into bunk and hypocrisy. (It might appear in that light to us at its high point, since we share the presuppositions that made it such.) When monarchy and court society collapsed, this mode followed, along with pageantry, tournaments, court masks, and other odd ceremonies and trappings of the noble life. But the social forms of that life did not altogether disappear; rather they were transmuted into other contexts—salon society, patrician and middle-class imitation of aristocracy—or maintained by an aristocracy being slowly moved out of its centrality in European power structures.

The distant relative of ennobling love that Stendhal calls "mannered love" is still very much in the air in the first half of the nineteenth century, if his treatise on love, *De l'amour* (1822), is a reliable indicator. Stendhal, it must be said, is a great admirer of sublime, ennobling love. In fact he was among the early rediscoverers of Andreas Capellanus and the courtly love of the twelfth century. He glorified that period as the youth of noble love and imagines himself as living in an age that has abased the grandeur of a formal, ceremonial love:

Society, still young, delighted in formalities and ceremonies which were then a mark of civilization, and which nowadays would bore us to extinction. . . . Everything *formal* in society, nowadays so insipid, had at that time all the freshness and tang of novelty. (*Love*, p. 165)

Stendhal includes excerpts from Andreas's *De amore* in his treatise on love. He also quotes sections of an Arab treatise on refined love and urges the publication of these and similar works, which have languished because "the few scholars who could read them have had their hearts desiccated by study and academic pursuits" (p. 176). Americans are especially guilty of the abasement of love, he claims, since their habit of being "reasonable" in all things makes passion impossible:

It is as though the springs of sensitiveness had dried up in these people. They are just; they are reasonable, but they are not at all happy . . . There is such a *habit of reason* in the United States that the crystallization of love there has become impossible. (p. 164; emphasis Stendhal's)

Stendhal idealized the medieval practice of courtly love as he understood it. Good love must be encumbered by restrictions, by laws, by formalities; passion must be hedged by modesty and wrapped in extravagant illusions:

Love is civilization's miracle. Among savages and barbarians only physical love of the coarsest kind exists. And modesty protects love by imagination, and so gives it the chance to survive. (p. 83)

His objection was clearly not to the formal, stylized character of courtly love, nor to its exalting effect, nor to love service, nor to modesty resisting uncultured sensuality, but rather to the expulsion of genuine feeling from the cultivation of gallantry. He could see in the practice of refined love in the Paris of his age only an instrument of vanity and ambition. It is courtly love grown cold and mercantile. What irritates him most is that what remains of formal love's ennobling force is only its social utility. It still is a source of prestige, it still enhances the reputation — and this means the debasement of passion.

In his novel *The Charterhouse of Parma*, the magnificent Contessa Pietranera (later Duchess Sanseverina), declares to her wealthy lover Conte N———, upon whom she is financially dependent, that she no longer loves him. The Conte accepts it with equanimity, but "well aware of the ways of the world," requests only that she tell no one what she has told him:

"If you will be so extremely kind as to continue to receive me with all the outward civilities accorded to a recognized lover, I may perhaps be able to find a suitable position." (p. 38)

She loses all respect for him, refuses his further support, returns his gifts, and lives a life of near-poverty in preference to his patronage. But the casualness of the Conte's request shows that he might have anticipated a better reception. The idea must have been widely accepted that the love of a high-placed noblewoman conferred a stature that could count as a job qualification. The Contessa is not following a social norm in rejecting him, but rather an individual sentiment that insists on passion in love. It is Cordelian behavior.

A nasty anecdote in Stendhal's treatise on love is based on a caricature of abased passion, love totally reduced to utility. It is called "An Example of Love among the Wealthy Class in France" and purports to be a letter Stendhal received from a certain "Goncelin" in response to the first edition of *De l'amour*. It concerns a woman named "Félicie Féline," married to a dull, rich man who has no interest in her. She herself is "arid and devoid of any genuine sensibility," but vain and ambitious and therefore in need of a lover. She fastens on a Swedish gentleman, a houseguest, sluggish but intelligent:

"This," said Félicie to herself, "is the man I must pretend to have for a lover. As he is the coldest of them all, his passion will do me the greatest honor." (pp. 319–20)

She goes on a two-month long trip with her husband and the Swede, who either ignores or misunderstands her advances. His indifference is no deterrent to Félicie's ambition:

If she had been able to circulate a formal announcement she would have notified all her friends and acquaintances that she loved M. Weilberg the Swede with a violent passion, and that M. Weilberg was her lover. (p. 320)

She does declare her love to her friends individually, of course, because it would have no use at all if it were not made public:

"If only you knew what an ardent soul, what frightening passions burn in this man who appears so cool and impassive! No, my dear, you would not despise me then!" (p. 321)

The two supposed lovers never speak of love when alone, but

In public it was quite a different matter; she spoke to him of nothing but love . . . Fortunately his knowledge of French was poor, and she managed to convey to all those present that he was her lover, without his being any the wiser. (p. 323)

The gist of the anecdote is clear: a woman needs a lover to maintain a certain image of herself; she can enhance her reputation, gain respect and admiration, by being the object of a grand passion. And the value of love in the stock market of social standing is so high that a shallow character would willingly stage it if she did not enjoy the real thing. Wealthy young wives can wear lovers the way they wear jewelry and think themselves badly dressed if they don't have one to put on.

To end I want to point to the remarkable reprise of ennobling love in Honoré de Balzac's novel *Lily of the Valley* (1836). Its main character, Félix, tells the story of the two great loves of his early life in a letter/report to a friend. After an unhappy youth, he falls in love at age twenty with a married woman, Countess de Mortsauf. They form a spiritual bond of love and seal it in a scene very like the "contracting" of love between Christine de Pizan's Duke of True Lovers and his Duchess, but dripping with sentimentality and heavy emotionality that, by dint of virtuosity and chutzpah, Balzac can sustain without losing the faith and confidence of at least this reader. On an evening walk, Félix speaks love to her too boldly and receives this rebuff:

"So, though the wife in me is invulnerable, never speak to me thus again. If you fail to respect this simple prohibition, I warn you, the door of this house will be closed against you for ever. I believed in pure friendship, in a voluntary brotherhood more stable than any natural relationship. I was mistaken!" (p. 73)

In her disappointment, she weeps, and Félix turns her tears into the sacramental meal of his new life:

Two large tears, sparkling in the moonlight, dropped from her eyes and rolled down her cheeks to her chin; but I held out my hand in time to catch them, and drank them with pious avidity, excited by her words . . .
    "This," said I, "is the first, holy communion of love. Yes; I have entered into your sorrows, I am one with your soul, as we become one with Christ by drinking His sacred blood. To love even without hope is happiness. . . . I accept the bargain which must no doubt bring me suffering. I am yours without reserve, and will be just whatever you wish me to be." (p. 74)

With this avowal begins "the purest love that ever burnt on earth" (p. 76), a "sanctified love" (p. 89), a "purely spiritual union" (p. 99), a "love far beyond the sphere of the senses." It draws constantly on religion for its articulation, beginning in a eucharistic ritual, moving through catechism:

"Speak, tell me, do you love me with a holy love?"
"With a holy love."
"And for ever?"
"For ever."
"As a Virgin Mary, to be left shrouded in her draperies under her spotless crown?"
"As a visible virgin."
"As a sister?"
"As a sister too dearly loved."
"As a mother?"
"As a mother I secretly long for."
"Chivalrously, without hope?"
"Chivalrously, but hoping." (pp. 156–57)

It inspires in Félix a religious devotion: "I will do for you what men do for God" (p. 80). The Middle Ages repeatedly provide the model to which the lovers appeal, alluded to in the catechism just quoted and cited explicitly in a reference to their love as "a relic of the Middle Ages, recalling the days of chivalry" (p. 186). It is compared with great spiritual courtly loves of the Middle Ages: "Can the tale of Petrarch's Laura be repeated?" (p. 74); "She loved as Laura de Noves loved Petrarch, and not as Francesca da Rimini loved Paolo" (p. 172). And like the pure love of chivalrous lovers, it refines, inspires, improves the man, infuses virtue, valor, grants redemption:

She became what Beatrice was to the Florentine poet, or the spotless Laura to the Venetian — the mother of great thoughts, the unknown cause of saving determinations, my support for the future. . . . She endowed me with the fortitude to conquer the conquerors, to rise after defeat, to wear out the stoutest foe. (p. 123)

She awakens "every noble feeling" in him (p. 76). She exalts him:

She bore me up to heights whither the shining wings of passion . . . could never carry me; to follow her flight a man would have needed to wear the white pinions of a seraph. (p. 123)

She has the effect of purifying his thoughts and banishing any that are not beyond reproach, "and so she was not only my happiness, she was also my virtue" (p. 175). She is the sole source of good in him: "Remember that all that is great in me comes from you" (p. 214).

   All that is sensual is banished, at least checked: "Never was the flesh more bravely or victoriously held in subjection" (p. 88). He is allowed to kiss her hand and no more — the back, not the palm, which is "the border line of sensuality." The price of this renunciation is torture, but it is richly rewarded:

In return for my flesh, left torn and bleeding in her heart, she shed on mine the unfailing and unblemished light of the divine love that can only satisfy the soul. (p. 123)

Their love does not require physical presence; it survives separation: "I am so entirely a part of your heart, that my soul is here when my body is in Paris" (p. 156). And yet the physical and the erotic denied take a toll. The suffering of the flesh for the sake of spiritual love is unnatural, desiccating, even deadly:

"Love without possession is upheld by the very exasperation of hope . . . A power is ours which we cannot abdicate, or we are not men. The heart, bereft of the nourishment it needs, feeds on itself and sinks into exhaustion, which is not death, but which leads to it. Nature cannot be persistently cheated." (p. 108)

These somber lines prefigure the end of the story: Félix's passionately sensual affair with Arabella, Lady Dudley, the death of Madame de Mortsauf, the failure of every kind of love for Félix and the desolation of his life.

Their love even echoes the courtly love of the Middle Ages to the extent of "raising the worth" and enhancing the reputation of the lovers in the eyes of society:

My passion, a relic of the Middle Ages, recalling the days of chivalry, became known. Perhaps the King and the Duc de Lenoncourt spoke of it. From this uppermost sphere, the story, at once romantic and simple . . . no doubt became known in the Faubourg Saint-Germain. (p. 186)

This leads to public notoriety. He is in demand as a guest, and traffics in high society—where he meets Arabella, Lady Dudley. Her soul seethes with volcanic passions and she has the inventiveness and wealth to satisfy them. She makes Félix into her god (obtaining a title of nobility for him: Vicomte Félix de Vandenesse) and worships him with a fervor that would shrink from no act of madness in seeking its satisfaction and showing its devotion. She has something of Heloise's self-abandonment in love, but even more, Isolde's commitment to the destructive nature of passion and to fulfillment beyond the grave. She loves love-death; death is romantic, the ultimate expression of devotion. (Cf. her speech in praise of self-immolation as an act of passionate love cited in the Introduction.) She courts love-death, flaunts it as a personal prerogative ("I was born in Lancashire, where women can die of love," p. 225), and cultivates its lethal, destructive side as an aristocratic distinction: "Walk over us, kill us, never let us encumber your life. Our part is to die, yours to live great and supreme" (p. 227).

And so Balzac has set the hero between two loves, one spiritual, one sensual; one eternal, the other "born anew from its death" (p. 193). But the end exposes the ideal character of the two loves as illusory, in fact false and sterile. Ultimately what is most active in the two loved women are the threats hidden in their names, the death-thirst of Madame Mortsauf and the arid deadliness of Arabella Dudley. All the promised benefits of devotion to flesh and spirit are thwarted by some disenchanting "reality" which gives the lie to human aspirations. The narrative trajectory is close to that of *The Book of the Duke of True Lovers*: first establish a paradigm of ideal love, then destroy it by revealing its false and destructive side. Having made him the beneficiary of two glorious love affairs, the narrator shows his hero gradually stripped of all love. Spiritual love fails because it is unnatural, beyond nature, divine, hence not of this earth. As Félix's affair with Lady Dudley develops, Madame de Mortsauf becomes progressively weak, frail, sickly, and ultimately dies. Lady Dudley abandons him in a humiliating snub. The daughter of Madame de Mortsauf, urged to marry Félix in her mother's will, rejects him as her future husband. The negation of love progresses even through the frames of the narrative, which closes with a letter from the woman to whom the entire story is addressed. She also rejects Félix as a lover, refusing a man whose heart is a "tomb for his two great loves," not a fruitful field.

*   *   *

An odd destiny for ennobling love in the modern period: it is virtually never seen as a viable mode of loving that establishes a life with dignity. Taken seriously (i.e. not as mere ceremonial form), it either destroys those who practice it or is rescued for normalcy through marriage. Its aspirations are as grand as its collapse is dismal. Its exalting force is an illusion; its claim of enhancing reputation a dangerous lie. The exhilaration that results from commitment to either side of the romantic dilemma, the flesh or the spirit, is short lived and illusory. The double gesture of Andreas Capellanus, first glorifying then condemning courtly love, repeats itself in a string of the best romances devoted to it. Ennobling love develops from the High Middle Ages to the present as the working out of an inevitable program of self-destruction built into in this mode of loving. It is an illusion as grand as the masques and shows and festivals of aristocratic society, staged for effect, fine and inspiring, but in contrast to other forms of ceremony and representation, destructive and dangerous.

The romantic solutions given to the unsolvable problem of reconciling virtue and sexual passion sustain a brilliant literature, but fail tragically as an ethic of love relations. The ethical aspects of courtly love were not viable as reality; they existed only as the shadow of an ideal of passionate male friendship inherited from earlier ages.

Appendix: English Translations of Selected Texts

ALCUIN, LETTER TO ARN OF SALZBURG

Your love letters, have come to me, sweeter than honey, more pleasant than refined gold, sealed with the sweetest little gifts. Believe me, sweetest father, that I could not read the little letters of the brothers and sisters from across the sea with such delight as [I read] your letters of love from beyond the mountains.
(Alcuin, Epist. 186, MGH Epist. 4, Epist. Karol. Aevi 2, p. 311)

ALCUIN, POEM TO AN ABSENT FRIEND

I

Sweet love laments with tears an absent friend,
A distant land denies him to my sight.
Rare is the loyalty among men that makes dear friends.
In the whirlwind of activities, he alone remains in my breast.
Better than silver, more precious than red gold,
He shines brighter than all treasures,
Whom the [whole] will and mind desires and seeks
To have, to hold, to love and to worship.
You are that one for me, joined to me in great love,
You are peace to my mind, sweet love to me.
May God watch over you in all eternity,
May you remember your Albinus at all times and in all places.
Farewell!

2

Oh would that the moment of wished-for love might come.
When will that day be when I may see you,
O beloved of God, youth famed for your knowledge.
Life, health and happiness be yours through the ages;
May beauty, goodness and wisdom be with you forever,
Honor and devotion, the praise and the glory of Christ.

3

Take then these slight verses with you, my brother and friend,
    Bear me always in your mind as your friend.
As you wander through the fields, the hills, the forests and rivers
    May Christ always guard your path.
Thrive ever in the prayers of the saints
    Both now and always, sweet friend. Farewell!

4

We shall end this song with the tears welling up while I write,
But the love in our breast is never-ending.
I've written this song weeping, dearest one,
And I believe that merciful Christ will wipe away the streams
Of tears from my eyes, and on the day he shows me the sight of your
    face,
My heart will find rest.

5

God, be his guardian while he sleeps, I beg you,
    Keep his bed safe, Christ, beneath your shadow,
Lest the thief in the night should come to this hall to snatch him away.
    And I ask that you be always his special God:
For you, O Christ, are a faithful protector to your servants
    Throughout the wide world, dear king and father.

6

And you, my faithful table-mate, transfer your office here [to this court],
If it's sweet wine you're after, my sweet friend.
Find happiness, I beg you, as a man of high standing in this court,
For I shall hasten to give you sweet wines.
But I shall tell everyone of the wondrous ceremonies I perform,
Because it's not right, I assure you, to imbibe strong wine.

7

Be present now, Christ, to bless our rich banquets here,
So that the food may satisfy your servants.
Feed our souls, we beg you, and our bodies
With sweet nourishment, nurture and strengthen them always.
For in your generosity you gave food and drink in barren soil
To your people when they prayed aright.

8

The frost is at hand, O youths; gather branches from the forest,
For behold how the snow is snowing, see how it billows.
Run all together now and gather logs for the hearth,
If you want to warm your chilled limbs at the fire,
And work the bellows of your cheeks with frequent puffs
I beg you, and so warm these shivering brothers at the fire.
. . . .

10

Living with tempered mind, the pupil of Christ in the court,
Rejoicing only at the simplicity of the good man,
Loveable in your services and filled with pure love
Leading a peaceful life by the rule of quiet,
Beloved of the people and worthy of high honor . . .
[The poem breaks off]

(Carmen 55, MGH Poet. Lat. Aevi Carol. 1, pp. 266ff.)

Alcuin, Poem (probably to Arn of Salzburg)

Love has penetrated my breast with its flame [. . .]
And love always burns with new heat.
Neither sea, nor land, hills nor forests or mountains
May stop or hinder the way of him
Blessed father, who always licks your innards,
Or washes your chest, O beloved, with his tears.
Why, O sweet love, should you bring bitter tears,
And why make bitter draughts flow from sweet honey?
If your sweet delights, O world, are mixed with bitterness,
Then good fortune must quickly give way to adversity.
All joys change, sad to say, to mourning,
Nothing is forever, all things are changeable.
Let us therefore flee from you with all the strength of our heart,
O perishable world, as you also flee from us.
And let us seek the delights of heaven
And the kingdoms which do not perish, with all our heart, our mind,
　　our hand.
Happy is the court of heaven, which never abandons a friend;
The heart which burns with love always [a word missing] what it loves.
Hasten there, father, snatch me up with your prayers, I pray with you,
　　[and take me to the place]
Where our love will never suffer separation.
Look with a happy heart, we pray,
On the puny gifts that great love has sent.
Recall that our most gentle master praised the two pennies
That the poor widow cast into the treasury of the temple [Mark 12, 42]
Sacred love is better than all gifts
And firm loyalty which abides and grows strong.
May divine gifts both follow you and preceed,
Dearest father, always and everywhere. Farewell.

                    (Carmen 11, MGH Poet. Lat. Carol. Aevi 1, p. 236)

Hildesheim Letter Collection, Letter from a Master to His Student (composed ca. 1073–1085)

No sooner had I heard what I breathlessly desired, hardly had my ears, wide
open and tensed with expectation, taken in the news that your life, which is my

own, and your affairs, which I regard as mine, were secure, hardly had I taken in your salutation, when at once my soul was suffused with such joy that the simple and undivided Easter celebration which others were intent upon became for me a double festival. The one was the gross, palpable, and corporal festivity all were celebrating; the other, inspired by your letter, is mine alone, private and unique — the festive and spiritual celebration of your love. Departing from you was like a descent into grave and gloomy Egyptian darkness where my mind was held captive, and as long as my unrelenting quest for news of your fortunes was to no avail, I strayed through the obstacles of the iniquitous and hostile desert, my mind assailed by various anxieties. But upon receiving your divine letters, by which you deified me, I was as one led into his own promised land, and my mind was restored to certainty and happiness. Therefore as they once did upon their flight from Egypt in reality, so I also thought it now behooved me to make my own paschal burnt offering without delay to celebrate the escape from my inner Egypt.

But if the shadowed thought of you and your sun-like words gave me so great a cause and occasion for joy, how much greater, how much fuller when you will enrich me with your bodily presence, and I rejoice to embrace you and speak with you, exult in this joy, and my whole body dances inwardly! How long shall I be deprived of your presence with no consolation? How long shall I be separated from you, my lord and most beloved? How long will you seem to turn your face away from your servant as though in anger? [cf. Psalm 26.9 (Rev. Std., 27.9)] Whither or to what distant place do you flee? But lest you think that these tearful interrogations are the result of despair, [I assure you that] I anticipate no small future benefit from my effusions, because the more I seek you with my constant desire, the greater will be my satisfaction at the dear and sweet delight of some day being with you. I consider our separation nothing other than the discipline of conserving what is one day to be shared together [*conservande olim conservantie disciplinatio*].

But as to the matter of which you reminded me — as you would remind someone forgetful of you and oblivious of your honor, supposing I might find it negligible that you press me into the throng of those who yawn from apathy [cf. Terence, *Andria* 181] — that I should inquire about an opportunity for your studies: I have played the loyal servant to you, my lord (let me speak thus, though it is not especially appropriate). I have made of those who were merely masters most humble servitors for my faithful lord. I have praised you so much to so many Frenchmen, Normans and Germans as so good and glorious that even without having seen you, from report alone, they would kindly promise their loyal services. Even though I am quite worthless either in letters or in this order of virtue, nonetheless I who am humble, lowly, and weak, somehow

strive to raise you up to whatever pinnacle of honors there is. Now you, who
have received as a gift of nature the highest nobility, an impressive beauty of
bodily shape, see to it, keep on your guard, and be ever vigilant that your noble
humility should make you beloved of all, approved of all, the intimate friend of
all, and that your probity of most holy manners should win you favor. For by
these means the zeal of your servants is firmed up and the prosperity of your
affairs made stable.

But while my soul now rejoices on nearly all accounts, yet there is one
point on which it mourns and sorrows more than a little. I have heard that you
propose to study with that same Heribert who not only himself did not study
at Beauvais, but recklessly and foolishly discouraged others from doing so. If
you realize this plan, you will reap more disgrace than either honor or profit
from it. Never at any time would he have or have had the courage to presume
to unpack his wares in lecturing, unless from some part of a book he had from
me. Nor if he had remained yet in France would anyone have paid two cents
for his own readings.

Restrain your steps, let the cautious man flee the reputed fool.

For it is not a greater vice to know little or nothing than to submit to the
instruction of the foolish — which is none. I give this advice not only to you
but to all who might know him.

Would that you would remain for me the same as you have always been!
Neither shall I set myself bounds, nor abandon safe places.
Go, if you wish to see the Indians or the cruel Parthians,
Or if you wish rather to send me out to Gothic shores,
Your devoted servant is prepared to go to either.
Or whatever you wish, nothing will tear me from you,
Neither death nor the sword, neither life nor any angel.
Where you drink, I drink; where you go, I follow.

If this letter of yours — it is no longer mine — should deserve whipping for
any fault, and I fear it does, then let its flaws be submitted to your judgment
and no other. [My letters] rush on their way to you unkempt like barefoot
country girls to their boy friends, having hastened in the middle of the night
on their way to you their lover, frivolously uncomposed, forgetting their cosmetics. And so much the worse on this most sacred of nights [i.e., Easter]. For
this reason they deserve great and severe punishment. Castigate them well and
as befits foolish and frightened women; and return them to me chastened.

Although I may desire many things, I will never persuade you to come if
it is contrary to your well-being and honor; far be from me any motive of

lechery. Whatever you decide to do, you must let me know through your man by Pentecost, because I am considering a project and must come to a final decision by then, [. . .] [unintelligible phrase: *non sive quod tu sive quod e.u.*]. Greet d.g. [= *dominum G.?*] as much as you can for me, both his foundation and his progress [? *et fundamentum et consecutivum*]. Regard these things as spoken to you alone and in all seriousness.

(Hildesheim Letter Collection, Epist. 36, pp. 76–79)

LETTER OF R. OF MAINZ TO THE STUDENTS OF THE WORMS SCHOOL (1032)

To the elect youth of Worms who pursue vigorously the studies and the arts of the Athenians, R. of Mainz—no Greek himself, in fact hardly risen to Latinity—[sends his wishes for] seamless friendship and unshaken fidelity.

The desire to receive the love of all has compelled us and compels us still to participate in the friendship of all good men, so that what we cannot dream of attaining through our own merits, we may at least attain through their support. Our wish to enter into such a love with you is all the more ardent and eager, since you have always cultivated the reverence of friends with such fervent and abundant piety. And we are grateful to you over and over again for your willingness to receive us into the community of your friendship with a pact of such intimate charity and such sincere affection.

And yet once the enmity between you and the Würzburg colleagues was reported to us and we learned that some practical advice is called for, we decided that it would be preferable for us to refrain from offering counsel lest now any trouble be thrust upon them through our instigation. And, consistent with our wishes to maintain the bond of friendship with all good men, we strive not to forfeit your affection while at the same time not offending them. So that we may enjoy the favor of all, therefore, we zealously strive, with our thoughts and our words in harmonious union, to be the advocates of all. And so in truth we know that it behooves the head placed in its lofty position to provide equally for all the appendages attached to it . . . We ask and we beg your diligence to recognize this point: that we desire your well-being no less ardently than theirs.

We ask you therefore to act as befits wise men who do nothing without counsel: call again for aid and counsel upon those whose advice has guided you in this matter from the outset, and as for those who have thus far been spared these matters, do not trouble them to judge any man, now that the affair, with God's aid, is so close to a positive conclusion . . .

But now lest I who have flown so far on the wings of Icarus should plunge into the great sea rushing past below, I shall for a while remain silent and choose salubrious leisure, hoping humbly that God will send you his guardian angel of peace to protect you and them lovingly. Farewell.

(*Ältere Wormser Briefsammlung*, Epist. 26, ed. Bulst, pp. 48–49)

BAUDRI OF BOURGUEIL, POEM TO A HAUGHTY BOY

Nothing pleases me but what is decorously pleasing,
Nor does anything displease me but what is displeasing.
Alexis is the proof of this, if you require proof.
It is agreed that whatever in you either pleases or displeases me
By rights should indeed please or displease me in you.
But now let us ask what should and what should not please:
Your appearance pleases, because it is both decent and beautiful:
Your downy cheeks, your blond hair and modest lips please;
Your voice is honey and balm to my ears,
Since it sings as sweetly as the sweet nightingale
Not yet fixed between girl's and boy's voice.
You will be a second Orpheus, unless age spoils your voice,
Age, which draws the line between girls and boys
When the cheek is clothed with the first down of youth
And the curve of the nose lends beauty to the face.
Your bright eyes touch me to the heart and core;
For I take these luminous orbs to be the constellation Gemini.
Your white skin and ivory breast suit these well.
A touch from this snowy body gives the hands sportive pleasure.
These are the things that properly should please me and others.
Especially since the lusts of youth do not stimulate you
Nor turn the divine art of your body into a reproach.
All this pleases me, all this I commend to my care.
I praise you for refusing to be Ganymede to Jove,
And I beg and urge you not to be corrupted by love.
But I have no praise for your rude manners:
It is crude to sport such haughtiness
That you'll hardly honor anyone with a sideways glance,
That with pursed lips and nose in the air you'll hardly ever deign to greet
    anyone,
Until at long last he has greeted you first.
Perhaps you think you alone rule on earth.

And you consider yourself a boy more excellent than others.
Narcissus, who lives in fable, was stand-offish too
And he gives an example to the haughty to relent.
Yours is not the only excellence in the world,
Nor will you rule alone on the earth:
The earth bears many trees and many lilies,
Many violets and many pleasant flowers.
Nor are you the only one on earth who is both chaste and beautiful.
There are many formed by greater beauty than yours
And commended by ivory coldness.
Chaste you are, and frosts have made many a one chaste;
Lovely you are, and nature has made many lovely.
Do not be arrogant because of what Nature has given you.
You are not the reason Nature creates.
She grants to many what she has briefly granted you,
And she puts one donkey in charge of another.
Stiff-necked and puffed up, you walk with your nose in the air.
Just this is what I blame, what I condemn in you.
This is a disgrace to you; this is what displeases me in you.
I despise your haughty airs and your unbending pose,
Your hard heart and your uncivil manners,
I despise pompous and flinty-hearted youths.
I love a humble appearance and despise a stiff neck.
Therefore if you wish, boy, to please me,
Put aside these lofty airs,
Smile at him who smiles at you, make fitting responses.
Learn to soften that stiff head and rigid eyes,
Learn a modest set of your eyes and to use them well.
You are a man; do not cock your head like a conceited boy.
Leave a savage gaze to the beasts; you are a man.
Be a graceful boy; and leave a stiff neck to the bulls:
You are a man; do not behave like a beast.
Your confidence in your beauty is too great.
Believe me: corrosive age will take your beauty from you.
The corruptible flesh will perish in a day;
When your dignity and beauty, the blossom on your skin — your pride
       and joy —
Will fade in an instant, when you will become someone else,
When your skin will shrivel and your flesh will decay,
When your lungs fill with fluid and coughing tortures you,
When the decay of your liver stirs up intestinal warfare.

Nature will one day reclaim those gifts she has lent you.

Therefore, O doom-destined youth, never again act with beastly
    arrogance,

Nor ever set a savage aspect in place of a lovely form.

If you wish my service, take heed of these verses.

In telling what pleases and what displeases me in you,

Let the reader judge whether my reproaches are just.

My complaint is certainly just, as is my lament.

You can satisfy it by correcting yourself.

(Carmen no. 3, ed. Hilbert, pp. 15–17)

MARBOD OF RENNES, "ON THE GOOD WOMAN"

In all things we receive from a generous God for the use of mankind, we think nothing more beautiful, nothing better than a good woman, who is flesh of our flesh and whose flesh we are flesh of, whom we justly love, urged by a law of nature as a social good even when she offends us. For, being the same creature, we live under the same condition and there is nothing which we do not bear in common, being in all things alike except for the distinction of sex. We are conceived in the same way, we eat the same foods, dress alike, our sadness and tears are moved by the same feelings, we judge with like intelligence what is good what is evil, what is just, what is sinful, and our mutual sentiments flow with equal eloquence. Amidst our peers we can perform equal duties: show gratitude, assign appropriate gifts, and give helpful counsel.

All these things man and woman can do in common, something we know is denied to brute animals. Many covet and confess their desire for these creatures which lack reason. But they have life and motion, and stand in the second rank of nature in relation to us.

All the growing things of the earth, herbs and flowers, nurtured and cultivated by heat mixed with moisture, which gives increase and generative power—human beings admire their beauty, knowing full well that they lack a soul and their life consists of growth. Thus the third rank instructs us to esteem them less.

Clothing, silver, jewels and gold, all that lacks vitality and yet is pleasant to look on, while very far removed from our mode of life, are assigned by the law of nature to the fourth rank, yet have admirable qualities, though denied life and motion.

Therefore since the dignity of woman is greater than all these things, more beautiful than silver, more precious than gold, more precious than gems, which lack the light of reason, we think it abundantly proven that she is more to be wondered at and more to be cherished.

We are joined by a bond of nature in just love, and while these issues, which each sex shares equally, arise from a single order of nature, still they are suited no less to men than to women.

But there are many things in which women's activity is preeminent and by which woman establishes her place in the world. Without her the race of mankind would perish altogether. For what good are your seeds lacking a field? Who could be a father if no woman were mother? Not to mention the hard and difficult trials of a pregnant woman, or the agonizing moments of painful labor by which our mother brought us in deep suffering to the light of day, soon forgetting those pains when compensated with a child. Who, I ask, pays back this debt with an appropriate love? Or who can claim he had no mother?

In many minor requirements of communal life, it is woman alone who ministers to you. For who, if not a woman, will take up the job of nourishing, without which no child can sustain life? Who will card the wool and linen? Who will endure turning the spindle, spinning and weaving?

But these things are so much a part of our life that the level of culture would be lowered if they were absent. And besides this, many other things that domestic life requires are more efficiently cared for by the special feminine skill, and she takes on many things that we in our arrogance pass over. She has a gentle touch in caring for the sick, and she assists with greater skill at the bedside, she prepares food and drink more diligently. Woman loves more and is better able to adapt precepts and to be shaped into the image of the Good like soft wax. The hard mind and stiff neck of man rebels against and hardly will take the yoke, denying all the time his inferiority. And furthermore the pursuit of virtue is more laudable in the more frail sex, her transgressions are minor. [Now follow a series of biblical and classical examples of the greater virtue and fortitude of women and the greater sinfulness of men (74–119).]

From these examples and from the arguments at the beginning of this song it is clear that woman deserves no blame for her womanhood alone, nor does man deserve praise for his manhood, but rather vice is blameworthy in both sexes, and virtue is equally praiseworthy in both.

(*Liber decem capitulorum*, "De muliere bona," ed. Leotta, pp. 112–130)

FROM THE REGENSBURG LOVE SONGS

It is a small gift we send and one useful to our manners and good
     character,

We thought it the least we could do at festive times.
Or rather it is our love that gives you these gifts, brother,
Fashioned of thought, not physical matter.
They are prompted by our lawful duties along with the telling flames [of
love],
And wish to show you that your poor sisters are not entirely without
resources.
They are the three daughters of Mercury and Philology,
Whom the father of genius has sent to serve us,
Lest our studies falter, bent under foolish tasks.
The wise Greeks called the first Euprophore,
Who receives good friends [lovers?] with affable and courteous speech.
The second is Eugiale, who duteously serves the guests thus received.
Placed third is Basilea [Basithea], the epitome of virtue,
Who enhances all she does through her chaste and decorous behavior.
We will give you these ladies, if you will, for your intimate use.
But with the proviso that you lead a special way of life,
Remaining far from those hostesses whose minds are as vagrant as their
bodies.
It is decorous for you serenely to venerate these three loyal maidens
wherever you are.
The warm waters of your birthplace make you glow with fire,
That wholesome fire by which love of virtue should be kindled.

(Regensburg Songs no. 27 (Paravicini, 36).

Adapted from Dronke's translation, Medieval Latin and the Rise, 2: 432)

EXCERPTS FROM "LETTERS OF TWO LOVERS," THE LOST LOVE LETTERS OF ABELARD AND HELOISE

Epistle No. 5 (Heloise to Abelard)

O faith of my joyous hope and my own with all devotion, for as long as I live,
may the bestower of all art and the bountiful enricher of the human mind fill
my innermost breast with skill in the art of philosophy, so that I can greet you
accordingly in my letters, most beloved, and beg your consent to my desires.

Farewell, farewell, hope of my youth.

(Epistolae duorum amantium, ed. Könsgen, p. 4)

Epistle No. 11 (Abelard to Heloise)

Oh you most famous vessel of all virtues and more sweet than honey, you my most faithful love and other part of my soul and my own in all loyalty. . . . God, from whom there neither is nor can be secrets, is my witness how purely, how sincerely, with what loyalty I love you. . . .

Now then, since I have not the leisure to write, I shout out a hundred wishes for your well-being, and I repeat it a thousand times. May your well-being surpass all.

(p. 11)

Epistle No. 22 (Abelard to Heloise)

He who without you is enshrouded in profound obscurity greets his jewel radiant with gentle light, may you glory incessantly in your natural splendor. The physicists are wont to tell us that the moon would not shine without the sun. Thus, deprived of this light, and bereft of all benefit of heat and radiance it shows to mortals a bleak and pallid sphere. Clearly the similitude of this thing is evident in you and me. For you are my sun, who always set me afire and illumine me with the jocund splendor of your face. I have no light if not from you. Without you I am dull, dark, frail, dead.

And, to confess the truth, it is a greater thing that you should accommodate me than that the sun should accommodate the moon: because the moon, approaching the sun, grows paler; I, the more I am moved by you, the closer I come to you, all the more do I burn, and so inflamed am I that, as you yourself have often observed, I become altogether flame, I am consumed to my very heart.

To what can I compare your innumerable gifts? for your sweet words are surpassed by such an abundance of deeds, that you seem to me poorer in words than in deeds. Amidst all those innumerable gifts by which you surpass all others, this is the most distinguished: that you do more than you say for your friend, poor in words, overflowing with deeds, and this is all the more glorious for you as deeds are more difficult than words. . . .

You are entombed for eternity in my breast. From this grave you will never rise as long as I live: there you lay yourself down, there you find repose. Until you join me in my dreams, you will not leave me in my dreams, but no sooner is my dream past and I open my eyes, than I see you before the light of heaven.

To others I direct my words, while my intentions stray to you. I trip again and again in my speech, since my thoughts wander elsewhere. Who then can deny that you are truly buried in me? . . .

Time, envious of our love, presses me, and yet you delay, as if we had leisure. Farewell.

(pp. 10–11)

Epistle No. 24 (Abelard to Heloise)

My soul, than which the earth can put forth nothing more radiant, nothing more dear to me, the flesh, which that same soul makes breathe and be moved, all that I owe my soul [I give to you] through whom I breathe and move.

The copious and always insufficient bounty of your letters proves two things to me most clearly, namely, your love and your loyalty. That is the meaning of the saying, "When the heart is full, the mouth speaks." . . .

I receive your letters so avidly since they are never long enough for me: they both inflame and satisfy my desire. I am like a man laboring in flames whom even a drink refreshes the more, the more it burns him. I swear to God that whenever I read them attentively, I am moved anew, in some new way, for my soul is cut by a joyous shudder, and my body is transformed, its bearing, its gestures are new. Those are truly praiseworthy letters, which impel the mind of the listener precisely where they want.

You often ask me, sweet soul of mine, what love is, nor can I excuse myself through ignorance, as if you were asking me about something of which I am ignorant. Now love has subjected me so completely to its reign that it is no longer a thing outside of me, but rather a member of my family and my household, or rather a thing residing inside me. Love then is a certain power of the soul which has no existence in itself nor is self-contained, but rather constantly flows out with a strong appetite and desire into another, and constantly longs to become identical with that other, so that of two separate wills one new being without distinction may be created. . . .

You must know that love, though it is a universal thing, yet it is so narrowed and reduced that I may boldly affirm that it now reigns in us and us alone, that it has made its home in me and in you. For the two of us have a love that is complete, watchful, pure; for nothing is sweet or restful to one of us unless it is sweet and restful in common; we approve equally and we reject equally; our understanding of all things is the same. It is easy to prove this assertion, because you often anticipate my thoughts; when I am planning to write something, you write it first, and, if I remember correctly, you have said the same thing about yourself.

Farewell, and as I you, so you too look upon me with inexhaustible love.

(pp. 13–14)

Epistle No. 50 (Abelard to Heloise)

To you, the only disciple of philosophy among all the girls of our age, the only one to receive all the gifts of the manifold virtues from Fortune, to you who alone are beautiful and comely, from him who only lives when he is certain of your favor. . . . You speak truly, oh sweetest of all women, when you say that the love that joins us is not the kind that joins those who seek their advantage, those who look for profit in friendship, those whose faith stands and falls with Fortune . . . those to whom in the end nothing is sweet that does not bring profit.

Not Fortune, but God has joined us with a different bond. I have chosen you from among many thousands for your innumerable virtues. The sole advantage I sought was to repose in you, to find consolation for all suffering in you, to seek of all worldly goods in your beauty alone refreshment and release from sorrows. You are my feast when I hunger, my drink when I thirst, my rest when I am tired, my warmth in cold, my shade from the heat. . . .

You have deigned to take notice of me perhaps because of some good opinion you may have formed of me. In many ways I am not your equal, to tell the truth in all ways I am not your equal, because you surpass me in the very things in which I seem to excel. Your genius, your eloquence, have grown strong beyond what your age and your sex can achieve. What about your humility, your affability that pleases all, your restraint and great dignity. Do they not elevate you above all others, do they not raise you aloft so that thence like a candelabra you may shed light and be marveled at by all?

(pp. 28–30)

THE METAMORPHOSIS OF GOLIAS

I

In that season when the sun had left the sign of the ram and entered that of the bull, when the face of the earth was adorned anew with flowers, I lay down beneath a pine whose buds were just new blown to refresh my tired limbs.

2

It seemed to me that I stepped into a forest glade whose foliage was just bursting forth from every side. Here winter's frost had wrought no harm nor disturbed the beauty of the place.

3

A gentle breeze murmured all about the glade, and the forest resounded with its steady gusts, and the rustle of its raucous force everywhere echoed forth sweet sounds.

4

In the very middle of that place, the forest fronds, forming as it were a host of tympanies, sounded forth a melody so sweet as to rival the last song of the swan.

5

From the epitrite, the sexcuple, the double union, there arises a harmony in consonant modulation, a harmony akin to that produced by those who sing on Mt. Helicon, and the entire glade resounds in proportion.

6

For when the breeze set the heart of the fronds to trembling and directed its steady beat against the branches, there resounded the chords of the diatessaron and the diapente, with the intervening semi-tone mixed in.

7

But now from the elevated part of the forest there arose a voice singing in tones more distinct, as a harmonious answer from on high to those in the lower parts, and now both strains rang out in mutual concord.

8

Here are heard the voices of sweet-singing birds, so that the forest rang with the sound of their complaints, a sound which in its diversity of harmonies prefigures the order of the seven planets.

9

The middle of the glade opened onto a broad meadow, tinged purple with violets and other flowers, and when I breathed in their sweet fragrance, it seemed to me as if I were born anew.

10

In that same meadow there stood a royal temple, raised up, its foundation of solid jasper, its walls the color of blue silk, its roof golden, covered with pictures inside and out.

11

When I glimpsed this scene, it dawned on me that that secret place contained divine mysteries that Vulcan must have forged with special art, everything bearing a concealed meaning, everything a symbol.

12

Here were depicted the nine sisters of Helicon, all the circles of the celestial region, and along with these and many other things, the fate of Adonis and the chains which caught Mars and Venus.

13

This same place is the temple of the universe, containing the patterns of all things and the objects formed from them, which the wondrous creator, master of the world, called into being and arranged in accordance with his Goodness.

14

From within I hear a richly modulated harmony, as if the goddesses themselves were convening here. For every instrument sings out in its individual voice, urging happiness.

15

The din of voices I heard in there is the proportional concord of things. For just as the voice of any one instrument is consonant with itself, in the same way all things are joined by a proportional musical nexus.

16

Within I see the king sitting on his high throne, leaning regally on his scepter, his consort at his side, both of them administering the things subject to them.

17

The king symbolizes that energy inherent in all things, though he stands for other things as well. The queen is that force which governs all the workings of the world, bringing forth the fruit of the trees, making the earth fecund.

18

The virgin Pallas went forth from the forehead of the king, who bound her at his side with a firm knot. Her face is altogether covered with a veil, nor does she unveil it to any but her initiates.

19

She is the mind of the Highest, the mind of divinity, commanding nature with laws and destinies, imposing in nature the laws and destinies she commands, the incomprehensible substance of Godhead, freed of the narrow straits of our puny state.

20

I see Mercury the celestial legate standing at the left hand of the deity, dressed all in purple as befits a bridegroom, his face lightly shaded with down.

21

By calling him a messenger I meant to point to the way in which graceful eloquence joins men together in bonds of affection; if I said that his face was shaded by down, it was to indicate the way in which elegance ought to lend color to your speech.

22

His bride, born of the family of the gods, is at his side, dressed in green and white silk, her face ruddier than a dewy rose which heat cannot wilt nor cold scar.

23

Unless speech is wed to wisdom, it is a vagabond, dissolute and impotent, and, profiting little, it advances little, like a ship off course for want of a pilot.

24

Prudence bestows wisdom as her own special gift. On the nuptial day in the congress of gods, she places the wreath on the virgin's brow, and the temple radiates with the glow cast from this gem in its midst.

25

The wreath signifies forethought, which lends circumspection to one's acts. The gem in the middle of the wreath symbolizes reason, whose task is to precede all action.

26

The magnificent sun wears a wreath on its head, from which innumerable rays break forth in all directions. The mystery here is neither hidden nor unapproachable. Rather its meaning is perfectly evident.

27

His face had a thousand different shapes and forms, the diadem on his head bright and unspoiled. This is the eye of the world and the maker of days, the life spirit and vital nourishment of living things.

28

Before the god stood four urns, redolent of the elements of all things, of bronzes varied in their appearance. These designate the four seasons of the year.

29

The residents of Helicon carry their instruments, as the perfect complement to this joy, and with their playing they applaud those divine secrets which seem to contain a mystical truth.

30

Nine there are in their order, the nine sang together, the nine held new lyres in their hands, and though with their fingers they strummed diverse strings, yet the resultant refrain was in full harmony.

31

What they represent is easily told. That good artificer created nine planets; eight of them give forth music, the ninth remains silent, for without motion there is nothing to give rise to sound.

32

Or perhaps they stand for the gifts which the artificer bestowed on Psyche, girding her about, clothing her, stamping their image on her as she descended through the circles of heaven during her trip to that frail dwelling, the flesh.

33

Three virgins stood there near Jove and turning toward him, embracing each other firmly, their arms intertwined. Their bodies facing in one direction, their faces in the other, all three of them are descended from the highest deity.

34

Largess is considered a gift of God. Let a gift received soon be repaid; let its memory be firmly held, so that things given singly may be returned twofold.

35

Now the silence is shattered by the shrill rattling of tambourines as Sylenus leads out a host of satyrs. Drunk and staggering he leads the dance, provoking laughter in one or two of the gods.

36

For the most part Venus reigns supreme in this crowd. Here one does homage to her, there another renders her service. At her side, as always, is her son, a naked boy and blind, his gaze aloof.

37

Naked, because his intentions can never be suppressed; blind, because reason has no power over him; a boy, because youth tends to wantonness; aloof, because he seldom stays long in one place.

38

The spear he brandishes is golden, curved slightly at its tip, a spear that never misses its mark, a formidable spear, since he who is pierced by it banishes chastity.

39

Pallas alone does combat with Venus, and does her worst with all her power. For Pallas disdains all that is pleasing to Venus, and Venus rarely keeps company with chastity.

40

Here various men and various attitudes do battle with each other who are unwilling to break with their accustomed habits. The battle rages among them whether Pallas or Aphrodite is the more worthy.

41

Psyche is held captive by the embraces of Cupid; Mars burns in fire for spouse Nerina; Janus shudders to part from his Argyo; only their offspring, Foresight, deserves to be loved.

42

Psyche is spellbound in the delights of the flesh; fate fluctuates in Mars; Nereus strays aimlessly; the artificer delights in his handiwork; what will happen afterward, God only knows.

43

The philosophers were present. Thales stood there wet, Crisippus with his numbers, Zeno weighed things out, Eraclius was afire, Perdix made circles, Samius set all things in proportion.

44

While Cicero implicated, Plato explicated; now Apius dissuades, now Cato persuades. Foolish Archelias considered fixed in space things located everywhere and nowhere.

45

Hysopullus brought his lady Ceta with him, Propertius brings Cynthia, Tibullus Delia, Tullius Terencia, Catullus Lesbia. The poets convened here, each with his beloved.

46

Each lady is fire and flame for her lover. The spark inflames Pliny for Calpurnia, Apuleius burns for his Prudentilla, everywhere the lover holds her beloved in her embraces.

47

They begin to create verses, modulating their meters variously, rattling off smooth-flowing, elegant ones, some in hendecasyllables, others in running meters. All they sing is elegant, nothing is rustic.

48

Here also that doctor of Chartres is present whose sharp tongue cuts like a sword. And with him is the bishop of Poitiers, prelate of prelates, the knight and castellan proper for all those seeking wedlock.

49

Amidst these and others in the remote glade was to be found the master who lives at the Petit Pont. Truth to tell, he disputed with thrusts of his I-shaped fingers and whatever he spoke became clear and intelligible in itself.

50

We saw the celebrated theologian of Lombardy, and along with Ivo, Peter Helias and Bernard, whose speech is balm and spikenard, and of these, many are devotees of Abelard.

51

Reginald the monk contended clamorously, cutting short this man and that with his subtle speech. He refuted one after another, not a man to sink into himself in contemplation, this man who caught even our Porphyry in his snares.

52

Present also is Robert the Theologian, a man pure of heart, and Manerius, second to none, lofty of spirit and profound of speech, no man on earth is more subtle.

53

Bartholomew is here also with his sharp features, rhetorician, dialectician, sharp of tongue, and likewise Robert Amiclas followed him along with many whom I pass over, not to diminish their number.

54

But now the bride seeks her courtier, her man of Pallet; where is he whose divine spirit altogether outshone all others; she longs to know why he withdraws and journeys about in other realms, whom she had nurtured at her own breast and bosom.

55

The throng of those educated by the philosopher cry out in protest: the monk-cowled primate of the monk-cowled tribe, thrice wrapped round in imprisoning tunics, has had silence imposed on so great a prophet.

56

This is the flock of evil, the flock of perdition, that wicked and impious brood of Pharaoh, putting on an outward show of religion, beneath which glows the spark of superstition.

57

This scum of a people, this sterile band, the cupidity of whose mind knows no bounds: flee them and shun them, snub them and make no answer, neither "yea" nor "nay."

58

The gods now pass judgment, and the decree stands: This flock shall be banished from the gathering, their ears stopped to the secrets of philosophy, their studies confined to the dungheap of the mechanical arts.

59

Let not any judgment rendered by so high a court be thought invalid, but rather let it be firmly obeyed: This monkish flock should be despised, therefore, and expelled from the schools of philosophy.

Amen

("Metamorphosis Goliae," ed. R. B. C. Huygens)

Notes

OF	Old French
PBB	Beiträge zur Geschichte der deutschen Sprache und Literatur
PL	Patrologia Latina, ed. J. P. Migne
RB	Revue Bénédictine
RS	Rerum Britannicarum medii aevi scriptores: Rolls Series
RTAM	Recherches de théologie ancienne et médiévale
TRE	Theologische Realenzyklopädie
ZfdPh	Zeitschrift für deutsche Philologie
ZrPh	Zeitschrift für romanische Philologie

Preface

1. *De quatuor gradibus violentae charitatis*, PL 196, 1207C.

2. *Leges Heinrici Primi*, ch. 49, 5a, ed. L. J. Downer (Oxford: Oxford University Press, 1972), p. 164. The passage is the central text in Michael Clanchy's study, "Law and Love in the Middle Ages."

Introduction

1. The model for Lear-Cordelia in Geoffrey of Monmouth's *History of the Kings of Britain* (ca. 1135) cautions against raising Shakespeare's adaptation into a marker of a one-time shift in Western sensibilities, however.

2. I.e., if the terms of the contest had not been carefully arranged in advance and agreed upon in private. Kings making major acts of state can tolerate surprises even less than modern diplomats and heads of state.

3. See the case of Sir Robert Carey demanding pay from Elizabeth of England, in Greenblatt, *Renaissance Self-Fashioning*, pp. 165–66.

4. Kent, King Lear's most loyal servant, is outraged by the king's disowning his daughter, not by the method he devises to determine his succession. He himself talked the talk of royal love. The king says to him, "Thou serv'st me, and I'll love thee" (1.4.89). The Shakespeare concordance shows the word "love" used as often to refer to the emotional ties between kings and courtiers as between young men and women.

5. Balzac, *The Lily of the Valley*, p. 195.

6. This assumes of course that, say, the Princess of Clèves is more a representative figure than the Marquis de Sade. The logic of Lady Arabella may also have been at work in the latter case, however.

7. My debt to John Boswell's *Christianity, Social Tolerance, and Homosexuality* (hereafter *CSTH*) but also my rejection of his premise that love between men in some sense implied homosexuality and that sex between men was casually tolerated prior to the thirteenth century, will be evident throughout. Love between men was widely admired, but sexual relations between men were not.

Chapter 1: Problems of Reading the Language of Passionate Friendship

1. Roger of Hovedon (Benedict of Peterborough), *Gesta Regis Heinrici II*, p. 7.

2. See Vern Bullough, "The Sin Against Nature and Homosexuality," and Brundage, *Law, Sex, and Christian Society in Medieval Europe* (late Middle Ages).

3. Roger of Hovedon, p. 126.

4. This is also clear in the chronicler's use of the phrase, "he loved him as his own soul" [dilexit eum rex . . . quasi animam suam]. It is a common enough phrase, but here it is probably an intentional reminiscence of the love of David and Jonathan: "Dilexit eum Ionathan quasi animam suam" (1 Samuel, 18.1); "diligebat enim eum quasi animam suam" (18.3); "sicut animam enim suam ita diligebat eum" (20.17). But the stress on intense love and lasting fidelity is puzzling and problematic given that their relationship quickly moved over to fierce competition. See John Baldwin, *The Government of Philip Augustus*, pp. 20–22.

5. Another witness describes the truce in some detail without indicating anything more than the restoration of peace and friendship. Gervase of Canterbury, *The Chronicle of the Reigns of Stephen, Henry II, and Richard I.*, p. 1.

6. In a later passage a mysterious hermit chastises Richard for "the vice of Sodom." (See below.)

7. MGH Poetae 1.236, no. 11, lines 2ff.

8. *Admonitio generalis*, MGH Leges 2, *Capitularia regum Francorum* 1.57, no. 22, article 49 (strict punishment for those who "sin against nature with animals or men").

9. Epist. 249, pp. 451–52. Boswell understates the force of the letter. It is one of the harshest this gentle man ever wrote: the student, Alcuin writes, is risking his former master's love, his own social position, and his own soul, by his indiscretions. Alcuin: don't cloud your reputation "with black blemishes" [*maculis nigris*]; "Where is your fear of hell? Your hopes of glory? Why do you not shudder to perpetrate what you should have been prohibiting to others?"; "Change your ways, I beg you" and pray "for your soul which will burn in the flames of Sodom"; correct "your most foul deeds" [*foedissima facta tua*]; he conjures the "terror" of the great judge, begs the student to "break the chain of this diabolical suggestion and of impious consent." Boswell on the letter (*CSTH* p. 191): "[Alcuin] registers no shock or outrage, simply annoyance . . . his primary objection is that the behavior in question is puerile, unbecoming to a scholar, and apt to lead to a bad reputation."

10. Epist. 120, *Anselmi Opera Omnia*, ed. F. S. Schmitt, 3.258–59. See the commentary by R. W. Southern, *St. Anselm and His Biographer*, pp. 72ff. On Anselm's letters of friendship, see also Adele M. Fiske, *Friends and Friendship in the Monastic Tradition* Sect. 15, pp. 1–32; Boswell, *CSTH*, pp. 218–20; B.P. McGuire, "Love, Friendship and Sex in the Eleventh Century: The Experience of Anselm," and his *Friendship and Community*, pp. 210–21.

11. See Southern, *St. Anselm and His Biographer*, p. 72.

12. See Boswell's reflections on the language of desire and love: *CSTH* and *Same Sex Unions*.

13. Eve Kosofsky Sedgwick, *Between Men*. The context of homosocial desire in early Christianity and the Middle Ages is, of course, very different from that which situates Sedgwick's texts. It excludes the female mediation which is the startling element in her book.

14. Against applying "homosexual"–"heterosexual" to earlier periods, Foucault, *History of Sexuality* 2.187–93. See also David Halperin, *One Hundred Years of Homosexuality*. Against Halperin's "social constructionism" ruling out the homo-/heterosexual dichotomy as anachronistic, see the review article by Ralph Hexter, "Scholars and Their Pals."

15. A question addressed by Niklas Luhmann in *Love as Passion*. He argues the socially constructed character of the experience.

16. *A History of Private Life*, 2.3–33 (Intro.), esp. pp. 4–7.

17. Peyer, *The Bridling of Desire*, pp. 14–15, points out that there is no word in medieval languages equivalent to the modern "sex." See also Baldwin, *The Language of Sex*. It is of course possible to find the regulators and moralizers commenting on sexuality, but not the participants in the culture of love and friendship.

18. Konstan points out a passage in Horace's *Satire* 2.5.32–33, where a social climber accosts a man in the street and declares, "'Your virtue has made me a friend of yours,'" with the clear intention of pinning on himself a badge of virtue. See *Friendship in the Classical World*, p. 159.

19. Cf. the report on a survey of women's responses to President Bill Clinton in the *International Herald-Tribune*, November 21, 1996, p. 9: "Women Turned Out for Clinton Because Power Is a Turn-On."

20. See the studies on charisma and royal power by Max Weber, conveniently collected in *Max Weber on Charisma and Institution Building*; Bloch, *Les rois thaumaturges*; Kantorowicz, *The King's Two Bodies*; Geertz, "Centers, Kings, and Charisma."

21. First Duino Elegy: "Die Schönheit ist des Schrecklichen Anfang, den wir noch gerade ertragen. / Wir bewundern es so, weil es gelassen verschmäht, uns zu zerstören."

22. "To His Highness . . . in the West . . . 1646," in R. S., *Shorter Poems and Translations*, ed. W. Bawcutt (Liverpool, 1964), p. 71. Cited and discussed in Smuts, *Court Culture and the Origins of a Royalist Tradition in Early Stuart England*, p. 245.

23. Also related is the experience known as "Stockholm syndrome." Terrorists take over a bank, threaten to kill the hostages, but then do not. One reaction of hostages under these circumstances is to experience gratitude, loyalty, even love for their captors. See F. Ochberg, "The Victim of Terrorism: Psychiatric Considerations," *Terrorism* 1 (1978), 147–68; Georges Gachnochi and Norbert Skurink, "The Paradoxical Effects of Hostage-Taking," *International Social Science Journal* 44 (1992), 235–46. (My thanks to Nehemia Friedland and Thomas Wallsten for these references.) See also the interesting report of the hostage-taking in Stockholm that gave its name to the "syndrome": Daniel Neil, "The Bank Drama," *New Yorker*, November 25, 1974, 56ff.

24. Odo of Cluny, *Vita Geraldi* 1.30, PL 133, 660A: " . . . he was loved by all because he himself loved all." Ibid., 1.25, 657B: " . . . the citizens and clerics of his territory . . . loved him with the affection due a father."

25. Middle Latin, *amor* also means "token" of love, or of service. See Niermeyer, *amor*. The Middle High German word *minne* (love) also has the meaning of "gift." Lexer, *MHD Taschenwörterbuch*, p. 140 (thanks to Britta Simon for this reference).

26. See Gerd Althoff, *Verwandte, Freunde und Getreue*; Francis Gentry, Triuwe *and* Vriunt *in the Nibelungenlied*.

27. See Gerd Althoff, "Empörung, Tränen, Zerknirschung." Also various essays in *Anger's Past*, ed. Barbara Rosenwein.

28. See Carl Schmidt, *Jus primae noctis: Eine geschichtliche Untersuchung* (Freiburg,

1881); Frances Litvack, *Le droit du seigneur in European and American Literature*; Alain Boureau, *Le droit de cuissage: la fabrication d'un mythe (XIIIe-XXe siècle* (Paris: Michel, 1995).

29. See Perella, *The Kiss Sacred and Profane*.

30. See Boswell, *Same-Sex Unions in Premodern Europe*, esp. pp. 61–65.

31. See Foucault, *The History of Sexuality*, esp. vol. 2. Also Konstan, *Friendship in the Classical World*.

32. See the entry "Homosexuality" by David Halperin in *Encyclopedia of Gay Histories and Cultures*, ed. George Haggerty, (New York: Garland, 1999).

33. English translation in John Boswell, *CSTH*, pp. 381–389.

34. Hovedon, *Chronica*, pp. 288–89. It is worth quoting the words of the hermit, which are confused in the translation of Henry Riley: "Esto memor subversionis Sodomae, et ab illicitis te abstine; sin autem, veniet super te ultio digna Dei." After some struggles, the king succeeds in giving up his "illicit" practices and correcting the "fetidness of his life" (*vitae suae foeditas*). He did penance and received his wife back, whom he had long neglected: " . . . abjecto concubitu illicito, adhaesit uxori suae, et facti sunt duo in carne una." For the dossier on the question of Richard's possible homosexuality, see Boswell, *CSTH*, pp. 231ff.; Brundage, *Richard Lionheart*, pp. 88ff., 287ff. Ulrike Kessler is skeptical about Richard's homosexuality: *Richard I. Löwenherz: König, Kreuzritter, Abenteurer*.

35. Cf. Boswell's treatment of Augustine and Aelred of Rievaulx in *CSTH*, pp. 134–35 and 222ff. Boswell does not deal with the problems posed for his interpretation by the loathing both men expressed in regard to their carnal leanings. They are difficult to resolve in terms of a tolerance or even indifference to homosexuality, but easy in terms of a tension between exalting and debasing friendship. See also Brian McGuire's analysis of Aelred's sexuality in *Brother and Lover*, esp. pp. 39–52, 59–67.

Chapter 2: Virtue and Ennobling Love

1. Aristotle, *Nicomachean Ethics*, 9.12.3, 1172a.

2. Plutarch, *Dialogue on Love*, 762B–D.

3. Andreas Capellanus, *De amore*, 1. 4, trans. Walsh (with liberties taken here), p. 39.

4. The exceptions to the statement grow in the course of the twelfth century, when sexuality itself became a subject of a discourse that developed without a particular interest in subjecting sexuality to the ethics of love. See Baldwin, *The Language of Sex*. On antiquity, see esp. Foucault's analysis in *History of Sexuality*, 2: 35–93. The best current guide to scholarship is David Konstan's *Friendship in the Classical World*, with extensive bibliography.

5. *Symposium*, 180C–184B. Cf. Plato, Seventh letter, 332C–334B: two types of friendship, one vulgar and facile, the other based on "a common liberal culture" (*eleutheras paideias*).

6. *Symposium* 178B–180B. Passage quoted, 180B.

7. *Nichomachean Ethics* 8.2–4, 1155b–1157a.

8. *Nichomachean Ethics* 8.11, 1161a–b.

9. *Nichomachean Ethics* 8.1.5, 1155a. Cf. Plato, Seventh Letter 332C: [The fact

that Dionysus had few friends and loyal followers marked him as a man of little virtue, since] "the possession or lack of these is the best indication of a man's virtue or vice."

10. See McGuire, *Friendship and Community*, pp. xxxiv–xxxxvi, 89; Reginald Hyatte, *The Arts of Friendship*; and Ullrich Langer, *Perfect Friendship*.

11. *De amicitia* 5.18. Cf. 14.50: " . . . good men love and join to themselves other good men, in a union which is almost that of blood-relatedness and nature . . . The good have for the good, as if from necessity, a kindly feeling which nature has made the fountain of friendship"; and 21.79: ". . . they are worthy of friendship who have within their souls the reason for their being loved."

12. This development is the subject of Foucault's *History of Sexuality*, Vol. 3, *The Care of the Self*.

13. One of the problems with Boswell's *CSTH* is the assumption that sexuality and the gratification of desire are necessarily implied or somehow present in the language of passionate friendship.

14. See McGuire, *Friendship and Community*, pp. 1–37. Also article, "Freundschaft", in TRE vol. 9.

15. Cf. McGuire, *Friendship and Community*: "The leading church writers of the West came from upper class society. The monasticism they created was of an aristocratic type that was based on Roman attitudes about friendship and alliances among good men" (p. 40); "the structure of christian friendship . . ." was "built on the foundation of classical tradition . . ." (p. 89; see also p. 39). It is worth stressing the point because of a widespread misconception, nurtured by the studies of Adele Fiske, that traditions of *amicitia* are somehow specifically monastic in character and origin. Bond, *The Loving Subject*, p. 49, casually assumes that monasticism had stamped the character of friendship prior to the twelfth century.

16. Ambrose, *De officiis* 3.22, PL 16, 182. Translation quoted here from Dronke, *Medieval Latin and the Rise*, 1.195.

17. A balder claim than Cicero's "Friendship cannot exist except among good men" (*De amicitia* 5.18), or that "virtue is the parent and preserver of friendship and without virtue friendship cannot exist" (6.20–21).

18. Brian McGuire's pre-twelfth-century sources (*Friendship and Community*) are in great part from worldly clerics, bishops, and archbishops. The near complete silence of the Benedictine Rule on friendship is significant (McGuire, p. 84).

19. See McGuire, *Friendship and Community*, pp. 77–82.

20. McGuire, *Friendship and Community*, p. 80: "Cassian was not concerned with how one monk can love another with affection, but with how a community of monks can live together in peace."

21. Quoted from McGuire, *Friendship and Community*, p. 81. Collatio 16, chap. 15, CSEL 13, p. 450. Cassian, *Conférences*, ed. Pichery, chap. 14, p. 234.

22. Cf. chap. 3, CSEL 13.440 (ed. Pichery, chap. 3, p. 225): True and unbroken love (*dilectio*) increases constantly in the double qualities of perfection and virtue of friends.

23. Benedictine Rule 2, 16–17: "Non unus plus ametur quam alius, nisi quem in bonis actibus aut oboedientia invenerit meliorem."

24. *Carmina*, pp. 24–39. *The Poems of St. Paulinus of Nola*, trans. Walsh, pp. 58–69.

25. I believe Raby characterized his poems well in calling them the expression of "that refinement of manner, that cult of friendship, and literature, which was one of the civilizing gifts of the ancient world" (*Secular Latin Poetry* 1.138).

26. For recent studies of Fortunatus's career and poetry, see Godman, *Poets and Emperors*, pp. 1–37; George, *Venantius Fortunatus: A Latin Poet in Merovingian Gaul*, pp. 35–61. See also George's translations and annotations of selected poems: Venantius Fortunatus, *Personal and Political Poems*. Fortunatus's poems are quoted here from Venantius Fortunatus, *Opera poetica*, ed. Leo.

27. 7.1a, lines 3–4, MGH, AA 4, ed. Leo, p. 129: "... me ... non trahit ingenium, sed tuus urguet amor." On Fortunatus and King Sigibert, see George, *Venantius Fortunatus* (1992), pp. 28–32, 40–43. See also George's translations and annotations of selected poems: *Venantius Fortunatus* (1995).

28. 7.1, 37, 43, ed. Leo, p. 154.

29. 7.16, lines 5–6, 33–34, 39, 49; ed. Leo, pp. 170–171.

30. 7.8, 33–38; ed. Leo, p. 162. Lupus was a member of Sigibert's court and a friend of Fortunatus. See George, *Venantius Fortunatus: A Latin Poet*, pp. 79–82. There are many other such references in the context of royal courts.

31. "Männerfreundschaft und Frauendienst bei Venantius Fortunatus."

32. Expressions of devoted friendship are *salutis opera*. Bk. 3, Carmen 26, 2, ed. Leo, p. 75; Bk. 10, Carmen 12d, 4, ed. Leo, p. 247. Epp, "Männerfreundschaft," p. 14.

33. Ibid., p. 16 and n. 27.

34. See Epp, p. 15–16, who raises the question of homosexuality but is skeptical that these expressions imply it.

35. See McGuire's commentary, *Friendship and Community*, pp. 98–100. Also Dronke, *Medieval Latin and the Rise*, pp. 200–209.

36. See McGuire, *Friendship and Community*, pp. 98–100. Also Verena Epp, "Männerfreundschaft und Frauendienst"; Inge Vielhauer, "Radegund von Poitiers (ca. 520–587)" (with a translation into German of Fortunatus's poem on the fall of Thuringia); and B. J. Rogers, "In Praise of Radegund."

37. Dronke accepts Wilhelm Meyer's distinction between the public and private poems to the two women (*Medieval Latin and the Rise*, p. 202).

Chapter 3: Love of King and Court

1. See Powis, *Aristocracy* esp. pp. 6ff.; and Elias, *Court Society*, pp. 117ff.

2. Wenzel, *Hören und Sehen*, pp. 21–25. Elias, *Court Society*, passim.

3. See Brunt, "'Amicitia' in the Late Roman Republic."

4. See Sharpe, *Criticism and Compliment*, pp. 23ff. on cults of Platonic love at Italian and English courts.

5. Smaragd, *Via Regia*, chap. 1, PL 102, 937B: "Vere enim haec ... regalis est virtus, quae ... dulcia cunctis oscula tribuit, et diligens omnes ulnis extensis amplectit [sic]". It is hard to agree with Peter Dinzelbacher that the Carolingian expressions of friendship were "restricted narrowly to monastic circles" ("Gefühl und Gesellschaft," p. 220) or with Brian McGuire that this is a specifically "monastic experience."

6. Godman, *Poets and Emperors*; Raby, *A History of Secular Latin Poetry*, 1: 178–209; von den Steinen, "Karl und die Dichter"; Schaller, "Vortrags- und Zirkulardichtung."

7. The erotic language has been much noted and little studied. Cf. Bischoff, "Gottschalks Lied für den Reichenauer Freund," p. 68, n. 34. Fichtenau, *Carolingian Empire*, pp. 93–94, I believe, very much underestimates, or underplays, the erotic strain

in court fellowship, clearly warding off thoughts of homosexual doings (p. 93: "From time to time we can discern also an erotic trait although it would certainly be wrong to exaggerate its importance"). Boswell, *CSTH*, pp. 188–92; McGuire, *Friendship and Community*, pp. 116–27; Fleckenstein, "Karl der Grosse und sein Hof," 24–50. Adele Fiske's study ("Alcuin and Mystical Friendship") is useful as a collection of sources but not as analysis. "Mystical friendship" and "union with God" are misleading terms when applied to Alcuin, the Carolingian court, and in general friendship prior to the twelfth century.

8. Quoted here from Godman, *Poetry of the Carolingian Renaissance*, No. 6, pp. 112–19. For commentary see Godman, *Poets and Emperors*, pp. 64–68; Schaller, "Vortrags- und Zirkulardichtung," pp. 29ff.

9. It is so prominent a feature of poetry celebrating the court that its absence in Theodulf of Orleans's court poems is striking. See Godman, *Poetry of the Carolingian Renaissance*, No. 15, pp. 150ff. Theodulf restricts the love motif to the king's family (cf. ll.91–112). See Schaller's commentary, "Vortrags- und Zirkulardichtung," pp. 17–24.

10. *Die Gedichte des Paulus Diaconus*, ed. Neff, Carmen 22, p. 103 (MGH Poetae 1, 51, Carm. 14, lines 9–16): "Non opus est claustris nec me compescere vinclis: / Vinctus sum domini regis amore mei . . . / Ut sacer inmenso Christi Petrus arsit amore, / . . . Sic . . . / Inflammat validus cor mihi vester amor."

11. Carm. 45; Poetae 1.257, line 1: "Carmina dilecto faciat mea fistula David"; "Te mea mens sequitur, sequitur quoque carmen amoris . . ." (line 17).

12. Carm. 74, MGH Poetae 1.295, lines 14–16: "Omnia vincit amor, nos quoque vincat amor. / Descripsi paucis partes et sidera caeli, / Te mandante, meo pectore magnus amor." Cf. Virgil, Ecl. 10.69.

13. Godman, *Poetry of the Carolingian Renaissance*, No. 25, p. 198 (MGH Poetae 1.367), lines 30–31 : "Ille duces magno et comites inlustrat amore; / Blandus adest iustis, hilarem se praebet ad omnes . . ." Godman's translation: "He bathes his dukes and counts in the brilliance of his great love, / he is gentle to the righteous and displays good humour to everyone." The poem, "Karolus Magnus et Leo Papa," was undoubtedly composed by a member of the court circle. Dümmler edited it among the works of Angilbert. On this work see Dieter Schaller, "Das Aachener Epos für Karl den Grossen." On the question of authorship, pp. 163–68. Schaller revives Einhard's candidacy.

14. 1.26; MGH Poetae 1.396: "Versibus incomptis, summo sed mentis amore, / Haec tibi conficiens, Caesar: dignare superne / Munera, quaeso, tui devoti sumere servi."

15. Theodulf, Carm. 35, lines 9–10; MGH Poetae 1.527: "Te nimium capitis sitiunt duo lumina nostri / Cernere teque cupit pectoris altus amor."

16. See Eberhardt, *Via Regia*, esp. on the letter of dedication, see pp. 104ff. On Charlemagne as recipient and the dating, pp. 262–63.

17. These lines in the Migne edition were rejected as "efféminé et absurde" by Donatien De Bruyne in favor of the older but less reliable ms. M, which omits the mentions of "sweet kisses" and "embraces" and speaks a language "qui soit digne de l'abbé et de la majesté royale." Friedel Rädle rescued the sentiments if not the priority of ms. G by reference to *Via Regia*, chaps. 1 and 19, which speak the same language of royal love, kisses and embraces. See the summary of the debate in Eberhardt, *Via Regia*, pp. 106–7.

18. MGH Epistolae 4, Epist. Karol. Aev. 2, p. 533.

19. Eberhardt argues that the abbacy of St. Mihiel of Verdun, bestowed by Charlemagne on Smaragd in 809, is the gift which stirred him to write the *Via regia*. See Eberhardt, *Via Regia*, pp. 73, 261–62. On Charlemagne as enricher of his court scholars and poets, see Fichtenau, *Carolingian Empire*, pp. 85–86. The opposition of the king's *magna munera* to the humble recipient, of his *magnus amor* to the *parva munera* he gives in return, is part of the court idiom. Cf. Alcuin's poem of thanks for gifts from Charlemagne, Carm. 38, MGH Poetae 1, p. 252, and to Arn of Salzburg, Carm. 11, line 22, p. 236: "[Aspice] . . . Parvula quae magnus munera misit amor."

20. Fleckenstein credits friendship with "eine so zentrale Rolle am Hofe . . . dass sie sogar für den höfischen Lebensstil bestimmend wurde"; the court, he says, developed "einen regelrechten Freundschaftskult" ("Karl der Grosse und sein Hof," p. 43). Fleckenstein in fact sees the combination of *familiaritas* and education as the factor which lent the Carolingian court its peculiar luster (p. 49).

21. See the passages from Alcuin discussed below.

22. Strong, *Art and Power*. Geertz, "Centers, Kings, and Charisma."

23. Schramm, *Herrschaftszeichen und Staatssymbolik*, and "Das Grundproblem dieser Sammlung: Die 'Herrschaftszeichen', die 'Staatssymbolik' und die 'Staatsrepräsentation' des Mittelalters," in Schramm, *Kaiser, Könige und Päpste*, 1.30–58; Kantorowicz, *The King's Two Bodies*; Althoff, "Demonstration und Inszenierung; Koziol, *Begging Pardon and Favor*; Wenzel, *Hören und Sehen*.

24. Alcuin, rejoicing at news of Charlemagne's safety, cries out, "O sweet love of mine, sweet presence of Christ . . ." ("O mihi dulcis amor, dulcis praesentia Christi . . . ," Carm 13, line 6; MGH Poetae 1, p. 237.) This makes the king into the embodiment of Christ for the poet. See the interpretation of von den Steinen, "Karl und die Dichter," p. 77. On the divine character of Carolingian kingship, the ruler as God and God as a ruler, see Fichtenau, *Carolingian Empire*, pp. 47–55. Also Wallace-Hadrill, "The *Via Regia* of the Carolingian Age," pp. 23–28.

25. See Peter Johanek, "König Artus und die Plantagenets"; Frances Yates, *Astrea: The Imperial Theme in the Sixteenth Century*; Stephen Greenblatt, *Renaissance Self-Fashioning*, pp. 165–66.

26. Kleinschmidt, "Minnesang als höfisches Zeremonialhandeln"; Müller, "Ritual, Sprecherfiktion und Erzählung."

27. See Jaeger, *Origins of Courtliness*, chap. 7.

28. *seniori tuo K[arolo], quisquis ille est* . . . "A Charles" had become a generic term for emperor.

29. Dhuoda, *Manuel*, ed. Riché, pp. 166–68. See Peter Dronke, "Dhuoda," in *Women Writers of the Middle Ages*, pp. 36–54. Manitius, 1.442–44. Also *Manuel* 3.9, p. 170: "Love [*ama*], cherish [*dilige*], and serve constantly the dignitaries of the royal court and their counselors . . . and any who shine with distinction at the court . . ."

30. Wolfram von den Steinen's incisive reading of Alcuin's love poems and letters to Charlemagne shows some of the problems of dealing with this discourse. He observes the charismatic, non-sexual character of their love: "' . . . meo pectore magnus amor'. Das ist es, was von Karl Ausstrahlt . . ." He notes that a comprehensive listing of the love declarations between the two men would show Alcuin virtually as an intoxicated devotee, even an idolatrous admirer of the emperor (" . . . er würde wie ein Trunkener oder schier abgöttisch erscheinen"), and asks, "What modern scholar would not prefer to avert his eyes?" ("Karl und die Dichter," pp. 75–76). Some of the hieratic

gay heroism of the circle of intellectuals around Stefan George (von den Steinen was on its fringe) may shine through his reading: "in den Worten [pulsiert] die männlich hingebende Liebe des Älteren zum Jüngeren, des Flaccus zu seinem David" (p. 75); "Die lebendige Erfahrung verdeutlichte ihm . . . jenen Meister der männlichen, tätigstrengen Liebe" (p. 77).

31. Carmen 55, pp. 266ff.

32. Alcuin, Carm. 55, line 1; MGH Poetae 1, 266: "Dulcis amor lacrimis absentem plangit amicum . . ."

33. Anselm of Canterbury regularly "recommended" his friends visiting other houses by letters of love. See Jaeger, "Ironie und Subtext in lateinischen Briefen."

34. Epist. 39, lines 8ff., p. 82:

O si . . . in tuo pectore spiritus esset prophetiae, ut . . . crederes . . . quam suavissimo sapore tui amoris pectus meum impleretur . . . Hos parvos apices magnae indices caritatis tibi dirigo, ut per hos intellegas quod vix intellegi potest. Sicut flamma potest videri, tangi autem non potest: ita caritas in litteris cerni potest, sed vix in animo scribentis sentiri valet. Quasi scintillae de igne sparguntur, ita dilectio litterarum officio volat.

Cf. Epist. 19, lines 11–15, p. 53, ; Epist. 209, line ll, p. 348; Epist. 83, lines 2–7, p. 126; Epist. 139, lines 15–17, p. 220; Epist. 191, lines 7–8, p. 318; Epist. 212, lines 39ff. p. 352. References from Fiske, "Mystical Friendship," p. 571.

35. Epist. 78, lines 15–17, p. 119. Cf. Epist. 59, p. 102; Epist. 78, p. 119; Epist. 80, p. 129; Epist. 159, p. 257. References from Fiske, "Mystical Friendship," p. 573. "Caritate vulnerata ego sum." (Cf. Song of Songs 4.9: "caritate/amore languescor." Var: "caritate vulnerata sum.")

36. Epist. 275, lines 30–31, p. 432.

37. Carm. 21, lines 21–22, p. 242: "Qui in caritate manet, portat in pectore Christum / Vera quidem caritas est deus omnipotens." See Fiske, "Mystical Friendship," p. 565.

38. *Viscera* = innards? The most sensitive parts of the body? difficult to translate. The intention is clearly to intensify the level of intimacy by setting the softest and most sensitive organ (tongue) against the "innermost" and most sensitive part of the friend (*viscera*). Boswell's translation, "breast," is understandable but misleading and I have preferred the far less appetizing but more accurate "innards."

39. Fiske's consistent reading in "Mystical Friendship."

40. The motif is anticipated in Paulinus of Nola and Venantius Fortunatus. Cf. Fortunatus, ed. Leo, MGH AA 4.1, p. 284 (Appendix 16, lines 5–7): "quam locus ille pius qui numquam abrumpit amantes, / quo capiunt oculis quos sua vota petunt / in medio posito bonitatis principe Christo . . ."

41. Cf. Epist. 113, to Arn, p. 166, lines 17ff.: "[I instruct you in this way for the sake of charity] . . . lest love which burns in the heart within should seem mute outwardly in words. Words seem given to men for this purpose: that they may pour into the ears of brothers the heart's secrets. For this purpose letters are written, that where the sound of words cannot reach, the medium of letters will penetrate, that the signs of mutual love may be shown to the fraternal gaze in letters, so that presence may arise in the love of souls, where there is absence of bodies because of the distance of

places. O happy, blessed life, where what is loved is always seen and what is seen never grows hated, where God is eternal love to all, eternal praise, glory and beatitude." Also Epist. 157, p. 255, to Arn (whose name means "eagle" in German): "O that my eagle would come to pray at Saint Martin's, so that I may embrace his most soft and gentle wings in that place, and I may hold the one whom my soul loves. Nor will I let him go before I introduce him into my mother's house and he kisses me with the kiss of his mouth [Song of Songs 1.1], and we shall share our rejoicing at the arrangement of love." [*ordinata caritate*] Also Epist. 185, lines 6ff., p. 311, (to Arn): "[I would have written if my letter could have been delivered] . . . but written in my heart is the memory of your name with the pen of charity, not with perishable wing, but with permanent gentleness, often sighing from the intimate feeling of my heart, 'When will that day come when I may embrace my eagle and press the neck of the venerable father with sweet embraces?'"

42. Alcuin to Arn, Epist. 193, lines 29ff., p. 319: "O si mihi translatio Abacuc esset concessa ad te: quam tenacibus tua colla strinxissem, o dulcissime fili, amplexibus; nec me longitudo aestivi diei fessum efficeret, quin minus premerem pectus pectore, os ori adiungerem, donec singulos corporis artus dulcissimis oscularer salutationibus. Sed quia hoc peccata mea inpediunt, ut in tardo corpore fieri valeat, quod possum, instantius efficiam; pennam caritatis lacrimoso intingens gurgite, ut suavissima salutationis verba scribantur in cartula . . . O dura divisio gravis ponderis in corpore, o dulcis coniunctio in dilectionis visceribus . . . In Christo sit unitas, sine quo nulla perfecta est caritas."

43. Alcuin to Charlemagne, Epist. 118, MGH Epist. 4, Ep. Karol. Aevi 2, p. 173.

44. Alcuin to Charlemagne, Epist. 121, p. 176.

45. It is not easy to render the exact thought of the half line, *dulcis praesentia Christi*. The paratactical formulation may suggest "sweet as" the presence of Christ, or he may intend the sequence, "sweet are: love, Christ's presence, your studies and your voice." The former is more correct intuitively, the latter grammatically, though jarring in its logic.

46. The idea of friendship or love as a response to virtue is evoked more than cited in a panegyric to Pope Leo III:

Notus in orbe procul, meritorum laude venustus,
Virtutum titulis nomen amoris habens.

Far-famed in the orb, beautified by the praise of your merits,
You are loved for the fame of your virtues. (Carm. 15, lines 7–8, p. 238).

47. He wrote to friend Abbot Adalhard of Corbey: "Let us be seed-sowers of peace among Christian peoples" [Pacis enim seminatores simus inter populos christianos] (Epist. 9, lines 20–21, p. 35).

48. Cf. Epistolae 74, 178, 187, 275, 284. Also *Carmen* 104 and 105. (This is far from complete.)

49. For instance his attempts to restore peace in Northumbria after the accession of King Aethelred in 790. See his Epist. 16 and 18. He addresses Aethelred and others ravaging his beloved homeland in terms of loving friendship.

50. Epist. 149, p. 242–45. He identifies himself in the salutation (as in other letters to Charlemagne) as *veteranus miles*.

51. "Softening harsh minds" is a duty of the counselors of kings, closely connected with music, to which there is abundant evidence from the tenth and eleventh centuries. See Jaeger, *The Envy of Angels*, pp. 143–58. Also on the connection of friendship and music, Ziolkowski, "Twelfth-Century Understandings and Adaptations of Ancient Friendship," pp. 68–69.

52. "amicus dicitur quasi animi custos." Cf. Isidor, *Etymologiarum Libri XX*, ed. Lindsay, Bk. 10. The extension of Isidore's etymology (*amicus = animi custos*) to the duties of a ruler is new to me.

53. Gottschalk's poem. See Bischoff, "Gottschalk's Lied." Walafrid Strabo. See Boswell, *CSTH*, pp. 191–93.

54. See letters in Epist. 5, Epist. Karol. Aevi 3, pp. 114–15, Einhard's letter of moral correction to the emperor Lothar (written in 830) is nearly frosty in its terse expressions of love: " . . . aeque vos atque piissimum dominum meum, patrem vestrum, semper dilexi . . ." (lines 29–30, p. 114); "Amo vos, Deus scit, et ideo tam fiducialiter ammoneo . . ." (line 23, p. 115).

55. Agobard of Lyon speaks very clearly in a letter on church administration, Epistolae 5, pp. 153–58: "Each who is set in a position of authority over others, be they clerics or monks, is an adulterer if he shows himself so benevolent, gentle and affable as to win over the hearts of his subjects to his love and to his own praise, and such a one ought never to assume the care of souls" (p. 156, line 42–157, line 1). The letter is in various passages directed against personal friendships, in every case mistrusts them as a sign of wicked worldly ambition (the context of the above passage), and the author is at pains to direct the emotion of love away from the *proximus* and to the *sponsus* (cf. p. 157, lines 10–12).

56. Ruotger, *Vita Brun.*, chap. 3, AQDGMA 22, p. 184: " . . . tantus amor colligavit domesticos, ut nihil umquam in quolibet potentissimo regno coniunctius videretur." *Coniunctus* has the double meaning of "alliance" and "loving union," as in *conjugium* (marriage, "conjugal"). Cf. Alcuin to his unnamed friend, Carm. 55, lines 9–10, pp. 266ff.: " . . . mihi magno *coniunctus* amore, / Tu requies mentis, tu mihi dulcis amor." Alcuin to Arn, Epist. 193, p. 320, line 3: "o dulcis *coniunctio* in dilectionis visceribus." Einhard says of Charlemagne's cultivation of close friends, "colebatque sanctissime quoscumque hac adfinitate sibi *coniunxerat*" (*Vita Karoli*, chap. 19, p. 18).

57. See Althoff and Keller, *Heinrich I. und Otto der Grosse*, pp. 157ff.; Althoff, *Amicitiae et Pacta*.

58. Searching through volume 5 of the MGH Poetae series is not rewarding on the topic of love. The volume contains a love poem which the most recent editor calls "the oldest European love poem," from a man to a girl, "Deus amet puellam". MGH Poetae 5, p. 553–54. See the commentary by Dronke in *Medieval Latin and the Rise*, pp. 264–68. A remarkable text to be sure, but not in the tradition of court poetry and other testimony on court love from Carolingian times on.

59. See McGuire, *Friendship and Community*, pp. 146–52.

60. In the entire letter collection there are two quotations from *De amicitia*, and they are peripheral. See the index in Weigle's edition.

61. *valde illum dilexit*. MGH SS 4, p. 833, line 23.

62. Petrus Damiani, *Vita Romualdi*, chap. 25, PL 145, 975C.

63. *Epistolae Bambergenses* 6 and 7, ed. Jaffé, p. 487. See below, Chapter 5.

64. *Vita Meinwerci* chap. 10: *Das Leben des Bischofs Meinwerk von Paderborn*, ed. F.

Tenckhoff, MGH, Script. rer. germ. in us. schol. 59 (Hannover: Hahn, 1921; rpt. 1983), p. 17.

65. MGH SS 11, p. 600, lines 31–32. The work, called simply *Ad Heinricum IV imperatorem*, consists of individual works written in the third quarter of the eleventh century instructing the young king in manners and imperial customs and traditions. They were collected into a single work between 1086 and 1090. Benzo was probably an Italian, possibly a Greek. See Jaeger, *Origins of Courtliness*, pp. 122–25, 171.

66. Edition by Ernst Dümmler, "Drei Gedichte aus Frankreich," pp. 222–30. See Jaeger, *Envy of Angels*, pp. 57–59 (citing earlier literature).

67. On the translation of *psalmatio regum* see Jaeger, *Envy of Angels*, p. 393, n. 25.

68. McGuire's chapter title for the period from the late ninth through the mid-eleventh century is "The Eclipse of Monastic Friendship." See *Friendship and Community*, pp. 134–79.

69. *Vita Maioli* 1.7; PL 142, 902B. See McGuire's discussion: *Friendship and Community*, pp. 170–71 and n. 125.

70. See Jaeger, *Envy of Angels* and Zielinski, *Der Reichsepiskopat*.

Chapter 4: Love, Friendship, and Virtue

1. Edition, translation, textual and historical commentary, Fridel Rädle, "Satyra de amicicia . . . (Clm 29111): Das Freundschaftsideal eines Freigelassenen." Earlier literature listed here. See also Jaeger, *The Envy of Angels*, p. 313.

2. The genre term in the eleventh century described a poem "criticizing vice and praising virtue." See "Satyra de amicicia," ed. Rädle, p. 178, with reference to U. Kindermann, *Satyra*.

3. See Ziolkowski's edition of the Cambridge Songs (hereafter CC), with introduction, text and translation: *The Cambridge Songs (Carmina Cantabrigiensia)*. The two standard editions are those of Strecker, *Die Cambridger Lieder*, and Bulst, *Carmina Cantabrigiensia*.

4. "En habes, perdulcis amor, / quod dedisti intactum / ante amoris experimentum" (Stanza 8, lines 4–6).

5. On this connection and on the Ciceronian strains in the poem, see Ziolkowski, "Twelfth-Century Understandings and Adaptations of Ancient Friendship," pp. 65–69.

6. *Cambridge Songs*, ed. and trans. Ziolkowski, pp. 158–61. The poem is datable to prior to 1050 by a reference to it in Amarcius Sextus. See *Cambridge Songs*, ed. and trans. Ziolkowski, pp. xliv–xlvi.

7. E.g., no. 14A "Nam languens / amore tuo", no. 27, "Iam dulcis amica, venito"; no. 40, "Levis exsurgit zephirus" (a woman's lament for her absent lover); no. 49 "Veni, dilectissime." See Dronke, *Medieval Latin and the Rise*, pp. 271–277. Werner Ross, "Die Liebesgedichte im Cambridger Liederbuch (CC)." Also of interest, the compiler has copied out five laments of women for their dead husbands from Statius's *Thebaid*: CC no. 29, 31, 32, 34, and 46. These are the only verses excerpted from classical sources, and they clearly are thematically linked.

8. See Ziolkowski's commentary, *Cambridge Songs*, pp. 306–9; also Boswell, *CSTH*, pp. 186–87.

9. As Ziolkowski points out, *Cambridge Songs*, p. 306.

10. For the theme of chastity in the Cambridge Songs, see CC nos. 17 (esp. stanza 5, line 4), 18, 23, 26, 36. The excerpts from Boethius, *Consolation of Philosophy*, also touch on the theme: CC nos. 69 and 74.

11. On *Ruodlieb*, see Dronke, "Ruodlieb: The Emergence of Romance," in his *Poetic Individuality*, pp. 33–65.

12. Cf. the words of the minor king to the legates of the greater: "To requite evil acts with good is a grand form of revenge" (*ultio grandis*, 4.141). Cf. also 5.40–41.

13. "dans / Oscula fert more, grandi nos liquit amore." (4.166–67).

14. 4.174: [He speaks] "with a restrained smile"; 4.203: "The king spoke smiling and as though making a joke"; 5.17: "The king received him with a benevolent smile."

15. Cf. 5.17–31.

16. 5.418: *mi kare*; 5.420: *dilectissime*; 5.422: *karissime cunctigenorum*.

17. On the contemporary relevance of the ideal of revenge restrained and the connection of *Ruodlieb* with the court of Emperor Henry III, see Hauck, "Heinrich III und der Ruodlieb."

18. On *amor* as an ethical ideal at the fictional court in *Ruodlieb*, see Helena Gamer, "Studien zum Ruodlieb."

Chapter 5: Love in Education

1. Most omit it. Exceptions are Jaeger, *Paideia*, esp. vol. 2, pp. 174–97; also vol. 1, pp. 194–96; vol. 3, pp. 186–88; and H.-I. Marrou, *A History of Education in Antiquity*, pp. 26–35. And above all, Foucault, *History of Sexuality*, vols. 2 and 3. Hellenic pederasty is one of the subjects in which this relationship is studied, but ordinarily within the more general frame of history of sexuality. See Konstan, *Friendship in the Classical World*, pp. 37–39. I do not know any study of pederasty in the Middle Ages.

2. Quintilian *Institutio Oratoria* 2.9. The teacher-student relationship is regularly compared to that of parent-child. Cf. William of Conches, glosses on Priscian, ed. Jeauneau, *RTAM* 27 (1960), 233: "Magister quodam modo gignit discipulum in sapientia, scilicet melius ei esse confert quam verus pater," and 224 [the first masters, loving their pupils with the affection of a father, composed writings for them.] John of Salisbury, *Policraticus*, 7. 14 [Teachers to be loved as parents.]

3. On "charismatic pedagogy," see Jaeger, *Envy of Angels*, pp. 76–81 and passim. William of Conches defines "reverence" as "The virtue which accords the honor due to men of some gravity or men elevated in a position of authority. It enjoins us to imitate prominent men . . . We must choose a good man and hold his image ever before our mind's eye, and thus we will live as if he were observing our each and every act." *Moralium Dogma Philosophorum*, ed. Holberg, p. 26, lines 16ff.

4. *Nichomachean Ethics*, 8.1, 1155a; 8.11, 1161a–1161b.

5. *Vita Adalberti* (ca. 997), chap. 23, MGH SS 4, p. 591, lines 32ff. The translation of *dulcissimus cubicularius* as "sweetest chambermate" reduces a double meaning to a single. On the wordplay, see McGuire, *Friendship and Community*, p. 154. It is worth noting that after telling about their love, kisses, embraces and sleeping habits, the biographer wards off anticipated criticism by saying this did not happen out of vainglory and love of the world. That is, the charge that needs warding off is worldly ambition, not homosexuality.

6. *Epistolae Bambergenses* 6 and 7, ed. Jaffé, pp. 484–97.

7. Ed. Jaffé, p. 486 (alluding to Psalm 42.1).

8. It is significant that in all of the ruler-tutor pairs mentioned above from the Middle Ages, the document attesting to the love relationship contains the moral instruction of the teacher to the student.

9. See Jaeger, *Envy of Angels*, pp. 36–117.

10. See Worms Letter Collection, *Die ältere Wormser Briefsammlung*, ed. Bulst, Epist. 8, 20, 21, 26, 34, 49, 56, 60, 61. See McGuire, *Friendship and Community*, pp. 185–88.

11. Worms Collection, Epist. 60, 61, pp. 100–105.

12. Ibid., p. 102: "Hactenus quidem dilexi vos propter virtutem, propter quam Tullius docet nos *eos etiam diligere, quos numquam vidimus.* Propter eam nimirum vos dilexi, amavi vos propter verum amorem, posthac amabo vos propter timorem" (emphasis by Bulst, with reference to Cicero, *De amicitia* 8.28).

13. P. 105: "Diligamus ergo nos ea dilectione, qua Deus est, amemus nos invicem . . . diligamus nos omni amoris fortitudine, omni constantia, tota perfectione. . . . Diligam vos propter Deum et propter vestram amabilem virtutem . . ."

14. For an analysis of the texts and the circumstances, see Jaeger, *Envy of Angels*, pp. 66–74. Also "Ironie und Subtext in lateinischen Briefen."

15. The last line is confusing. It puzzled both Strecker (*Tegernseer Briefsammlung*, p. 130) and Bulst (Worms Letter Collection, p. 123). But the sense is fairly clear: Many who can't end their disputes will marvel at the model of conciliatory restraint and loving friendship these two friends provide.

16. Worms Letter Collection, Epist. 26, ed. Bulst, pp. 48–49.

17. See the analysis in Jaeger, *Envy of Angels*, pp. 226–29. Guibert's teacher received his education at a cathedral school in the first half of the eleventh century.

18. "Quorum innutritus curiae," Guibert of Nogent, *De vita sua*, chap. 4, ed. Labande, pp. 26–28.

19. Guibert, *De vita sua*, chap. 6, ed. Labande, p. 38; trans. Bland and Benton, p. 49.

20. See Halphen, "Un pédagogue," in his *A travers l'histoire du moyen âge* (Paris: Presses Universitaires de France, 1950), 277–85.

21. *De vita sua*, chap. 5, ed. Labande, p. 32. On this aspect of Guibert's education, see Jaeger, *Envy of Angels*, pp. 226–29.

22. *Wibaldi epistolae*, Epist. 167, p. 277.

23. *Carmen ad Astralabium*, p. 107, lines 9–12.

24. E.g., Epist. 4, 8, 34, 36, 37, 44, 48, 49, 55, 57. See discussion in McGuire, *Friendship and Community*, pp. 188–94.

25. Hildesheim Letter Collection, Epist. 37, ed. Erdmann, *Briefsammlungen*, pp. 79–81. The writer quotes Cicero, *De amicitia* 18.65, claiming, "Friendship cannot exist except among good men" ("'Amicitiam nisi inter bonos esse non posse'").

26. Epist. 44, p. 88. Possibly Hezilo, later bishop of Hildesheim writing as a student to Bishop Gebhard of Regensburg (according to Erdmann with ref. to Sudendorff).

27. McGuire believes it is from an older to a younger student (*Friendship and Community*, p. 189), and the puerile character of much of the letter argues for it. But the addressee depends on the writer for recommendations; the writer is able to make contact with "very many" French, Norman, and German *magistri* and to help his friend

reach the highest offices (p. 77, lines 17–25); he instructs him in the behavior proper to a man of his ambitions (p. 77, lines 26–31); he claims that Master Heribert teaches nothing he has not received from him, the writer of the letter (p. 78, line 5). This makes his rank of master clear.

28. Hildesheim Letter Collection, Epist. 36, pp. 76–79.

29. Ibid., p. 77, line 18: "hec, que magis proprie dicere nequeo, dicam." The phrase might also mean, "these things, which I cannot say more properly, I shall say." The logic of *que dicere nequeo, dicam*, seems to me to favor giving *que* the force of "although." The implication is "were I speaking more properly, I could not talk this way" — i.e., he knows he is speaking *minus proprie*.

30. The criticism of the Würzburg master that provoked the overwrought Worms-Würzburg polemics appears to have been mild and jesting.

31. "Hec tibi soli, ecce, puta serio dictum." McGuire reads it differently: "Think seriously about what has been said" (*Friendship and Community*, p. 191). But *serio* must modify *dictum*, not *puta*. I think the stronger reading sees two different direct objects of *puta*: *hec tibi soli* and *serio dictum*. McGuire's reading requires that *puta* change its meaning from "regard as" to "think about." It also requires *dictum* to agree with *hec*, which it does not.

32. It also shows the writer's awareness that his penchant for irony and cynical virtuosity requires assurance of the general seriousness of the letter's message.

33. Though it falls apart oddly in the last two paragraphs, which are in part garbled and unintelligible.

34. Cf. *De amicitia* 8.28. On "distant love" see below, Chapter 8.

35. See Jaeger, *Envy of Angels*, pp. 106–16, 256–60.

36. *Carmina*, ed. Hilbert, no. 3, pp. 15–17. See Boswell, *CSTH*, p. 245.

37. "Forma *placet*, quia forma *decet*, quia forma *venusta* est" (line 7); "Nec solus *castus* nec solus es ipse *decorus*" (line 39); "Dedecet hoc in te" (line 50); "*decus* atque *decor*" (line 68, emphasis added). The alignment of propriety, beauty, and chastity is programmatic for the poem.

38. Cf. Alcibiades's speech, *Symposium* 216Dff. [Since I imagined that he was courting me for my beauty, I thought myself lucky, since all I had to do was gratify his desires, and I could learn all he knew, "for I had an enormously swollen opinion of my youthful charms."] Alcibiades tells of the various ruses by which he courted Socrates. When he finally maneuvers him into the most intimate situation — the two sleep together without slaves or chaperones — Socrates "showed superiority and contempt, laughing my youthful charms to scorn" (219C), and Alcibiades got up in the morning the same as if he had slept with his brother or father, not his "lover."

39. Cf. *The Correspondence of Marcus Cornelius Fronto*, 1: 18–33, 74–79.

40. *Carmina*, ed. Hilbert, no. 193, p. 258, 112.

41. *Metalogicon* 1.8, ed. Hall, p. 26–27, trans. McGarry, p. 30 (emphasis added): " . . . castigatione philosophiae et virtutis exercitatione repressit, et domuit." Baudri plots the route by which lascivious love develops into wise love and youthful lust to the life of the wise man in an allegorical reading of the story of King Pretus and his wife Antia, who fell in love with Bellerophon. *Carmina*, ed. Hilbert, no. 154, lines 989–1088, pp. 231–33. It is instructive to compare the version in Fulgentius (3.1), Baudri's source, quoted in the edition of Abrahams, *Baudri de Bourgueil, Oeuvres poétiques*, p. 313, n. 46. For Fulgentius the story is about three stages of love from its onset to

consummation. Baudri takes that shell and adds the language of *mores*: virtue and chastity opposing *lascivia*; self-control, restraint, modesty set against lust, ending in the "birth of wisdom, the splendor of [self-]mastery, which like a powerful horse bears you upward to the stars" (lines 1087–88).

42. *Rodulfi Tortarii Carmina*, ed. Ogle, and Schullian, pp. 256–67 (Epistula 2).

43. A sampling: a Latin prose version from around 1150 tells the *Vita Sanctorum (!) Amici et Amelii*; an Old French chanson de geste, *Ami et Amile* (ca. 1200); an Anglo-Norman romance, *Amis e Amilun* (also ca. 1200); a verse legend in Alemannic dialect, *Amicus und Amelius*; Konrad von Würzburg's MHG verse novella *Engelhard* (late thirteenth century). Vincent of Beauvais took the story into his *Speculum Historiale* (l. XXIII, c. 166ff.), and Jacobus da Voragine in his *Legenda Aurea*; an OF miracle play, *Amis et Amille* (fifteenth century). See Peter Dembowski, "Ami et Amile," in *Dictionary of the Middle Ages* 1.234. Dembowski points out that the two friends are still revered as saints in parts of Italy.

44. See Jaeger, *Origins of Courtliness*, pp. 43–46.

45. Aelred, *Spiritual Friendship*, 3.89, trans. Laker, p. 114, ed. Hoste, p. 336: "Accedat huc in sermone iucunditas, hilaritas in vultu, suavitas in moribus, in oculorum etiam nutu serenitas, in quibus haudquaquam mediocre in amicitia condimentum."

46. Dronke, *Medieval Latin and the Rise*, 2:422–47. See Dronke's commentary in ibid., 1:221–29, and *Women Writers of the Middle Ages*, pp. 91–92.

47. *Carmina Ratisponensia*, ed. Paravicini, I will quote here from Dronke's text and translation, comparing with Paravicini.

48. Schnell excludes them from the discussion of courtly love: *Causa Amoris*, pp. 154–55.

49. Dronke, *Medieval Latin and the Rise*, 1:221–29.

50. Carmen 39 (Paravicini, no. 51), p. 439. The Liège group is departing for the winter, and the nuns console themselves and bait the men by reference to Count Hugo and his many friends. If the women find the manners of these secular rivals flawless, then the Liège clerics will be swept aside and can weep at their rejection.

51. It is hard to agree with Paravicini's reading of the poems as school exercises, not based on experience: "*Amor* und *dilectio* finden Ausdruck wie Erfüllung im Dichten" (*Carmina Ratisponensia*, p. 10).

52. E.g., Carmen 28 (Paravicini, no. 37), p. 431, lines 3 and 11:

Iam non est tutum   contendere carmine tecum! . . .
Longe precellis,   longe me carmine vincis . . .

Carmen 29 (Paravicini, no. 37), p. 432:

Treicius vates   iustas reperit sibi clades,
Presumens vestrum   scribendo lacessere sexum . . .
Sic satis exemplis   me commonitum memoratis
Hanc ut devitem   (quia non sum par tibi) litem.

53. Especially skilled is the weaving together of love and poetry in Carmen 28, ed. Dronke, pp. 431–32.

54. Carmen 5 (Paravicini, no. 6), ed. Dronke, p. 424:

Mittit vestalis   chorus ad vos xenia pacis,
Concedens vestre   dominandi iura caterve,
Sic tamen, ut precium   Virtus sibi reddat honestum.

55. The dating of his poems is notoriously difficult. See Gerald Bond's introduction in *The Poetry of William . . . IX Duke of Aquitaine*, pp. xlix–l. *Terminus post quem* for his activity as a poet is 1102.

56. See Brinkmann, *Entstehungsgeschichte des Minnesangs* and Bond, *Loving Subject*.

57. See Ziolkowski, "Twelfth-Century Understandings and Adaptations of Ancient Friendship," p. 78. He wonders why Ovid has so monopolized the naming of the age: "Without toppling the monument to Ovid that has been erected over the past century, a statue of Cicero could be added . . ."

58. I am following Ralph Hexter, *Ovid and Medieval Schooling*.

59. Hexter, *Ovid and Medieval Schooling*, p. 158. On the formula, "Ethicae subponitur" in reference to Ovid's works, also p. 100.

60. C. S. Lewis's thesis that courtly love may owe its formation partly to "Ovid misunderstood" has not found acceptance, though it is evident from the glosses how badly he was understood. (See *The Allegory of Love*, pp. 6–8.) But Lewis made the effect into the cause. The schoolmasters and students who commented on Ovid's erotic poetry had a preformed conception of noble, chaste love which they imposed on Ovid. They did not form that conception from him.

61. *Carmina*, nos. 97 (Florus to Ovid) and 98 (Ovid to Florus), ed. Hilbert, pp. 104–12.

62. See Jaeger, *Origins of Courtliness*, p. 143.

63. The text presented and discussed by John Baldwin, *Language of Sex*, pp. 23–25 and edited as Appendix 3, p. 251. Also more broadly on Ovid and Andreas Capellanus as instructors in love, *Language of Sex*, pp. 19–25. See also Jaeger, *Envy of Angels*, pp. 319–22.

64. *Carmina Burana*, no. 105, ed. Hilka and Schumann, rev. Bischoff, pp. 373–76.

Chapter 6: Women

1. On the exclusivity of friendship (*philia*) in ancient Greece, see Konstan, *Friendship in the Classical World*, pp. 90–91, who finds men-women friendships in Greece mainly between prostitute and client. On men-woman friendships in Rome, p. 146

2. See the articles on Jerome, Fortunatus, and Boniface in *Meine in Gott geliebte Freundin*, ed. Signori; also Epp, "Männerfreundschaft." Of course, men had loved women and written poetry to them. But they had not publicly proclaimed their love to give honor to the beloved and to receive it from loving her. See esp. Dronke, *Medieval Latin and the Rise*. The one bit of testimony to a sense of the lover raised in stature by loving a woman is the poem "Deus amet puellam," composed not later than the early tenth century, though I do not share Dronke's reading of the poem as close to a Dantean glorification of woman (pp. 264–71). We can assume that men experienced passion for women and vice versa, but this love had no language, certainly none rooted in virtue.

3. Cf. Isidore, *Etymologiae* 11.2.17: "Vir nuncupatus, quod maior in eo vis est quam in feminis; unde et virtus nomen accepit . . . Mulier vero a mollitie, tanquam

mollier detracta littera vel mutata, appellata est mulier." Quoted in Marie-Thérèse d'Alverny, "Comment les théologiens et les philosophes voient la femme," 111.

4. Cf. Bumke, *Höfische Kultur*, p. 504, summing up the results of the tradition of scholarship: "What courtly love is seems less certain today than a hundred years ago." Historians and literary scholars have reached a consensus that the representation of women in courtly literature is radically at odds with the "reality" of women's position in court society (Bumke, *Höfische Kultur*; Schnell, "Die 'höfische' Liebe als 'höfischer' Diskurs über die Liebe"). For reviews of research, see Boase, *The Origin and Meaning of Courtly Love*; Liebertz-Grün, *Zur Soziologie des "amour courtois"*; Schnell, *Causa Amoris*, with bibliography and extensive review of research; Peters, "Höfische Liebe: Ein Forschungsproblem."

5. Poetae 1, p. 511, lines 691–710. Translation quoted here from Godman, *Poetry of the Carolingian Renaissance*, p. 167.

6. Hildebert, Carmen 50, *Carmina minora*, ed. Scott, pp. 40–41. The motif of woman, the ruin of great men, is prominent in the correspondence of Abelard and Heloise and Abelard's "Planctus" on Samson. See Dronke, *Poetic Individuality*, pp. 135–43. On Hildebert's attitude to women, see von Moos, *Hildebert von Lavardin*, pp. 208–27.

7. Carm. 23, PL 171, 1659C:

Filia Fulconis, decus Armoricae regionis,
   Pulchra, pudica, decens, candida, clara, recens,
Si non passa fores thalamos, partusque labores,
   Posses esse meo Cynthia judicio.
Sed quia juncta mari castae nequit aequiparari,
   Est etiam potior virginitatis honor.

Cf. also Carm. 24 (to the Queen of the English), PL 171, 1660; his hymn to Mary Magdalene, PL 171, 1647f.; Carm. 12 ("Commendatio castitatis"), PL 171, 1653; Carm. 14, 15 (hymns to virgins), PL 171, 1654–55. Also Hildebert, Carm. 4 ("Ad reginam Anglorum"), ed. Scott, p. 2; Carm. 19 ("De Lucretia"), ed. Scott, p. 9; Carm. 27 ("Epitaph. Bone virginis"), ed. Scott, p. 18; Carm. 30 ("Super quandam matronam"), ed. Scott, p. 19; Carm. 35 ("Ad Mathildam Reginam"), ed. Scott, p. 22.

8. See Jaeger, "Courtliness and Social Change," esp. pp. 294–95.

9. Elliott shows that opposition of the reform movement to clerical marriage and concubinage made women into a particular object of attack (*Spiritual Marriage*, pp. 98–104). I believe that this is the historical background for the Loire circle's warnings to and against women. It also shows how the exaltation of women can keep company with and grow out of criticism.

10. Anselm, Epist. 168, 169, *Opera Omnia*, ed. Schmitt, 4.43–50. On these letters and the historical circumstances see R. W. Southern, *St. Anselm and His Biographer*, pp. 185–88, and Southern, *St. Anselm: A Portrait in a Landscape*, pp. 262–64.

11. For reasons that escape me, Southern sees in these two letters a return to the "eloquent fervor of personal attachment" common in his letters as prior and abbot of Bec (*Anselm: A Portrait*, p. 263). The runaway nun Gunhild can only have felt a chill around the heart at the dour reduction of affection to an imposed duty in the archbishop's greeting, "the charity by which I wish all men to be saved and the office laid upon me require me to love you with fraternal and paternal affection." Epist. 168, trans. Fröhlich, 2.64; ed. Schmitt, 4.43.

12. See Peter Damian's comment that to embrace a female body is to embrace a corpse. *Epistolarium*, bk. 1, Epist. 15, PL 144, 232D–233A. Also Bultot, *La Doctrine du Mépris du monde*, p. 25. More generally on his attitude to women, Elliott, *Spiritual Marriage*, pp. 102–3.

13. Heinrich von Melk, "Von des todes gehugde," 19, 1–19, *Religiöse Dichtungen*, ed. Maurer, 3.337.

14. Cf. Anselm's letter 167 (trans. Fröhlich, 2.62–63; ed. Schmitt, 4.41–42) to Countess Ida of Boulogne, also notorious for her amours, more loving and restrained in his chastening of worldliness.

15. Following the study of Latzke, "Der Fürstinnenpreis," esp. 46ff.

16. See Diane Bornstein, "Antifeminism," in *Dictionary of the Middle Ages*, 1.322–25; R. Howard Bloch, *Medieval Misogyny and the Invention of Western Romantic Love*.

17. The exception is of course praise of female saints and of the Virgin Mary. The point remains, unregenerate secular women are praised for approaching, entering, excelling in the religious life, not for virtues inherent to their sex and certainly not for their ability to infuse men with those virtues. One might look for an exception to this in the poem entitled "De muliere forti," from the early eleventh century, MGH Poetae 5.601–10, a verse meditation on Proverbs 31.10–31 adapted from Bede's proverb commentary. But the *mulier* is the church in its relation to its bridegroom, Christ. A nun Hadewig, *nobilissima femina* (p. 602, lines 14–15), is mentioned in the prologue and final lines. She is the earthly embodiment of the *mulier fortis*, "as long as she serves the good life chastely" (p. 610, lines 276ff.). Peter Damian's letters to noblewomen, including the Empress Agnes, are instructive on the representation of the high noblewoman in the mid-eleventh century. Praise of virtue is always coupled with reminders of mutability and urgings to the religious life.

18. See Alcuin Blamires, *The Case for Women*. Especially useful is his collection of translated texts, *Woman Defamed and Woman Defended*. When the manuscript of this book was finished, I came upon the new study by Rüdiger Schnell, *Frauendiskurs, Männerdiskurs, Ehediskurs: Textsorten und Geschlechterkonzepte in Mittelalter und früher Neuzeit*. It gives by far the most differentiated view of anti-feminism and shows the positive view of woman as far wider than has been imagined.

19. See Archibald R. Lewis, *The Development of Southern French and Catalan Society*, pp. 123–24, 391–92. The classic study of women as owners and administrators of land in the earlier Middle Ages is Herlihy, "Land, Family, and Women in Continental Europe." The problem is analyzed and the scholarship broadly reviewed by Bond, *Loving Subject*, pp. 129–57, with extensive bibliography for France. See also Duby, "Women and Power."

20. Edited with commentary by André Boutemy, "Une version médiévale inconnue de la légende d'Orphée," in *Hommages à Joseph Bidez et à Franz Cumont*, Collection Latomus 2 (Brussels: Latomus, 1941), 43–70. See the commentary in Jaeger, *Envy of Angels*, pp. 132–33, 141–45.

21. See my article, "Orpheus in the Eleventh Century."

22. Cf. Dronke, *Women Writers of the Middle Ages*, pp. 84–92, and Bond, *Loving Subject*, pp. 141–43. A poem from perhaps a decade later by a nun complaining against "slanderers of poetry" who think that "it is not for religious women to compose verses" suggests that it had become a conflicted question. For text and translation of the poem, see Bond, *Loving Subject*, pp. 166–69.

23. On the rise of the cult of Mary Madgalene, see Victor Saxer, *Le culte de Marie Madeleine en Occident des origines à la fin du moyen âge* (Paris: Clavreuil, 1959). On the connection with views of woman in the later eleventh century, see Bond, *Loving Subject*, pp. 140–41.

24. Cf. Song of Songs 4.9: "caritate/amore languescor."

25. Cf. 14.26ff.: [Ruodlieb commends the marriage to his relatives] "It behooves us all to consent to this marriage, so that a man of such character and such excellent virtues is not dishonored, but rather is separated from that foul whore who has more than deserved burning."

26. 16.17ff.: [find a woman] "Per cuius mores tibi nec minuantur honores."

27. *Encomium Emmae Reginae*, ed. and trans. Alistair Campbell, Camden 3rd Ser. 72 (London: Offices of the Royal Historical Society, 1949), p. 32. The encomium was commissioned by Emma herself and the image of the queen and wife it draws clearly had her approval. The passage is cited and analyzed, along with other portraits of "conqueror" women, by Searle, "Emma the Conqueror."

28. Jaeger, *Envy of Angels*, passim.

29. Other than the praise of particular virtues, the female panegyrics Latzke cites do not have the motif of woman the moral equal or the moral improver of man.

30. The widow of books 10–12 is also *hera* and *domina* over a castle and land. On women as landowners, see the study by Herlihy, "Land, Family, and Women."

31. See Dronke, *Poetic Individuality*, pp. 33–65, on this passage, 58–59. Also Bond, *The Loving Subject*, p. 257, n. 33.

32. Not having been included complete in the Migne edition of Marbod's *Carmina* (PL 171), they are scattered through various publications. Esp. Bulst, "Liebesbriefgedichte Marbods." Others in Werner, *Beiträge zur Kunde der lateinischen Literatur des Mittelalters*.

33. All except the last three in the "Liebesbriefgedichte" edited by Bulst fit this description. Also, *Beiträge*, ed. Werner, Carm. 8, p. 65.

34. "Liebesbriefgedichte," ed. Bulst, p. 192. PL 171, 1667 ("Vos qui diligitis bona"), 1669 ("Demonis inventum scelerum"), 1655 ("Egregium vultum"), *Beiträge*, ed. Werner, Carm. 9, pp. 6–7.

35. PL 171, 1491.

36. PL 171, 1653 ("Ut flos in pratis"), 1654 ("splendidior stella simplex").

37. *Marbodi Liber Decem Capitulorum*, ed. Leotta (earlier edition, *Marbodi ep. Redonensis liber decem capitulorum*, ed. Bulst). The work dates ca. 1102. That sets it contemporary with the poems of Baudri treated in the next section, but Marbod began writing poems of love and misogyny earlier than his student Baudri. We are looking at a late work that preserves the simple dualism of whore-*domina* alongside the complexities that enter the discourse with Baudri. See Bulst's *Studien zu Marbods Carmina varia und Liber decem capitulorum*.

38. *Liber decem capitulorum*, "Chapters" 3 and 4. Bulst uses the titles given in the Editio princeps (1524), "De meretrice" and "De matrona," Leotta those given in the two major twelfth-century manuscripts, "De muliere mala," "De muliere bona." On the titles, see Leotta's introduction to his edition, pp. 12–13.

39. Both poems are translated in Blamires, *Woman Defamed and Woman Defended*, pp. 100–103 ("De meretrice") and pp. 228–32 ("De matrona"). Translations in the text are my own.

40. See McLaughlin, "Peter Abelard and the Dignity of Women: Twelfth-Century Feminism in Theory and Practice," 287–334.

41. See Jaeger, "Courtliness and Social Change."

42. A formulation of Hildebert in his poem to Queen Mathilda of England, wife of Henry I, Carm. 35, line 13, ed. Scott, p. 22: *muliebris gloria sexus*.

43. *Carmina*, ed. Hilbert, no. 137, p. 190, lines 35–40. Baudri told the nun Constance also that no other woman had received his poems, but this does not belie his claim that at one point he included women after exclusively writing to males.

44. See Bond, "*Iocus amoris*," pp. 42–69.

45. "Ad Dominam Constantiam," *Carmina*, ed. Hilbert, no. 200, pp. 266–71. See Dronke, *Women Writers*, pp. 85–91; Bond, "*Iocus amoris*," and *The Loving Subject*, pp. 42–69. The translation is for the most part my own, though I have consulted Dronke's and Bond's translations (*Loving Subject*, pp. 171–81) and borrowed from them occasionally. For another commentary on the poem, see Ruhe, *De amasio ad amasiam*, pp. 25–27.

46. Cf. lines 51–52: "Your writings have stirred my feelings for you / And your Muse has joined me to you deep within." In an extravagant conceit, Baudri depicts himself as the conquering Christian hero, having taken the Greeks captive, and leading them into servitude for the community at Bourgueil. Each and every "Greek trifle" can educate them, as Greek slaves educated the Romans:

Athens is conquered and led captive to Bourgueil,
Barbaric Greece now serves at Bourgueil. (129–30)

Burgulii victae nunc captivantur Athenae,
  Barbara nunc servit Grecia Burgulio.

And now he invites Constance to the mutual study of their works to whet their taste for "lofty things."

47. *Carmina*, ed. Hilbert, no. 139, p. 192, lines 1–6.

48. Ibid., no. 193, p. 255, lines 16–17.

49. Cf. no. 193, lines 25–28:

Now I am sterile to you, now I am like an impotent man;
I cannot improve you but I can love you.
But don't be too anxious about our love.
I who now am sterile will some day bear children.

Nunc tibi sum sterilis, nunc sum tamquam vir inanis;
  Non prodesse queo, sed queo diligere.
Non omnino tamen nostrum verearis amorem;
  Qui modo sum sterilis, quandoque parturiam.

50. Cf. lines 81–82: "Ipse tue semper sum virginitatis amator, / Ipse tue carnis diligo mundiciam." I assume that the thick irony of a formulation like "virginitatis amator" would not have escaped the recipient or any comparably literate reader.

51. See Dronke's comments on the tone of the Baudri-Constance letters in *Women Writers*, pp. 86–91.

52. Even if she had not yet taken vows, the fact of living in a convent could be interpreted as acceptance in advance of the monastic vows. See Anselm of Canterbury's letters 168 and 169, discussed earlier in this chapter.

53. *Carmina*, ed. Hilbert, no. 201, pp. 271–76. Translation of her poem in Bond, *Loving Subject*, pp. 183–93. As if to demonstrate formally her will to match him point for point, her poem has exactly the same number of lines as his (178). Dronke, *Women Writers*, pp. 85–91, reads her poem as an intricate, witty play on Ovidian themes, with Constance slipping in and out of roles of the women in love of the *Heroides*.

54. Pointed out by Dronke, *Women Writers*, p. 89.

55. He confesses his own levity in the poem to Constance: "I am not the grim type. Everything I do is a jest. A light-hearted nature has made life a game for me" (144–45).

56. Cf. lines 38, 40, 42–43, 46, 48 (identical with 38), 49–50, 71–73, 79–80, 83.

57. *Carmina*, ed. Hilbert, no. 99, p. 117, lines 185–95.

58. Ibid., no. 217, p. 287.

59. Ibid., no. 134, pp. 149–85; ed. Abrahams, no. 196. See Brinkmann, *Entstehungsgeschichte*, pp. 21ff. and Bond, "*Iocus amoris*," pp. 180–81. Also on Adela of Blois generally and Baudri and Adela, Bond, *Loving Subject*, pp. 129–57. Abrahams dates the poem between 1099 and 1102 (p. 232). Bond (p. 260, n. 56) argues for an earlier date, 1096.

60. The educating force of love is present in other poems of this circle to women, however. See Brinkmann, *Entstehungsgeschichte*, p. 25. Baudri writes to Domina Emma: "If your order allowed disciples, I would wish to be your disciple. Gather me now beneath your love, o virgin, I have gathered you beneath mine." *Carmina*, ed. Hilbert, no. 139, p. 192, lines 17–20.

61. Ed. Dronke, Carm. 27 (Paravicini, no. 36), pp. 430–31.

62. On this confused passage I am following Paravicini's text, which construes the grammar more consistently than Dronke's.

63. Now the standard text, Trall, ed., "'Parce continuis?" I quote with reference to Trall's line numbering. The poem was earlier tentatively attributed to Abelard with some plausibility. See Wilhelm Meyer, "Zwei mittellateinische Lieder in Florenz," in *Studi letterari e linguistici dedicati a Pio Rajna* (Milan, 1911), pp. 149ff. ("Über Liebe und Freundschaft; ein Gedicht Abaelards?"). Raby, "*Amor* and *amicitia*," pp. 609–10. The ascription rests on the congruence of "Parce" lines 133–35:

Do quietem fidibus.
finem, quaeso, luctibus
tu curas alentibus.

with the ending of Abelard's "Planctus" on Saul and Jonathan:

do quietem fidibus;
vellem ut et planctibus
sic possem et fletibus.

But the ascription has not taken. For other commentary, see Dronke, *Medieval Latin and the Rise*, pp. 341–52; Ziolkowski, "Twelfth-Century Understandings," pp. 74–76.

64. Lines 29–30: "non altis sermonibus / solis loquar fidibus." It is probably an Orphic pose. He is clearly learned and in command of "lofty sentiments" (*alti sermones*).

65. See Glendinning, "Pyramus and Thisbe in the Medieval Classroom."

66. *Recueil des historiens des Gaules et de la France*, ed. Leopold Deslisle (Paris, 1878), 16: 23.

67. The letter has recently been analysed by Ursula Peters and Rolf Köhn in a joint article: "Höfisches Liebeswerben oder politisches Heiratsangebot?" They work out the historical background in detail, but interpret it as proposing a secret and politically explosive liaison.

68. See D'Alverney, "Comment les théologien et les philosophes voient la femme," p. 116–17; McLaughlin, "Peter Abelard and the Dignity of Women," passim.

69. Cf. also the poem by Petrus Pictor, "de mala muliere," *Carmina*, ed. van Acker, CCCM 25 (Turnholt: Brepols, 1972), carm. 14 and 16, esp. 14.255–91.

70. See Jaeger, *Envy of Angels*, pp. 264–67; Henri Platelle, "Le problème du scandale: les nouvelles modes masculines aux XIe et XIIe siècles," *Revue Belge de Philologie et d'Histoire* 53 (1975): 1071–96; Bond, *Loving Subject*, pp. 106–10.

71. *De vita sua*, pp. 78–82; trans. Benton, 65–66. Pointed out in Bezzola, *Origines*, 2.2.468–69.

Chapter 7: Sublime Love

1. This is not to deny its presence in Arab eroticism. See Nelli, *L'érotisme des troubadours*, 1: 87–97. Also Boase, *Origin and Meaning of Courtly Love*.

2. Leo Spitzer, *L'amour lontain de Jaufré Rudel*, pp. 1–2.

3. To call it "the basis of all troubadour poetry" is overstating it. Some of Jaufré Rudel's fellow troubadours found the idea of "amor de lonh" peculiar, even unmanly. See the article on Jaufré by L. Rossi, in *Lexikon des Mittelalters*, 7.1069. Also Bumke's treatment of *amor purus* in *Höfische Kultur* (pp. 513–16). For every example Bumke cites of chaste love, he can also show an ironical or critical perspective on it. Contemporaries could view this ideal as extreme, unattainable, even "unnatural."

4. *The Life of Ailred of Rievaulx*, chap. 2, p. 2; chap. 3, pp. 5ff. The biography dates ca. 1170.

5. Ibid., chap. 2, p. 2: "Rex vehementer amabat eum"; "amore complexus est."

6. Ibid., chap. 3, pp. 5ff.

7. See the analysis of Aelred's court service in McGuire, *Brother and Lover*, pp. 40–52. Also in Jaeger, *Origins of Courtliness*, pp. 37–39.

8. *Brother and Lover*, esp. pp. 39–52, 59–67.

9. *Spiritual Friendship*, Prologue, 2–3, trans. Laker, p. 45; ed. Hoste, p. 287.

10. The same is true of Walter Daniel's description of Aelred's clash with the boorish knight. The gentle, loving victory over the boorish knight reads like an illustration of *De amicitia* 21.77:

even these [disputes, abuse and invective] are to be borne, and such respect is to be paid to the old-time friendship that he may be in the wrong who committed the offence and not he who suffered it.

11. *Spiritual Friendship*, 1.25–26, trans. Laker, p. 56; ed. Hoste, p. 293:

IVO: Cum tanta sit in amicitia vera perfectio, non est mirum quod tam rari fuerunt hi quos veros amicos antiquitas commendavit . . . Quod si nostris, id est christianis temporibus, tanta est raritas amicorum, frustra, ut mihi videtur, in huius virtutis acquisitione desudo, quam me adepturum, eius mirabili sublimitate territus, iam pene despero.
AELREDUS: . . . virtuosae mentis est sublimia semper et ardua meditari . . .

12. He does not name them, but the first may have been a monk named Simon whose early death Aelred laments in the *Speculum caritatis* (1.98, chap. 34, *Opera Omnia*, ed. Hoste, p. 57), the other Geoffrey of Dinant. See Powicke, *Aelred of Rievaulx and His Biographer Walter Daniel*, p. 50; McGuire, *Friendship and Community*, pp. 310–14, and *Brother and Lover*, pp. 64–66.

13. 3.120, ed. Hoste, pp. 345–46: "Et primum quidem virtutum eius contemplatio illi meum inclinavit affectum."

14. Trans. Laker, p. 127; ed. Hoste, p. 346: "plurimis exemplo fuit, admirationi multis, mihi gloriae et delectationi."

15. 3.89, trans. Laker, p. 114; ed. Hoste, p. 336: "in sermone iucunditas, hilaritas in vultu, suavitas in moribus, in oculorum etiam nutu serenitas." On these qualities as courtly virtues, see Jaeger, *Origins of Courtliness*, pp. 128–73 and *Envy of Angels*, pp. 96–116.

16. 2.19, trans. Laker, p. 74; ed. Hoste, p. 306. Aelred would agree with Abelard, who wrote to his son Astralabius, "Brothers there are many, but a friend among them is rare" ("sunt multi fratres sed in illis rarus amicus" — *Carmen ad Astralabium*, ed. Rubingh-Boscher, line 119). Aelred describes Christ's love for John in these terms in the *Speculum caritatis*, 3.110, chap. 39, ed. Hoste, p. 159: "licet a piissimo magistro discipuli omnes summae caritatis dulcedine foverentur, huic tamen hoc cognomen familiarioris affectus praerogativa concessit, ut diceretur discipulus ille, quem amabat Iesus."

17. 3.82–83, trans. Laker, p. 112; ed. Hoste, p. 334.

18. 3.85, trans. Laker, p. 113; ed. Hoste, p. 335: "Haec amicitia tam sublimis est et perfecta, ut ad eam aspirare non audeam."

19. Baudri of Bourgueil regularly makes his friends aware that his friendship is "special," opposed both to "carnal" and to "common" or "communal." Urging the nun Agnes to guard her virginity, he writes, "This letter I send you is not for everyone [*communis*], it savors of the special. Its special savor comes from the fact that it sings a song of love" [Quod tibi mando, vale communis epistola non est; / Non est communis, que speciale sapit. / Hec speciale sapit, quia carmen cantat amoris]. *Carmina*, ed. Hilbert, no. 138, p. 191, lines 3–5). Godfrey of Reims he calls "Tu . . . alter ego non ut communis amicus, / Sed specialis . . ." (no. 99, p. 118, lines 213–14); the *specialis amor* he proposes to Lady Constance is set against carnal (common, vulgar) rather than communal love (no. 200, p. 268, lines 77–80), as is the "special way of life" enjoined on the Liège master in Regensburg Song no. 27.

20. 2.41, trans. Laker, p. 80; ed. Hoste, p. 310 (quoting Cicero, *De amicitia* 18). Cf. 2.10, trans. Laker, p. 71; ed. Hoste, p. 304: "[Friendship] manifests all the virtues by its own charms; it assails vices by its own virtue"; 2.38: "[Friendship] can

begin among the good, progress among the better and be consummated among the perfect . . . it springs from an esteem for virtue" (trans. Laker, pp. 78–79; ed. Hoste, p. 309); 2. 55: "friendship cannot endure except among the good" (trans. Laker, p. 83; ed. Hoste, p. 312); 2.63: [the friendship of David and Jonathan] "was consecrated from the contemplation of virtue" (trans. Laker, p. 85; ed. Hoste, p. 314); 3.59: "we are speaking of true friendship, which cannot exist except among the good . . ." (trans. Laker, p. 105; ed. Hoste, p. 328); 3.80: "This is true and eternal friendship, which . . . here belongs to the few where few are good, but there belongs to all where all are good" (trans. Laker, p. 111; ed. Hoste, p. 333).

21. Aelred did indeed stir resentment in Rievaulx, in part by his practice of limiting access to his presence to all but a handful of close friends. See McGuire, *Friendship and Community*, pp. 333–38. In both the theory of *Spiritual Friendship* and in the governance of the community at Rievaulx, Aelred's friendship, says McGuire, was "almost too personal and too special as a recommendation for the monastery as a whole."

22. Ivo notes that neither in pagan nor in Christian times have there ever been many able to do so (1.25). Cf. 2.9; 2.38.

23. McGuire (*Friendship and Community*) and Hyatte (*The Arts of Friendship*, esp. pp. 43–86) both distinguish between the elitism of personal friendship and the communal *caritas* important to the ordered life of the monastery, but they concentrate on the latter and allow it to subsume texts which fall into the category of "sublime," "special" friendship.

24. A "use" of the more elite, restrictive form of friendship not touched on in the theoretical or epistolary writings on friendship is the influence that men in authority can bring to bear to create peace and settle conflicts in communities. See the study by Julian Haseldine, "Friendship and Rivalry."

25. See the studies by Alfred Karnein, *De amore in volkssprachlicher Literatur*; also various essays in Karnein's *Amor est passio*. Also Rüdiger Schnell, *Andreas Capellanus: Zur Rezeption des römischen Rechts in "De Amore"*.

26. See Karnein, *De amore in volkssprachlicher Literatur*. The extremes to which Andreas can tempt interpreters are checked in an article by Monson, "Andreas Capellanus and the Problem of Irony."

27. The structure is suggested by the model of Ovid's *Ars amatoria* and *De remedia amoris*. See Karnein, "Andreas Capellanus, Ovid, and the Consistency of *De Amore*," in his *Amor est passio*, pp. 23–40.

28. *Andreas Capellanus on Love*, 1.470–72, ed. and trans. Walsh, p. 181.

29. Later in the work Andreas approves "pure love" in his own voice (6.6.24–25, 38–39, pp. 245, 249).

30. Stated paradigmatically by Suger of St. Denis in his second book on the consecration of the church of St. Denis, chap. 1, ed. and trans Panofsky, pp. 82–83: [those who wish to participate in divine reason] "forget carnal desires to the admiration and amazement of others" [Carnalia desideria in admirationem et spectaculum aliorum obliviscuntur].

31. 1.6.91, p. 65; 1.6.147, p. 81; 1.6.211, p. 101; 1.6.217, p. 103: "Nothing in the whole world is more desirable than love, because from love comes instruction in every good deed, and without it no man in the world could achieve any good"; 1.6.286, p.

123: "Only men of great soul deserve to know the intimate secrets of mistresses, and to obtain their love"; 1.6.305, p. 127; 1.6.403, p. 159; 1.6.412, p. 161; 1.6.472, p. 181; 1.6.513, p. 193; 2.1.10, p. 227; 2.8.46, p. 283: [Rule of love 18] "Honesty of character alone makes a man worthy of love." "Honesty of character" (*probitas morum*) is one of the five means of acquiring love (1.6.1, p. 41). This quality is set above beauty and eloquence, indeed, it can confer beauty on a plain lover: "Honesty of character gains a love that shines with honesty of character. . . . Honesty of character alone truly enriches a man with nobility, and makes him thrive with glowing beauty" (1.6.11, 14, p. 45).

32. Cf. 1.6.468, p. 179 (a woman "advances her fame" under the impulse of love; if she refuses this, "she will not deserve to obtain a praiseworthy husband, nor to achieve the full effect of any great experience"); 1.6.477, p. 183 (a man capable of "chaste love" is "most worthy of every distinction"); 2.7.27, p. 261: "Any woman desirous of winning the world's praises is bound to devote herself to love." "Raising worth" can refer to moral worth or social standing. It is connected with the process by which men are educated through the influence of women. Cf. 2.7.28, p. 261: "This lady by her teaching so strengthened her love in worthy manners, whilst granting him kisses and embraces, that through her he attained the highest worth of character, and deserved praise for general honesty." This whole line of thought is squarely contradicted in 3.24–28, p. 295.

Chapter 8: Love Beyond the Body

1. *Peter Abelard's Ethics*, ed. and trans. Luscombe, p. 4, lines 15–17.

2. *Metalogicon* 1.8.

3. Bernard, *Sermo in Cant.* 1.11, *S. Bernardi Opera*, 1.8: "Est quippe nuptiale carmen, exprimens castos iucundosque complexus animorum, morum concordiam, affectuumque consentaneam ad alterutrum caritatem."

4. Paulinus of Nola spoke of "chaste lust" (*casta voluptas*) as Christ's compensation to the faithful for renouncing earthly pleasures. Carm. 10, lines 61ff.

5. "Eine Bamberger Ars Dictaminis," ed. Bittner, p. 155, lines 1–3: " . . . Godescalce, tibi, nostro carissime cordi, / Immo pars animae, rerum dulcissime, nostrae, / Dimidiumque fere . . ."; line 7: "frater amate"; line 15: "nostro dulcissime cordi"; line 18: "o mi dulcis amice"; line 19: "mi dulcis frater, quo non michi carior alter."

6. Carm. 27, ed. Dronke, *Medieval Latin and the Rise*, p. 430, line 14: "Ex habitu casto quod agit decorans et honesto."

7. CB no. 59, stanza 5: "Questio per singulas / oritur: honesta / potiorque dignitas / casta, vel incesta?"

8. "Amoris solamine / virgino cum virgine; / aro non in semine, / pecco sine crimine."

9. On the "five stages" of love, see Baldwin, *The Language of Sex*, p. 164 and n. 123.

10. See Douglas Kelly, " 'Li chastiaus . . . Qu'amors prist puis par ses esforz,' " 61–78.

11. See Bumke, *Höfische Kultur*, pp. 503–29 and Schnell, "Die Höfische Liebe als höfischer Diskurs." Bumke's treatment of "fulfilled and unfulfilled love" (pp. 513–16) argues the unreality of chaste love. But I think the texts he cites show the opposite: not

only that chaste love is in the center of the debate on "what is love?" but that it was admired and looked at in awe. Admiration in some parts does not exclude ridicule in others and vice versa.

12. Cited in Bumke, *Höfische Kultur*, p. 514.

13. Ibid.

14. *Le Breviari d'Amor de Matfre Ermengau*, esp. lines 27323–84, in *Les Troubadours II: le trésor poétique de l'Occitanie*, ed. and trans. René Nelli and René Lavaud, pp. 666–67. Cited in Benton, "Clio and Venus," p. 30 and n. 36.

15. *De amore* 1.4, ed. Walsh, p. 39: "amor reddit hominem castitatis quasi virtute decoratum." [Love renders man, as it were, beautiful with the virtue of chastity.]

16. Cited and translated in Douglas Kelly, *The Medieval Imagination*, p. 19.

17. See Jaeger, *Envy of Angels*, pp. 159–64, 184–86. Also Udo Friedrich, "Überwindung der Natur."

18. Hexter, *Ovid and Medieval Schooling*, p. 158.

19. *The Epistles on the Romance of the Rose*, ed. Charles Frederick Ward (Chicago, 1911), p. 94, lines 446–54. Cited in Kelly, *The Medieval Imagination*, p. 17.

20. See Thum, *Aufbruch und Verweigerung*, and Dyan Elliott, *Spiritual Marriage*. Also in early Christianity, see Brown, *Body and Society*.

21. Also worth mentioning: "The countess of Die (born 1140) would allow the lover embraces and kisses that must stop short of the consummation that is the husband's prerogative." Cited from Jo Ann McNamara, "The *Herrenfrage*," p. 24, n. 28.

22. RS 67: 2, p. 303 chap. 3. On Becket and courtliness, see Jaeger, *Envy of Angels*, pp. 297–309.

23. Boutière and Schutz, *Biographies des troubadours*, p. 17. Quoted with English translation in L. T. Topsfield, *Troubadours and Love*, p. 42.

24. On the genesis of the legend out of Jaufré's poems, see Monson, "Jaufré Rudel et l'amour lointain." Along with scholarship on Jaufré generally, I am following Spitzer's reading of the "love" as directed to an unknown lady, not to the holy land or the virgin Mary. See Spitzer, *L'amour lointain*. See also Baldwin, *Language of Sex*, pp. 152–53 and n. 102.

25. In this partial paraphrase I am following the text of *The Songs of Jaufré Rudel*, ed. Pickens, pp. 164–68.

26. See Zade, *Der Troubadour Jaufré Rudel*.

27. Marie de France, *Lais*, ed. Ewert, "Lanval," lines 110ff. Pierre Bec points out the distinction between the two motifs, distant love and love before first sight, but accepts the kind of love implied as fundamentally related. See his "'Amour de loin' et 'dame jamais vue,'" with useful bibliography.

28. *Lays of Desiré, Graelent and Melion*, ed. Grimes, lines 71ff.

29. For further examples in Old French sources, see Guerreau-Jalabert, *Index des motifs narrativs dans les romans arthuriennes français en vers*, p. 187; Ruck, *An Index of Themes and Motifs in Twelfth-Century French Arthurian Poetry*, p. 105. For the German sources I am following Horst Wenzel, "Fernliebe und Hohe Minne."

30. *König Rother*, lines 1909–13.

31. *Partonopier und Meliur*, lines 1834–45.

32. *Des Minnesangs Frühling* (hereafter MF). Here Meinloh von Sevelingen, 1.1.1–2 (earlier editions 11, 1–2).

33. MF, Reinmar der Alte, 19.2.1–4 (earlier editions, 170, 8–11).

34. Paulinus of Nola writes to Augustine, "My loving brother in Christ, I have long known of your holy and dutiful labors . . . and beheld and embraced you, though we are apart, with my whole heart" (Epist. 6, *Letters of St. Paulinus of Nola*, 1.70); CSEL 29, pp. 39–40. And Venantius Fortunatus in a poem to Dynamius of Marseilles: "I await you, my love, revered Dynamius, whom my affection sees even though you are absent. . . . Torn from my sight, you are with me, bound to my heart" (6.9.1ff.; *Opera poetica*, ed. Leo, p. 149; *Personal and Political Poems*, trans. George, p. 55).

35. Cf. his letter to Abbot Moroald and the monks of Farfa: "Though with the eyes of the body I may never have seen you, yet I seem to see you with the eyes of the heart, and I love you very much, and in my eager mind I embrace the goodness of your life" [licet oculis carnis non vidissem, tamen oculis cordis vos videre videor et valde diligo; honestatemque vitae vestrae animo complector studioso] (Epist. 91, p. 135, lines 19ff.).

36. Anselm, Epist. 45, trans. Fröhlich, pp. 151–52; ed. Schmitt, 1.158.

37. Epist. 4, trans. Fröhlich, p. 81; ed. Schmitt, 1.104. Reputation stimulates love: "Dearly beloved, the more report testifies [to the *honestas* and holiness of your conduct] . . . the more your friend's heart is inflamed by the desire of seeing what he hears by loving" (Epist. 5, trans. Fröhlich, p. 83; ed. Schmitt, 1.106); distance is no hindrance: "no interval of earth or water lying between us can cut off my affection for you" (Epist. 51, trans. Fröhlich, p. 159; ed. Schmitt, 1.164); perhaps even a goad to love: "because I cannot have you I love you even more" (Epist. 79, trans. Fröhlich, p. 210; ed. Schmitt, 1.202); but his longing is constant for those he loves without knowing them: "my mind will not rest until my eyes have seen his face, my ears have heard his voice and my soul has enjoyed the presence of him who, without knowing me . . . freely took me on with such love" (Epist. 85, trans. Fröhlich, p. 221; ed. Schmitt, 1.210).

38. *Carmina*, ed. Hilbert, pp. 121–22, no. 105, lines 1–6:

Rumores de te frater michi rettulit unus
. . . mei quoniam non immemor esses . . .
. . . quia me vehementer amares
Meque semel visum pectore congereres.

39. Hildebert, Epist. bk. 3, Epist. 18, PL 171, 294. Also among Bernard's letters, Epist. 122, *Bernardi Opera* 7.302–3.

40. Epist. 65, *Opera* 7.160.

41. Cf. the speech of the nobleman to noblewoman:

"Though I appear before your eyes only rarely in the flesh, in heart and mind I am never out of your presence. My thoughts which dwell continually on you often set me in your company, causing me to gaze constantly with the eyes of the heart on that treasure on which my attention lingers." (1.6. 198, p. 97)

42. This seems to me a more probable context for "distant love" than the "spatialization of social distance" suggested by Köhler, "Amor de lonh." Montaigne is clearly continuing a Ciceronian tradition when he claims to have loved his friend, La Boétie, prior to seeing him. Langer, *Perfect Friendship*, makes this point, also with reference to the Princesse de Clèves.

Chapter 9: Sleeping and Eating Together

1. See Boswell, *CSTH*, pp. 223–24 and plate 13. A well-known capital from Autun depicts the three Magi wearing their crowns and sleeping in a single bed. See Schiller, *Ikonographie der christlichen Kunst*, 1.110; Réau, *Iconographie de l'art Chrétien*, 2.2.252–53. My thanks to Klaus van Eickels for these references. See his study, "*Homagium* and *Amicitia*," p. 139 and n. 26.

2. Gregory of Tours, *Historia Francorum*, 9.19, ed. Giesebrecht and Buchner, 2.256: "... Sicharius ... magnam cum eo amicitiam patravisset et in tantum se caritate mutua diligerent, ut plerumque simul cibum caperent ac in uno pariter stratu recumberent ..." The prelude to their reconciliation, 7.47.

3. Nithard, *Hist.* 3.6, ed. Müller, pp. 37–38.

4. Petrus Damiani, *Vita Romualdi*, chap. 25, PL 145, 975C. See above, Chapter 3.

5. *Vita Adalberti*, chap. 23, MGH SS 4, 591: Otto III's adviser and courtier, Bishop Adalbert of Prague, became his "sweetest chamber-mate," they were together night and day and slept in the same room because "he loved him."

6. I do not know sleeping together as a gesture of friendship in antiquity. Alcibiades and Socrates slept together, but with the full expectation on the part of Alcibiades of being ravished by his master. Cicero's voice in the *Republic*, Scipio, expressed shock at the Lacadaemonian custom of young men sleeping together with their lovers separated only by their cloaks. Cicero, *De republica* 4.4.113. Cited in Marrou, *History of Education in Antiquity*, p. 366: "They permit everything but intercourse ... embracing and sleeping together with their cloaks separating them."

7. Though Althoff, *Amicitiae et Pacta*, only notes two cases. Others in van Eickels, "*Homagium* and *Amicitia*," pp. 138–39 and n. 26–28 and "Two Princes in One Bed: A Neglected Ritual of Peace-Making."

8. The king's bed probably had a public, representative role as important as the throne or the seat at table. Thietmar of Merseburg reports that the duke of Saxony, Hermann Billung, in 972 usurped royal prerogatives in "rebellious" fashion by occupying the emperor's (Otto I's) place among the bishops at table and in the emperor's bed. Thietmar, *Chronicle*, ed. Holtzmann, 2.28: "in medio episcoporum ad mensam loco imperatoris sederet lectoque dormiret." See the commentary by Gerd Althoff, "Das Bett des Königs in Magdeburg." Georges Duby points out a passage in a charter of the Abbey of Andres telling how a feudal tenant of Count Manasses of Guines, seeking approval of his donation to the abbey in 1117, came to the count and countess, who received him, "the two of them seated on their bed." Duby's commentary: "The bed: it was like a conjugal throne ..." ("Women and Power," p. 72). For some observations on the political use of the bed, see Hyams, "What Did Henry III of England Think in Bed," pp. 94–96. Literature offers examples: Eilhart of Oberge comments with surprise on the sleeping arrangements mentioned in his supposed source, a Breton lay, that place Tristan's bed in the same room with King Mark's (cited in Dürr, *Nacktheit und Scham*, p. 189 and n. 37; see also p. 183). Cf. the situation in the Spanish *Amadis of Gaul* by Garci Ordonez de Montalvo (1508) bk. 1, prol. and chap. 1: The king of Gaul falls in love with the daughter of his host, the King of Brittany, but their love trysts are hindered because the two kings sleep in the same bedroom (not the same bed, however). The lovers must invent an excuse that will remove the king diplomatically from his favorite's bedchamber. (Thanks to Stephanie Pafenberg for this reference.)

9. *Metalogicon* 4.42; trans. McGarry, p. 274.

10. A certain ambiguity remains in the word *concubitus*. It can mean simply "sleeping together." Cf. German *Beischlaf*. But Marbod does not make a distinction in this poem between sleeping together and sexual intercourse.

11. Quoted from Werner, *Beiträge zur Kunde*, p. 89, no. 200. The lines cited are missing in the Migne edition, PL 171, 1669.

12. The Benedictine Rule forbids holding hands and imposes strict surveillance on the dormitory (RB, chap. 22). See McGuire, *Friendship and Community*, pp. 82–83; Boswell, *CSTH*, p. 188.

13. See Elliott, *Spiritual Marriage*, p. 111 and n. 68. Bond, *Loving Subject*, pp. 138–40. Ernst Werner, "Zur Frauenfrage und zum Frauenkult im Mittelalter." The practice is evidently a renewal of the socalled *syneisactentum* or spiritual marriage practiced in the early church and in Irish monasticism. See Elliott, *Spiritual Marriage*, pp. 32–38; Werner, "Zur Frauenfrage," pp. 272–73; the article by Hans Achelis, "Virgines subintroductae (Syneisaktoi)," in *Schaff-Herzog Encyclopedia of Religious Knowledge* (New York and London: Funk and Wagnalls, 1911), 125–26.

14. PL 171, 1481 (Epist. 6). Cited in Bond, *Loving Subject*, p. 138.

15. PL 157, 181–84.

16. For an analysis of this event, see Brian McGuire, *The Difficult Saint*, pp. 48–52. The relevant texts by Geoffrey of Clairvaux are not part of his biography of Bernard. See Robert Lechat, "Les fragmenta de vita et miraculis S. Bernardi par Geoffroy d'Auxerre," *Analecta Bollandiana* 50 (1932): 94–95.

17. It seems to me conceived at least in part as an illustration of Bernard's idea of a "natural language" of the body, far more spontaneous and truthful than learned language. See his interpretation of the "bride's belch," *Sermo 67 in Cant.*, 2.3–3.4.

18. It bears comparison with the legend of St. Julian the Hospitaler. Suffering under a curse, he is redeemed when he helps a leper ford a river at night, then takes the half-frozen man into his own bed, though he recognizes him as a leper. See *Acta Sanctorum*, January vol. 3, ed. Bolandus, pp. 589–90 (Jan. 29). The legend was popular and widespread. It is included in Jacobus da Voragine's *Golden Legend*. Caxton's version is given in *Butler's Lives of the Saints*, 1.314–16 (Feb. 12). In Flaubert's version (*Trois contes*), the leper asks Julian to lie down in bed with him, take off his clothes, and warm his diseased body by the touch of his own.

19. Laying on of hands is a common form in the *Liber miraculorum*.

20. See *Vita prima* 1.13–14, PL 185, 234–35 and McGuire's comments, *The Difficult Saint*, pp. 51–52.

21. Walter Map, *De Nugis Curialium*, Dist. 1, chap. 24, pp. 80–81.

22. *De speculo caritatis* 3.109–10, ed. Talbot and Hoste, p. 159. See the comments of Boswell, *CSTH*, pp. 225–26. and of Ruth Mazo Karras, "Friendship and Love in the Lives of Two Twelfth-Century English Saints."

Chapter 10: Eros Denied, Eros Defied

1. See Bynum, *Holy Feast, Holy Fast*. Also Karras, "Friendship and Love."

2. Comm. in Matthew bk. 12, 741–62; ed. Haacke, CCCM 29, pp. 382–83 (PL 168, 1601). This is followed some thirty days later by a dream of Christ floating down

from on high to settle in Rupert's bed and press his body against his own "in a manner that words cannot express." Upon awakening, Rupert still feels the "sweet weight," still exults in the memory of the melting of his soul and the "living and true delight" (*voluptas*) (781–97; pp. 383–84). The intensification of carnal pleasure marks stages in a rising understanding of the word of Christ.

3. *The Life of Christina of Markyate, a Twelfth-Century Recluse*, chap. 72, ed. and trans. Talbot, pp. 160–63.

4. The ambiguity is possible because *limen* is both lintel and threshold, both lower and upper boundary of a doorway.

5. The title of the lead essay in M.-D. Chenu's *Nature, Man, and Society in the Twelfth Century*, ed. and trans. Jerome Taylor and Lester K. Little (Chicago and London: University of Chicago Press, 1968).

6. See George Economou, *The Goddess Natura in Medieval Literature* (Cambridge, Mass.: Harvard University Press, 1972); Andreas Speer, "Kosmisches Prinzip und Mass menschlichen Handelns: *Natura* bei Alanus ab Insulis," in *Mensch und Natur im Mittelalter*, ed. Albert Zimmermann and Andreas Speer, Miscellanea Mediaevalia 21 (Berlin: de Gruyter, 1991), 1.107–28.

7. "*Quid suum virtutis*": *Eine Lehrdichtung des 11. Jahrhunderts*, ed. Anke Paravicini, Editiones Heidelbergenses 21 (Heidelberg: Winter, 1980), lines 1023–24. See Jaeger, *Envy of Angels*, pp. 146–47.

8. But see also Keith Busby, "Diverging Traditions of Gauvain in Some of the Later Old French Verse Romances," in *The Legacy of Chrétien de Troyes*, ed. Norris Lacy, Douglas Kelly, and Keith Busby (Amsterdam: Rodopi, 1988), 1: 93–109.

9. On accused queens and the motif of the accused queen or princess, see Alfred Karnein, "Mechthild von der Pfalz as Patroness: Aspects of Female Patronage in the Early Renaissance," *Medievalia et Humanistica* n.s. 22 (1995), 141–70, esp. 144–48 ("The Maligned Lady"); Donald J. Kagay, "Countess Almodis of Barcelona: 'Illustrious and Distinguished Queen' or 'Woman of Sad, Unbridled Lewdness,'" in *Queens, Regents and Potentates*, ed. Theresa M. Vann (Dallas, Tex.: Academia, 1993), 37–47; Margaret Schlauch, *Chaucer's Constance and Accused Queens* (New York: New York University Press, 1927).

10. Boccaccio, *The Decameron*, p. 825 (Tenth Day, conclusion).

11. The further away from the king's presence, the more it became possible. Cf. the scurrilities of Archbishop Conrad of Salzburg on the court of Henry IV of Germany, or those of Gerald of Wales on the English court.

12. A tantalizing bit of commentary prior to Polydore Vergil is an oblique comment in the tract of Mondonus Belvaleti on the order (1463). He says that "There are many who claim that this order took its rise from the female sex." *Tractatus ordinis serenissimi domini regis Anglie vulgariter dicti la Gerretiere* (Cologne, 1613), p. 7. Quoted in Beltz, *Memorials of the Most Noble Order of the Garter*, p. xiii, n. 2. The author's coyness is so obtrusive as to constitute evidence in itself; he must be keeping something quiet. At least it would seem to bear on Polydore Vergil's comment that historians of the garter have kept silent on its origins for fear of touching on issues so sensitive as to threaten insult of majesty.

13. Beltz was the first to take this line, but made clear that it was conjecture: *Memorials*, p. xlvii. Cf. Juliet Vale, *Edward III and Chivalry*, pp. 76ff.; Richard Barber,

Edward, Prince of Wales, p. 8off.; Keen, *Chivalry*, p. 194. Rejection of Margaret Galway's case for a liaison between Edward and Joan of Kent as a motive in founding the order is pretty much unanimous ("Joan of Kent and the Order of the Garter," *University of Birmingham Historical Journal* 1 [1947], 13–50). But recently James L. Gillespie has suggested that the contemporary testimony on Jean le Bel might imply a connection between Joan and the founding of the order ("Ladies of the Fraternity of Saint George and of the Society of the Garter," *Albion* 17 [1985], 260–61). For a thorough and balanced discussion see D'Arcy Boulton, *The Knights of the Crown: The Monarchical Orders of Knighthood in Later Medieval Europe*, esp. pp. 152–61.

14. Pointed out by Israel Gollancz, *Pearl: An English Poem of the Fourteenth Century* (London: Nutt, 1891), pp. xliff. See also Oscar Kargill and Margaret Schlauch, "The *Pearl* and Its Jeweler," *PMLA* 43 (1928): 118–23; a number of studies by Henry L. Savage, summarized in his *The Gawain-Poet: Studies in His Personality and Background* (Chapel Hill: University of North Carolina Press, 1956). The position taken by Barber and Vale is not reconcilable with a connection between *Sir Gawain* and the order. Since that connection is generally accepted, they need to come to terms with it or revise their position (or refute the connection). Boulton mentions the belt of the Gawain romance in connection with the Order of the Garter (*Knights of the Crown*, p. 158), but not the recurrence of the motto or the shame symbolized by the green belt that requires positing a similar meaning of the order's garter.

15. *Polydori Vergilii Urbinatis Anglicae historiae libri XXVI* (Basel, 1534).

16. See the study by Denis Hay, *Polydore Vergil: Renaissance Historian and Man of Letters* (Oxford: Oxford University Press, 1952), pp. 109ff.

17. *Anglica Historia*, p. 373: " . . . garter lingua Anglica, id ligaculum significet quo mulieres tibiarum tegmenta sibi ligant."

Chapter 11: Value, Worth, Reputation

1. Würzburg poem (Worms Letter Collection), lines 127–35. See above, Chapter 5.

2. Anselm, Epist. 58, trans. Fröhlich, p. 170; ed. Schmitt, 1.172.

3. Epist. 42, trans. Fröhlich, p. 145; ed. Schmitt, 1.153.

4. Epist. 45, trans. Fröhlich, pp. 151–52; ed. Schmitt, 1.158–59.

5. Bernard of Clairvaux, Epist. 116, *Opera* 7.296.

6. On this much studied motif see esp. Schutz, "The Provençal Expression 'Pretz et valor'"; Cropp, *Le vocabulaire courtois des troubadours de l'époque classique*, pp. 426–32, 435–38.

7. Peire Vidal, no. 24, st. 4; ed. Avalle, p. 193. Marcabru asks the emperor for his generosity, calls on the empress to help him and promises, "intercede for me, and I'll make your merit grow greater" (no. 23, st. 8; ed. Dejeanne, p. 113). The same poet asserts that loving in the courtly way makes a man behave well and a lady grow better (*meillurar*) but if a woman is faithless "her worth must surely decline" (no. 15, st. 5; ed. Dejeanne, p. 62). In a lament on the decline of love, Giraut de Borneilh says that since skilled minstrels no longer praise noble women, "their merit is in ruins" and much ill spoken of them (no. 65, st. 4; ed. Kolsen, vol. 1, p. 416). Aimeric de Péguilhan makes

love the sole source of joy and honor: "no man who's not in love . . . has ever joy or honor; for just as good sense is worth more than folly, so he is worth more who serves, and is more to be honored" (no. 19, st. 3; ed. Shepard and Chambers, p. 116).

8. See Schnell, *Causa Amoris*, pp. 66–71; Chênerie, *Le chevalier errant*, pp. 457–72; Kasten, *Frauendienst*, pp. 156–57, 181.

9. Dietmar von Eist, 3.2.1–4 in *MF* (earlier editions 33, 23–26).

10. Albrecht von Johansdorf, 12.7.3–6, *MF* (earlier editions 94, 11–14).

11. *The Romance of Yder*, ed. and trans. Adams, pp. 48–49, lines 664–68. See also 3660ff., 3718ff.

12. Also the Countess of Flanders is quoted in one of the judgments of the courts of love in the same sense: "Any woman desirous of winning the world's praises is bound to devote herself to love" (2.7.27, p. 261).

13. *Autobiographie*, ed. Labande, 78–82. *Self and Society in Medieval France*, trans. Benton, 65–66. Pointed out in Bezzola, *Origines*, 2.2.468f.

14. *Ethics*, ed. and trans. Luscombe, p. 16–17.

15. For instance, Schnell, "Höfische Liebe als höfischer Diskurs," p. 288: [in courtly love] "Ideale [waren] avisiert . . ., die mit den Normen der Adelswelt nicht in Einklang zu bringen waren"; Fleckenstein, epilogue to *Curialitas*, p. 469: "Es handelt sich offenbar um ein reines Kunstprodukt aus Bildung, Spiel, und Erotik, das heisst: ein schwebendes Gebilde dem schon am Hofe selbst alles andere als eine alltägliche Existenz zukam." Also Bumke, *Höfische Kultur*, pp. 503–29; Willms, *Liebesleid und Sangeslust*, pp. 4–8, 163–99 and passim and Johnson, "Down with Hôhe Minne!"

16. Bernard, Epist. 123, *Opera* 7.304.

17. See esp. on Andreas's irony Karnein, *De amore in volkssprachlicher Literatur*. For a persuasive answer to the tendency to find hidden sexual allusions and to dissolve all statements in *De amore* into irony, see Monson, "Andreas Capellanus and the Problem of Irony."

18. For some methodological considerations, see my article, "Courtliness and Social Change."

19. See my *Origins of Courtliness*.

20. See "Courtliness and Social Change," p. 298.

21. *Partonopier und Meliur*, 1834–40.

22. Willigis of Mainz (d. 1011) is said to have instructed "lovers of virtue" more by the "language of his conduct" (*lingua morum*) than by his speech. MGH, SS 15:2, p. 745, lines 31–32.

23. From a letter of Wibald of Stablo, *Wibaldi epistolae*, Epist. 167, p. 286. Hildebert of Lavardin addressed Bernard in the salutation of a letter as "the one in the church with the ability to educate others to virtue, in word as in example" (Hildebert, Epistolae bk. 3, Epist. 18, PL 171, 294C; among Bernard's letters, Epist. 122, *Opera* 7.303.

24. On the parallel of schoolmaster and courtly damsel as administrators of virtue, see Duby, *Love and Marriage in the Middle Ages*, p. 33.

25. *Tristan*, lines 636–40; trans. Hatto, p. 50.

26. Ibid., 8290–97; trans. Hatto, p. 150, here with minor variations.

27. Esp. evident in the brief tract ascribed to Richard de Fournival (mid-thirteenth century), "Amistié de vraie amour," ed. Pickford.

28. Graelent *and* Guingamor: *Two Breton Lays*, ed. and trans. Weingartner, pp. 6–7, lines 85–106.

29. Konrad Fleck, *Flore und Blancheflur*, lines 69–92.

30. See the dossier of essays on the subject: *Ritterliches Tugendsystem*, ed. Eifler.

Chapter 12: Heloise and Her Orbit

1. A perceived "wave" of homosexuality, inveighed against by Peter Damian in the eleventh century and Alan of Lille in the twelfth, and argued in modern scholarship by John Boswell, may be a factor: love between men and women needs to coopt male love's claim to virtue and cast itself as the legitimate form of ennobling love. See the parallel case in Elizabeth Keiser's *Courtly Desire and Medieval Homophobia*.

2. See Hans Peter Dürr, *Nacktheit und Scham*.

3. *Carmina*, ed. Hilbert, no. 99, p. 117, lines 189–91: ". . . si quid vellem, si quid vehementer amarem, / Esset amoris tunc nescia carta mei. / Non promulgetur confessio carmine nostra." See the discussion above, Chapter 6.

4. On misogyny and courtly love, see Bloch, *Medieval Misogyny and the Invention of Romantic Love*. See also the discussion above, Chapter 6.

5. Baudri's rich phrase is narrowed by our "act of love." "Love-work" would come closer.

6. See Foucault's vols. 2 and 3 of *History of Sexuality*. One of the ironies of that work (or those parts of it) is that it is not about sexuality per se, but the managing, the control, the dominance, the discipline imposed on sexuality.

7. Peter Brown, *Body and Society*, esp. on Augustine.

8. See Chapter 1, n. 34 and the discussion of "Helen and Ganymede."

9. *Epistolae duorum amantium*, ed. Ewald Könsgen. For discussion see Dronke, *Abelard and Heloise in Medieval Testimonies*. Both Dronke and Könsgen cautiously avoid an ascription to Abelard and Heloise, though the evidence for it Könsgen gives is strong. When this manuscript was in its last stages, I learned of the new book by Constant Mews, which places the ascription to Heloise and Abelard beyond question: *The Lost Love Letters of Heloise and Abelard: Perceptions of Dialogue in Twelfth-Century France*.

10. Cf. *Epistolae duorum amantium*, Epist. 24, p. 13 (Abelard to Heloise):

I receive your letters so avidly. . . . because they both inflame and satisfy my desire. I am like a man laboring in flames whom even a drink refreshes the more, the more it burns him. I swear to God that whenever I read them attentively, I am moved anew, in some new way, for my soul is cut by a joyous shudder, and my body is transformed, its bearing, its gestures are new.

The woman calls the man "sweet medicine for my body" (Epist. 76, p. 44, language shared with the Tristan romance, where sickness equals desire or longing, medicine equals sexual gratification. Also: "no one can cure my love except you alone" (Epist. 21, p. 9). She compares herself with stones heated to the melting point: "In the same way my body is consumed by love" (Epist. 82, p. 46). Epist. 113, p. 62 (Abelard to Heloise):

What are those things that lie concealed beneath your dress?
[At the thought] my mind finds no rest.
I wish to caress those things whenever they enter my mind.

11. Epist. 82, p. 46: "I shall never know joy except from you, / Both sorrow and grief pursue us constantly."

12. Epist. 24, pp. 13–14. For English translation see Appendix.

13. Cf. the salutation to Epist. 99, p. 55 (Abelard to Heloise): "To her who knows well the laws of love and fulfills them perfectly . . ." Epist. 113, p. 61 (*jura amoris*); Epist. 12, p. 6 (*amoris regula*); Epist. 50, p. 28 (*amicicie legibus*). The phrases are Ciceronian. Cf. *De amicitia* 13.44 (*lex amicitiae*) and 17.63 (*ius amicitiae*).

14. On the Augustinian character of the vocabulary, see Hannah Arendt, *Love and St. Augustine*, esp. pp. 9–17.

15. *Carmina minora*, Carm. 46, ed. Scott, p. 37, lines 7–10 (see *Epistolae duorum amantium*, ed. Könsgen, p. 94):

parcius elimans alias Natura puellas,
    distulit in dotes esse benigna tuas.
in te fudit opes, et opus mirabile cernens,
    est mirata suas hoc potuisse manus.

16. Easily surveyed in Könsgen's thorough annotation.

17. An allusion to the Song of Songs 5.10: "electus ex milibus" (Könsgen, p. 29), not only the arrogance of this writer ("inter *multa* milia").

18. Abelard says, "In many ways I am not your equal, to tell the truth in all ways I am not your equal, because you surpass me in the very things in which I seem to excel" (Epist. 50, p. 29).

19. Heloise writes,

May the ruler of heaven be our mediator, and the companion of our loyalty. Farewell, and may Christ, king of kings, save you, sweetest of men, into eternity. Prosper in him who rules all things on earth (Epist. 3, p. 3).

Cf. Epist. 52, p. 30 and passim.

20. Epist. 54, p. 31; Epist. 81, p. 46 (Heloise to Abelard): "let those who wish to separate us perish!" Epist. 85, p. 49 (Heloise says that deceiving "envious intriguers" fuels the fire of their love). Epist. 28, p. 17 (Abelard to Heloise): "Let those who envy us have plenty to envy and let them slowly wither at our bounty."

21. Epist. 75, p. 43:

We shall be able to love wisely, rare as that may be . . . because we shall both look after our reputation cautiously and still mix our joys with the highest sweetness!

Epist. 101, p. 56 (Abelard to Heloise):

Now I speak more cautiously with you, you may notice, I approach you more cautiously, shame tempers love and embarassment restrains it, lest it run wild, thus fulfilling our sweet prayers, but gradually undermining the fame that we have attained.

22. See the treatment of this dilemma by Denis de Rougement, *Love in the Western World*, which for all its historical mistakes still offers an incisive analysis.

23. Epist. 28, p. 17: "Let those who envy us have plenty to envy and let them slowly wither at our bounty." It is an Abelardian posture — to boldly confront and draw out the envy and malice of his opponents — a posture that contributed to his downfall.

24. Still standard commentary is the marvelous essay of Etienne Gilson on Heloise's "pure love" in *Heloise and Abelard*. Gilson also pointed out the Ciceronian source of her arguments against marriage. See also the important biography/study of Abelard's life by Clanchy, *Abelard: A Medieval Life*, esp. pp. 149–72.

25. The standard edition of the personal letters is by J. T. Muckle, "The Personal Letters Between Abelard and Heloise" (hereafter Muckle), passage cited p. 81. Quoted here from *The Letters of Abelard and Heloise*, trans. Betty Radice (hereafter Radice), p. 133. I treat the entire corpus of writings between Abelard and Heloise, including of course the *Historia calamitatum*, as authentic. After a long period of doubt in the authenticity of the personal letters, the efforts to argue inauthenticity have proven as futile as they were fervent. There are no persuasive arguments that Heloise did not write the letters ascribed to her. After Barbara Newman's study arguing Heloise's authorship, "Authority, Authenticity, and the Repression of Heloise," the burden of proof is on the doubters. It will take a shrewd scholar to disprove their authenticity after 150 years of failure arguing that position.

26. I discuss its uniqueness in the context of twelfth-century attitudes toward discipline and moral training in *Envy of Angels*, pp. 233–34.

27. See the commentary by Raymond Cormier, *One Heart, One Mind*.

28. Abelard himself interpreted Heloise's posture in this way (rebellion and tenacity, not weakness) in his poem to their son Astralabe, though he also reduced it to the physical: "Some delight so in past sins that they never truly repent them. . . . That is the frequent complaint on this point of our Heloise, which she often used to make as much to herself as to me: 'If there were no salvation for me unless I repented our past, then no hope would remain for me; too sweet are the joys of what we did.'" Peter Abelard, *Carmen ad Astralabium*, p. 127, lines 375–82.

29. Muckle, p. 80: "Quo modo etiam poenitentia peccatorum dicitur, quantacumque sit corporis afflictio, si mens adhuc ipsam peccandi retinet voluntatem . . ."

30. Epist. 1, Radice, p. 113; Muckle, p. 70: " . . . eo te magis mihi obnoxium, quo te semper . . . immoderato amore complexa sum."

31. Radice, p. 113; Muckle, p. 70: "me ipsam pro iussu tuo perdere sustinerem. Et quod maius est dictuque mirabile, in tantam versus est amor insaniam ut quod solum appetebat, hoc ipse sibi sine spe recuperationis auferret."

32. Radice's translation might appear at first glance to speak a modern language of romantic love. But I cannot improve on it and think it likely that the same extravagant language, rich with slippage between tabooed and sublime emotion, between destruction and exaltation through love, is inherent also in Heloise's phrasing: "immoderatus amor" [a love beyond all bounds]; "in tantam versus est amor insaniam" [my love reached such heights of madness.] Heloise recognizes her own extravagance: "quod maius est dictuque mirabile."

33. Radice, p. 74; *Historia calamitatum*, ed. Monfrin, p. 79, lines 553–57: "suspirans vehementer et lacrimans perorationem suam tali fine terminavit: 'Unum, inquid, ad ultimum restat ut in perditione duorum, minor non succedat dolor quam precessit amor.'"

34. Heloise quotes the very formula of tragedy in describing the course of their love: "The higher I was exalted when you preferred me to all other women, the greater my suffering over my own fall and yours, when I was flung down; for the higher the ascent, the heavier the fall" (Epist. 3, Radice, p. 129; Muckle, p. 78). On tragedy in the Middle Ages, see Henry Ansgar Kelly, *Chaucerian Tragedy*.

35. Epist. 3, Radice, p. 133; Muckle, p. 81.

36. Epist. 3, Radice, p. 130; Muckle, p. 80.

37. See her arguments against marriage, both in Abelard's version (*Hist. cal.*, Radice, pp. 70–74; ed. Monfrin, pp. 75–79, lines 425–558) and in her letter, Epist. 1, Radice, pp. 114–15; Muckle, p. 71).

38. Epist. 1, Radice, p. 114; Muckle, p. 71.

39. Epist. 1, Radice, p. 114; Muckle, p. 71: "Sanctus hic error et beata fallacia in coniugatis ut perfecta dilectio illaesa custodiat matrimonii foedera non tam corporum continentia quam animorum pudicitia."

40. See Gilson's chapter "The Ethics of Pure Love," in *Heloise and Abelard*, pp. 47–65.

41. Radice, p. 113; Muckle, pp. 70–71. Abelard most likely formed his idea of divine love from the example of Heloise. This is the thesis developed by Weingart, *The Logic of Divine Love*. Cf. the following passage from Abelard's commentary on Paul's letter to the Romans:

So sincere was the love of Christ for us that not only did he die for us, but in all things he did for us he sought not his own advantage, temporal or eternal, but ours; he acted not with any intention of his own reward, but only out of a desire for our salvation . . .

The true affection of a father for a son or of a chaste wife for her husband, is when they love them even though they may be useless rather than others who may be more beneficial to them. Nor can their love be diminished if they suffer some disadvantages for their sake, because the full cause of love remains in those whom they love while they have them, not in the advantages they gain through them. (ed. Buytaert, pp. 201ff.)

See also Clanchy, *Abelard*, pp. 164–72.

42. See Gilson, *Heloise and Abelard*, pp. 56–57. The devotion to the person alone, *te pure, non tua*, is common enough in the confessions of virtuous friendship from the Middle Ages to the present. We can add to Gilson's references Bernard of Clairvaux, Epist. 107, *Opera* 7.268, 17ff.: "te non tua diligimus . . . Pure . . . nos amantes"; and Hildebert, Epist. 6, PL 171, 149C (to Countess Adela of Blois): "te puro et simplici amore complector."

43. Muckle, p. 70, n. 78: "valde perdulciter ac blande per totum agis."

44. "On Friendship," Michel de Montaigne, *Essais*, ed. Pierre Villey and V.-L. Saulnier (Paris: Presses Universitaires de France, 1965), p. 188. See the commentary of Langer, *Perfect Friendship*, esp. pp. 168–70.

45. Abelard's phrase: "So intense were the fires of lust which bound me to you that

I set those wretched, obscene pleasures, which we blush even to name, above God as above myself" (Epist. 4, Radice, p. 147; Muckle, p. 89).

46. On the dynamics of affirmation through tragedy see A. D. Nuttall, *Why Does Tragedy Give Pleasure?* (Oxford: Clarendon Press, 1996).

47. In Dronke, *Abelard and Heloise in Medieval Testimonies*, p. 31.

48. "Metamorphosis Goliae," ed. Huygens. See the reading by John R. Clark, "Love and Learning in the 'Metamorphosis Golye Episcopi.'" Clark stresses the connection between love and learning fundamental to the poem and demonstrates its twelfth-century origins by reference to the poem's sources in late antiquity.

49. St. 13: *templum universitatis*. I have a hunch that "temple of the university" would complement the associations of the term. The poem is among other things an allegory of education and a vision of an ideal setting for education.

50. See the problems of an identification by Winthrop Wetherbee, *Platonism and Poetry*, pp. 133–34, and Benton, "Philology's Search for Abelard in the 'Metamorphosis Goliae.'"

Chapter 13: The Loves of Christina of Markyate

1. The chapter title is both indebted to and set against Thomas Head's useful article, "The Marriages of Christina of Markyate," which did not pose "the marriages" as the thematic dominant, just an important theme. Answering with "the loves" is not meant polemically, though I see love as a structuring element of the *Life* much more than marriage.

2. See Cormier, *One Heart, One Mind*, introduction, pp. 71–75 on Christina. This study is remarkable for anticipating in a few brush strokes major themes of Caroline Bynum's and John Boswell's work, and of the present study. I have also learned much from the article by Karras, "Friendship and Love." Robert Hanning's reading of the *Life* is still interesting for the topic of individuality in the twelfth century. Also analyzing Christina's marriages, Carol Symes, *Aspects of Marriage and Sexuality in the Miracle Literature of Twelfth-Century England* and Christopher N. L. Brooke, *The Medieval Idea of Marriage*.

3. *The Life of Christina of Markyate*, ed. and trans. Talbot.

4. See Holdsworth, "Christina of Markyate."

5. See Renna, "Virginity in the Life of Christina of Markyate and Aelred of Rievaulx's Rule." He also sees a progression in the male figures (p. 87).

6. Karras's commentary, "Friendship and Love," pp. 315–17," is especially insightful on this point.

7. See Renna, "Virginity in the *Life* of Christina."

8. "Utinam tenuissem te extra civitatem." Talbot weakens the formulation in his translation: "I wish I could have you with me outside the town." There is tremulous anxiety in the past perfect of the subjunctive (*tenuissem*), not renderable in English: that I "might have had" you. It implies, "I know what an impossible request this is." Also, why *tenere* instead of the sober and unambiguous *loqui*? The writer wanted to imply a lover's whispered hopes, not a servant's directions.

9. Talbot translates, "When dawn is breaking." The writer's "Apparente aurora" (p. 86) is poetic language, however. The biographer wants allure in his formulations, at least in this episode. "Prima luce" would have been the more literal formulation.

10. Talbot renders *sodalis* as "accomplice," though this word too participates in the ambiguity of the scene, meaning both "conspirator" and "companion."

11. Chrétien, *Chevalier de la charette*, lines 941ff.

12. Her parents try to weaken her resolve with worldly allurements, but she matches them wit for wit, "deceiving their cunning" [illorum delusa calliditas], and heightening her "invincible prudence" (p. 49); they encourage her to drink wine, but she resists, and thus "her parents had been outwitted in this" [in hoc illusi] (pp. 50–51); they send Christina's husband into her room at night to consummate the marriage by force if necessary, and she talks him into a chaste marriage, which the parents regard as just another of "her deceitful tricks" [ambagibus fallentis] (pp. 50–51). Repeatedly, the parents' efforts to have the marriage consummated take the structure of plot and counterplot; they lay *insidias* and *laqueos* (p. 54), which Christina foresees, thwarts, eludes, repeatedly showing herself "intelligent, prudent in affairs, efficient in carrying out her plans" [acumen in sensu . . . providencia in gerendis . . . efficacia in deliberatis . . .] (pp. 67–68). The parents plot secretly in *clandestina conventicula*, and Christina calculates "how she could counter any plots they might make against her" (pp. 68–69). The series of plots and counterplots ends when the husband, Burthred, again finding himself "deceived" — "homo delusus abscessit" (p. 94) — finally vows to give up such attempts and ultimately allows the annulment of the marriage.

13. This is the insight of Symes, *Aspects of Marriage and Sexuality*, pp. 44–57, and Head, "Marriages." Also Brooke, *The Medieval Idea of Marriage*.

14. Christina and Roger conceal the fact that they are living together, "for they feared scandal to their inferiors and the fury of those who were persecuting the handmaid of Christ" (p. 103). Late in the story the devil is so frustrated by Christina's virtue that he

plotted to break her steadfastness by creating false rumours and spreading abroad unheard-of and incredible slanders through the bitter tongues of his agents. (p. 131)

She is accused of "every imaginable evil" but her faith keeps her safe from the "malice" of "perverse minds." Also in her love for Abbot Geoffrey of St. Albans she is persecuted "with gossip, poisonous detractions, barbed words." Some of her detractors "spread the rumour that she was attracted to the abbot by earthly love" (p. 173).

15. See Renna, "Virginity." Also Newman, "La mystique courtoise: Thirteenth-Century Beguines and the Art of Love," Chap. 5 of her *From Virile Woman to Woman-Christ*, pp. 137–67.

16. See Karras's reading of the scene, "Friendship and Love," pp. 315–16.

17. "multo eum excoluit affectu. miroque sed sincero dilexit amore" (pp. 138–39).

18. "Desudat illa virum accumulare virtutibus" (pp. 154–55).

Chapter 14: Virtuous Chastity, Virtuous Passion

1. See W. T. H. Jackson's essay, "Faith Unfaithful."

2. Chrétien, *Yvain*, lines 18–28. Also the troubadour Giraut de Borneil complains that all pleasure has passed from the world and "worth" (*pretz*) is banished. He

has given up his attempt to rescue these values. Minstrels no longer praise noble ladies; therefore their "worth" is in ruins. Their lovers now prefer to practice deceit than to praise them (Giraut de Borneil, *Sämtliche Lieder*, ed. Kolsen, 1.412–20, No. 65 ("Per solatz revelhar"). Hartmann von Aue also expresses a sense of living in a joyless age, lightened by the tales of King Arthur and his court (*Iwein*, lines 53–58).

3. Gottfried, *Tristan*, lines 12279–86; trans. Hatto, p. 203.

4. Chrétien had a very different and more sanguine sense of the history of chivalry and learning: they were recent imports to France from cultures which had declined, and he predicts, or wishes a great future for them. See *Cligés*, lines 30–44.

5. Lewis, *Allegory of Love*, pp. 4, 11.

6. Dinzelbacher, "Über die Entdeckung der Liebe im Hochmittelalter."

7. See the entire excursus on the decline of love, *Tristan*, 12209–357; trans. Hatto, pp. 202–4.

8. Hugo Sotovagina, in *Anglo-Latin Satirical Poets*, ed. Wright, RS 59.2, p. 219: "Non amor est hodie quo se Pylades et Orestes, / Quo se amaverunt Laelius et Scipio. / Fidens vel fidus rarus in alterutrum." Cf. Cicero, *De amicitia* 4.15, 5.20. On nostalgia at friendship lost in the Renaissance, see Langer, *Perfect Friendship*, pp. 164–86.

9. *Spiritual Friendship* 1.25, trans. Laker, p. 56; ed. Hoste, p. 293:

Cum tanta sit in amicitia vera perfectio, non est mirum quod tam rari fuerunt hi quos veros amicos antiquitas commendavit. Vix enim, ut ait Tullius, tria vel quatuor amicorum paria in tot retro saeculis fama concelebrat. Quod si nostris, id est christianis temporibus, tanta est raritas amicorum, frustra, ut mihi videtur, in huius virtutis acquisitione desudo, quam me adepturum, eius mirabili sublimitate territus, iam pene despero.

10. Heloise to Abelard, Epist. 5, Radice, p. 167; Muckle, p. 246. The biblical reference (Matt. 24.12: "because iniquity shall abound, the love of many shall wax cold") is changed so that a senile world and not "iniquity" is responsible for frigidity, gendered masculine in Heloise's text. On the motif in literature, see Dean, *The World Grown Old in Later Medieval Literature*, passim. On the cooling of charity with reference to Heloise's statement, ibid., pp. 62–66; as a literary motif ("The decline of Love"), pp. 99–102.

11. CB no. 105, 6.3–4:

"vigor priscus abiit,   evanuit iam virtus.
Me vis deseruit,   periere Cupidinis arcus!"

See the discussion in Chapter 5.

12. *Serm. in Cant.* 2.1.1. Cf. Richard of St. Victor, *De gradibus charitatis*, chap. 4, PL 196, 1204C–D. And Peter of Blois, *De amicitia Christiana*, prol. PL 207, 871A. Peter writes his work, he explains, out of the pain he feels for this "common evil."

13. See James W. Marchand, "Wolfram's Bawdy."

14. As in the meeting in the garden late in the romance, where they are united like poured bronze.

15. Cf. Wolfram's excursus blaming "Frau Minne" for corruption, shame, criminality, pardoning her only when "Frau Liebe" accompanies her (291, 1–30).

16. *Paradiso*, canto 33, lines 139–45. See Dronke, "L'amor que move il sole e l'altre stelle."

17. See the reading of this excursus by Tomasek, *Utopie in Tristan*, pp. 180–211.

Chapter 15: The Grand Amatory Mode of the Noble Life

1. See Ingeborg Glier, *Artes amandi*.

2. Keen includes many examples in "Chivalry and Courtly Love," in his *Nobles, Knights, and Men-at-Arms*, pp. 21–42.

3. *Book of Chivalry*, sections 12 and 19, ed. Daeuper and Kennedy, pp. 94, p. 118.

4. "Avoir bonne et vray amour." Th. Frimmel and J. Klemme, "Ein Statutenbuch des Ordens vom goldenen Vliesse," *Jahrbuch der kunsthistorischen Sammlungen des allerhöchsten Kaiserhauses* 5 (1887), p. 213. Cited in Melville, "Rituelle Ostentation," p. 223.

5. Keen, "Chivalry and Courtly Love," in *Nobles*, p. 32.

6. *Le livre des faits de Jacques de Lalaing*, in *Oeuvres de G. Chastellain* VIII, ed. K. de Lettenhove (Brussels, 1886), p. 15. Cited in Keen, "Chivalry and Courtly Love," in *Nobles*, p. 36.

7. Christine de Pizan, *The Book of the Duke of True Lovers*, trans. Fenster and Margolis, pp. 47–48.

8. Duby, *France in the Middle Ages*, p. 180.

9. Greenblatt, *Renaissance Self-Fashioning*, pp. 165–69. And Frances Yates, "Elizabethan Chivalry: The Romance of the Accession Day Tilts," in *Astrea*, pp. 88–111; Strong, *The Cult of Elizabeth*.

10. What follows summarizes Christine de Pizan, *The Book of the Duke of True Lovers*, pp. 101–3.

11. See the interpretation of this phrase and a shrewd reading of the love and friendship theme in the novel by Langer, *Perfect Friendship*, pp. 176–86.

12. See Richter, "Winckelmann's Progeny" and Rasch, *Freundschaftskult und Freundschaftsdichtung im deutschen Schrifttum des 18. Jahrhunderts*.

13. See Tobin, "In and Against Nature."

Bibliography

PRIMARY TEXTS

Abelard, Peter (see Peter Abelard).

Acta Sanctorum. Ed. Joannes Bolandus. Paris and Rome: Palmé, 1866.

Aelred of Rievaulx. *Aelredi Rievallensis Opera Omnia*. Ed. A. Hoste and C. H. Talbot. CCCM 1.1. Turnholt: Brepols, 1971.

———. *Spiritual Friendship*. Trans. Mary Eugenia Laker. Cistercian Fathers Series 5. Kalamazoo, Mich.: Cistercian Publications, 1977.

———. *Spiritual Friendship*. Trans. Mark F. Williams. Scranton, Pa.: University of Scranton Press; London and Toronto: Associated University Presses, 1994.

Aimeric de Peguilhan. *The Poems of Aimeric de Peguilhan*. Ed. and trans. William P. Shepard and Frank M. Chambers. Evanston, Ill.: Northwestern University Press, 1950.

Alcuin. *Alcuini Carmina*. Ed. Ernst Dümmler. MGH Poetae Latini Aevi Carolini 1.160–351.

———. *Alcuini Opera Omnia*. PL 100–101.

———. *Alcuini sive Albini epistolae*. Ed. Ernst Dümmler. MGH Epistolae 4, Epistolae Karolini Aevi 2. Pp. 1–481. Berlin: Weidmann, 1895.

———. *Monumenta Alcuiniana*. Ed. Philipp Jaffé. Bibliotheca rerum Germanicarum 6. Berlin, 1873; repr. Aalen: Scientia, 1964.

Ambrose. *Sancti Ambrosii Mediolanensis episcopi De officiis ministrorum libri tres*. PL 16, 23–194.

Andreas Capellanus. *Andreas Capellanus on Love*. Ed. and trans. P. G. Walsh. London: Duckworth, 1982.

Angilbert. *Angilberti (Homeri) Carmina*. Ed. Ernst Dümmler. MGH Poetae 1, 355–366.

Anglo-Latin Satirical Poets and Epigrammatists of the Twelfth Century. Ed. Thomas Wright. 2 vols. RS 59. London, 1872; repr. Wiesbaden: Kraus, 1964.

Anselm of Canterbury (Bec). *The Letters of Anselm of Canterbury*. Trans. Walter Fröhlich. 3 vols. Cistercian Studies Series 96, 97, 142. Kalamazoo, Mich.: Cistercian Publications, 1990–1994.

———. *Sancti Anselmi Cantuariensis Archiepiscopi Opera Omnia*. Ed. F. S. Schmitt. 6 vols. Edinburgh: Nelson, 1946–1961.

Aristotle. *The Nicomachean Ethics*. Trans. H. Rackham. Loeb Classical Library. Cambridge, Mass.: Harvard University Press, 1926, repr. 1962.

Balzac, Honoré. *The Lily of the Valley*. Trans. Ellen Marriage and Clara Bell. Works of Honoré de Balzac 9. Philadelphia: Avil, 1901.

Baudri of Bourgueil. *Baldricus Burgulianus Carmina*. Ed. Karlheinz Hilbert. Editiones
    Heidelbergenses 19. Heidelberg: Winter, 1979.
——. *Oeuvres poétiques de Baudri de Bourgueil (1046–1130): Edition critique publiée d'après
    le manuscrit du Vatican*. Ed. Phyllis Abrahams. Paris: Champion, 1926; repr. 1974.
Bernard of Clairvaux. *Sancti Bernardi Opera*. Ed. J. Leclercq, Charles H. Talbot, H. M.
    Rochais. Rome: Editiones Cistercienses, 1957.
Bertran de Born. *The Poems of the Troubadour Bertran de Born*. Ed. William D. Paden Jr.,
    Tilde Sankovitch, and Patricia H. Stäblein. Berkeley: University of California
    Press, 1986.
Boccaccio, Giovanni. *The Decameron*. Trans. G. H. McWilliam. London: Penguin,
    1995.
Butler, Alban. *Butler's Lives of the Saints*. Ed Herbert Thurston and Donald Attwater. 4
    vols. New York: P. J. Kenedy, 1956.
Die Cambridger Lieder. Ed. Karl Strecker. MGH Script. rer. Germ. in us. schol. 40.
    Berlin: Weidmann, 1926.
The Cambridge Songs (Carmina Cantabrigiensia). Ed. and trans. Jan Ziolkowski. New
    York and London: Garland, 1994.
Carmina Burana: Die Lieder der Benediktbeurer Handschrift. Ed. Alfons Hilka and Otto
    Schumann, rev. Bernard Bischoff. Munich: Deutscher Taschenbuch Verlag, 1979.
Carmina Cantabrigiensia. Ed. Walther Bulst. Editiones Heidelbergenses 17. Heidel-
    berg: Winter, 1950.
Cassian. *Conférences*. Ed. and trans. Eugène Pichery. Sources Chrétiennes 54. Paris:
    Editions du Cerf, 1958.
Chrétien de Troyes. *Le chevalier de la charette*. Ed. Mario Roques. Paris: Champion,
    1952.
——. *Cligès*. Ed. Stewart Gregory and Claude Luttrell. Cambridge: D. S. Brewer,
    1993.
——. *Yvain ou Le Chevalier au Lion*. Ed. Jan Nelson, Carleton W. Carrol, and Douglas
    Kelly. New York: Appleton-Century-Crofts, 1968.
Christine de Pizan. *The Book of the Duke of True Lovers*. Trans. Thelma S. Fenster with
    lyric poetry trans. Nadia Margolis. New York: Persea Books, 1991.
Cicero. *De senectute, De amicitia, De divinatione*. Trans. William Armistead Falconer.
    Loeb Classical Library 154. Cambridge, Mass.: Harvard University Press, 1979.
Demosthenes. *The Erotic Essay, Funeral Speech, Exordia, and Letters*. Loeb Classical Li-
    brary. Cambridge, Mass.: Harvard University Press, 1949.
Dhuoda. *Manuel pour mon fils: introduction, texte critique, notes*. 2d ed. Ed. Pierre Riché,
    trans. Bernard de Vregille and Claude Mondésert. Sources Chrétiennes 225. Paris:
    Editions du Cerf, 1991.
"Drei Gedichte aus Frankreich." Ed. Ernst Dümmler. *Neues Archiv* 2 (1877), 222–30.
Einhard. *Einhardi Vita Karoli Magni*. 4th ed. Ed. G. H. Pertz and Georg Waitz. MGH
    Script. rer. germ in us. schol. Hannover: Hahn, 1880.
——. *Two Lives of Charlemagne: Einhard and Notker the Stammerer*. Trans. Lewis
    Thorpe. Harmondsworth: Penguin, 1983.
The Epistles on the Romance of the Rose. Ed. Charles Frederick Ward. Diss. University of
    Chicago, 1911.
Epistolae Bambergenses. Bibliotheca rerum germanicarum 5. Ed. Philipp Jaffé. Berlin,
    1869; repr. Aalen: Scientia, 1964.

Epistolae duorum amantium: Briefe Abaelards und Heloises? Ed. Ewald Könsgen. Mittellateinische Studien und Texte 8. Leiden: Brill, 1974.

Fleck, Konrad. *Flore und Blancheflur: Eine Erzählung von Konrad Fleck.* Ed. Emil Sommer. Bibliothek der gesammten Deutschen National-Literatur 1. Abt. Bd. 12. Quedlinburg and Leipzig: Basse, 1846.

Fortunatus, Venantius. *Venanti Honori Clementiani Fortunati Opera Poetica.* Ed. Fridericus Leo. MGH Auct. Antiquiss. 4. Berlin: Weidmann, 1881.

——. *Personal and Political Poems.* Trans. Judith George. Texts for Historians 23. Liverpool: Liverpool University Press, 1995.

Fronto, M. Cornelius/Marcus Aurelius. *The Correspondence of M. Cornelius Fronto.* Trans. C. R. Haines. Vol. 1. Loeb Classical Library. Cambridge, Mass.: Harvard University Press; London: Heinemann, 1928.

Geoffroi de Charny. *The Book of Chivalry of Geoffroi de Charny: Text, Context, and Translation.* Ed. Richard W. Kaeuper and Elspeth Kennedy. Philadelphia: University of Pennsylvania Press, 1996.

Gerbert of Aurillac (Pope Sylvester II). *Die Briefsammlung Gerberts von Reims.* Ed. Fritz Weigle. MGH Briefe der deutschen Kaiserzeit 2. Weimar: Böhlau, 1966.

Giraut de Borneil. *Sämtliche Lieder des Trobadors Giraut de Bornelh.* Ed. Adolf Kolsen. 2 vols. Halle: Niemeyer, 1907.

Gottfried von Strassburg, *Tristan.* Ed. Friedrich Ranke. 11th ed. Dublin and Zurich: Weidmann, 1967.

——. *Tristan with the 'Tristran' of Thomas.* Trans. A. T. Hatto. Harmondsworth: Penguin, 1985.

Graelent *and* Guingamor: *Two Breton Lays.* Ed. and trans. Russell Weingartner. Garland Library of Medieval Literature 37, ser. A. New York and London: Garland, 1985.

Gregory of Tours. *Historia Francorum.* Gregor von Tours, *Zehn Bücher Geschichten.* Ed. and trans. Wilhelm Giesebrecht and Rudolf Buchner. 2 vols. Ausgewählte Quellen zur Deutschen Geschichte des Mittelalters 2–3. Berlin: Deutscher Verlag der Wissenschaften, 1967.

Guibert of Nogent. *Autobiographie: de vita sua.* Ed. Edmond-René Labande. Classiques de l'Histoire de France au Moyen Age 34. Paris: Les Belles Lettres, 1981.

——. *Self and Society in Medieval France: The Memoirs of Abbot Guibert of Nogent.* Trans. C. C. Swinton Bland, rev. with commentary by John F. Benton. Toronto: University of Toronto Press, 1970.

Hartmann von Aue. *Iwein: Eine Erzählung von Hartmann von Aue.* Ed. G. F. Benecke and Karl Lachmann. 6th ed. Berlin: De Gruyter, 1959.

Hildebert of Lavardin. *Hildebertus Carmina minora.* Ed. A. B. Scott. Leipzig: Teubner, 1969.

Hildesheim Letter Collection. *Briefsammlungen der Zeit Heinrichs IV.* Ed. Carl Erdmann and Norbert Fickermann. MGH Briefe der deutschen Kaiserzeit 5. Weimar: Böhlau, 1950.

Isidore of Seville. *Etymologiarum sive Originum Libri XX.* Ed. W. M. Lindsay. Oxford: Clarendon Press, 1911.

Jaufré Rudel. *The Songs of Jaufré Rudel.* Ed. Rupert T. Pickens. Studies and Texts 41. Toronto: Pontifical Institute of Mediaeval Studies, 1978.

John of Salisbury. *Metalogicon.* Ed. J. B. Hall. Corpus Christianorum Continuatio Mediaevalis 98. Turnholt: Brepols, 1991.

——. *The Metalogicon of John of Salisbury: A Twelfth Century Defense of the Logical and Verbal Arts of the Trivium*. Trans. Daniel D. McGarry. Berkeley and Los Angeles: University of California Press, 1962.

König Rother. Ed. Theodore Frings and Joachim Kuhnt. Altdeutsche Texte für den akademischen Unterricht 2. Halle: Niemeyer, 1961.

Konrad von Würzburg. *Konrads von Würzburg Partonopier und Meliur*. Ed. Franz Pfeiffer and Karl Bartsch. Berlin: De Gruyter, 1970.

Lafayette, Madame de. *The Princesse de Clèves*. Trans. Robin Buss. London: Penguin, 1992.

The Lays of Desiré, Graelent and Melion: Edition of the Texts with an Introduction. Ed. E. Margaret Grimes. New York: Institute of French Studies, 1928.

The Life of Christina of Markyate: A Twelfth Century Recluse. Ed. and trans. C. H. Talbot. Oxford Medieval Texts. Oxford: Clarendon Press, 1959.

Marbod of Rennes. *Beiträge zur Kunde der lateinischen Literatur des Mittelalters aus Handschriften gesammelt*. Ed. Jakob Werner. 2d ed. Aarau: Sauerlander, 1905.

——. "Liebesbriefgedichte Marbods." Ed. Walther Bulst. In *Lateinisches Mittelalter: Gesammelte Beiträge*, ed. Walter Berschin, 182–96. Supplemente zu den Sitzungsberichten der Heidelberger Akademie der Wissenschaften, Phil.-hist. Klasse 3 (1983). Heidelberg: Carl Winter, 1984. Originally in *Liber floridus: Festschrift Paul Lehmann* (St. Ottilien: Eos, 1950), 287–301.

——. *Marbodi ep. Redonensis liber decem capitulorum*. Ed. Walther Bulst. Heidelberg: Winter, 1947.

——. *Marbodi Liber decem capitulorum*. Ed. Rosario Leotta. Rome: Herder, 1984.

Marcabru. *Poésies complètes du troubadour Marcabru*. Ed. J.-M.-L. Dejeanne. Toulouse: Privat, 1909.

Marie de France. *Lais*. Ed. Alfred Ewert. Oxford: Blackwell, 1947.

"Metamorphosis Goliae." Ed. R. B. C. Huygens. In "Mitteilungen aus Handschriften." *Studi Medievali* ser. 3.3 (1962), 764–72.

Des Minnesangs Frühling. Ed. Hugo Moser and Helmut Tervooren. 38th ed. from the edition of Lachmann, Haupt, reworked by Vogt and von Kraus. Vol. 1: Texts. Stuttgart: Hirzel, 1988.

Nithard. *Nithardi Historiarum libri IV*. Ed. Ernst Müller. 3rd ed. Script rer. Germ in us. schol. Hannover and Leipzig: Hahn, 1907.

"'Parce continuis': A New Text and Interpretative Notes." Ed. David A Trall. *Mittellateinisches Jahrbuch* 21 (1986), 114–24.

Paulinus of Nola. *Letters of St. Paulinus of Nola*. 2 vols. Trans. and annotated P. G. Walsh. Ancient Christian Writers 35 and 36. London: Longmans, 1967.

——. *The Poems of St. Paulinus of Nola*. Trans. and annotated P.G. Walsh. Ancient Christian Writers 40. New York: Newman Press, 1975.

——. *Sancti Paulini Nolani Epistulae*. Ed. G. Hartel. CSEL 29. Prague, Vienna, Leipzig: Tempsky, 1894.

——. *Sancti Paulini Nolani episcopi carmina*. Ed. G. Hartel, CSEL 30. Prague, Vienna, Leipzig: Tempsky, 1894.

Paulus Diaconus. *Die Gedichte des Paulus Diaconus: Kritische und erklärende Ausgabe*. Ed. Karl Neff. Quellen und Untersuchungen zur lateinischen Philologie des Mittelalters 3, 4. Munich: Beck, 1908.

Peire Vidal. *Poesie*. Edizione critica e commento a cura di D'Arco Silvio Avalle. Milan and Naples: Ricciardi, 1960.

Peter Abelard. *Carmen ad Astralabium: A Critical Edition*. Ed. Josepha M. A. Rubingh-Boscher. Groningen: J.M.A. Rubingh-Boscher, 1987.

——. *Historia calamitatum: Texte critique avec une introduction*. Ed. Jacques Monfrin. Paris: Vrin, 1959.

——. *The Letters of Abelard and Heloise*. Trans. Betty Radice. Harmondsworth: Penguin, 1974.

——. "The Personal Letters Between Abelard and Heloise." Ed. J. T. Muckle. *Mediaeval Studies* 15 (1953), 47–94.

——. *Peter Abelard's Ethics*. Ed. and trans. D. E. Luscombe. Oxford: Clarendon Press, 1971.

——. "The Letter of Heloise on Religious Life and Abelard's First Reply." *Mediaeval Studies* 17 (1955), 241–53.

Peter of Blois. *De amicitia Christiana*. PL 207, 871–96.

Plato. *Lysis, Symposium, Gorgias*. Trans. W. R. M. Lamb. Loeb Classical Library. Cambridge, Mass.: Harvard University Press; London: Heinemann, 1925.

Plutarch. *Moralia*. Vol 9, *The Dialogue on Love*. Trans. W. C. Helmbold. Loeb Classical Library. Cambridge, Mass.: Harvard University Press; London: Heinemann, 1961.

Quintilian. *The Institutio Oratoria of Quintilian*, trans. B. E. Butler. Loeb Classical Library. Cambridge, Mass.: Harvard University Press; London: Heinemann, 1958.

Regensburg Love Songs: *Carmina Ratisponensia*. Ed. Anke Paravicini. Editiones Heidelbergenses 20. Heidelberg: Winter, 1979.

Die religiösen Dichtungen des 11. und 12. Jahrhunderts. Ed. Friedrich Maurer. 3 vols. Tübingen: Niemeyer, 1970.

Richard de Fournival. "Amistié de vraie amour." Ed. C. F. Pickford. *Bulletin of the John Rylands Library* 34 (1952), 333–65.

Richard of St. Victor. *De gradibus charitatis*, PL 196, 1195–1207.

——. *De IV gradibus violentae charitatis*. PL 196, 1207–24.

Rodolfus Tortarius. *Rodulfi Tortarii Carmina*. Ed. Marbury B. Ogle and Dorothy M. Schullian. Rome: American Academy, 1933.

Roger of Hovedon. *Chronica*. Ed. William Stubbs. RS 51:3. London: Longmans, 1870.

Roger of Hovedon (Benedict of Peterborough), *Gesta Regis Heinrici II*. Ed. William Stubbs. RS 49:2.

The Romance of Yder. Ed. and trans. Alison Adams. Cambridge: D. S. Brewer, 1983.

Ruodlieb: Faksimile-Ausgabe des Codex Latinus Monacensis 19486 der bayerischen Staatsbibliothek München und der Fragmente von St. Florian. Ed. Benedikt Konrad Vollmann. 2 vols. Wiesbaden: Reichert, 1985.

"Satyra de amicicia . . . (Clm 29111): Das Freundschaftsideal eines Freigelassenen." Ed. Friedel Rädle. In *Lateinische Dichtungen des X. und XI. Jahrhunderts: Festgabe für Walther Bulst zum 80. Geburtstag*. Ed. Walther Berschin and Reinhard Düchting, 162–85. Heidelberg: Schneider, 1981.

Servatus Lupus. *Epistulae*. Ed. Peter K. Marshall. Leipzig: Teubner, 1984.

Smaragd of St. Mihiel (St. Michael of Verdun). *Via regia*. PL 102, 933–70.

Stendhal (Marie-Henri Beyle). *The Charterhouse of Parma*. Trans. Margaret Shaw. London: Penguin, 1978.

——. *Love*. Trans. Gilbert Sale and Suzanne Sale. London: Penguin, 1975.

——. *Scarlet and Black*. Trans. Margaret Shaw. London: Penguin, 1979.

Die Tegernseer Briefsammlung. Ed. Karl Strecker. MGH Epistolae selectae 3. Berlin: Weidmannsche Buchhandlung, 1925.

Theodulf of Orleans. *Theodulfi Carmina*. Ed. Ernst Dümmler. MGH Poetae 1: 2, 437–578.

Les Troubadours II: le trésor poétique de l'Occitanie. 2 vols. Ed. and trans. René Nelli and René Lavaud. Paris: Desclée de Brouwer, 1966.

Ulrich of Bamberg. "Eine Bamberger Ars Dictaminis." Ed. Franz Bittner. *Historischer Verein für die Pflege der Geschichte des ehemaligen Fürstbistums Bamberg* 100 (1964), 145–71.

Venantius Fortunatus (see Fortunatus, Venantius).

Walter Daniel. *The Life of Ailred of Rievaulx by Walter Daniel*. Ed. and trans. M. M. Powicke. New York: Oxford University Press, 1951.

Walter Map, *De Nugis Curialium: Courtiers' Trifles*. Ed. and trans. M. R. James, rev. C. N. L. Brooke and R. A. B. Mynors. Oxford Medieval Texts. Oxford: Clarendon Press, 1983.

Walther von der Vogelweide. *Leich, Lieder, Sangsprüche: 14., völlig neu bearbeitete Auflage der Ausgabe Karl Lachmanns*. Ed. Christoph Cormeau. Berlin and New York: De Gruyter, 1996.

Wibald of Stablo. *Wibaldi epistolae*. Bibliotheca rerum Germanicarum, vol. 1: Monumenta Corbeiensia. Ed. Philipp Jaffé. Berlin, 1864; repr. Aalen, 1964.

William IX of Aquitaine. *The Poetry of William VII, Count of Poitiers, IX Duke of Aquitaine*. Ed. and trans. Gerald Bond. New York: Garland, 1982.

William of Conches. *Das Moralium Dogma Philosophorum des Guillaume de Conches: Lateinisch, Altfranzösisch und Mittelniederfränkisch*. Ed. John Holberg. Uppsala: Almquist and Wiksells, 1929.

Wolfram von Eschenbach. *Parzival*. Ed. Karl Lachmann. 6th ed. Berlin: De Gruyter, 1965.

Worms Letter Collection. *Die ältere Wormser Briefsammlung*. Ed. Walther Bulst. MGH Briefe der deutschen Kaiserzeit 3. Weimar: Böhlau, 1949.

Studies

Allen, Peter L. *The Art of Love: Amatory Fiction from Ovid to The Romance of the Rose*. Philadelphia: University of Pennsylvania Press, 1992.

Althoff, Gerd. *Amicitiae et Pacta: Bündnis, Einung, Politik und Gebetsgedenken im beginnenden 10. Jahrhundert*. MGH Schriften 37. Hannover: Hahn, 1992.

——. "Das Bett des Königs in Magdeburg: Zu Thietmar II, 28." In *Festschrift für Berent Schwineköper zu seinem Siebzigsten Geburtstag*, ed. Helmut Maurer and Hans Patze. Sigmaringen: Thorbecke, 1982: 141–53.

——. "Demonstration und Inszenierung: Spielregeln der Kommunikation in mittelalterlicher Öffentlichkeit." In *Spielregeln der Politik*, 229–57.

——. "Empörung, Tränen, Zerknirschung: 'Emotionen' in der öffentlichen Kommunikation des Mittelalters." *Frühmittelalterliche Studien* 30 (1966), 60–79.

——. *Spielregeln der Politik im Mittelalter: Kommunikation in Frieden und Fehde*. Darmstadt: Primus, 1997.

——. *Verwandte, Freunde und Getreue: Zum politischen Stellenwert der Gruppenbin-*

dungen im frühen Mittelalter. Darmstadt: Wissenschaftliche Buchgesellschaft, 1990.

Althoff, Gerd and Hagan Keller. *Heinrich I. und Otto der Grosse: Neubeginn auf karolingischem Erbe*. Göttingen: Muster-Schmidt, 1994.

Arendt, Hannah. *Love and St. Augustine*. Ed. Joanna Scott and Judith Stark. Chicago: University of Chicago Press, 1996.

Baldwin, John W. *The Government of Philip Augustus: Foundations of French Royal Power in the Middle Ages*. Berkeley: University of California Press, 1986.

———. *The Language of Sex: Five Voices from Northern France Around 1200*. Chicago: University of Chicago Press, 1994.

———. *Masters, Princes and, Merchants: The Social Views of Peter the Chanter and His Circle*. 2 vols. Princeton, N. J.: Princeton University Press, 1970.

Barber, Richard. *Edward, Prince of Wales and Aquitaine: A Biography of the Black Prince*. London: Allen Lane, 1978.

Bec, Pierre. "'Amour de loin' et 'dame jamais vue': Pour une lecture plurielle de la chanson VI de Jaufré Rudel." In *Miscellanea di studi in onore di Aurelio Roncaglia*, 1: 101–18. Modena: Mucchi, 1989.

Beltz, George F. *Memorials of the Most Noble Order of the Garter*. London: Pickering, 1841; repr. New York, 1973.

Benton, John F. "Clio and Venus: An Historical View of Medieval Love." In *The Meaning of Courtly Love*, ed. F. X. Newman. Albany: State University of New York Press, 1968: 19–42.

———. "Philology's Search for Abelard in the 'Metamorphosis Goliae.'" *Speculum* 50 (1975), 199–217.

Bezzola, Reto. *Les origines et la formation de la littérature courtoise en Occident (500–1200)*. 4 vols. Paris: Champion, 1944–63.

Bischoff, Bernhard. "Gottschalks Lied für den Reichenauer Freund." In *Medium Aevum Vivum: Festschrift für Walther Bulst*, ed. Hans Robert Jauss and Dieter Schaller. Heidelberg: Winter, 1960: 61–68.

Blamires, Alcuin. *The Case for Women in Medieval Culture*. Oxford: Clarendon Press, 1997.

———, ed. *Woman Defamed and Woman Defended: An Anthology of Medieval Texts*. With Karen Pratt and C. W. Marx. Oxford: Clarendon Press, 1992.

Bloch, Marc. *Les rois thaumaturges: Etude sur le caractère surnaturel attribué à la puissance royale en France et en Angleterre*. Paris: Gallimard, 1983.

Bloch. R. Howard. *Medieval French Literature and Law*. Berkeley: University of California Press, 1977.

———. *Medieval Misogyny and the Invention of Western Romantic Love*. Chicago: University of Chicago Press, 1992.

Boase, Roger. *The Origin and Meaning of Courtly Love: A Critical Study of European Scholarship*. Manchester: Manchester University Press, 1990.

Bond, Gerald A. "*Iocus amoris*: The Poetry of Baudri of Bourgueil and the Formation of the Ovidian Subculture." *Traditio* 42 (1986), 143–93.

———. *The Loving Subject: Desire, Eloquence, and Power in Romanesque France*. Philadelphia: University of Pennsylvania Press, 1995.

———. *The Poetry of William VII, Count of Poitiers, IX Duke of Aquitaine*. New York: Garland, 1982.

Boswell, John. *Christianity, Social Tolerance, and Homosexuality: Gay People in Western Europe from the Beginning of the Christian Era to the Fourteenth Century*. Chicago: University of Chicago Press, 1980.

——. *Same-Sex Unions in Premodern Europe*. New York: Villard, 1994.

Boulton, D'Arcy. *The Knights of the Crown: The Monarchical Orders of Knighthood in Later Medieval Europe, 1325–1520*. Woodbridge: Boydell Press, 1987.

Boutière, Jean and A. H. Schutz. *Biographies des troubadours: textes provençaux des XIIIe et XIVe siècles*. Paris: Nizet, 1964.

Brinkmann, Hennig. *Entstehungsgeschichte des Minnesangs*. Halle: Niemeyer, 1926; repr. Darmstadt: Wissenschaftliche Buchgesellschaft, 1971

——. *Geschichte der lateinische Liebesdichtung im Mittelalter*. Halle: Niemeyer, 1925.

Brooke, Christopher N. L. "Aspects of Marriage in the Eleventh and Twelfth Centuries." In *Proceedings of the Fifth International Congress of Medieval Canon Law*, ed. Stephan Kuttner and Kenneth Pennington. Monumenta Iuris Canonici C.6. Vatican City: Biblioteca Apostolica Vaticana, 1980.

——. *The Medieval Idea of Marriage*. Oxford: Clarendon Press, 1989.

Brown, Peter R. L. *The Body and Society: Men, Women, and Sexual Renunciation in Early Christianity*. New York: Columbia University Press, 1988.

Bruggen, Elke. "Minnelehre und Gesellschaftskritik im 13. Jahrhundert: Zum Frauenbuch Ulrichs von Lichtenstein." *Euphorion* 83 (1989), 72–97.

Brundage, James A. *Law, Sex, and Christian Society in Medieval Europe*. Chicago: University of Chicago Press, 1987.

——. *Richard Lion Heart*. New York: Scribner, 1974.

Brunt, P. A. "'Amicitia' in the Late Roman Republic." *Proceedings of the Cambridge Philological Society* n.s. 11 (o.s. 191) (1965), 1–20.

Bugge, John. *Virginitas: An Essay in the History of a Medieval Ideal*. International Archives of the History of Ideas, Series Minor 17. The Hague: Nijhoff, 1975.

Bullough, Vern L. "The Sin Against Nature and Homosexuality." In *Sexual Practices and the Medieval Church*, ed. Bullough and James A. Brundage. Buffalo: Prometheus Books, 1982: 55–71.

Bullough, Vern L. and James A. Brundage, eds. *Handbook of Medieval Sexuality*. New York: Garland, 1996.

Bulst, Walther. *Studien zu Marbods Carmina varia und Liber decem capitulorum*. Nachrichten von der Gesellschaft der Wissenschaften zu Göttingen, phil.-hist. Klasse 4, N.F. 2, no. 10. Göttingen, 1939.

Bultot, Robert. *Christianisme et valeurs humaines: A. La doctrine du mépris du monde*. Part 4, vol. 1. Louvain: Nauwelaerts, 1963.

Bumke, Joachim. *Höfische Kultur: Literatur und Gesellschaft im hohen Mittelalter*. Munich: Deutscher Taschenbuch Verlag, 1986.

Chênerie, Marie-Luce. *Le chevalier errant dans les romans arthuriens en vers des XIIe et XIIIe siècles*. Geneva: Droz, 1986.

Clanchy, Michael. *Abelard: A Medieval Life*. Oxford: Blackwell, 1997.

——. "Law and Love in the Middle Ages." In *Disputes and Settlements: Law and Human Relations in the Medieval West*, ed. John Bossy. Cambridge: Cambridge University Press, 1983: 47–68.

——. *The Symbolism of Love in Medieval Thought*. Soc. Scient. Fennica, Hensligfors, 1970.

Clark, John R. "Love and Learning in the 'Metamorphosis Golye Episcopi.'" *Mittellateinisches Jahrbuch* 21 (1986), 156–71.

Conner, Paul. *Friendship Between Consecrated Men and Women and the Growth of Charity*. Thesis. Rome: Pontificia Facultas Theologica Institutum Spiritualitatis Teresianum, 1972.

Cormier, Raymond J. "Medieval Courtly Literature, Royal Patronage, and World Harmony." *Aevum* 2 (1990), 269–77.

——. *One Heart, One Mind: The Rebirth of Virgil's Hero in Medieval French Romance*. University Miss.: Romance Monographs, 1973.

——. "Old Views and New Trends: Observations on the Problem of Homosexuality in the Middle Ages." *Studi Medievali* 25 (1984), 587–610.

Cropp, Glynnis M. *Le vocabulaire courtois des troubadours de l'époque classique*. Geneva: Droz, 1975.

D'Alverny, Marie-Thérèse. "Comment les théologiens et les philosophes voient la femme." *CCM* 20 (1997).

Dean, James M. *The World Grown Old in Later Medieval Literature*. Cambridge, Mass.: Medieval Academy of America, 1997.

Delhaye, Philippe. "Deux adaptations du *De Amicitia* de Cicéron au XII siècle." *RTAM* 15 (1948), 304–31.

Derrida, Jacques. "The Politics of Friendship." *Journal of Philosophy* 85 (1988), 632–44.

Dinzelbacher, Peter. "Pour une histoire de l'amour au moyen-âge." *Le Moyen Age* 93 (1987), 223–40.

——. Sozial- und Mentalitätsgeschichte der Liebe im Mittelalter." In *Minne ist ein swaerez spil: Neue Untersuchungen zum Minnesang und zur Geschichte der Liebe im Mittelalter*, ed. Ulrich Müller. Göppingen: Kümmerle, 1986: 75–110.

——. "Über die Entdeckung der Liebe im Hochmittelalter." *Saeculum* 32 (1981), 185–208.

Dörrie, Heinrich. *Der heroische Brief*. Berlin: De Gruyter, 1968.

Dover, K. J. *Greek Homosexuality*. London: Duckworth, 1976.

Dronke, Peter. *Abelard and Heloise in Medieval Testimonies*. Glasgow: University of Glasgow Press, 1976.

——. "L'amor que move il sole e l'altre stelle." *Studi Medievali* 6 (1965), 389–422.

——. "Andreas Capellanus." *Journal of Medieval Latin* 4 (1994), 51–63.

——. *Medieval Latin and the Rise of the European Love Lyric*. 2 vols. 2d ed. Oxford: Oxford University Press, 1968.

——. *Poetic Individuality in the Middle Ages*. Oxford: Clarendon Press, 1970.

——. *Women Writers of the Middle Ages: A Critical Study of Texts from Perpetua (+203) to Marguerite Porete (+1310*. Cambridge: Cambridge University Press, 1984.

Duby, Georges. *France in the Middle Ages 987–1460 From Hugh Capet to Joan of Arc*. Trans. Juliet Vale. Oxford: Blackwell, 1993.

——. *The Knight, the Lady, and the Priest: The Making of Modern Marriage in Medieval France*. Trans. Barbara Bray. New York: Pantheon, 1983.

——. *Love and Marriage in the Middle Ages*. Trans. Jane Dunnett. Chicago: University of Chicago Press, 1994.

——. "Women and Power." In *Cultures of Power: Lordship, Status and Process in Twelfth-Century Europe*, ed. Thomas N. Bisson. Philadelphia: University of Pennsylvania Press, 1995: 69–85.

Dürr, Hans Peter. *Nacktheit und Scham: Der Mythos vom Zivilisationsprozess*. Frankfurt: Suhrkamp, 1994.

Eberhardt, Otto. *Via Regia: Der Fürstenspiegel Smaragds von St. Mihiel und seine literarische Gattung*. Münstersche Mittelalter-Schriften 28. Munich: Fink, 1977.

Eickels, Klaus van. "*Homagium* and *Amicitia*: Rituals of Peace and Their Significance in the Anglo-French Negotiations of the Twelfth Century." *Francia* 24 (1997), 133–40.

———. "Two Princes in One Bed: A Neglected Ritual of Peace-Making in the Middle Ages," forthcoming.

Eifler, Günter, ed. *Ritterliches Tugendsystem*. Wege der Forschung 56. Darmstadt: Wissenschaftliche Buchgesellschaft, 1970.

Elias, Norbert. *The Court Society*. Trans. Edmund Jephcott. New York: Pantheon, 1983.

Elliott, Dyan. *Spiritual Marriage: Sexual Abstinence in Medieval Wedlock*. Princeton, N.J.: Princeton University Press, 1993.

Epp, Verena. "Männerfreundschaft und Frauendienst bei Venantius Fortunatus." In *Variationen der Liebe: Historische Psychologie der Geschlechterbeziehung*, ed. Thomas Kornbichler and Wolfgang Maaz. Tübingen: Diskord, 1995.

Fabre, Pierre. *Saint Paulin de Nole et l'amitié chrétienne*. Bibliothèque des Ecoles Françaises d'Athènes et de Rome 167. Paris: E. de Boccard, 1949.

Fichtenau, Heinrich. *The Carolingian Empire*. Trans. Peter Munz. Oxford: Blackwell, 1957.

Fiske, Adele. "Alcuin and Mystical Friendship." *Studi Medievali* (1961), 551–75.

———. *Friends and Friendship in the Monastic Tradition*. Civoc Quaderno 51. Cuernavaca, Mexico: Centro Intercultural de Documentación, 1970.

Fleckenstein, Josef. "Karl der Grosse und sein Hof." In *Karl der Grosse: Lebenswerk und Nachleben, vol. 1: Persönlichkeit und Geschichte*. Düsseldorf: Schwann, 1965: 24–50.

———, ed. *Curialitas: Studien zu Grundfragen der höfisch-ritterlichen Kultur*. Göttingen: Vandenhoeck and Ruprecht, 1990.

Foucault, Michel. *The History of Sexuality*. Vol. 2, *The Use of Pleasure*. Trans. Robert Hurley. New York: Vintage, 1990.

———. *The History of* Sexuality. Vol. 3, *The Care of the Self*. Trans. Robert Hurley. New York: Vintage, 1988.

Fraisse, Jean-Claude. *Philia: la notion d'amitié dans la philosophie antique*. Paris: J. Vrin, 1974.

Frappier, Jean. *Amour courtois et table ronde*. Publications Romanes et Françaises 126. Geneva: Droz, 1973.

Freytag, Hartmut. "Höfische Freundschaft und Geistliche *Amicitia* im Prosa-Lancelot." In *Wolfram-Studien IX: Schweinfurter 'Lancelot'-Kolloquium 1984*, ed. Werner Schröder. Berlin: Schmidt, 1986: 195–212.

Friedrich, Udo. "Überwindung der Natur: Zum Verhältnis von Natur und Kultur im *Strassburger Alexander*." In *fremdes Wahrnehmen-Fremdes wahrnehmen*, ed. Wolfgang Harms and C. S. Jaeger. Stuttgart: Hirzel, 1997: 119–36.

Gamer, Helena. "Studien zum Ruodlieb." *Zeitschrift für deutsches Altertum* 88 (1957/58), 249–66.

Geertz, Clifford. "Centers, Kings and Charisma." In *Local Knowledge: Further Essays in Interpretative Anthropology*. New York: Basic Books, 1983: 121–46.

Gelsomino, Remo. "S. Bernardo di Chiaravalle e il *De amicitia* di Cicerone." *Studia Anselmiana* 43 (1958), 180–86.

Gentry, Frank. Triuwe *and* Vriunt *in the Nibelungenlied*. Amsterdamer Publikationen zur Sprache und Literatur 19. Amsterdam: Rodopi, 1975.

George, Judith W. *Venantius Fortunatus: A Latin Poet in Merovingian Gaul*. Oxford: Clarendon Press, 1992.

——, trans. *Venantius Fortunatus: Personal and Political Poems*. Translated Texts for Historians 23. Liverpool: Liverpool University Press, 1995.

Gillingham, John. *Richard the Lionheart*. London: Weidenfeld and Nicolson, 1978.

——. "Some Legends of Richard the Lionheart: Their Development and their Influence." In *Richard Coeur de Lion in History and Myth*, ed. Janet L. Nelson. London: King's College Centre for Late Antique and Medieval Studies, 1992: 51–69.

Gilson, Etienne. *Heloise and Abelard*. Chicago: Regnery, 1951; repr. Ann Arbor: University of Michigan Press, 1972.

Glendinning, Robert. "Pyramus and Thisbe in the Medieval Classroom." *Speculum* 61 (1986), 51–78.

Glier, Ingeborg. *Artes amandi: Untersuchung zu Geschichte, Überlieferung und Typologie der deutschen Minnereden*. Münchener Texte und Untersuchungen zur deutschen Literatur des Mittelalters 34. Munich: Beck, 1971.

Godman, Peter. *Poets and Emperors: Frankish Politics and Carolingian Poetry*. Oxford: Clarendon Press, 1987.

——, ed. and trans. *Poetry of the Carolingian Renaissance*. London: Duckworth, 1985.

Gold, Penny Shine. *The Lady and the Virgin: Image, Attitude, and Experience in Twelfth-Century France*. Chicago: University of Chicago Press, 1985.

Gould, Thomas. *Platonic Love*. London: Routledge and Kegan Paul, 1963.

Gravdal, Kathryn. *Ravishing Maidens: Writing Rape in Medieval French Literature and Law*. Philadelphia: University of Pennsylvania Press, 1991.

Greenblatt, Stephen. *Renaissance Self-Fashioning: From More to Shakespeare*. Chicago: University of Chicago Press, 1980.

Guerreau-Jalabert, Anita. *Index des motifs narrativs dans les romans arthuriennes français en vers: XIIe-XIIIe siècles*. Geneva: Droz, 1992.

Halperin, David M. *One Hundred Years of Homosexuality and Other Essays on Greek Love*. New York and London: Routledge, 1990.

Haseldine, Julian. "Friendship and Rivalry: The Role of Amicitia in Twelfth-Century Monastic Relations." *Journal of Ecclesiastical History* 44 (1993), 390–414.

Hauck, Karl. "Heinrich III und der Ruodlieb," *PBB* 70 (1948), 372–419.

Haug, Walter. "Gottfrieds von Strassburg 'Tristan': Sexueller Sündenfall oder erotische Utopie." In *Kontroversen alte und neue: Akten des VII. Internationalen Germanisten-Kongresses Göttingen 1985*, ed. Albrecht Schöne, 1. Tübingen: Niemeyer, 1986: 41–52.

Head, Thomas. *Hagiography and the Cult of the Saints: The Diocese of Orléans, 800–1200*. Cambridge Studies in Medieval Life and Thought ser. 4. Cambridge: Cambridge University Press, 1990.

——. "The Marriages of Christina of Markyate." *Viator* 21 (1990), 75–101.

Heathcote, Sheila J. "The Letter Collections Attributed to Master Transmundus." *Analecta Cisterciensia* 21 (1965), 35–109, 167–238. Esp. 195–97 for letters of friendship.

Hempen, Daniela. *The Negotiation of Gender and Power in Medieval German Writings.* Dissertation, University of British Columbia, 1998.

Herlihy, David. "Land, Family and Women in Continental Europe." *Traditio* 18 (1962), 89–120.

Hexter, Ralph. *Ovid and Medieval Schooling: Studies in Medieval School Commentaries on Ovid's* Ars amatoria, Epistulae ex ponto, *and* Epistulae Heroidum. Münchener Texte und Untersuchungen. Munich: Arbeo, 1986.

———. "Scholars and Their Pals." *Helios* 18 (1992), 154–57.

Higonnet, Ethel Cardwell. "Spiritual Ideas in the Letters of Peter of Blois." *Speculum* 50 (1975), 218–44.

Holdsworth, Christopher. "Christina of Markyate." In *Medieval Women*, ed. Derek Baker. Studies in Church History, Subsidia 1. Oxford: Oxford University Press, 1978: 185–204.

Hult, David. "Gaston Paris and the Invention of 'Courtly Love.'" In *Medievalism and the Modernist Temper*, ed. R. Howard Bloch and Stephen G. Nichols. Baltimore: Johns Hopkins University Press, 1996: 192–224.

Hutter, Horst. *Politics as Friendship: Origins of Classical Notions of Politics in the Theory and Practice of Friendship*. Waterloo, Ontario: Wilfried Laurier University Press, 1978.

Hyams, Paul. "What Did Henry III of England Think in Bed and in French About Kingship and Anger?" In *Anger's Past: The Social Uses of an Emotion in the Middle Ages*, ed. Barbara H. Rosenwein. Ithaca and London: Cornell University Press, 1998: 92–126.

Hyatte, Reginald. *The Arts of Friendship: The Idealization of Friendship in Medieval and Early Renaissance Literature*. Brill's Studies in Intellectual History 50. Leiden: Brill, 1994.

Jackson, W. T. H. "Faith Unfaithful: The German Reaction to Courtly Love." In *The Meaning of Courtly Love*, ed. F. X. Newman. Albany: State University of New York Press, 1968: 55–76.

Jaeger, C. Stephen. "Charismatic Body — Charismatic Text," *Exemplaria*, 9 (1997), 117–137.

———. "Courtliness and Social Change." In *Cultures of Power: Lordship, Status, and Process in Twelfth-Century Europe*, ed. Thomas N. Bisson. Philadelphia: University of Pennsylvania Press, 1995: 287–309.

———. *The Envy of Angels: Cathedral Schools and Social Ideals in Medieval Europe, 950–1200*. Philadelphia: University of Pennsylvania Press, 1994.

———. "Humanism and Ethics at the School of St. Victor in the Early Twelfth Century." *Mediaeval Studies* 55 (1993), 51–79.

———. "Ironie und Subtext in lateinischen Briefen des 11. und 12. Jahrhunderts." In *Gespräche, Boten, Briefe: Körpergedächtnis und Schriftgedächtnis im Mittelalter*, ed. Horst Wenzel. Berlin: Schmidt, 1997: 177–92.

———. *The Origins of Courtliness: Civilizing Trends and the Formation of Courtly Ideals, 939–1210*. Philadelphia: University of Pennsylvania Press, 1985.

———. "Orpheus in the Eleventh Century." *Mittellateinisches Jahrbuch* 27 (1992), 141–68.

Jaeger, Werner. *Paideia: The Ideals of Greek Culture*. Trans. Gilbert Highet. 2d ed. 3 vols. New York: Oxford, 1945.

Javelet, Robert. "L'amour spirituel face à l'amour courtois." In *Entretiens sur la renais-*

sance du 12e siècle, ed. Maurice de Gandillac and Edouard Jeauneau. Paris: Mouton, 1968: 309–36.

Johanek, Peter. "König Artus und die Plantagenets." *Frühmittelalterliche Studien* 21 (1987), 346–89. Johnson, L. P. "Down with Hôhe Minne!" *Oxford German Studies* 13 (1982), 36–48.

Jordan, Mark D. *The Invention of Sodomy in Christian Theology*. Chicago: University of Chicago Press, 1997.

Kantorowicz, Ernst. *The King's Two Bodies: A Study in Mediaeval Political Theology*. Princeton, N.J.: Princeton University Press, 1957.

Karnein, Alfred. "Amor est passio: A Definition of Courtly Love." In *Court and Poet*. Ed. G. S. Burgess. Selected Proceedings of the Third Congress of the International Courtly Literature Society. Liverpool: F. Cairns, 1980: 215–21.

———. *Amor est passio: Untersuchungen zum nicht-höfischen Liebesdiskurs des Mittelalters*, ed. Friedrich Wolfzettel. Trieste: Parnaso, 1997.

———. *De amore in volkssprachlicher Literatur: Untersuchungen zur Andreas-Capellanus-Rezeption in Mittelalter und Renaissance*. Heidelberg: Winter, 1985.

Karras, Ruth Mazo. "Friendship and Love in the Lives of two Twelfth-Century English Saints." *Journal of Medieval History* 14 (1988), 305–20.

Ingrid Kasten. *Frauendienst bei Trobadors und Minnesängern im 12. Jahrhundert*. Heidelberg: Winter, 1986.

Keen, Maurice. *Chivalry*. New Haven, Conn.: Yale University Press, 1984.

———. *Nobles, Knights and Men-at-Arms in the Middle Ages*. London and Rio Grande: Hambledon Press, 1996.

Keiser, Elizabeth B. *Courtly Desire and Medieval Homophobia: The Legitimation of Sexual Pleasure in "Cleanness" and its Context*. New Haven, Conn.: Yale University Press, 1997.

Kelly, Douglas. *The Medieval Imagination: Rhetoric and the Poetry of Courtly Love*. Madison: University of Wisconsin Press, 1978.

———. "'Li chastiaus . . . Qu'amors prist puis par ses esforz': The Conclusion of Guillaume de Lorris's *Rose*." In *A Medieval French Miscellany*, ed. Norris J. Lacy. Lawrence: University of Kansas Press, 1972.

Kelly, Henry Ansgar. "Gaston Paris's Courteous and Horsely Love." In *The Spirit of the Court: Selected Proceedings of the Fourth Congress of the International Courtly Literature Society (Toronto 1983)*, ed. Glyn S. Burgess and Robert A. Taylor. Dover, N.H.: D. S. Brewer, 1985: 217–23.

———. *Chaucerian Tragedy*. Woodbridge and Rochester, N.Y.: D. S. Brewer, 1997.

Kendrick, Laura. *The Game of Love: Troubadour Wordplay*. Berkeley: University of California Press, 1988.

Kessler, Ulrike. *Richard I. Löwenherz: König, Kreuzritter, Abenteurer*. Graz: Styria, 1995.

Kindermann, Udo. *Satyra: Die Theorie der Satire im Mittellateinischen: Vorstudie zu einer Gattungsgeschichte*. Erlanger Beiträge zur Sprach- und Kunstwissenschaft 58. Nüremberg, 1978.

Kleinschmidt, Erich. "Minnesang als höfisches Zeremonialhandeln." *Archiv für Kulturgeschichte* 58 (1976), 35–76.

Köhler, Erich. "Amor de lonh oder: Der 'Prinz' ohne Burg." In *Orbis Mediaevalis: mélanges de langue et de littérature médiévales offerts à Reto Bezzola*, ed. Georges Güntert et al. Bern: Francke, 1978: 219–34.

Konstan, David. *Friendship in the Classical World*. Cambridge: Cambridge University
    Press, 1997.
Koziol, Geoffrey. *Begging Pardon and Favor: Ritual and Political Order*. Ithaca, N. Y. and
    London: Cornell University Press, 1992.
Kühnel, Jürgen. *"Du bist mîn, ich bin dîn": Die lateinischen Liebes- und Freundschaftsbriefe
    des CLM 19411*. Litterae 52. Göppingen: Kümmerle, 1977.
Kuzniar, Alice, ed. *Outing Goethe and His Age*. Stanford, Calif.: Stanford University
    Press, 1996.
Langer, Ullrich. *Perfect Friendship: Studies in Literature and Moral Philosophy from Boccac-
    cio to Corneille*. Histoire des Idées et Critique Littéraire 331. Geneva: Droz, 1994.
Latzke, Therese. "Der Fürstinnenpreis." *Mittellateinisches Jahrbuch* 14 (1979), 22–65.
Lazar, Moshé. *Amour courtois et "fin' amors" dans la littérature du XIIe siècle*. Paris:
    Klincksieck, 1964.
Leclercq, Jean. "L'amitié dans les lettres au moyen-âge." *Revue du Moyen Age Latin* 1
    (1945), 391–410.
——. "Deux opuscules sur la formation des jeunes moines." *Revue d'Ascétique et de
    Mystique* 33 (1957), 387–99.
——, ed. "Epistulae Fiscannenses: Lettres d'amitié, de gouvernement et d'affaires
    (XIe-XIIe siècles)." *Revue Mabillon* 43 (1953), 5–31.
——. *Monks and Love in Twelfth-Century France*. Oxford: Clarendon Press, 1979.
Legros, Huguette. "Le vocabulaire de l'amitié, son évolution sémantique au cours du
    XIIe siècle." *CCM* 23 (1980), 131–39.
Lewis, Archibald R. *The Development of Southern French and Catalan Society, 718–1050*.
    Austin: University of Texas Press, 1965.
Lewis, C. S. *The Allegory of Love: A Study in Medieval Tradition*. London: Oxford
    University Press, 1936; repr. 1972.
Liebertz-Grün, Ursula. *Zur Soziologie des "amour courtois": Umrisse der Forschung*. Bei-
    hefte zum Euphorion 10. Heidelberg: Winter, 1977.
Liebeschütz, Hans. "Theodulf of Orleans and the Problem of the Carolingian Renais-
    sance." In *Fritz Saxl 1890–1948: A Volume of Memorial Essays from His Friends in
    England*, ed. D. J. Gordon. Toronto and New York: Nelson, 1957: 77–92.
Litvack, Frances. *Le droit du seigneur in European and American Literature*. Birmingham,
    Ala.: Summa, 1984.
Lochrie, Karma. *Margery Kempe and Translations of the Flesh*. Philadelphia: University
    of Pennsylvania Press, 1991.
Luhmann, Niklas. *Love as Passion: The Codification of Intimacy*. Trans. Jeremy Gaines and
    Doris L. Jones. Cambridge, Mass.: Harvard University Press, 1986.
Marchand, James W. "Wolfram's Bawdy." *Monatshefte* 69 (1977), 131–49.
Marrou, Henri-Irène. *A History of Education in Antiquity*. Trans. G. Lamb. Madison:
    University of Wisconsin Press, 1956.
Matter, E. Ann *The Voice of My Beloved: The Song of Songs in Western Medieval Chris-
    tianity*. Philadelphia: University of Pennsylvania Press, 1990.
McEvoy, James. "Friendship and Love." *Irish Theological Quarterly* (1983–84), 35–47.
——. "Notes on the Prologue to Saint Aelred of Rivaulx's *De spirituali amicitia*, with a
    Translation." *Traditio* 37 (1981), 396–411.
——"*Philia* and *Amicitia*: The Philosophy of Friendship from Plato to Aquinas."
    Sewanee Medieval Colloquium: Occasional Papers 2 (1984), 1–23.

McGuire, Brian Patrick. *Brother and Lover: Aelred of Rievaulx*. New York: Crossroad, 1994.

———. *The Difficult Saint: Bernard of Clairvaux and His Tradition*. Kalamazoo, Mich.: Cistercian Publications, 1991.

———. *Friendship and Community: The Monastic Experience 350–1250*. Cistercian Studies Series 95. Kalamazoo, Mich: Cistercian Publications, 1988.

———. "Love, Friendship, and Sex in the Eleventh Century: The Experience of Anselm." *Studia Theologica* 28 (1974), 111–52.

McLaughlin, Mary Martin. "Abelard and the Dignity of Women: Twelfth-Century Feminism in Theory and Practice." In *Pierre Abélard-Pierre le Vénérable: les courants philosophiques, littéraires, et artistiques en Occident au milieu du XIIe siècle*. Paris: Editions du Centre National de la Recherche Scientifique, 1975: 287–334.

McNamara, Jo Ann. "Chaste Marriage and Clerical Celibacy." In *Sexual Practices and the Medieval Church*, ed. Vern L. Bullough and James A. Brundage. Buffalo, N. Y.: Prometheus, 1982.

———. "The *Herrenfrage*: The Restructuring of the Gender System, 1050–1150." In *Medieval Masculinities: Regarding Men in the Middle Ages*, ed. Clare A. Lees. Medieval Cultures 7. Minneapolis and London: University of Minnesota Press, 1994.

McNamara, Jo Ann, and Suzanne Wemple. "The Power of Women through the Family in Medieval Europe, 500–1100." In *Women and Power in the Middle Ages*, ed. Mary Erler and Maryanne Kowaleski. Athens: University of Georgia Press, 1988: 83–101.

McNamara, Marie A. *Friendship in Saint Augustine*. Studia Friburgensia, n.s 20. Fribourg: University Press, 1958.

Melville, Gert. "Rituelle Ostentation und pragmatische Inquisition: Zur Institutionalität des Ordens vom Goldenen Vliess." In *Im Spannungsfeld von Recht und Ritual: Soziale Kommunikation in Mittelalter und Früher Neuzeit*, ed. Heinz Duchhardt and Gert Melville. Cologne: Böhlau, 1997: 215–271.

Mews, Constant. *The Lost Love Letters of Heloise and Abelard: Perceptions of Dialogue in Twelfth-Century France*. New York: St. Martin's Press, 1999.

Monson, Don A. "Andreas Capellanus and the Problem of Irony." *Speculum* 63 (1988), 539–72.

———. "Jaufré Rudel et l'amour lointain: les origines d'une légende." *Romania* 106 (1985), 36–56.

Moore, John C. "Love in Twelfth-Century France: A Failure in Synthesis." *Traditio* 24 (1968), 429–43.

Moos, Peter von. *Hildebert von Lavardin, 1096–1133: Humanitas an der Schwelle des höfischen Zeitalters*. Pariser Historische Studien 3. Stuttgart: Hiersemann, 1965.

Müller, Jan-Dirk. "Ritual, Sprecherfiktion und Erzahlung: Literarisierungstendenzen im späteren Minnesang." In *Wechselspiele: Kommunikationsformen und Gattungsinterferenzen mittelhochdeutscher Lyrik*, ed. Michael Schilling and Peter Strohschneider. Heidelberg: Winter, 1996: 43–76.

Nelli, René. *L'érotisme des troubadours*. 2 vols. Paris: Union Générale d'Editions, 1974.

Nelson, Deborah Hubbard. "Christine de Pisan and Courtly Love." *Fifteenth-Century Studies* 17 (1990), 281–89.

Neuhausen, Karl A. "Zu Cassians Traktat De amicitia (Coll 16)." In *Studien zur Litera-*

tur der Spätantike, ed. Christian Gnilka and Willy Schletter. Antiquitas 1. 26. Bonn: Habelt, 1975: 181–218.

Newman, Barbara. "Authority, Authenticity, and the Repression of Heloise." *Journal of Medieval and Renaissance Studies* 22 (1992), 121–57.

——. *From Virile Woman to WomanChrist: Studies in Medieval Religion and Literature*. Philadelphia: University of Pennsylvania Press, 1995.

Offermanns, Winfried. *Die Wirkung Ovids auf die literarische Sprache der lateinischen Liebesdichtung des XI. und XII. Jahrhunderts*. Wuppertal: Kastellaun, 1970.

Olsen, Glenn W. "One Heart and One Soul (Acts 4:32 and 34) in Dhuoda's 'Manual'." *Church History* 61 (1992), 23–33.

Pepin, Ronald E. "*Amicitia jocosa*: Peter of Celle and John of Salisbury." *Florilegia* 5 (1983), 140–56.

Perella, Nicolas J. *The Kiss Sacred and Profane: An Interpretive History of Kiss Symbolism and Related Religio-Erotic Themes*. Berkeley: University of California Press, 1969.

Peters, Ursula. "Höfische Liebe: Ein Forschungsproblem der Mentalitätsgeschichte." In *Liebe in der deutschen Literatur des Mittelalters*, ed. Jeffrey Ashcroft et al. Tübingen: Niemeyer,
1987: 1–13.

Peters, Ursula and Rolf Köhn. "Höfisches Liebeswerben oder politisches Heiratsangebot?: Zum Brief der Konstanze von Bretagne an Ludwig VII. von Frankreich." *PBB* 111 (1989), 179–95.

Peyer, Pierre J. *The Bridling of Desire: Ideas of Sex in the Later Middle Ages*. Toronto: University of Toronto Press, 1993.

Powicke, F. M. *Aelred of Rievaulx and His Biographer Walter Daniel*. Manchester: Longmans, 1922.

Powis, Jonathan. *Aristocracy*. Oxford: Oxford University Press, 1984.

Putz, Marianne. "Hohe Minne in den Carmina Burana." *Amsterdamer Beiträge zur älteren Germanistik* 30 (1990), 51–60.

Raby, F. J. E. "Amor and Amicitia: A Medieval Poem." *Speculum* 40 (1965), 599–610.

——. *A History of Secular Latin Poetry in the Middle Ages*. 2d ed. 2 vols. Oxford: Clarendon Press, 1967.

Rasch, Wolfdietrich. *Freundschaftskult und Freundschaftsdichtung im deutschen Schrifttum des 18. Jahrhunderts vom Ausgang des Barock bis zu Klopstock*. Halle: Niemeyer, 1936.

Réau, Louis. *Iconographie de l'art chrétien*. Paris: Presses Universitaires de France, 1957.

Reiss, Louise Horner. "Tristan and Isolt and the Medieval Ideal of Friendship." *Renaissance Quarterly* 33 (1986), 131–137.

Renna, Thomas. "Virginity and Chastity in Early Cistercian Thought." *Studia Monastica* 26 (1984), 43–54.

——. "Virginity in the *Life* of Christina of Markyate and Aelred of Rievaulx's *Rule*." *American Benedictine Review* 36 (1985), 79–92.

Richter, Simon. "Winckelmann's Progeny: Homosocial Networking in the Eighteenth Century." In *Outing Goethe and his Age*, ed. Alice Kuzniar. Stanford, Calif.: Stanford University Press, 1996: 33–46.

Rist, John M. *Augustine: Ancient Thought Baptized*. Cambridge: Cambridge University Press, 1994.

Rogers, B. J. "In Praise of Radegunde: A Commentary on the Love Poetry of Venantius Fortunatus." *Language and Style* 4 (1971), 264–72.

Ross, Werner. "Die Liebesgedichte im Cambridger Liederbuch (CC): Das Problem des 'Frauenliedes' im Mittelalter," *Der Altsprachliche Unterricht* 20 (1977), 40–62.

Rougemont, Denis de. *Love in the Western World*. New York: Harper and Row, 1974.

Ruck, E. H. *An Index of Themes and Motifs in Twelfth-Century French Arthurian Poetry*. Cambridge: D. S. Brewer, 1991.

Ruhe, Ernstpeter. *De amasio ad amasiam: Zur Gattungsgeschichte des mittellateinischen Liebesbriefes*. Beiträge zur romanischen Philologie des Mittelalters 10. Munich: Fink, 1970.

Schaller, Dieter. "Das Aachener Epos für Karl den Grossen." *Frühmittelalterliche Studien* 10 (1976), 134–68.

———. "Vortrags- und Zirkulardichtung am Hof Karls des Grossen." *Mittellateinisches Jahrbuch* 6 (1970), 14–36.

Schiller, Gertrud. *Ikonographie der christlichen Kunst*. Gütersloh: G. Mohn, 1966.

Schnell, Rüdiger. *Andreas Capellanus: Zur Rezeption des römischen Rechts in "De amore"*. Münstersche Mittelalterschriften 46. Munich: Fink, 1982.

———. *Causa amoris: Liebeskonzeption und Liebesdarstellung in der mittelalterlichen Literatur*. Bern: Francke, 1985.

———. *Frauendiskurs, Männerdiskurs, Ehediskurs: Textsorten und Geschlechterkonzepte in Mittelalter und Früher Neuzeit*. Frankfurt and New York: Campus, 1998.

———. "Die 'höfische' Liebe als 'höfischer' Diskurs über die Liebe." In *Curialitas: Studien zu Grundfragen der höfisch-ritterlichen Kultur*, ed. Josef Fleckenstein. Göttingen: Vandenhoeck and Ruprecht, 1990: 231–301.

Schramm, Percy Ernst. *Kaiser, Könige, und Päpste: Gesammelte Aufsätze zur Geschichte des Mittelalters*. 4 vols. Stuttgart: Hiersemann, 1968–1970.

Schultz, James A. "Bodies That Don't Matter: Heterosexuality Before Heterosexuality in Gottfried's *Tristan*." In *Constructing Medieval Sexuality*, ed. Karma Lochrie, Peggy McCracken, and James A. Schultz. Minneapolis: University of Minnesota Press, 1997: 91–110.

Schutz, A.-H. "The Provencal Expression Pretz et valor." *Speculum* 19 (1944), 488–93.

Searle, Eleanor. "Emma the Conqueror." In *Studies in Medieval History Presented to R. Allen Brown*, ed. Christopher Harper-Bill et al. Woodbridge: Boydell, 1989: 281–88.

Sedgwick, Eve Kosofsky. *Between Men: English Literature and Male Homosocial Desire*. New York: Columbia University Press, 1985.

Sharpe, Kevin. *Criticism and Compliment: The Politics of Literature in the England of Charles I*. Cambridge: Cambridge University Press, 1987.

Signori, Gabriela, ed. *Meine in Gott geliebte Freundin: Freundschaftsdokumente aus klösterlichen und humanistischen Schreibstuben*. Bielefeld: Verlag für Regionalgeschichte, 1995.

Singer, Samuel. "Karolingische Renaissance." In *Germanisch-Romanisches Mittelalter: Gesammelte Aufsätze und Vorträge*. Zürich and Leipzig: Niehans, 1935.

Smuts, R. Malcolm. *Court Culture and the Origins of a Royalist Tradition in Early Stuart England*. Philadelphia: University of Penn Press, 1987.

Southern, R. W. *St. Anselm and His Biographer: A Study of Monastic Life and Thought, 1059-ca. 1130*. Cambridge: Cambridge University Press, 1963.

———. *St. Anselm: A Portrait in a Landscape*. Cambridge: Cambridge University Press, 1990.

Spitzer, Leo. *L'amour lointain de Jaufré Rudel et le sens de la poésie des troubadours*. University of North Carolina Studies in the Romance Languages and Literatures 5. Chapel Hill: University of North Carolina Press, 1944.

Stehling, Thomas. *Medieval Latin Poems of Male Love and Friendship*. New York: Garland, 1984.

———. "To Love a Medieval Boy." *Journal of Homosexuality* 8 (1983), 151–70.

Steinen, Wolfgang von den. "Karl und die Dichter." In *Karl der Grosse: Lebenswerk und Nachleben. Vol. 2: Das geistige Leben*. Düsseldorf: Schwann, 1965: 63–94.

Strong, Roy. *Art and Power: Renaissance Festivals, 1450–1650*. Woodbridge: Boydell, 1984.

———. *The Cult of Elizabeth: Elizabethan Portraiture and Pageantry*. London: Thames and Hudson, 1977.

Symes, Carol. *Aspects of Marriage and Sexuality in the Miracle Literature of Twelfth-Century England*. M. Litt. thesis. Oxford, 1990.

Taiana, Franz. *Amor purus und die Minne*. Fribourg: Universitätsverlag, 1977.

Thum, Bernd. *Aufbruch und Verweigerung: Literatur und Geschichte am Oberrhein im hohen Mittelalter: Aspekte eines geschichtlichen Kulturraums*. Waldkirch im Breisgau: Waldkircher Verlagsgesellschaft, 1980.

Tobin, Robert D. "In and Against Nature: Goethe on Homosexuality and Heterotextuality." In *Outing Goethe and His Age*, ed. Alice Kuzniar. Stanford, Calif.: Stanford University Press, 1996: 94–110.

Tomasek, Tomas. *Die Utopie im "Tristan" Gottfrids von Strassburg*. Hermaea N.F. 49. Tübingen: Niemeyer, 1985.

Topsfield, L. T. *Troubadours and Love*. Cambridge: Cambridge University Press, 1975.

Vale, Juliet. *Edward III and Chivalry: Chivalric Society and Its Context 1270–1350*. Woodbridge: Boydell Press, 1982.

Vielhauer, Inge. "Radegunde von Poitiers (ca. 520–587)." *Castrum Peregrini* 33 (1984), 5–40.

Wachinger, Burghart. "Was ist Minne?" *PBB* 111 (1989), 252–67.

Wack, Mary. *Lovesickness in the Middle Ages: The Viaticum and Its Commentaries*. Philadelphia: University of Pennsylvania Press, 1990.

Wallace-Hadrill, J. M. "The *Via Regia* of the Carolingian Age." In *Trends in Medieval Political Thought*, ed. Beryl Smalley. New York: Barnes and Noble, 1965: 23–28.

Weber, Max. *Max Weber on Charisma and Institution Building: Selected Papers*, ed. S. N. Eisenstadt. Chicago: University of Chicago Press, 1968.

Weingart, Richard. *The Logic of Divine Love: A Critical Analysis of the Soteriology of Peter Abailard*. London: Clarendon Press, 1970.

Wenzel, Horst. "Fernliebe und Hohe Minne: Zur räumlichen und zur sozialen Distanz in der Minnethematik." In *Liebe als Literatur: Aufsätze zur erotischen Dichtung in Deutschland*, ed. Rüdiger Krohn. Munich: Beck, 1983: 187–208.

———. "Das höfische Geheimnis: Herrschaft, Liebe, Texte." In *Schleier und Schwelle: Archäologie der literarischen Kommunikation V, Bd. 1.: Geheimnis und Öffentlichkeit*, ed. Aleida Assmann und Jan Assmann. Munich: Fink, 1998.

———. *Hören und Sehen, Schrift und Bild: Kultur und Gedächtnis im Mittelalter*. Munich: Beck, 1995.

Werner, Ernst. "Zur Frauenfrage und zum Frauenkult im Mittelalter: Robert v. Arbrissel und Fontevrault." *Forschungen und Fortschritte* 29 (1955), 269–76.

Wetherbee, Winthrop. *Platonism and Poetry in the Twelfth Century: The Literary Influence of the School of Chartres*. Princeton, N. J.: Princeton University Press, 1972.

White, Peter. "*Amicitia* and the Profession of Poetry in Early Imperial Rome." *Journal of Roman Studies* 68 (1978), 74–92.

White, Stephen D. "The Politics of Anger." In *Anger's Past: The Social Uses of an Emotion in the Middle Ages*, ed. Barbara Rosenwein. Ithaca, N.Y. and London: Cornell University Press, 1998: 127–52.

Willms, Eva. *Liebesleid und Sangeslust: Untersuchungen zur deutschen Liebeslyrik des späten 12. und frühen 13. Jahrhunderts*. Münchener Texte und Untersuchungen 94. Munich and Zürich: Artemis, 1990.

Winkler, John J. *The Constraints of Desire: The Anthropology of Sex and Gender in Ancient Greece*. New York: Routledge, 1990.

Yates, Frances. *Astrea: The Imperial Theme in the Sixteenth Century*. London: Routledge, 1975.

Zade, Lotte. *Der Troubadour Jaufré Rudel und das Motiv der Fernliebe in der Weltliteratur*. Diss. Greifswald, 1919.

Zielinski, Herbert. *Der Reichsepiskopat in spätottonischer und salischer Zeit (1002–1125)*. Wiesbaden: Steiner, 1984.

Ziolkowski, Jan. "Twelfth-Century Understandings and Adaptations of Ancient Friendship." In *Mediaeval Antiquity*, ed. Andries Welkenhuysen, Herman Braet, and Werner Verbeke. Mediaevalia Lovaniensia Series 1, Studia 24. Louvain: Louvain University Press, 1995, 59–81.

Index